THE ACONCEPTUAL MIND

ADVANCES IN CONSCIOUSNESS RESEARCH

ADVANCES IN CONSCIOUSNESS RESEARCH provides a forum for scholars from different scientific disciplines and fields of knowledge who study consciousness in its multifaceted aspects. Thus the Series will include (but not be limited to) the various areas of cognitive science, including cognitive psychology, linguistics, brain science and philosophy. The orientation of the Series is toward developing new interdisciplinary and integrative approaches for the investigation, description and theory of consciousness, as well as the practical consequences of this research for the individual and society.

Volume 11

Pauli Pylkkö

The Aconceptual Mind

Heideggerian themes in holistic naturalism

Kyyt viherti katsehesta,
suusta lensi yölepakot,
jalan alta ahmat nousi,
käden päällä kärpät juoksi,
korppi koikkui päälaella,
haaskalinnut hartioilla.

Kaikki tiesi, min inehmot,
kaikki taisi, min jumalat;
ei sitoa sinistä tulta,
aarnihautoja avata.

Eino Leino, *Helkavirsiä I* (1903)

Contents

Acknowledgements

This book would not have been written without the quite unconventional seminars which were arranged in 1993-1996 in the Helsinki academic underground. Because at least fifty persons attended the seminars it is not possible to thank them all separately. Special thanks go to Dr. Tere Vadén who used to travel from Tampere in order to be present and whose contribution was essential for the thematic development of the seminar. He has also read the manuscript, and his comments have shaped my work up to the last, published version. Dr. Paavo Pylkkänen's activity and initiative was particularly important, not the least in the area of quantum theory and its interpretation. Through his excellent international contacts, he transmitted some of the recent topics and discussions to our seminar, and this energized the course of our work which was constantly threatened by petty provincialism. Our often quite fancy and speculative discussions were guided back to the solid ground by Dr. Markus Lammenranta's sober and sharp arguments. Mr. Gareth Griffiths whose many comments have helped me to improve the manuscript connected our seminar discussions to continental philosophy and aesthetic issues. Tapio Hyvönen, Ari Peuhu, Tiina Seppälä, Jouko Seppänen, Leena Thurlin, Arto Tukiainen and many others contributed to the spirit of the seminar. Leena Thurlin and Arto Tukiainen have also read the manuscript and their comments have helped me to find the final version of the work.

Professor Gordon Globus (Irvine) and Dr. Maxim Stamenov (Sofia) who are the editors of John Benjamins's series *Advances in Consciousness Studies* have patiently guided my work with innumerable comments and provided critique and encouragements without which the book would never have seen daylight. My work had already been inspired by professor Globus's writings for some time before I met him personally in Lapland 1995. During the rewriting of the manuscript, it was the presence of his spirit that I felt most intensively behind my shoulder. The presence was not always fictitious but was actualized by a considerable number of lively and spontaneous e-mail responses from Southern California. They enlivened the gloomy arctic nights and alleviated the mental dystrophy in which a Finnish philosopher almost always works.

Professor Dominique Janicaud (Université de Nice), professor Jens Allwood (Göteborg) and professor Dieter Haselbach (Bonn) have helped me to see my work from the outside angle which has, hopefully, made it more resistant to critique. Professor Janicaud read the opening chapter of the manuscript, and his critique, especially his comments on Heidegger and naturalism, helped me to design the future disposition of the work. Several intensive discussions with professor Allwood have inspired me to sharpen the linguistic aspect of my work, especially as regards the problem of nationally and culturally unique meanings. Professor Haselbach has read the essay on Nazism (Chapter 7) and his comments and suggested references to literature, especially on the economic aspect of National Socialism, have helped me to see some inadequacies of my work and, hopefully, to overcome them.

* * *

Some of the chapters of this book have appeared elsewhere as different versions. *'Dasein' naturalized* (Pylkkö, 1995c) was published in *Analecta Husserliana*, Vol. XLIX, pp. 203-218; *On surprise* (Pylkkö, 1995b) has appeared in *Semiotica*, 109-3/4, 1996, pp. 283-309; *Gaming without subjects* (Pylkkö, 1994a) appeared in *The British Tradition in the 20th Century Philosophy*, edited by Klaus Puhl and Jaakko Hintikka, The Ludwig Wittgenstein Society, Kirchberg am Wechsel; and *Nationally unique meanings* has appeared under a different title in *New Directions in Cognitive Science, Proceedings of the International Symposium, Saariselkä, 4-9 August 1995, Lapland, Finland*, edited by Paavo Pylkkänen and Pauli Pylkkö, the Finnish AI Society, Otaniemi, Finland (see Pylkkö, 1995d).

Heidegger with a grain of salt

In the seventeenth song of *Kalevala*, which is said to belong to the oldest layer of the work, Väinämöinen who has run out of poetic inspiration visits a mythical shaman, Antero Vipunen, in order to find a remedy. Vipunen appears to be deceased, almost decayed already, or at least his body can hardly be separated from the thick vegetation of the forest where he used to live. Väinämöinen's problem is that he is unable to find the *right words* for a song which he needs to sing in order to finish the sail boat which he is constructing. Väinämöinen belongs to a new generation of shamans and is eager to learn Vipunen's ancient wisdom, but Vipunen who is both suspicious and flattered at the same time is not willing to yield and sing the right words. Though their relationship is sore and turns eventually violent, it doesn't lack harsh and virile mutual respect. Väinämöinen enters into Vipunen's mouth by force and demands to hear the missing words. Vipunen is unyielding and decides to get rid of Väinämöinen by swallowing him. Down in Vipunen's stomach, Väinämöinen makes Vipunen's life intolerable with a sword and fire until Vipunen is eventually forced to sing.

Kalevala depicts the contents of the secret song only indirectly and cursorily. Instead, it presents an impressive and detailed *loitsu* (incantation) with the help of which one is supposed to find relief for a stomach ailment! The seventeenth song of *Kalevala* is a phallic and carnivorous, even anthropophagic, vision of how the oral tradition is passed from one generation to another, such that the traditional wisdom is veiled in an apparently irrelevant medical *loitsu*.

A difficult and complex master-disciple relationship is not a Finnish privilege but a familiar theme in many cultures. For example, the relationship between Husserl and Heidegger oscillated between love and hate, and later

Heidegger and his disciples reperformed similar stormy scenes. It seems that the landscape around Heidegger's legacy is filled with demons of suspicion, erotic rivalry, jealousy and aggression, and even today it is hardly possible to write about Heidegger's thinking without participating in a perpetual philosophical *Walpurgisnacht* which is taking place within the sphere of his influence.

The epoch of Heidegger's formative years, as well as Heidegger's character, were so violent, harsh and saturated with a nihilistic spirit that peaceful master-disciple relations would have been a small-scale miracle. Heidegger's epoch overflowed with wars, revolutions, street fights, mass murders and genocides, and Heidegger himself had serious problems with his character, some of which were almost certainly related to sex and violence. Therefore it's no wonder that as soon as a modern scholar decides to study Heidegger and his times, a strange tension begins to build up between the scholar and his subject matter, a distant repercussion of the Vipunen-Väinämöinen conflict. A typical Heidegger scholar lives most probably in the comfortable and relatively affluent circumstances of a modern democratic welfare state (or its American version) and its academic subculture where such perils of life as hunger and violence are relatively rare, whereas Heidegger's epoch and Heidegger's work are saturated by nihilism, spiritual destitution, anxiety and violence. Even if it were theoretically possible for us to understand Heidegger, his epoch and its problems, it is understandable if our unwitting and not necessarily conscious scholarly reaction is aversive. The aversion may be so strong that we have to concede that actually we don't *want* to understand Heidegger and his epoch, that we don't want to get engaged in it, at least not too intensively. It is all too painful and embarrassing.

Our reaction is often reinforced by the atmosphere which still surrounds the study of the Nazi epoch. In the mid nineties, echos of the Allied war propaganda can still be heard, and the victors' view of the war continue to exercise its influence upon our studies by suggesting simplistic explanations. The prevailing attitudes are convenient indeed because they help us to find such relief which only distance can serve. We still need a comfortable distance in order to separate our own life from the crimes of the Nazis. By painting their crimes with exceptionally sinister colors, we hope to absolve ourselves. Yet it is far from clear that all of our most cherished philosophical, political and religious ideas and movements, such as Enlightenment, Socialism, Democracy and Christianity, are free of the very ingredients which gave rise to the crimes of the Nazis. For example, it is not obvious that the crimes which the Nazis committed were a direct and easily comprehensible consequence of the National-Socialist philosophy and ideology. At least, it isn't more obvious than that the crimes which have been committed in the name of Progress, Socialism, Democracy and Christianity were a direct and easily comprehensible consequence of their respective philosophy and ideology. For very obscure reasons we don't think that the present-day Christianity is responsible for the genocides which have been carried out earlier on behalf of it, whereas the genocides of which the National-Socialist regime was responsible are still almost automatically associated with Nazi philosophy. It would be very nice indeed if we could pinpoint the factors which led the Nazis from Nazi philosophy to the disaster of wars and genocides. But we simply cannot do that. One reason for this failure may be that similar factors are latently effective in our thinking today, and only 'nonphilosophical,' say economic, reasons prevent us, that is, the enlightened West, from waging wars and committing genocides similar to those of the Nazis.

Be the reason of this selectivity of absolvment as it may, Heidegger's times lie almost transcendentally far from our present sphere of experience in the modern welfare state and its academic circles. And we have accepted this distance, and the conveniently simplified picture of the era which amplifies the distance, to such an extent that such renowned theorists of Nazi thinking as Philippe Lacoue-Labarthe and Jean-Luc Nancy may unabashedly declare that they have not read the essential literature of the epoch because it is, as they say, abominable and monotonous. The question is not only that by retaining the simplifying experiential distance we fail to understand Nazism, but that we fail to understand our own epoch, its ideas and thinking, and eventually, we fail to understand ourselves. For what is the 'monotonous' literature of the Nazi epoch in this case? Are also Benn, Jünger, Pound, Brasillach, Céline, Blanchot, Koskenniemi, Montherlant, Marinetti, D'Annuzio, Hamsun, Schmitt, Müller-Armack and Freyer abominable and monotonous? Those who want to discharge these writers hurry to add: 'Yes, but they are good writers!' the underlying idea being that one cannot be a Nazi and a good writer at the same time.

Though the circle is blatant it is obviously not blatant enough because it vitiates a great deal of writing about Nazism and Fascism. When it turns out that a writer or philosopher whom we have appreciated has a Nazi past our first reaction is: 'This must be a mistake! His work is too good to be related with Nazism in any other than a superficial way.' But if we have learned to know a person first and primarily as a Nazi or Fascist, and we happen to read his work later, our reaction tends to comply with the convenient stereo-type: 'It is clearly pure propaganda and low in literary and philosophical value.' Yet, which European government has today a head who could write a decent introduction to Marxist philosophy or review international philosophy congresses as Mussolini did?

Both of the above sketched reactions are straightforward *non sequiturs*, and the problem is not at all limited to the study of Nazism alone. It is not seldom that we read a report, say, of the life of a serial killer in which the reporter tells us, sometimes even in one sentence, that, on the one hand, the murders are completely incomprehensible, but, on the other hand, a typical 'serial killer's behavioral pattern' could be discerned already in the killer's childhood. This kind of ambiguity is common in the literature which deals with serious crimes, social anomalies, mental diseases, political revolutions, wars, genocides, and so on. On the one hand, Lacoue-Labarthe and Nancy claim that the Nazi crimes are incomprehensible; on the other hand, they claim that there exists a Nazi *logic*! Furthermore, there is no way to find out whether a Nazi piece of work is abominable and monotonous except by studying it; and an interesting piece of writing may turn out, not only to be written by a National Socialist, but to be closely related to National-Socialist thinking and aesthetics, as is the case, for example, with Heidegger, Jünger, Müller-Armack, Schmitt and many others.

If not recognized, the circular and ambiguous strategies can cause confusion. Thus, for instance, because German Expressionism is highly appreciated in painting, cinema, drama and poetry, its close relations with Nazism have often been suppressed. On the other hand, because we know that certain buildings were commissioned and used by the Nazi leaders and administration, they are automaticly said to be distasteful, even if practically every European and American capital is filled with buildings which are, not only of a similar style, but clearly of less aesthetic value. In addition, a whole generation of relatively interesting German philosophers (Bäumler; Klages; Heyse; Jünger) who may not have been as luminous thinkers as Heidegger but are certainly worth of reading (if compared, say, to the faceless army of philosophers which the recent global academic industry has produced) have been labelled as uninteresting and incompetent due to their Nazi connections. The strategy is understandable but not acceptable. In order to be accepted at all, a former National-Socialist must be an exceptionally good writer or philosopher, as is the case for example with Heidegger; after the acceptance, a purification machinery is put on to clean him up and obfuscate his Nazi past. If the poor fellow isn't of Heidegger's stature, he can be simply forgotten. The unavoidable result is that we don't really understand today what happened in Central Europe between the great Wars, and our self-understanding is undermined.

It may be ethically perfectly justifiable to say as follows: 'Nazi Germany was the unprecedented Evil Empire, and I don't want to be in any contact with it; because understanding Nazism means that I have to expose myself to the *Nazi experience*, I decline to understand it.' This is an acceptable view as long as one also declines to write publicly about Nazism. But it turns problematic and hard to defend when highly qualified authors, such as Lacoue-Labarthe and Nancy, *write about matters which they don't actually want to understand.*

This is a problem which concerns, not only the understanding of Nazism, but the philosophical and scientific description of human experience in general. Western academic scholars live in artificially restricted and domesticated experiential circumstances with which the great majority of people of the world are not familiar. For example, the experience of such cultures which never produced industrial technology and mathematical natural science, and which did not create permanent contacts with the sphere of Western culture, may be so different from any standard Western experience, especially the academic and scientific experience, that every Western, technology-based approach to such an experience, including the standard scientific approach, will either ignore some aspect of it, turn it to something which it originally wasn't, or simply destroy it. The gap between cultures may be transcendental, and it is possible that the so-called *intercultural communication* communicates only Westernized copies of experience from one culture into another. Analogously, philosophical views and scientific explanations of human experience, say, in consciousness studies, tend to edit, clean up and unify human experience just in order to mitigate its variety and make life easy and comfortable for scholars.

With the problem of understanding Nazism, this boils down to the following. There seldom exists a sharp line between understanding and accepting. Actually, in many languages, including English, 'understanding' is used also in a sense which means by and large the same as 'accepting.' For example, said with a suitable intonation in a proper context, 'I don't understand him' means the same as 'I don't accept what he has done.' To some extent, understanding always requires re-experiencing, and one cannot re-experience and hence understand something without, at least, pretending that one accepts what one is trying to understand. This willful act of pretending resembles the fictive attitude: one can return from the fictive world to the everyday world, but something alien remains alive in the mind after the return too. Thus understanding Nazism presupposes minimally some kind of pretension, temporary suspension of judgement, during which the scholar of the epochal experience adopts fictitiously the role of the persons whose experience he is studying. Obviously, this is not a completely innocent or harmless enterprise. It requires that one is able to adopt simultaneously several, mutually incompatible experiential roles. It may be a reasonable decision to keep a healthy distance from such spooky experiments.

In the following pages, such a distance is not kept, and the approach will be experiential. But Heidegger will not be handled softly either: what is vital in his thinking is sieved out and planted into a foreign soil, and the rest is renounced or reversed with no regret. This is Väinämöinen's approach to Vipunen's secret. Yet it is proper to honor Heidegger's name, even with our slightly anthropophagic title (cf. Derrida, 1989), because his work turned the phenomenological movement to an asubjectivistic direction, toward a post-phenomenological era. In what follows, one of the leading ideas will be that now the postphenomenological thinking should take a naturalistic turn, and it should do it without adopting the metaphysical machinery of standard scientific realism. Hopefully, the new, *anomalous naturalism* will be both more aware and more critical of the metaphysical origins of standard science than the old one because it is naturalism that we need in our attempt to ascend away from the experiential hell of Heidegger's times. The ascending is supposed to happen *after* we have attained some understanding of the era. This doesn't mean that we believe that we can comprehend the horrors of the Nazi epoch just by doing philosophical analysis, for example, by adopting an ethical stance. Not all Evil can be tamed by reason and ethics.

But we will frequently encounter the problem of boundary: where does Heidegger's ideas end and something else begin. Here we cannot avoid practicing mental anthropophagy: Like Väinämöinen's encounter with Vipunen, the new interpretation is always violent, also when it depends on the old one. One cannot cut a slice out of the organism of Heidegger's thinking, plant it anew and expect the slice not to suffer any immunological disorders.

Yet it may be possible to carry out the operation, and it may be even necessary to do so if we don't want to raise the hell once again. Thus we must not expect the resulting hybrid to be recognized and acknowledged as *Heideggerian* any more. Interpretative purity and piety are not on our agenda, just as they were not on Heidegger's. Nobody can expect us to adopt a submissive attitude to the Nazi epoch and to one of its leading thinkers. Not even Heidegger himself could expect that because his own interpretations, for example of Husserl, Kant or Descartes, were not particularly pietistic either. Thus, experiential intensity doesn't imply submissiveness. On the contrary, the only alternative to the aggression of the head-on experiential approach is the academic detachment. But here, as well as in the study of foreign cultures in general, experiential detachment implies ignorance.

Heidegger's thinking is like a field of energy which affects everything. Even in those areas where the influence is hard to recognize, it is inseparably everywhere. Take, for example, the notions of *democracy* and *tolerance*. We would not like to abandon them completely, but still, after Heidegger everything looks different. If there will ever be a tenable and interesting view of democracy and tolerance, it has to be able to face the Heideggerian challenge. After that has happened, what we will end up with, namely an *a*subjective view of democracy and tolerance, may differ so much from the old subject-centered notions that we shouldn't, perhaps, use the words *democracy* and *tolerance* any more. And here the anthropophagic factor becomes effective: not everything in Heidegger is equally useful for us, and, strictly speaking, the possibility of *ametaphysical* democracy or tolerance wasn't one of Heidegger's own problems because *he* wouldn't have hesitated to abandon the ideals of democracy and tolerance altogether.

Hence, as we attempt to revise Heidegger's stance and change some of the meanings which he created we must first make a serious effort to understand the stance and its background, and this understanding cannot succeed without an experiential commitment. We haven't understood Heidegger and his times if we haven't re-experienced his thinking, as well as what some of his contemporaries experienced. Though this re-experience is mainly *our* experience and takes place mostly in our own cultural context, it will not leave our minds intact, pure and innocent: it will definitely change us to something that we were not before, and that will alter also the meanings of Heidegger's key words as they are now used by us. It is not possible to write about Heidegger today without altering their meanings. Already understanding them superficially, tentatively or conditionally would somewhat change them. Assimilating them to a new meaning context will change them crucially.

Consider, for example, Heidegger's relation to *natural science* and *philosophical naturalism*. Heidegger views the prospects of natural science and naturalism in a bleak light indeed. But it is possible that he confounded science with classical science and was, therefore, unable to give credit to the *ametaphysical* tendencies of recent natural science, for example to those of the quantum theory. Yet, if we will ever find a view of natural science which doesn't depict nature as a set of entities and which doesn't picture natural science purely as a metaphysical enterprise, our notion of science will differ crucially, not only from Heidegger's view, but from the standard view of natural science and from the standard self-image of natural science too. It will, again, be something else, perhaps to such an extent that it doesn't deserve to be called *natural science* any more. Perhaps it should be called "man's interactive thinking of nature" or "nature as a human experience." And, as is the case with the prospects of democracy, this whole question of nondogmatic science is not really one of Heidegger's own questions because *he* believed that natural science is necessarily doomed to philosophical naiveté.

Also regular philosophical work and its language are saturated with metaphysical attitudes. One of the main difficulties of the kind of writing which appears on the following pages is to keep the reader's mind attuned to the subtle and evasive ametaphysical connotations of philosophical language. The language of Western philosophy is not *only* a dusty store of metaphysical dichotomies, but a considerable ametaphysical tradition, for example from Hume to Mach and onwards, can be discerned even in such philosophy that was produced in the immediate vicinity of modern natural science.

Difficulties with metaphysical language are not alleviated by the naiveté of the standard scientific attitude. While most scientists adopt this attitude and the related habit of straightforward realism and objectivism, one of the most important recent results of physical science, namely the quantum theory, quite openly suggests that the habit is a philosophical dead end. Colloquial language is not of much help either because it is the original breeding ground of many deep-trenched metaphysical dichotomies. New language and interpretation is needed, but not necessarily new vocabularies. Some guidelines might be found in Niels Bohr's heroic attempts to design adequate *atheoretical language* in which microphysical phenomena could be spoken of; another source is later Wittgentein's relentless attacks on any theoretical and explanatory attitude toward language. Both of these views are, however, riddled with difficulties.

One reaction to the problem of metaphysical language is the tendency to design neologisms, new vocabularies which are, from the outset, intended to be free of metaphysical dichotomies. But this neologistic line of working isn't intrinsically more promising than the revisionist line which hopes to make language users more aware of the metaphysical dichotomies upon which a great deal of their language is traditionally based, because a new vocabulary which is initially intended to be ametaphysical or atheoretical may just as easily be mistaken as metaphysical and theoretical as any old one. It is not a too modest goal for a philosopher to say that he attempts to *hear* what he is saying, if hearing in this case requires sensitivity for the ametaphysical connotations and subtleties which almost *every* vocabulary, even the most corrupted one, potentially contains.

One reason for adopting the revisionist strategy is that overly externalist and mechanical language is a problem, not only for postphenomenological thinkers, but for many scientists and philosophical naturalists too. And it may not be as easy for a scientist to adopt a new vocabulary as it is for a postphenomenological thinker whose work is not expected to be tied to a strictly regimented vocabulary in the first place. It may be reassuring for such scientists to know that Heidegger did not only descend to the *Angst*-ridden experiential hell of the Expressionist Weimar culture with the help of his poetically attuned language but was also the undisputed master of dichotomy destruction with a perfect ear for the metaphysical connotations of the German vocabulary.

But regardless of the differences in working and thinking strategies, the view that the human mind is originally *aconceptual* is something which both the postphenomenological thinkers and the advocates of philosophical naturalism may find attractive. Obviously, in order to reach a truce between these apparently diverging traditions of thinking, both columns, the postphenomenological and the naturalist one, have to make some concessions. In order to avoid philosophical naiveté, naturalism must adopt genuinely holistic thinking habits and distance itself, not necessarily from properly interpreted quantum theory and neuroscience, but from dogmatic realism, objectivism and scientism. Analogously, postphenomenological thinking must learn to tolerate ametaphysically interpreted natural science and confer on it a role as nontrivial thinking whose results may occasionally guide and inspire philosophical thinking too. If there is no foundation, then philosophical insight may arise from any area of human interest, including nondogmatic and nonfoundational natural science. In Heidegger's vocabulary, though not in his opinion, the relationship between philosophical thinking and natural science will be that of *nearness* (Nähe) and *belonging-together* (Zusammengehören), not that between the foundation and superstructure.

If the human mind and language are originally aconceptual experience which is not controlled by a rational, representative and autonomous subject, then the study of the human mind and language cannot simply begin with concepts and theories. Something which is aconceptual cannot be understood comprehensively in any purely conceptual framework. In what follows, we begin with aconceptual and asubjective experience, and suggest that this is, not only a naturalistically acceptable starting point, but perhaps even the only really naturalistic alternative. From this kind of amorphous and astructural experience, things, objects and concepts may be derived as special, reified forms of experience which will, however, always remain partly entangled with their low aconceptual origin. Any science, including modern natural science, which tries to free itself from dogmatic objectivism, must study the preconceptual and preobjectual stage of (human and nonhuman) experience and derive its objects from it.

The aconceptual experience which will be considered in the sequel is asubjective and, therefore, it is not possible to characterize it comprehensively in terms of such notions as person, rationality, intentionality or consciousness. *Experience* covers here both nonhuman experience and nonpersonal human experience. It is collective, or, properly speaking, it can be so holistic that it destroys the boundaries which are said to separate persons from one another. This makes the problem of solipsism and privacy less acute in this context. This view of experience which covers experience of all times everywhere represents a movement away from the unsettled *Sein-Dasein* dualism which dominates Heidegger's *Being and Time* (1927/1992), toward such *Zusammengehören* of Being and Human Being which appears in *Identity and Difference* (1957). In our terms, experience in general (which may include also nonanimate experience) and human experience belong to one another and are almost nothing without one another.

It is the notion of aconceptual experience which we will use when it is time to approach Nazism. The thesis is that, for those who participated in the movement, Nazism was an intensive aconceptual experience and, therefore, Nazism cannot be described and understood adequately without recourse to aconceptuality or some other respective notion. Now, we notice immediately that, because of its aconceptual nature, the above sketched experiential approach to Nazism will be extremely difficult to accomplish. Nazism cannot be understood adequately if we resort only to theoretical or conceptual tools. In other words, *no* theory or conceptual approach will ever be able to deal properly with Nazism, that is, without leaving crucial aspects of the Nazi experience unaddressed.

Because the aconceptual origin of meaning is best appreciated if language is studied in an ethnic or national context where unique meanings dwell, there is no way to avoid the political dimension of the problem of aconceptuality, not even in the naturalistic context. Heidegger's political shadow follows us everywhere even if we seem to be dealing with problems which remain apparently far from the Nazi field of experience. The view that there are ethnically and nationally unique meanings which are not translatable from one culture into another is not a view which conforms easily with the enlightened picture of man as a rational being. The enlightened picture presupposes that man is a being who has access to universal meanings and crosscultural rationality upon which meaning-preserving communication can be established. Heidegger was deeply aware of the temptation and power which this universalist picture exercises upon our minds, and, therefore, his work challenges us to question, not just the dominance of technology, but also our modern, enlightened view of man, rationality, communication and intercultural relations.

One of the underlying questions which cannot, however, be directly answered here but upon which, hopefully, some light will be cast, is the following: If the modern picture of man, or metaphysics of subjectivity as it is often called, ties democracy and modern technology (Technik) into an inextricable framework, the *Gestell*, can the overwhelming power of technology be challenged and controlled within any democratically organized society? This was one of the questions which the later Heidegger used to ponder, and it seems that his answer was negative. He thought that democracy was a naive errand boy of modern technology and contributed to the global annihilation of locally cultivated meanings and cultural variety. The following pages are written in order to show that naturalization and cultural relativization of

Heidegger's position might open a new vista onto this field of ultimate questions.

But in order to see this question in a proper light, we must not obscure Heidegger's stance and picture him kindly as a nice modern man with enlightened ideas of democracy, equality, intercultural communication and progress. Heidegger was a harsh man, a thinker who was obsessed by his *deinon*, by his primordial urge to think violently. Both early Heidegger's urge of authenticity and later Heidegger's view of language as unique and aconceptual experience are hard to reconcile with the modern view of man, say, with the ideals of Enlightenment, technological progress and modern welfare state ideology. The authentic *Dasein* experience dissolves the boundary which separates the subject from the object, and this dissolution threatens the autonomy and rationality which is traditionally believed to characterize a democratic individual. Heidegger's authenticity is hard, violent and horrorful. It is only with violence that truth as *aletheia* can be disclosed to us.

Similarly, later Heidegger's vision of such new thinking which is subtle enough to live in the neighborhood of poetry suggests that original thinking can be carried out only in a native language. Only those who were born as native speakers within the cultural sphere which produced modern philosophy and technology can address seriously and creatively such ultimate problems as the essence of technology and its relation to democracy. It is native language which lives and thinks in us, and new thinking arises from the perpetually evolving and unfolding aconceptual experience which only poetically tuned language can beget. Persons, individuals or subjects are unable to produce anything genuinely new or unique because what is genuinely new and unique doesn't arise from conscious intentions. Similarly, no value debate or rational decision making is able to challenge the power which technology exercises upon our minds because ethics, critical debate and rationality are notions which are thoroughly and unavoidably saturated with technological attitudes.

The violent aspect of authenticity and the inequality which is implied by such philosophical localism which makes meanings interculturally untranslatable are philosophical difficulties which must not be suppressed. We cannot just ignore these problems, and, at the same time, pretend to be taking Heidegger seriously as a thinker. The possibility that naturalization, relativization and non-Western localism might open a new network of paths onto the problem field of language, meaning and experience, and through that, to the problems of technology and democracy, is based on the idea that recent natural science itself has reached the end of the objectivist program on which it was founded in the early seventeenth century. This situation didn't result from any good or democratic intentions which we might entertain in order to control technology. The power of technology cannot be challenged by good intentions alone, but it is possible that the 'irrational' aspects of quantum theory, as Wolfgang Pauli used to call them, can unwittingly contribute to that goal instead. The essence of technology, the overwhelming *Gestell*, which has shaped our thinking and experience into a mechanical form, may, due to such new notions as quantum inseparability, indeterminacy and nonlocality, be able to generate the semen of its own destruction.

Similarly, democracy which is based on the program to unify locally varying human experience has turned life in a welfare state into a monotonous boredom and slow ecological disaster. At the same time, it destroys unique local cultures with no regret. The new network of thinking paths is opened by the possibility that non-Western thinking, or thinking in the Western periphery, because of its marginal position and its immediate connection to asubjective and aconceptual local experience and a nontechnological environment, may provide a revitalizing point of view to these problems. However, it may be the case that this new thinking doesn't solve the original Central-European problem but, rather, a foreign interpretation of that old problem. Therefore, the possible solution, too, must be creatively reinterpreted back into its original cultural home.

* * *

Chapter 1 (*'Dasein' naturalized*) attempts to bring some of Heidegger's most central notions (Dasein; Angst) closer to naturalism and cultural relativism, and, through that, undermine the obvious tendency of elitism, cultural solipsism and chauvinism which threatens Heidegger's view of authenticity.

Chapter 2 (*Is modern science necessarily onto-theo-logical?*) studies Heidegger's relationship with natural science and shows that Heidegger's view of natural science was dominated by classical natural science. Therefore he was unable to appreciate certain ametaphysical tendencies of recent natural science. If his view of science had not been tied only to classical science, his view of technology would have been different too.

Chapter 3 (*What is 'noncomputational' in recent consciousness studies?*) surveys the different meanings of the word *noncomputational* and tries to demonstrate that some recent results of quantum theory and neuroscience comply with the experiential and ametaphysical view of the human mind which is pursued by postphenomenological thinking. The alliance of holistic naturalism and postphenomenological thinking will also provide the proper meaning for *noncomputational*.

Chapter 4 (*On surprise*) shows that any adequate approach to the understanding of surprise, for example aesthetic surprise, must connect surprise to aconceptual experience. Surprise is described in terms of games and players, and therefore the respective ametaphysical notions must be designed.

Chapter 5 (*The unique language problem*) criticizes Wittgenstein's notion of 'language game' and compares it with later Heidegger's view of language. Wittgenstein's aversion toward experiential notions prevented him from dealing with unique meanings. The Chapter also suggests that philosophical discourse on language might benefit from shifting the focus of discussion from the public-privacy problem to the unique-universal problem. In other words, unique is not necessarily private.

Chapter 6 (*Gaming without subjects*) deals with the problem of asubjectivism, both in the naturalistic and postphenomenological contexts. The key question is how games can be understood without metaphysics of subjectivity. As an example, the question of ametaphysical democracy is raised.

Chapter 7 (*Is Nazism humanism?*) is a critique of Lacoue-Labarthe and Nancy's view of Nazism and of their view of Heidegger's relationship with Nazism. It sketches an alternative, experiential and aconceptual view of Nazism and tries to understand Heidegger's engagement in the light of the alternative view.

Chapter 8 (*Culturally unique meanings*) deals with the problem of philosophical localism and untranslatability, and tries to answer the question whether philosophical problems have to be addressed in a native language. It attempts to show that there are unique and preontological ways to understand some expressions of certain non-Western languages. Therefore such languages cannot be comprehensively translated into other languages, especially not to Western languages (Indo-European languages). Ontological relativism and linguistic relativism do not provide an adequate explanation to this situation but have to be enforced by ontological nihilism.

CHAPTER ONE

Dasein naturalized

Naturalization to the rescue

Dasein is in bad shape, as if a disease had overtaken the most central notion of Martin Heidegger's thinking. The symptoms of the disease include the almost inevitable elitism, preclusion of democracy, discrimination on the ground of language, cultural background and ethnicity, intolerance, and, yes, ultimately Nazism, too. There is no doubt that Heidegger reserved a special philosophical and historical task for the German people (see, for example, *Introduction to Metaphysics*, Heidegger, 1935/1978, p. 50). The Germans were supposed to be the chosen nation whose poets and thinkers possess the special competence which is needed in grasping the essence of *Technik* (technology) and liberating mankind from its dominance. The Germans possess this competence, says Heidegger, mainly because their language is particularly closely related to the original language of Western thinking, Ancient Greek, especially as it was spoken before Aristotle. In its pre-Aristotelian phase, Ancient Greek was not yet seized by the spell of *Seinsvergessenheit* (forgetfulness of Being) and was therefore able to disclose the temporal openness of Being (Sein).

In Heidegger's infamous *Der Spiegel Interview* (1967/1988, published for the first time in 1976), we find a dialogue in which Heidegger first contends that if the dominance of *Technik* will ever be challenged, the challenge and resulting change will arise from the same cultural and ethnic soil where *Technik* was originally conceived. Heidegger: "I am convinced that a change can only be prepared from the same place in the world where the modern technological world originated." (Meine Überzeugung ist, dass nur von demselben Weltort aus, an dem die moderne technische Welt entstanden ist, auch eine Umkehr sich vorbereiten kann [...]) A bit later *Der Spiegel* asks: "Do you think that the Germans have a specific qualification for this change?" Heidegger answers: "I am thinking of the special inner relationship between the German language and the language and thinking of the Greeks. This has been confirmed to me again and again by the French. When they begin to think they speak German. They insist that they could not get through with their own language." (Der Spiegel: "Glauben sie, dass die Deutschen eine spezifische Qualifikation für diese Umkehr haben?" Heidegger: "Ich denke an die besondere innere Verwandschaft der deutschen Sprache mit der Sprache der Griechen und deren Denken. Das bestätigen mir heute immer wieder die Franzosen. Wenn sie zu denken anfangen, sprechen sie deutsch; sie versichern, sie kämen mit ihrer Sprache nicht durch.) To this Heidegger adds that thinking can be translated as little as poetry.

This may sound rather depressing to anyone who was not born as a German or who did not learn German in early childhood. In "The nature of language" (Heidegger, 1957-58/1971; but see also Heidegger, 1953/1982), Heidegger had already brought thinking to the nearness of poetry. This liaison which in itself is happy has ungainly implications in the Heideggerian context: those who are not Germans or who have not learned German early enough to speak it with natural fluency have no access to the paths of genuine thinking, thinking creatively about the central problems of the Western philosophical and technological tradition. Even within the sphere of regular scientific views, the liaison would make thinking sensitive to the finest phonological, syntactic, semantic and pragmatic subtleties which, just as original poetic language, can be produced and understood only by native speakers. And if there are aspects of language which cannot be described in regular scientific terms, this problem of nativeness may become even more difficult. In Heidegger's thinking, the condition of native sensitivity and subtlety makes serious thinking, for example, thinking of the essence of *Technik* without *Seinsvergessenheit*, untranslatable, and ultimately, a local German enterprise. This is a blow which hits hard on those of us whose first language doesn't belong to the Indo-European family and whose social, cultural and historical origin lies far from the cradle of *Technik*. One of the unfortunate implications of Heidegger's view is that thinkers and poets whose cultural background is alien to the Greek-German Axis are bound to trifle with problems which are of secondary importance if considered from the central-European perspective.

And if the foregoing didn't sound bad enough, there is worse to come. The authenticity of the *Dasein* experience is something that the Everyman (das Man) is unable to handle. The *Angst* (asubjective Anxiety) which is related to the authentic experience of *Dasein* is too much for him. Authentic experiential contact with Nothing (Nichts) is so painful and filled with horror that most of us would avoid it as long as possible (see especially "What is metaphysics?" Heidegger, 1929/1988). It is not just that some of us are natively less well disposed to face such experience, or that some of us lack the proper social and historical background to deal with the experience. All this could be accepted even by a naturalistically oriented egalitarian. If his version of naturalism is anomalous enough (see Preface), he may even concede that the authentic *Dasein* experience is so threatening because it dissolves the subject-object boundary, and that it is the firmness of this boundary which makes painful experience manageable in the everyday life. Along with the breakdown of the subject-object contrast, the protective control which the rational consciousness exercises over the rest of the mind is lost, and the authentic *Dasein* experience which is totally absorbing and beyond intellectual control may ravish what is left of us.

According to Heidegger, the access to this kind of wild experience of being which emerges only in the nearness of the Nothing is reserved only for a selected group of people, for a sort of philosophical, religious, artistic and political elite. That the elite can be discerned from the less fortunate average people rests on the idea that experiential authenticity can be kept strictly separate from inauthenticity, and it is this idea that may be naturalistically questionable. Even if there were very little one can actually do in order to produce or cause the authentic *Dasein* experience and even if it remained conceptually or rationally inaccessible, this wouldn't yet make it naturalistically incomprehensible. Indeed, those who actually manage to go through exceptionally intensive experiences may not be able to do so by a volitional and conscious decision. But still, even if that sounds plausible, all naturalistically oriented views should avoid projecting such strong dichotomies, as that of the authentic and inauthentic in Heidegger, upon natural phenomena.

In his rectorial address, "The self-assertion of the German university," Heidegger (1933/1990) didn't hesitate to associate his *Dasein* philosophy with the National-Socialist revolution, and it is quite obvious that, according to his view, it was National Socialism and, in particular, the person of Adolf

Hitler who could provide the best historical circumstances where the German *Geist* (Spirit) could encounter the opening of its *Dasein* and face its historical destiny. It was the destiny of the German nation to provide the third alternative between America (democracy) and Russia (Bolshevism) and thus save the spirit of the West from the mediocrity of the average man. The average man, the enlightened modern man of the West who believes in equality and democracy, is too weak to encounter the possible openness of his *Dasein* and must not be relied on when it is the proper time to settle the destiny of the German *Dasein*.

Richard Wolin (1990) has pointed out that Heidegger's view of the authentic *Dasein* experience leads Heidegger's thinking to a kind of avant-garde elitism whose historical origins can be traced back to German right-wing radicalism. It may be difficult to spell out what such words as *right* and *left* are supposed to mean in the political scene of the Weimar Republic, but it seems obvious that some kind of *national and revolutionary elitism* attracted Heidegger. Many influential National Socialists, Heidegger among them, came from working-class or *petit bourgeois* families and thought that a humble family background should not prevent them from assuming a leading role in political and academic circles. Born leaders could be born in shady alleys, and, as can be seen from *Der Spiegel interview* (but see also *Letter to Herbert Marcuse*, Heidegger, 1947/1993), it was radical social and political depolarization, reconciliation of political and social antagonisms, that Heidegger expected from the National Socialist revolution.

A somewhat similar radical elitism characterized Stefan George's estheticism, and it is not by chance that George was one of the poets whom Heidegger often cites. *Dasein* was a widely used existential term in the German literary and philosophical circles between the wars. Even the protagonist of Joseph Göbbels's novel *Michael* (1929, p. 13) is called *Daseins-menschen*. *Dasein* was also one of Ernst Jünger's favorite terms as can be noticed, for example, from his *Das Kampf als inneres Erlebnis* (1922) where he describes war with ecstatic, pseudo-religious Expressionist terms. For Jünger war was the genuine father of his generation and it was only in war, as near to destruction and Nothingness as possible, where modern man can reach the intensity peak of his inner experience. The essence of modern technology reveals itself in war. Michael Zimmerman (1990) has studied this rather necrophilic background of Heidegger's notions of *Dasein* and authenticity and their relation to Jünger's thinking. It was, in particular, Jünger's vision of technology that left a strong impact upon Heidegger's thinking. One of the common denominators of Heidegger and Jünger, which is not studied by Zimmerman (in his 1990 study), is Expressionism, but the historical roots of Heidegger's *Dasein* notion and his views of authenticity date back much further. It is, perhaps, Schopenhauer's *Wille*, its application in Richard Wagner's work, and its more skeptical and naturalistic version as Nietzsche's respective *Wille* which are the genuine historical precedents of Heidegger's *authenticity*.

Regardless of how the political dimension of Heidegger's thinking should be interpreted, it cannot be denied that the door which in Heidegger's thinking leads toward the authentic *Dasein* experience is designed to be extremely narrow and categorically separated from the inauthentic. This narrowness arises from the peculiar *dualistic* application of ethnic, linguistic, historical and other criteria which inevitably bring with them some air of discrimination. Especially if these criteria are not thought to be universal, they may unwittingly lead us to cultural isolation, even to a kind of cultural solipsism. Thus it seems that the remedy for the aforementioned disease has to be searched for somewhere between the *Scylla and Charybdis* of the pretentious universalist position, with its hidden intolerance, and cultural solipsism, which leads to the breakdown of intercultural dialogue. It is doubtful that Heidegger himself ever realized that his work actualized the danger of either intolerant universalism or cultural solipsism. Almost certainly he didn't associate Nazism with either of them because for him Nazism was the only genuinely antimetaphysical political movement of his times. Analogously, he didn't realize that his reaction to recent natural science was overly defensive.

But is the disease curable? Some light (including Wolin's and Zimmerman's work) has already been cast upon the network and history of the discriminatory and dualistic criteria. But perhaps there is more to be done. I think that there exists a promising remedy for the disease. The remedy is naturalization. *Naturalization* represents a strong antidualistic attitude: some of the most central notions of Heidegger's thinking must be exposed to a treatment which dissolves naturalistically untenable dichotomies. For example, I suggest that the notion of *Dasein* can be submitted to a sort of naturalization treatment which, hopefully, will cure it and release it from its unappealing symptoms. In what follows, I hope to be able to show that through naturalization the Heideggerian *Dasein* can be politically neutralized to such an extent that even the spirit of democracy can be preserved to some extent, though it may be the case that we will have to alter somewhat the standard meaning of *democracy*. Not surprisingly, we will have to alter also the meaning of *naturalism* and distance it from standard scientific realism. Our hope is that we would not have to sacrifice cultural uniqueness when we try to avoid the dangers of cultural solipsism; and that we don't have to retain a defensive distance to some antimetaphysical inclinations of recent natural science. Uniqueness is not privacy, and not all science is metaphysical.

The price of the treatment will be that we end up with something which will be called *meaning relativism* and *environmental relativism* (cultural and natural relativism), and this may not sound like Heidegger any more. Therefore, a warning is in order: due to the application of Väinämöinen's strategy (cf. Preface), the resulting naturalized notion of *Dasein* may have less in common with the original Heideggerian notion than what is perhaps expected. We could say that the remedy is more like intensive psychological therapy than the administration of drugs: after the remedy has been applied, the patient, the notion of *Dasein*, will not be the same as it used to be. We might even agree with someone who thinks that the new notion differs so much from the old one that it doesn't deserve to be called *Dasein* any more. Yet it is proper to acknowledge its Heideggerian origin.

From *Angst* to *Furcht*

Let us begin with the difference between *Angst* (asubjective dread) and *Furcht* (fear as a subjective attitude) as it is depicted by Heidegger ("What is metaphysics," 1929/1988; see also *Being and Time*, 1927/1992, especially Section 40, 228-235). *Angst* has no object, says Heidegger, and therefore the subject-object contrast isn't actualized in the *Angst* experience. Thus in anxiety, as we come close to the Nothing, our experience is not directed to any definite entity. In Heidegger's words: "... anxiety does not 'see' any definite 'here' or 'yonder' from which it comes (1927/1992, p. 231). (... die Angst 'sieht' nicht ein bestimmtes 'Hier' und 'Dort'... 1927/1986, p. 186). Entities do not disappear but they lose completely all relatedness to human affairs. The Nothing reveals itself in anxiety (Die Angst offenbart das Nichts, 1929/ 1988) and discloses entities in their concealed strangeness.

Contrary to this, the nature of *Furcht* is more or less like that of any emotion or propositional attitude. Whatever it is that is experienced as fearsome, it is always encountered as an entity. As an attitude, fear always has an object, namely, the object toward which the attitude is directed. Therefore, in the state of fear, we are able to recognize ourselves as subjects and distinguish ourselves from the object of the feeling. Thus we can, if that is what we want, submit the emotion of fear to scientific consideration and, to some extent, approach it from the regular scientific angle.

From a naturalistic point of view, the strict dichotomy of *Furcht* and *Angst* is hardly tenable, although it may be acceptable to try to get rid of the subject-object contrast. Thus we should not accept Heidegger's blunt declaration (1929/1988) that science relates *only* to entities. Instead, we should say: only dogmatic science does that. Dissolution of the subject-object dualism was, for example, one of Ernst Mach's central endeavors (Mach, 1897; 1906; see also Feyerabend's brilliant essay on Mach, 1987, pp. 192-218). But Mach and other naturalists, including Wilhelm Ostwald, who rejected the standard scientific realism, didn't expect the dissolution of the contrast to take place only in special extreme experiences. Contrary to Heidegger, they assumed that the contrast may be dissolved already in experience with quite normal intensity. If the contrast of subject and object can be softened already in quite a normal experiential situation, then, according to the kind of antirealistic naturalism which we are considering here, we should not design the contrast of *Furcht* and *Angst* to be too crisp. Rather, we should make it less acute than what Heidegger had in mind. *Angst* isn't anything categorically more than something that is ranked high on the intensity scale of *Furcht* feeling. When the intensity grows, the contrast of subject and object tends to become less sharp but, to a small extent, it may be present even in the highest ranking fear. Therefore, no such philosophical role remains to be played by extreme or pure experience which would separate it categorically from inauthenticity.

Heidegger seems to have thought that by dissolving the subject-object contrast, *Angst* can be separated from regular feelings and elevated to a special antinaturalistic status. This would be a plausible line of thinking if the evaporation of the subject-object contrast is something that takes place only in extreme experience. However, already in quite regular situations, we go through many sensations, emotions and attitudes where the border line of the subject and object is blurred, though it may be that common sense tends to ignore or marginalize them as 'unimportant' or 'irrelevant' cases. For example, auditive perception often lacks objectuality and it may be difficult to tell when and where one sound ends and another begins. Individuation criteria of musical sounds are sometimes most obscure, and within a suitable musical 'individuation system,' practically any two sounds can be defined to be 'identical with each other' regardless of their empirically observable differences. This shows that musical sounds are not object-like external entities with mind-independent individuation conditions. Furthermore, it is possible to educate visual perception to be less objectifying, such that its impressions apprehend, say, immediate colors and shapes, not full-fledged external things of which we tend to say that they *have* color and shape. Sounds are not really external objects at all, and it is quite possible to experience colors and shapes without attributing them to external physical objects. If a more drastic example is needed, in the hypnogogic state of falling asleep when the wakeful consciousness isn't fully in control any more, there often occur experiences during which the organization of the subject begins to evaporate and experience flows freely without the perspective and hierarchy which characterizes the controlling presence of subject. In this kind of pre-sleep state, what we call "external" in colloquial language becomes inseparably entangled with "internal." The converse is also possible: that suddenly in the middle of a dream we become conscious of the fact that we are dreaming, and sometimes we may even consciously influence the course of the dream events and reach those rare moments of life when the future events obey our conscious will.

Neither should *Angst* be associated *only* with the ultimate encounter with Nothing. The presence of nothingness, in some more common and naturalized sense, can be experienced even if the regular subject-object contrast is weakly activated (in some naturalistically acceptable way). When we are afraid of a violent person our fear isn't necessarily directed only to the violent person as such. Our fear contains residual ingredients of general animal horror which is aroused by the possibility of becoming injured or destroyed. Though this kind of dread has no clear object to which it is directed, it is not impossible to conceive a naturalistic explanation for it. We could also say that any experience, no matter how intensive it is, is always associated with a center, a kind of local perspective or point of view which isn't necessarily yet a full subject but something from which the subject may eventually arise. Especially, *Angst* cannot be abstract dread of pure Nothing. Rather, it is 'decentered' or decentralized dread, the intensity of which is not rationally proportional to (but bigger than) the threat which the source of violence and annihilation provides. *Angst* in the naturalized sense is the experience of intensive fear which is released by the disintegration of a subject or a presubjective experiential center.

Such words as *intensity, center* and *source* are not used here in a sense which associates them to common sense or to the regular thinking habits of science, say classical physics and classical logic. Thus *center* (presubject, see Chapter 2) is not a concept, and it has no external reference either, and *intensity* is not a quantitative notion of empirical science. This doesn't make *intensity* a purely normative notion either. Centerization (formation of centers) is a process of experiential articulation which, as a result, produces (experience of) external objects and internal concepts. When the articulation is finished, and the internal and the external have been polarized, an experiential center emerges which may gradually assume the role of a self. But the polarization is never perfect, and even afterwards the internal and the external always remain inseparable to some extent. Also the tendency to substantiate that what is not (which is revealed by such a nominalization as *nothing* and double nominalization as *nothingness*) suggests that completely non-reified or object-free experience is impossible. Thus naturalization, as it is here understood, doesn't require that all experiences have an external object toward which they are directed or which is said to cause the experience. Though being drunk is an experience which can be said to be caused by alcohol, it is not clear that a person who feels drunk feels so *only* because he has perceived the changes which alcohol has caused in his body or behavior. Being drunk may be an experience which is aroused by the reorganization or disorganization of the subject (and its perceptual processes), and thus the experience may lack the object toward which the subject's experience can be said to be directed. Analogously, among the many interpretations which we can give to such expressions as "being afraid of dying," there is one which doesn't relate the experience to any object as such. It is possible to associate the expression with the experience which we have when our own conscious subjectivity is going through the process of dissolution. Of course, if the notion of *experience* would be equated with *subjective experience*, we could not describe the kind of experience in which subject is dissolved.

In addition, regular fear is not always personal and can be excruciating even if the possibility of destruction threatens, not the person himself, but, say, a member of his family. In terms of a clear-cut subject-object distinction, it would be difficult to explain why we can be so intensively concerned with the future of our family members, friends and relatives. These examples show that, even in some of our most frequent experiences, the subject-object contrast is weaker and less obviously present than what Heidegger seems to have thought.

Holistic experience which is not shaped by a crisp subject-object contrast seems to be even more typical of small children and nonhuman mammals, including primates, than adult humans. We may assume that small children and some nonhuman mammals do not have access to as external objects and as purely internal feelings, let alone to as sharply articulated concepts, as adult humans do. Even adult humans can occasionally re-experience this lost holism in religious, erotic and esthetic life.

In short, Heidegger's attempts to separate *Angst* from regular fear and elevate it to a special, philosophically privileged position are naturalistically questionable. Experience as such doesn't provide ground for such a categorical or dualistic separation. Something analogous can be said of Heidegger's contrasting of negation as a regular cognitive operation and pure Nothing (Heidegger, 1929/1988). In both contrasts, in *Angst-Furcht* and Nothing-negation, human experience is all too holistic, diffuse, inseparable, perpetually changing and inarticulate to support any categorical dichotomy. We could say that experience of Nothing isn't more than a particularly intensive experience of negation; or, that negation is a weak experience of Nothing. In the same spirit we could say that perceiving represents a particularly vivid and concrete case of thinking; and thinking a delayed and schematic way of perceiving. This doesn't imply that we could characterize Nothingness comprehensively in terms of the notion of negation; or, in general, that we could characterize intensive experience purely in terms of conceptual attitudes. There is something mutually inaccessible in their relationship, almost transcendental (assuming that *transcendental* is used to mean 'not completely intertranslatable'). This kind of experiential inaccessibility which becomes manifest as untranslatability originates from experiential inseparability and can be understood in a naturalistically acceptable way, that is, without categorical dichotomies.

Certainly some feelings are more intensive than others, and, certainly, in some cases the centered perspective (the alleged subject) becomes or remains less articulated than in some other cases. Thus experiential intensity should be associated with the dissolution of structure. But what is not obvious is why more intensive feelings should be elevated to a categorically different and dualistically more important philosophical position than less intensive feelings. Therefore we should be skeptical of the view that there are philosophically privileged, elite experiences in this particular meaning of *elitism*.

There are philosophers, Heidegger among them, who seem to think that extreme intensity of an experience separates the experience categorically from other experiences. A philosopher who wants to advocate some kind of naturalism should add to this that a philosophical view, concerning for example language and mind, is bound to remain inadequate if it deals only with extreme cases of experience excluding, ignoring or degrading regular ones. The description of extreme cases should be related to regular cases, and every adequate view should allow extreme experience to grow continuously from regular experience. But, similarly, a view which is able to deal only with regular cases and which would exclude intensive experiences as something purely anomalous or irrelevant would be equally inadequate. Natural phenomena can be unique. Intensive experiences, including religious and mystical experiences, madness, perversions and ultimate apersonal experiences are also in nature. What is not there is dualism and identity. In other words, an adequate philosophical view of experience should be able to deal in a satisfactory way with all varieties of experience and with their mutual relations.

So, in rejecting Heidegger's categorical dichotomy of the authentic and the inauthentic we are not denying that there are intensive experiences, even extreme ones, or that they are philosophically interesting. Such experiences may also be transcendentally inaccessible for a mind which is attuned only to regular intensities or to finding regularities, identities and symmetries. But, according to naturalism, even the highest pinnacle of what is called the "authentic Dasein experience" remains within the realm of emotions. As an emotion, it is something psychological. Here *psychological* refers neither to Brentano's sense nor to the sense which associates it to standard empirical research. The former is too dualistic and the latter is unable to deal with the aconceptual dimension of experience. But whatever the proper (nondogmatic, anomalous) meaning of *psychological* is, extreme experience, as something psychological, remains open to social, anthropological and other historical influences, and its purity is lost. (More about the possibility of nondogmatic natural science in the next chapter.)

But then, what is *not* lost? What is it that is naturalistically acceptable, interesting and even desirable in *Dasein*? *It is the aconceptual and atheoretical nature of authentic Dasein experience*, namely, that there is experience which is so unstructured with respect to conceptuality that even the contrast of the interior and the exterior (subject and object; subject and predicate) isn't yet discernable. This is experience that cannot be captured by such conceptual or theoretical tools which cut everything into logical and grammatical structure. That the human language and mind is to be described primarily in terms of this kind of primitive and primordial experience is a view that naturalism can and should adopt (for more detailed views, see Pylkkö, 1993a).

In what follows, a special task is reserved for the letter *a*. When a word, *w*, is prefixed with it, the resulting word, *aw*, represents an attempt to move beyond the dichotomy which is presupposed in the meaning of *w*. Thus *aconceptual* doesn't equal in meaning *nonconceptual* but represents an attempt to dissolve the conceptual-nonconceptual dichotomy. Similarly, *amechanical* means something that precedes the contrast of the mechanical and the nonmechanical. This use of the letter *a* holds for all of the following chapters. The sense in which the meaning of the word *aw* is said to *precede* that of *w* and *nonw* cannot be expressed in any regular theoretical language if *w* occurs in that language. This is so because all meaningful use of the language most probably presupposes the very dichotomy (of *w* and *nonw*). If we want to emphasize that the *preceding* in question is empirical or historical, we prefer to use the prefix *pre-*.

The human mind was there before external objects and the human language before concepts. Therefore, experience is not to be described in terms of externalization and conceptualization alone. There is much more to the mind than what can be conceptualized and experienced as external or internal objects. And, if cognition is something that can be comprehensively conceptualized, then, trivially, there is more to the mind than cognition alone. Though pleasures and horrors vary in intensity, they have almost no structure, and, most certainly, they cannot be reduced to logical or grammatical structure. Neither should we say that pleasure and horror are purely either external or internal things. Yet they belong to the human mind. The human mind and language is, first of all, aconceptual experience which is immediate and present before internal or external objects enter the scene of the mind and organize it.

It is not only our modern culture and its technology which lure us to explain our experience in terms of 'things' or 'external objects,' both concrete and abstract. The desire for objects runs deeper, namely in our genes. For the sake of argument, let us adopt here some notions of the biological sciences and leave their modification for the next chapters. Our nervous system, due to its genetically determined structure, *almost* forces us to perceive and think in terms of external objects. For example, contour enhancement, color constancy and constancy of objects under rotation are genetically supported abilities of the human visual system which enhance the thing-oriented ontology. Biological evolution itself seems to have misguided us by providing us with a nervous system whose conception of knowledge is less than elegant and which contradicts the best of our physical theory, quantum theory, especially as it is known after the inseparability implications of Bell's theorem. That we can be aware of this shows that the very same evolution has, fortunately, been less than perfectly consistent and has equipped us with several, mutually exclusive, rivalling conceptions of knowledge. That is why it was said above that our nervous system forces us, not fully, but only *almost* to perceive and think in terms of external objects.

Aconceptual experience

Let us take immediate and unstructured primitive experience as our philosophical starting point. This unarticulated and prelogical experience which we call *aconceptual* is what mind and language primarily *is*. It is not yet organized by concepts. Because we associate subjectivity strongly with the conceptual organization of experience we say also that, in aconceptual experience, there is no such hierarchy and perspective which characterize the subject's presence. The experience is, so to speak, holistically everywhere, without center, or it has a center which is not yet fully organized. The intensity of aconceptual experience varies perpetually and aconceptuality is the main source of experiential intensity. Thus, we *don't* say that when a person has a regular everyday experience with external common sense objects, like sticks and stones, that his experience is as intensive as the ultimate apersonal experience of a tantric mystic or political zealot. Nature isn't that democratic. There is a difference in experiential intensity involved.

If we decide to describe aconceptual experience verbally, we have (infinitely) many different discourses available, ranging from poetry and religious language to neurobiological and connectionist language. One of the main restrictions that we want to impose upon these languages, as well as upon an adequate description of these languages, is that they should not resort to strong structural notions, especially not to standard logical, grammatical, Newtonian and ethical notions. Any attempt to use such notions would preclude the possibility of finding an adequate description. This restriction makes metaphysical or *a priori* individuals and all sort of substances unavailable. By accepting this, we also renounce some central dogmas of common sense, including crude versions of folk psychology, folk ontology and folk semantics, and, along with common sense, all standard common-sense-based conceptions of mind, language and science. The restriction is a consequence of a requirement which says that a notion can be said to be naturalistically acceptable only if it can be constructed in experiential, neural, behavioral, social and historical terms, and this requirement will renounce most of the standard grammatical, logical and ethical notions, as well as the notions of classical science, as normative fictions.

Now, intensive aconceptual experience, as it reaches up to certain extreme stages, is what remains of the authentic *Dasein* experience after naturalization. The aconceptual experience is unstructured and holistic to such an extent that even the so-called authentic cannot be sharply distinguished from the inauthentic. The experience is essentially impure and open to all sort of natural, social and historical influences and disturbances. But even at its most extreme level, the experience has grown continuously and without categorical gaps from everyday experience, though everydayness here is not common-sensically explainable. This means, among other things, that our present-day everydayness is, through its aconceptual nature, already ineradicably contaminated by the scientific culture. Thus, no way to experiential purity is available. Even our most intensive religious, political and aesthetic experiences carry ingredients which originate from the scientific attitude.

George Bataille's *l'expérience intérieure* is an interesting description of such extreme experience (Bataille, 1943/1988; see also Arnaud & Excoffon-Lafarge, 1978). Some elitist inclinations may threaten also Bataille's *l'expérience* as the following comments suggest: "I call experience a voyage to the end of the possible of man. Anyone may not embark on this voyage..." (Bataille, 1943/1988, p. 7). It runs in the original text as follows: "J'appelle expérience un voyage au bout du possible de l'homme. Chacun peut ne pas faire ce voyage,...", (Bataille, 1943/1992, p. 19). But by and large Bataille's *l'expérience* differs from 'regular experience' only by its degree of intensity, not by belonging to a special superior antinaturalistic category of experience. Therefore, Bataille's notion lends itself more easily (with fewer modifications) to a naturalized interpretation than Heidegger's "authentic Dasein experience." The danger of antinaturalistic elitism lurks, however, behind some characterizations of *l'expérience*, too. For example, Bataille's tendency to purify the arousal of *l'expérience* from all external causes, like esthetic causes, shades the notion with some antinaturalistic connotations. In a proper treatment which would not have trivialized the notion, Bataille could have allowed something to *influence* the experience. This influence cannot, however, be causal in any classical sense of the word.

Bataille distances his *l'expérience* from all sorts of conceptualizations and systematizations, even if they are supposed to be realized in religious language. There is more to the human mind than what any single system of conceptualization can ever capture. As such, this isn't yet an antinaturalistic tendency at all. On the contrary, the naturalistic attitude must concede that man's relationship with nature cannot be exhausted by a single, logically consistent theory. Bataille says that if one tries to describe extreme experience with the word *God* one has already changed the experience to something else (Bataille, 1943/1988, p. 4): "If I said decisively: 'I have seen God,' that which 'I see would change." In the original: "Si je disais décidément: 'j'ai vu Dieu', ce que je vois changerait." (Bataille, 1943/1992, p. 16). The word *God* carries with it, and is supported by, the whole machinery of lifeless theological rationalization. Bataille's approach is decidedly *a*theological. He rejects also classical phenomenological analysis of extreme experience because classical phenomenology is biased to the side of consciousness in the description of the human mind. And consciousness is, of course, the most faithful ally of logical and grammatical structure. If consciousness is part of experience, it belongs to the most corrupted and compliant department of it. According to Bataille's view, proper description of mind shouldn't be carried out from any such point of view which is dominated or controlled by consciousness. Thus the inner experience has very little to do with the transcendental or *a priori* conditions of knowledge in the Husserlian or Kantian sense. Yet the experience is to some extent conceptually inaccessible, that is, it transcends any single, consistent rationalization.

Even such inner experience which lies beyond or below conceptual reason is not necessarily completely ineffable. It can be described as long as our descriptions do not assume structure, objectification and externalization, and as long as descriptions of the language which is used to describe experience do not resort to structure, objectification and externalization either. So, we must be particularly careful with language when we are dealing with *l'expérience*. Otherwise, it may happen that official language, the language of science, religion, metaphysics and administration, blocks our way back to *l'expérience*. In Bataille's words: "Although words drain almost all life from within us [...] there subsists in us a silent, elusive, ungraspable part" (1943/ 1988, p. 14). In the original: "Bien que les mots drainent en nous presque toute la vie [...] il subsiste en sous une part muette, dérobée, insaissible." (Bataille, 1943/1992, p. 27).

If Bataille's *l'expérience* is mystical in some sense, we are dealing here with an earthly, or as we may prefer to say, "naturalized," version of mysticism. The experience is natural but not theoretically accessible, or not at least comprehensively so. Inner experience leads us nowhere, and nothing deep or high lies behind it. It is not a medium or path toward something hidden or more profound than experience itself. This kind of 'natural mysticism' has its origin in unstructured and often less than noble experiences which everyone of us has had in infancy, and which, after infancy, are still available for almost all of us in erotic life, in some art, in dreams and nightmares, in adventure, in being close to danger and death, and, perhaps, in experimenting with some drugs. This kind of down to earth mysticism of intensity doesn't promise salvation or the final answer. If it is transcendental, it is in Schopenhauer's sense, namely, by being something that evades concepts (Vorstellungen) (cf. Chapter 4).

What an advocate of naturalism has to remind us here is that Bataille almost always speaks of extreme experience ("l'expérience allant au bout du possible") and its philosophical role. This was his calling. But most people are not willing to be lost in such experiences, and, even if willing, not actually capable of dealing with them, let alone capable of utilizing them in their thinking. If accepting this observation implies a *possibility* of elitism, it is a possibility that must be accepted. Yet such pejorative expressions as *das Man* need not be attributed to these persons. Also their knowledge may be genuine, that is, knowledge which arises from experience, though this experience remains less intensive. According to naturalism, there is no knowledge without experience, and the neural story of what experience is is worth consideration. Some experiences are more intensive than others, but any experience may serve as an origin for some knowledge.

Genuine naturalism cannot afford to adopt an overly defensive attitude toward extreme experiences. Also they belong to nature, namely, to the nature of man and some other animals. Even what is called *Angst* by Heidegger has a biological and evolutionary description, though that may today be quite inadequate, and may always remain so. We enter into elitism and cultural solipsism only when we separate intensive experiences into a special category and make them accessible through a gate which can be opened only by those who satisfy some dualistic discriminative criteria. For example, one day a genetic description may be given of experiential intensities because some people may be natively more prone to intensive experience than others. But it would be naturalistically extremely implausible that experiential intensity would appear only among, say, the Germans or Swabians. Analogously with linguistic criteria. Languages express ethnically and nationally unique experiences which may even be untranslatable, and, therefore, experiential intensity of one linguistic community may be verbally inaccessible in another. But it would be naturalistically implausible that only one language or language family could be able to monopolize the description of intensive aconceptual experience.

Experiential relativism

What we have done so far is that we have torn down the categorical wall which separates Heidegger's authentic *Dasein* from what might be called "regular experience," and, simultaneously, what separates the Nothing from the regular psychological operation of negation. The resulting notions are *neither* regular notions of empirical science *nor* notions which are categorically separated from the empirical world. They are nondogmatically naturalistic notions which allow us to move close to properly interpreted natural science without committing ourselves to objectivism or externalism.

We could have chosen another path toward a similar position. We could have taken seriously the later Heidegger's view of language. In "The nature of language" (1957-58/1971), Heidegger has ended up with a view according to which the meaning of a verbal expression for a speaker consists of the *experiences* which the speaker has had with the expression. Heidegger invites us to experience something unexpected with language, that is, "to undergo an experience with language ("... mit der Sprache eine Erfahrung zu machen," Heidegger, 1957-58/1985). This experience will overwhelm and transform us ("... es uns umwirft und verwandelt") to something that we were not before. Yet it is not an intentional enterprise which is controlled by the conscious subject. During the experience one may find the authentic *home or abode of the Dasein* in language ("... der Mensch den eigentlichen Aufenhalt seines Daseins in der Sprache hat..."). Our *Dasein* is so ineradicably in our language that we could say that we *are* our language.

But obviously, experiences which any two or more persons attach to the allegedly same verbal expression can never be identical with each other, and the direction in which an experience will transform a person represents something genuinely unpredictable only if the change is unique, something that no one else (including the person himself) has gone through before. Therefore, meaning (of what we carelessly call "one and the same expression") varies from person to person (which means that actually there is no "one and the same expression" after all). Experience is also open to social, ethnic, linguistic and other historical influences from the speaker's environment because the experiences which the speaker is able to attach to an expression do not arise in a cultural vacuum. There are no pure, nonhistorical or completely nonsocial experiences which remain constant and which would not vary as a function of the environment where they take place. Even the greatest joy, dread and rage are influenced by the environment where they arise. But this doesn't mean that meanings are culturally determined. Nature puts limits to such determination attempts.

This points toward a naturalized reinterpretation of the later Heidegger's view of language. The interpretation challenges the peculiar *universalist trait* of Heidegger's thinking and claims that it is actually in conflict with the basic tendency of Heidegger's work. The naturalistic interpretation questions also all such rivalling interpretations which make languages and cultures solipsistically isolated. Actually, these two views, the universalist and the solipsistic one, may, in some obscure and ambiguous way, originate from a common view of meaning. Analogously, both misunderstanding and obsessive securing of identities originate from a common view of meaning. According to the naturalistic interpretation, the later Heidegger's view will eventually lead us to meaning relativism, or more accurately, to *meaning relativism with respect to experience*. No meaning without experience, and no experience without perpetually changing environment. Here *experience* covers more than just perceptual experience, and *environment* covers both cultural and natural environment and is not supposed to be independent of experience. Thus the so-called 'misunderstanding' is understanding with strange or exceptional conditions.

This is not to suggest that Heidegger himself ever took a decisive step toward such relativism, let alone toward naturalism, as it is here recommended. Here we are approaching the no-man's land, the divide which separates a Heidegger interpretation from Heidegger-inspired thinking (cf. Preface). This is so because Heidegger would not have liked the next natural step either, which is that we direct the thrust of relativism to the central notions of Heidegger's own vocabulary, starting with "authentic Dasein experience." This may happen with the following question: What guarantees that all great thinkers and poets actually do deal with only *one* question, as Heidegger used to claim, namely, with the question of Being (Seinsfrage)? In other words, how do we know that they all are speaking of one and the same Being when they use, say, the words *Sein* and *Dasein*?

The answer which accords with naturalism is that nothing guarantees that all great thinkers and poets deal with only one Big Question. This is so because one thinker or poet *cannot* mean by his words *Sein* or *Dasein* the same as another thinker or poet, even if he or she desperately wants to do so. Experiences which they attach to these words are never identical. Thus, desperate attempts to mean the identical leads only to misunderstanding. In other words, the words *Sein* and *Dasein* necessarily bear different meanings to different thinkers and poets due to the unique cultural, historical, ethnic, social and linguistic background and environment which have shaped their experiences. Therefore, *Dasein* also becomes relativized. Actually, if a thinker uses the words *Sein* and *Dasein* and wants to make them mean something intensive, then he *cannot* mean and shouldn't even try to mean by them what Heidegger allegedly had in mind.

Genuine naturalism views language and mind in terms of experience. Experience as such and our neural conception of experience support each other at least in this respect: just as any two experiences are never identical, two neural processes aren't identical either. Even what is colloquially called 'one and the same person' can never return to a previous experience; analogously, his brain processes never return to a previous state. In other words, there are no persistent brain states. Experience is unique and irreversible.

This relativizes all meaning to a "unique experiential history." We could have also said "unique neural history." But this doesn't mean that we are dealing only with an experiential-neural history of *one* person (solipsism) because neural naturalism blurs the boundaries of persons, too, and it makes no sense to speak of experience only in terms of 'one' nervous system. Rather, we should speak of the experiential history of a community or even of the human species. For example, a reasonable unit for many linguistic considerations is a human community, that is, a network of neural networks which are linked together by perception, other experiences and behavior and which share a common way of life. But even species solipsism which this view might imply can be avoided because the experience of the human species cannot be strictly separated from nonhuman animal experience.

From this kind of relativized point of view, human experience is wild, untamed and culturally extremely heterogeneous: no universal logic, grammar, ontology, religion, ethics or science is able to unify it without violating the local uniqueness and variety of experience. And our notion of *experience* may be so wide that it covers phenomena from humans down to the 'behavior' of electrons. After meaning relativism has been accepted, the suggestion according to which a special task has been assigned to the German people and the German language is seen from a new angle. If there is such a special task, "special" means also "local, without universal bearing." The German *Dasein* experience is just one among others, and other cultures may provide a background for experiences which are just as extreme and philosophically interesting as that which the German culture is able to produce. For example, thinkers whose cultural background lies far from southern Germany may find interesting solutions to the problems of technology, particularly because their language is *not* related to Greek and German. This is so because the structure of the Indo-European languages may have contributed, not only to the ascent of Western technology, but to the amplification of its difficulties.

This kind of relativism fails to give us comprehensive or meaning-preserving translations. If there is any hope of ever finding acceptable conditions for *intercultural dialogue*, the conditions will be based neither on any common conceptual ground nor on rational patterns of conjoint action. For example, science is unable to provide such a ground or rationality of action. This view is perfectly naturalistic; actually, its negation, the universality claim of Western science, is deeply antinaturalistic. In addition, this kind of relativism doesn't automatically guarantee equality among cultures because every standard notion of equality presupposes either that a universal conceptual ground can be found or a common rationality unites human action. Thus, for example, we cannot preclude the possibility that the Germans and their language have been vital in shaping the modern Western culture, including philosophy, technology and science. What we can preclude is that this was dictated by a historical necessity, or, that by some kind of fate, it *must* be the Germans and their language which will help us in understanding the essence of metaphysics and technology in the future too.

This view accords with what was earlier attained through the naturalization of some of Heidegger's basic notions. As the borderline between *Angst* and *Furcht* was demolished, *Angst* was exposed to natural, social and historical influences and its purity was lost. Every culture has its own version of *Angst* and its own reaction to *Technik*. And contrary to what Heidegger has suggested, *Seinsfrage*, or its local counterpart, has been recognized in many non-European cultures, not least in early Buddhist philosophy (for which, see Kalupahana, 1992). Of course, we may begin to wonder at this phase of our essay if *Seinsfrage* is the proper word for a local, non-German question of being. In addition, *Seinsvergessenheit* in the Western culture hasn't been completely overwhelming. A great deal of nineteenth century European literature and philosophy did deal with the *Seinsfrage*. What must be conceded is that the global technologization and unification of human experience has advanced faster than anybody could predict, and the cultivation of ametaphysical tendencies in the West has been neglected.

It also seems that Heidegger exaggerated the extent to which externalization and reification characterizes modern natural science. Perhaps this misconception arose simply because Heidegger equated natural science with the classical Newtonian science. This may have misled him to overestimate the amount to which modern science is dominated by reification and objectivism. The consequences of this misinterpretation may turn out to be severe if it has unwittingly helped the metaphysical camp to secure its positions. The possibility of antirealism which the so-called Copenhagen interpretation and especially the inseparability implications of Bell's theorem have opened to us make quantum theory look much less *onto-theo-logical* than what one would have expected had Heidegger been right about the essence of science (see the next chapter). In quantum theory, subject and object have become entangled and their boundary appears to be highly conventional, and the existence of separable physical objects has been questioned. Therefore, Heidegger's vision of the cultural situation of the West is far from accurate, and, what is central for the theme of this chapter, his discriminatory pro-German attitudes which he expressed so blatantly in many writings, not the least in *Der Spiegel interview*, can be disarmed.

Tolerance and dominance

Through naturalization and meaning relativism we have ended up at environmental relativism (including both the cultural and natural aspects). The kind
of relativism which we are interested in here is possible only if we can
distinguish *culturally tolerant* from *culturally intolerant*. An idea is culturally
tolerant, or culturally contingent, if it can be widely distributed, say through
proper interpretation, over cultural boundaries, such that the uniqueness of
the foreign culture where it is applied is not seriously threatened. Otherwise
an idea is said to be culturally intolerant. Tolerance is thus an inherent ability
of some ideas and experiences to live among and deal with other ideas and
experiences without annulling them. For example, let us assume that an idea
presupposes a definite conception of rationality, personhood and morality.
The idea is culturally intolerant if those who have adopted it have to characterize those who have not adopted it as irrational nonpersons who lack
morality. Thus *cultural tolerance* (contingency), as it is here understood, is
not primarily a relation among persons but among collective experiences,
cultures and ideas, though we may occasionally use a personal tone of
expression. Therefore, cultural tolerance, as such, doesn't necessarily mini-
mize violent reactions among persons or nations. Actually, every interpretation itself is already somewhat violent.

A culturally tolerant idea can be locally modified and assimilated so that
its new cultural context doesn't feel that its uniqueness is fatally in danger.
Therefore, a culturally tolerant idea may be helpful in finding an interesting
solution to a problem which arose originally within another culture, that is,
within a culture which didn't itself produce the idea. (I didn't realize until
recently that some of the views here resemble Feyerabend's cultural relativism as it is expressed, for example, in his "Notes on relativism" which is the
first essay, pp. 19-89, of *Farewell to Reason*, 1987.)

The issue of tolerance is not particularly closely related to the problem of
fundamentalism or fanaticism. Even culturally tolerant ideas can be propa-
gated fanatically, and vice versa, culturally intolerant ideas can be marketed
with extremely suave methods. The issue is that some ideas tend necessarily
to annihilate or degrade other ideas. For example, it is possible that a Siberian
shaman (culture) tolerates a Western scientist and even praises the scientist's
skills and sees them as powerful forms of magic. At the same time, it wouldn't
be too surprising if the scientist's attitudes were not reciprocally tolerant, and

he thought that the shaman's knowledge is not as serious, good or valuable as his own knowledge. This is not just stupidity on the scientist's part. It is plausible that his system of beliefs necessarily implies that kind of an attitude. It is a common attitude within modern Western natural science to picture traditional non-Western knowledge and science, as well as non-scientific Western knowledge, simply as colorful nonsense. Actually it may be hard or even impossible to reconcile standard modern scientific attitude with ideas and experiences of non-Western cultures without annulling or distorting them.

Culturally intolerant ideas are overwhelming and dominating. They don't mix easily with alien ideas and they cannot be questioned without questioning a great deal of their background, too. Their advocates often present them as universal ideas, and, therefore, there is the flair of 'cultural necessity' or inherent coercion around them. Because the claim of universality is pretentious, culturally intolerant ideas attempt to reach global dominance with the help of *cultural unification*. Cultural unification is characterized by a low level of experiential intensity. A great deal of Western logic and grammar, classical natural science, ideas of the Enlightenment (quantitative equality; unificatory democracy; universalist tolerance) and Christian theology is culturally intolerant, though often tacitly so, and its claim of universal validity is questionable. Contrary to this, modern Western poetry and the conception of man related to it are often culturally tolerant because it is inherent in the poetical culture that poems are local and untranslatable. In order to understand foreign poetical works, a lot of patience and skill is needed. The understanding is possible only with the help of *interpretation* in which the poetical work is recreated within a new cultural context. The ways of recreation are always partly unpredictable and no universal method exists to find out what they are. An attempt to reach meaning identity may actually hinder or distort the interpretation because identity-seeking attitudes tend to diminish experiential intensity.

The origin of tolerance lies in accepting natural and experiential indeterminacy. Every serious naturalist says that either the objects to which culturally intolerant ideas refer are not (do not exist) at all, or if a community defines some ideas in a culturally intolerant way and the objects to which they refer must, in some sense, be said to 'be,' then their demand of universality is pretentious and they are actually just local fictions. Thus, it is understandable that culturally intolerant ideas suffer of lowered intensity when they are exported outside of their original context. In other words, either we say that the objects which grammar, logic, regular democracy, Christian theology and Newtonian science assume do not exist in any naturalistically acceptable way; or, if they are in some sense said to exist (because, for example, they are followed and accepted by Western academics), their demand of universality is not valid and they are actually nothing more than local fictions which cannot be exported without reducing their intensity.

Heidegger suggested that classical logic and Western natural science are culturally intolerant and denounced their claim of universal applicability. What he failed to appreciate is that the twentieth century natural science, especially after the invention of quantum theory, isn't as obviously culturally intolerant as the old science used to be. By introducing such notions as chance, indeterminacy and inseparability, the quantum theory forces us to distance ourselves from realism and objectivism, and this makes it easier for us to understand what *uniqueness* could mean in the context of philosophical naturalism. So, though modern natural science is a local Western product, not all Western science is automatically intolerant and saturated with equally rigid metaphysical thinking habits.

Unfortunately, Heidegger didn't denounce the obvious cultural intolerance of his own *Sein* philosophy. Therefore, there is always a danger that his thinking will be interpreted either in a universalist or solipsistic way. He even attempted to purify "authentic Dasein experience" of all naturalizing and relativizing ingredients which could have made it culturally tolerant. By introducing tolerance, we open *Dasein* to *intercultural interpretation* and foreign influence. This doesn't yet make *Dasein* peaceful or nonviolent. On the contrary, by acknowledging irreducible cultural uniqueness we deny the possibility of such intercultural communication which is based on the idea of a ground of common meaning. This may fuel violence just as easily as peace in intercultural personal or national relations because both alternatives may be based on a proper interpretation. Culturally tolerant shamanism doesn't preclude the possibility that a shaman resorts to violence in his attempt to preserve the uniqueness of his culture against the unification pressures of the Western science. Thus tolerance doesn't imply nonviolence. A culturally unified world which is dominated by modern technology and democracy will be peaceful indeed.

I have tried to show how naturalization can make *Dasein* and other Heideggerian notions culturally more tolerant, as well as more resistant to cultural solipsism. If Heidegger's *Dasein* notion is taken too literally in a

German context, it will encourage cultural solipsism; if it is taken too literally in a non-German context, it tends to become unificatory and lose some of its intensity. This thinking exercise is the remedy which, I hope, can amend the disease which holds *Dasein* in its grip and release it from the symptoms which were described at the beginning of this chapter. This doesn't mean, however, that all consequences of the disease are straightforwardly negative, or that the body of Heidegger's thinking could be sharply separated from the disease. No, such externality would betray the nature of disease in general: diseases belong ineradicably to our nature and result from biological evolution just as our health does. Many repercussions of *Dasein*'s disease are ambiguous, and already the incubation of the disease may have enhanced the vitality of the organism, the body of Heidegger's thinking. Diseases sometimes reveal the hidden potentialities of the organism.

The origin of the disease lies in Heidegger's ambiguous claim of universal applicability and necessity for his *Dasein* notion. The claim may have contributed also to the appearance of strong aversive reactions to Heidegger's thinking in some quarters and eventually forced Heidegger to adopt a position of cultural solipsism and isolation. For example, Heidegger didn't hesitate to speak of *the* question of Being (die Seinsfrage) as if there was only *one* such question. This ambiguous universalism implies a special kind of cultural intolerance and precludes *cultural variety*. But as soon as Heidegger's universalist tendencies are shown to be pretentious, a new difficulty threatens: cultural solipsism, isolationism and political elitism. Cultural solipsism can be overcome only by a proper notion of intercultural interpretation (see Chapter 8), whereas the core of elitism can be undermined by an antidualistic view of experiential intensity. The remedy of naturalization, as it is here devised, provides a contingently tolerant view to *Dasein*, such that even the most extreme and bizarre cases of any local *Dasein* experience are made accessible over ethnic barriers via proper intercultural interpretations, and even the most intensive and horrific experiences are opened to the so-called Everyman. Later (Chapter 8) we will consider the Finnish context and the peculiar mode of human *Dasein* which can be expressed only by the word *ollaan*. Of course, we may wonder whether the word *Dasein* is still proper in this kind of altered use.

After naturalization, all versions of the *Dasein* notion and all varieties of *Dasein* experience become *interpretable* (but not translatable or 'communicable') over cultural, ethnic, linguistic and social boundaries. Clearly, this doesn't make the notion or experience universal. The anomalous *Dasein*, as well as *naturalism* and related notions, remains German and Western in its origin. But a Western point of view is not necessarily intolerant. When a tolerant Western notion is applied in a non-Western context, the notion is influenced by the new context and becomes smoothly transformed into something else. At some phase of the transformation, we have to decide whether or not we want to use the old name for a new experience.

Through naturalization and relativization of *Dasein*, something of the spirit of democracy can, perhaps, be saved, at least to the extent to which the Everyman is willing to utilize his possibilities. Underlying all genuine tolerance lies a view which doesn't want to reduce the human mind into concepts and reason alone but acknowledges an irreducible role for the aconceptuality, uncertainty and indeterminacy in the human experience. Because of the aconceptual origin of the mind, no universal rationality or conceptual ground is ever able to unify the human experience comprehensively, though such unification processes have attained almost a global range today. Unfortunately, regular democracy and the related individualistic notion of tolerance belong to the processes of experiential unification and are therefore tacitly quite intolerant.

Ultimately, all concepts are originally local, that is, seamlessly connected to the aconceptual experience of local communities; it is the intolerant nature of the concept and the clumsy application of it to a foreign environment that deprives the concept of intensity. Still, after naturalization and relativization, intensity of experience, amplified by its original aconceptuality, preserves its philosophical weight and vitality. The alliance of relativism and naturalism denounces both metaphysical realism and all universalist conceptions of meaning. Thus the hope that our concepts are able to approach and grasp the structure of the so-called reality is lost. But it is exactly this loss that retains an important role for the intensity of experience as a source of philosophical insight and understanding.

CHAPTER TWO

Is modern science necessarily
onto-theo-logical?

The difference between *Sein* and *Seiende*

In his *Identity and Difference* (1957/1969), Heidegger used the attribute *onto-theo-logical* to designate such thinking which is unable to recognize the difference between Being (Sein) and entities (Seiende). Onto-theo-logical thinking is representative and, therefore, bound to endorse the dichotomy of subject and object. It is typical of ontology, theology and logic that, because of their representative nature, they deal only with entities and are forced to ignore the question of Being and pass it eventually into forgetfulness. Onto-theo-logic is the core of the Western metaphysical tradition and, according to Heidegger, metaphysics dominates modern Western culture through technology (Technik) and natural science. Though the whole possibility of metaphysics rests on the difference between Being and entities, metaphysics is unable to think of the difference.

Hence, it is typical of metaphysical thinking that it is unable to think of its own essence. Instead, metaphysics has considered entities as such and as a whole and searched for a foundation of knowledge which it pretends to have found in the *Logos*, in the immutable structure of onto-logic and theo-logic. For example, within the onto-logic of natural science the world is seen as a set of entities (Seiende), such that each entity is determined by a logical kind of scientific identity. In the onto-theo-logical context, the human mind becomes a mechanism or device whose main purpose is to reflect entities and their relations. As such a mechanism, the human mind is unable to think of the difference between Being (Sein) and beings (Seiende). Thus, onto-theo-logical thinking blocks the mind's access to the proper understanding of what it is. In the proper self-understanding, Being and the Being of man belong to one another or together in a kind of act of intertwinement, assimilation and mutual surrendering.

Also theology is metaphysics because it endeavors to approach its subject matter, the essence of God, representatively. In this respect, theology is a genuine science. As we saw in the previous chapter, this conceptual and representative nature of theology was something of which also George Bataille wanted to remind us (Bataille, 1943/1988). According to Bataille, every attempt to describe the inner experience (l'expérience intérieure) with theological terms, including the term *God* itself, transforms the experience to something else, to something that it wasn't earlier, before the attempt took place. Inner experience, in Bataille's sense, defies conceptual and representative description.

Heidegger's choice of words in the expression *onto-theo-logic* suggests also that he may have thought that natural science itself is a kind of modern theology. Just like theologians, scientists seek for an immutable foundation and first cause. A scientific realist believes that there is an external world which is independent of our experience, that the world is to some extent experience-transcendent (purified of experience), as we might say, and that we can reflect the structure of some department of the reality with the help of the terms of our theories. Furthermore, it is thought that scientific theories form a consistent and gradually improving description of the reality. But, according to Heidegger, the human experience itself doesn't provide any evidence for such a categorical separation of experience and world. Therefore, a theological conviction is needed, a conviction that behind or below our experience there lies a mind-independent but comprehensible reality. One might even say that this conviction is the only theological conviction which the modern man takes seriously.

The parallel question: Is nondogmatic philosophical naturalism possible?

The question whether modern science is necessarily onto-theo-logical runs parallel with another question which comes close to the original one but which presumably did not attract Heidegger's attention. The question is this:

Is *a*-onto-theo-logical (or, as we will also say, *nondogmatic*) naturalism possible? In other words, is it possible to design a version of philosophical naturalism which surpasses onto-theo-logic and takes Being and the human experience of it seriously? Is it possible to conceive the difference between Being and entities within the natural sciences and within philosophical naturalism? Or, is modern science doomed to handle only entities and accept the dogma that the subject and the object both can and must be kept clearly separated?

In order to make sense, the question concerning the possibilities of nondogmatic naturalism requires that naturalism is incompatible with all versions of traditional psycho-physical dualism. All traditional versions of dualism rest heavily on the idea that there exists a conscious subject which reflects the things of the world with the help of its concepts, and that it is the freedom of the subject's will that vaults man above the causally closed world of things. But, assuming that this kind of dualism has taken the existence of rational subjectivity as a precondition of all knowledge, dualism is hardly able to tell us how subjects emerge. Of course, psycho-physical dualism is important as a sign which indicates the presence of a serious crisis in our thinking about the human mind, and naturalism, including the nondogmatic versions, cannot avoid encountering some dualities either. For example, already the best of our physical theories, namely quantum theory, presupposes a whole bunch of dualities (particle/wave; determinism/indeterminism; systemic/holistic; and so on) which every adequate interpretation has to face.

Analogously, materialism, including such materialism which hopes to be antireductionistic, is hardly able to show a proper place for human experience among material things. Could it thus have anything interesting to tell us about such experience which is often, though misleadingly perhaps, called 'inner experience' and which is characterized by the ultimate inseparability of subject and object? And, could traditional materialism which presupposes the concept of *thing* tell us anything interesting about the conditions under which things arise?

Normal materialism and scientific realism are hard to reconcile with the quantum theory as it is understood within the Copenhagen interpretation (see d'Espagnat, 1981, especially pp. 27-48), especially after the Bell's theorem, whereas the possibility of some kind of nondogmatic or anomalous naturalism is still open to us. But let us go a step further and assume that, during some cognitive processes and experiences, there occur brain phenomena which cannot be described adequately without quantum-theoretical notions. An immediate consequence of this situation is that the human brain and its environment form, at least at the microphysical level, an indivisible whole. But if this is the case then also every normal version of materialism and realism which is based on the very separability and independence of the brain and the extra-brain environment is in trouble. Even without microphysical considerations, if human experience is incorrigibly holistic, such that it has no systemic structure, all such versions of naturalism which require that the reality is independent of the human mind are untenable. There is no such thing as "holistic realism."

Now, a materialist and scientific realist might try to defend himself as follows. If our best scientific theories tell us that the world is holistic, diffuse and chaotic, then let it be so. This, however, is no reason to abandon materialism and realism which encompass every scientist's natural stance. Even if the world is a whole or totality in which no subsystems or constituents can be discerned and kept separate from one another, the world nevertheless exists independently of our mind and theories, and our concepts can picture relatively reliably how things are in the world. What is essential in the realistic stance is that the realist assumes that it is *reasonable* to believe that there exists a reality independently of our mind and language, and that this holds also in those cases when our perception, thinking, linguistic expressions and theories turn out to be inadequate or partial. The realist can even require that scientific knowledge must always be expressed in mechanical and easily computable terms, and still claim that the holistic aspects of the reality which we must acknowledge can always be approximated reasonably well. The approximation can be less than perfect, but this is no reason to question the existence of the mind-independent reality.

But this line of thinking would cause severe difficulties for our materialist and realist because a brain or mind which is inseparably entangled with the world could hardly claim to have reached brain-independent, and therefore mind-independent, knowledge of it. Thus, the least we can say is that the belief in the existence of the mind-independent reality cannot be based on empirical knowledge of the reality. Rather, the belief is based on a metaphysical presupposition which precedes all empirical knowledge. In general, the problem seems to be incorporated into the notion of *approximation*. The only notion of approximation with which a realist should feel comfortable is the one which can in principle be improved as long as is desired. As soon as this condition cannot be satisfied, we lose touch with the reality, and it is possible that, along with the growing complexity of our theories, our theoretical terms actually picture a gradually shrinking area of the reality, and our alleged approximations are, not approaching, but distancing us from the true picture of the so-called reality. A reality which is receding faster away than our concepts are approaching it is not really a reality at all because it would require a perfectly man-independent conception of knowledge, and that is an absurdity.

The question whether modern science is onto-theo-logical is thus also a question about the possibilities of naturalism. But if nondogmatic naturalism *is* possible, we will be forced to use the word *naturalism* in a highly anomalous way. *Naturalism* will mean man's peculiar willingness to understand his relation with nature. This requires openness to natural phenomena and sensitivity to the two-way influences which flow between man and nature. In anomalous naturalism, natural science is not supposed to approach nature from an external or objectifying perspective, as if nature consisted of a set of things the existence of which is independent of experience and lies somewhere outside of it. If the nondogmatic view can be defended and smuggled into the realm of natural sciences and philosophical naturalism, natural science and naturalism are not necessarily doomed to philosophical naiveté.

We can consider the question of the possibility of nondogmatic science also from a more restricted point of view, namely, from that of neuroscience and the so-called philosophy of mind. Is it possible to consider the relationship between human experience and a good neural description of the experience without adopting dogmatic attitudes?

At first glance, almost all work in neuroscience seems to be forced to adopt an external point of view as it approaches its subject matter. Contrary to this, experience (Erfahrung; Erlebnis; upplevelse; elämys; kokemus) is something that cannot be comprehensively objectified or reified because experience is what we *are*, and we are not outside of ourselves as things; or if we are there, say as living bodies, we are not *fully* there because there is also a body experience which is not fully external. And if we are something, say aconceptual experience or holistic experience, only to a small extent, that something will become an embarrassment to natural science, if natural science is, in principle, unable to deal with it.

Thus in order to approach human experience, neuroscience, and perhaps science in general, may have to distance itself from such externalism which characterizes classical materialism and scientific realism. In other words, it may turn out that every genuinely naturalistic attitude will eventually force us to challenge materialism and realism.

The circularity of external naturalism

Nondogmatic philosophical naturalism sees natural science as a human enterprise which, as any human enterprise, is just one manifestation and organization of human experience. The interests and goals of natural science intertwine inseparably with many other human interests and goals, and scientific discourse cannot be separated crisply from other human discourses, including philosophical discourse. As the discourses become entangled into an inseparable whole, we cannot tell which is more fundamental or primary. Rather, the interaction of philosophy and science is perpetual, providing criticism, incitement and fomentation in both directions. In this kind of entangled situation, a philosopher, or what is left of being a philosopher after the entanglement has taken place, doesn't have to take the *doxa* of dogmatic science (externalism; objectivism; and so on) for granted. For example, anomalous naturalism, in the above sketched sense, means by and large the same as *thinking of man's nature experience*. Naturalism which begins with external objects and which suppresses man's active initiative and constructive contribution in the research enterprise is dogmatic, and one part of this dogmatism arises from the repressed circularity of the enterprise.

Consider the following example. If we study, say with a MEG measurement device (for MEG, see Hämäläinen, et al., 1993), the magnetic fluctuations of cortical activities during and after a person has received some perceptual stimuli, then we have to assume that, during the research process itself, our perception works correctly and produces reliable observations. But how is our reliance justified? It is based on a theory of perception, even though the theory may be just one of the so-called folkpsychological theories. But if the subject matter of our research consists of perceptual processes, we should not have a well articulated preconception of what perception actually is and what makes it reliable. If we do have such a preconception, it may turn out that the theory which we are testing with the MEG devices is the same folkpsychological theory which we have already presupposed to be true or, at most, a theory which is based on that very folkpsychological theory.

Similar examples can be designed easily with respect to practically any psychological "faculty." If we work on a theory of language which accords, say, with the basic guidelines of the mainstream cognitive science, we have to express our theory in natural language. But then, obviously, we must have adopted a preconception of what natural language is and how it succeeds in communicating meanings from one scholar to another. Again, this preconception may only be a folklinguistic theory, but it is still possible that the genuine scientific theory which we are designing is nothing but an uncritical confirmation of the folklinguistic thinking habits which we have adopted without proper scientific discussion. Therefore, it is possible that our scientific theory is nothing but a complex academic way to say that folk linguistics and folk semantics are valid after all. And often we seem to be saying even more, namely, that folk linguistics and folk semantics is, in a sense, *necessary* (true in all research situations, so to speak) or true a priori (true *before* empirical research begins).

Even if there is no way to avoid this circularity, the least we can do is acknowledge and investigate it. But this is not what happens in standard neuroscience and cognitive science, or in dogmatic natural science in general. It is good to notice that at least one alternative approach to cognitive science, namely that of Francisco Varela's, is aware of the web of circularities in which cognitive science is entangled (see Varela, Thompson and Rosch, 1991, especially pp. 9-11). To become conscious of the ways of such circularities from the very beginning is a crucial part of what being *nondogmatic* and *nonnaive* means. A strong flair of paradox hovers around the obsession of objectivity which characterizes dogmatic science because dogmatic science, by its very definition, attempts to obliterate all traces of its humble human origin: it tries to attain knowledge which is purified of its ties to human experience. But there is something paradoxical in the idea of purely objective knowledge because it seems that nothing can be known of objects which are purely mind-independent. At the very moment when we learn something about an object, the object becomes entangled with our organs of perception and knowledge, and the object loses part of its objectivity. And we could add: the part which it loses is proportional to the amount of knowledge which we are gaining.

One way to settle the dilemma was suggested by the Finnish philosopher and physiologist, Yrjö Reenpää (1959). He went so far as to claim that sets of perceptual stimuli are actually conceptualizations or projections which *suc-*

ceed perceptions. Instead of the standard stimulus-perception schema, he recommended a reversed schema in which perceptions precedes conceptualized stimuli.

Nondogmatic naturalism

Let us consider what nondogmatic naturalism which tries to be conscious of such circularities as were considered above, might look like (for more, see Pylkkö, 1993a; the topic is developed also in the next chapter). Nondogmatic naturalism might begin its work with such *aconceptual experience* in which the contrast of the internal and the external is not originally present, and say that perception, thinking and speaking are different ways to articulate such experience. Whatever may eventually arise as a result of the articulation, a subject, for example, its concepts, external objects, and so on, will never be able to become fully independent of or separated from the primordial aconceptual origin but will always remain partly entangled with it. What articulates the aconceptual experience is an *association*, a primitive operation which is itself neutral with respect to the contrast of the psychical and the physical, in a somewhat similar way as *Mach's elements* were intended to be neutral.

Neuroscience could describe this association in terms of trained or self-organizing neural networks but such a description will remain dogmatic as long as neural networks are understood as external mechanisms or formalisms. Anyway, all human concepts, including the most sophisticated scientific concepts, are never more than ways to organize human experience into a more or less feasible form with the help of associations. As Wilhelm Ostwald used to put it, things are experiences, namely experiences which have been reified into permanent structures. Things are not, of course, experiences of one single subject, but collective experiences which, in connectionist language, can be said to arise from the conjoint activities which a network of brains generates. Such a network of neural networks comprises what, in more colloquial terms, is called a *community*.

This doesn't mean that the world or being is "created" or "constituted" by a subject and its concepts because both subjects and concepts arise from the aconceptual experience as a result of a special kind of articulation process the end product of which, namely the so-called subject, "reflects" the objective part of the experience. The objective part of experience is called "reality" or the "world of things." So, the subject and the object depend on each other, and their articulation from aconceptual experience goes in parallel and ends up eventually in the appearance of a full-fledged conscious subject which finds itself surrounded by the causally related objects of the so-called external world. We could say that the subject is the conceptual structure of experience which makes the perception and knowledge of objects possible.

From the point of view of an emerging subjectivity, it is other subjects, especially the mother, and their bodies that form the most important part of the world of objects, and, therefore, it can be claimed that it is the environment of social games where the subject gradually becomes recognized as a "unity," namely as a competent participant in a game. In short, the subject is a competent player, an entity which is able to participate in a game and which arises from diffuse aconceptual experience as the participant's playing skills gradually evolve. To put it bluntly: first comes the mother, and then, due to the mother-child differentiation, the external world. This picture is intended to resemble to some extent George Herbert Mead's view of the social origin of subjectivity (cf. Mead, 1910; see also Chapter 4).

For example, in experimental neuroscience, say, in such neuroscience in which EEG and MEG measurements are carried out, we need not accept the dogmatic presupposition that, in measurement situations or in more theoretical scientific work, our pretheoretical observations, reasoning and language work reliably and that there is a conception, say a folk-psychological view, of perception, reasoning and language which is *a priori*, let alone universally, true. (An analogous argument applies, for example, to quantum theory.) On the contrary, we may assume that our pretheoretical ("pre" with respect to the theory which we are designing) conception of what perception, reasoning and language is, is designed tentatively but consciously to serve the interests of the scientific enterprise, and the enterprise may later modify the conception just as the conception is allowed to constrain the scientific work.

Even this small critical step would distance naturalism from the crudest form of dogmatism because, after we have taken the step, we cannot resort in our scientific work on cognition to an *a priori*, necessary and reliable preconception of what cognition actually is. But, of course, the price of the step is that, as soon as we take it, we must admit that we are not dealing with perception, reasoning and language in any objective, universal or general sense, and the theory of cognition which we are designing and for which we are arranging the EEG and MEG measurements will not be an objective, universal and general theory of perception, reasoning and language either. Rather, it will be a theory which applies only to such special cases of cognition which were chosen in a benevolent way in order to make them comply nicely with the expected results of measurements and with related theoretical views.

Benevolence implies here normality. Therefore, we must also say that the theoretical work itself, not only tells us what we are, but also shapes, conditions and transforms our mind toward a certain direction, namely toward a direction where our perception, reasoning and language actually become a model of our theoretical work. Eventually, our actual experience and cognition will satisfy the theoretical picture which we are designing. The theoretical work transforms what we experience and think, that is, what we actually *are*, toward a state where what we are will eventually satisfy the theoretical model. It would be naive to claim, for example, that the two or three millennia of logical and grammatical studies, amplified by institutionalized education, would not have influenced our language and thinking experience. We might summarize our view of this kind of influence by saying that dogmatic science is not only a device which helps us to describe the world and ourselves as such but an asubjective power which, unwittingly perhaps, transforms us toward a certain direction, namely, toward a direction in which anything (in nature or in ourselves) that doesn't comply with the prevailing scientific view is little by little forgotten or ignored and all that does comply with it is enhanced, emphasized and extolled as 'real.'

Standard science is trivially *onto-theo-logical*

Unfortunately, what I have sketched above, a picture and tentative self-image of anomalous science, is not what prevails in the academic world. The prevailing picture seems to be that such sciences as psychology and linguistics are actually able to describe human cognition and language in a manner which doesn't have a profound impact on what cognition and language are. The role of the human mind and language in the generation of theories is supposed be innocent, not seriously problematic or viciously circular, and the human language and mind are supposed to be what they are, independently of our theories about them. It is not unreasonable to claim that, in this respect, most scientists are dogmatic, that regular science tends to be highly dogmatic and the self-image of science presents science as a dogmatic enterprise.

Standard science is as circular as its confidence in common sense is unshakable. The problem is not that standard science accepts common sense, but that it accepts common sense uncritically and that it often chooses to accept the most mechanical and unreflective part of it. Even common sense has many aspects, and not all of them are equally reified and naive. The first critical step would be to notice that it is not rare that scientific theories unwittingly both accept and contradict some aspects of common sense. The next step away from naiveté would be to acknowledge that scientific theories themselves are unable to provide a single consistent and complete explanation of their field. For example, twentieth century physicists hold an array of mutually incompatible theories (for example, classical physics; special relativity; quantum theory). And eventually, common sense itself is incoherent and strongly influenced by a perpetually changing natural, historical and cultural environment, not the least because of the impact which science exercises upon it. There is neither *a priori*-like *Lebenswelt* nor pure ordinary language to which we can return when we need guidance and condolence. Both are already hopelessly contaminated by different technological, scientific and academic ideas (cf. Chapter 5). It is vital to notice that the fact that dogmatic science accepts common sense in an uncritical way doesn't imply that dogmatic science would be particularly good in explaining what common sense is. The opposite seems to be the case. Uncritically adopted foundations fall easily into inaccessible obscurity.

The standard scientific attitude still views the world as a set of external things, language as a set of labels for the things and actions, and the human mind as a mechanism which handles the labels and related concepts in order to say something about the things. Often science itself is seen as a continuation of common sense, though it should be quite easy to note that the common sense of the prescientific era of the West was quite different from the common sense which we follow today, and that neither of them is able to provide a consistent point of view. Yet, a considerable part of the present-day Western common sense accords with the standard scientific outlook, not the least because the very common sense has been shaped by the scientific tradition, and, simultaneously, the primary task of science was to explain the easily understandable aspects of common sense things.

One central difficulty of the common-sense-based science is this: how

could standard natural science at the same time be based on common sense
and explain why common sense things behave as they allegedly do (analogously, how could scientific psychology be based on folk psychology and be
able to explain it) ? For example, linguistics is seen as a science which
explains how labels of things (grammatical subjects) and actions (grammatical predicates) can be organized to produce meaningful strings (sentences)
which represent how things are in the world. Yet it is well known that this
subject-predicate view cannot be developed systematically, and, among other
things, it cannot explain how language is used even in science itself. For
example, the thing-label view of naming is unable to explain how quantum
physicists are able to speak of superposed quantum phenomena, assuming
that they actually *are* able to do that.

It takes a man of Hume's stature to acknowledge that though common
sense is necessary for conducting of our ordinary life and thinking, common
sense is unable to face critical philosophical analysis, and if the same critical
eye is turned to standard common-sense-based science, the result is equally
disastrous. There are hardly more moving words in the literature of Western
thinking than the conclusion of the Book I of *Treatise* (1739-40/1987, Section
VII, pp. 263-274) where the author acknowledges the limits of rational
thinking. It is human vanity which prevents us from acknowledging the limit,
and therefore the power of self-deception reigns among laymen and scientists, as well as among many philosophers. We are drawn toward this deception by the social warmth that participation in a collective deception always
elicits. The best that philosophical work can ever hope to do is to shed the
cool, lonely and weak light of disillusion upon the human condition. A great
deal of this disillusion arises when we realize how limited the power of
ordinary reason is.

If we hope that our knowledge can be both comprehensive and consistent
simultaneously, philosophy may teach us that we cannot have that much.
Whichever discourse we choose, it will sooner or later reveal its limits beyond
which the jurisdiction of a new discourse has to be assumed. But then, the new
discourse will never be fully reconcilable with or translatable into the old one.
This is what is denied by dogmatic science. For example, dogmatic natural
science declines to pay attention to such indeterminacies and uncertainties
which have been introduced to physics by some of the most critical thinkers of
the field. According to Niels Bohr (1933; see also Pais, 1991, pp. 309-323 and
420-451; Jammer, 1974, pp. 85-107 and 247-251; Faye, 1991, pp. 127-146), a

new notion, namely, *complementarity*, has to be introduced into the philoso-phy of natural science if we want to understand natural phenomena, for example, how microphysical phenomena are related to macrophysical ob-jects. Many pairs of concepts (particle/wave; space-time/causality; position/momentum) which we have learned either from common sense or classical physics cannot be applied to microphysical phenomena simultaneously with desired accuracy. Yet both of the aspects of each pair are necessary for a complete picture.

Wolfgang Pauli (1954; see also Laurikainen, 1988; and Pylkkö, 1996b) went even further by claiming that the research program of natural science which was launched in the early seventeenth century has, with the invention of quantum theory, come to the end of its road. The reason for this is that the research program was initiated with overly optimistic expectations as regards the prospects of finding a comprehensive and consistent rational explanation of natural phenomena. Quantum theory frustrated these expectations seri-ously. This is so mainly because of the collapse of the wave function, the existence of which is accepted by most of the well known interpretations. The collapse forces us to accept a step from the deterministic and mechanical Schrödinger equation to statistical measurement results, and this step from determinacy to indeterminacy lacks rational foundation. The theory is unable to explain why this sudden burst of chance and indeterminacy happens. Wolfgang Pauli drew the conclusion that nature has eventually disclosed its *irrational* face which had been covered for about three hundred years under the thin mask of exaggerated rationality. The mask's scaffold is the carefully built edifice of classical science and classical logic.

If science actually is what dogmatic scientists claim, namely, a project which searches for general and consistent laws of how external things behave, then the answer to our original question whether modern science is onto-theo-logical is trivially: *yes*. If the credo that science reveals to us what the lawful relations of external things are is tenable, and if the related folklore of how the human mind and language are related to the things is basically correct, then modern science is certainly very onto-theo-logical indeed, the epitome of philosophical naiveté. Alternatives for dogmatic science, as well as for the dogmatic self-image of science, are rare and often classified as scientifically irrelevant or even unscientific.

But is science necessarily what average scientists believe it is? Similarly, is natural language really what average speakers believe it is? Is it possible that people do not really know or understand any more what they are doing when they speak, and what they are speaking of? Is it possible that a whole civilization misunderstands its own nature by forgetting the proper meanings of its central cultural products, including language? Analogously, could a psychological theory dispense with folk psychology and change people in a direction which deviates radically from the conception of man which prevails in the culture which produced the psychological theory? Or, is psychology forced to adopt some *a priori* folk-psychological truisms in order to get started?

Heidegger seems to have thought (in *Being and Time*, 1927/1992 for example) that nondogmatic science is impossible, and, in this respect, his view accords surprisingly well with the implicit view which dogmatic scientists themselves hold. According to Heidegger, the world view of modern natural science is either dualistic (Cartesian) or, what is even worse, materialistic or crudely pragmatic, in which case the chances that it succeeds in dealing well with human experience are, if possible, even weaker. Therefore, Heidegger's picture of science and the self-image of dogmatic science are not, after all, too far from one another, though Heidegger, unlike many dogmatic scientists, thought that the scientific attitude is necessarily limited in its ability to approach human experience and that science arises within the *Dasein* experience and is, therefore, not independent of it.

That scientific knowledge has to be derived from the human experience and, as a special way to organize human experience, remains always entangled with it, is a view which dogmatic science would never accept. If it accepted the view it would have to acknowledge the active and constructive role that the human mind plays in the conception of scientific knowledge, and that would eventually make a part of human experience scientifically inaccessible. Dogmatic science wants to see all experience scientifically accessible and, at least in principle, explainable. This would mean that science can reach up to the reality in a way which renders the role of the human experience marginal, passive and even irrelevant.

Dasein, including the everyday *Dasein*, shouldn't in this respect be equated with the common sense world as the latter is understood by the present-day Western common sense itself because common sense says that the common sense world, that is, the reality, would be out there without colloquial language and common sense knowledge too. A crucial part of the reality would be out there had man never existed. That scientific knowledge is understood as a refined continuation of common sense knowledge means that both of them, common sense knowledge and common-sense-based science, are true because there is a reality out there, and the attitude of that reality toward both of them, that is, common sense and science, is equally indifferent.

Nothing analogous can be said of the *Dasein* in any sense of the word which comes even close to that of Heidegger's. *Dasein* is a broad philosophical notion and its meaning cannot be captured by average common sense. For example, man is occasionally able to attain authenticity in his experience of *Dasein* and this carries man far away from the sphere of everyday experience. In the *Dasein* analysis, there is no man-independent reality out there with a complete and consistent structure awaiting consideration by human reason. Being and man's *Dasein* depend on each other and are inseparably entangled with one another. That Heidegger was not particularly relativistic in his thinking and was inclined to think that the scientific community may be able to reach a rationally justifiable unanimity doesn't mean that Heidegger would have thought that scientific knowledge (or the everyday aspect of the *Dasein*) is primary, fundamental or independent with respect to other branches of knowledge or that scientific explanation is able to cover human experience comprehensively. According to Heidegger, scientific knowledge, especially that of modern natural science, is essentially *limited* and *deficient* in its applicability, and modern man has drastically overestimated its philosophical weight in the human context. Therefore, we must be careful not to confound Heidegger's pragmatism with, say, the American versions of pragmatism which move much more closer to common sense knowledge than Heidegger, and which are also overly optimistic as regards the comprehensiveness of scientific rationality.

For similar reasons, we should not be too eager to associate the *Dasein* notion of *Being and Time* closely with a *natural ontological attitude* (as happens in Dreyfus. 1991, p. 254). A person who has first adopted the natural ontological attitude and then believes that science is a seamless continuation of this attitude cannot really ponder over the limits of scientific rationality. If he would try that, he would eventually violate the very natural attitude which he has presupposed. A person who has first adopted the natural ontological attitude and then moves on to the scientific world by extending the attitude to new areas cannot radically question the scientific attitude by pretending, for example, that the natural ontological attitude itself is scientifically inaccessible. Because dogmatic science is a seamless continuation of the natural dogmatic attitude, there is nothing in the attitude which couldn't be explained by the very science. For example, every attempt to argue that time as it is known to modern science (and modern Western common sense) was around before man entered the scene of world history *and* that there is a *Dasein* which is in principle scientifically inaccessible leads us to intolerable dualism. This kind of dualism deflates Dreyfus's Heidegger interpretation (Dreyfus, 1991). Either dinosaurs lived on the earth before and independently of man's being, and *Dasein* is philosophically superfluous and dispensable; *or*, alternatively, we put *Dasein* to real work and derive time, space, causation, nature, science and eventually also dinosaurs from it. This derivation is not antirealistic in the normal sense of the word because it is not the subject and its cultural sphere from which we derive the basic concepts of science. The origin of scientific intolerance and the inherent tendency toward dominance lies at the heart of the very natural ontological attitude itself. Unlike *Dasein*, the natural ontological attitude is incapable of authentic openness. It simply lacks *deinon*, and the abyss into which *deinon* can push us.

But with these reservations, the science which in Heidegger's analysis can be found in the Being-in-the-World was actually very dogmatic science after all. It is not anomalous or sophisticated science which is capable of self-reflection and investigating its own limitations. It is naive science which doesn't bother to wonder why nature reveals to us only those aspects of itself which happen to fit to our mathematical and technological concepts, as if, not only time, but mathematics and technology had existed before man.

Mechanicalness

Heidegger would probably have maintained that standard cognitive science is one of the most typical examples of onto-theo-logical thinking, belonging to the worst tradition of Western *Seinsvergessenheit*. He would, most probably, have thought similarly of standard connectionism. Standard connectionist models are, after all, purely external descriptions of neural or pseudoneural principles, and, therefore, unable to deal with the human experience comprehensively and enlighten man's relation to Being (see Pylkkö, 1995a). Nevertheless, Heidegger might have given some reluctant credit to connectionism because of its obvious inclination toward subconceptuality and elimination.

For example, it seems that connectionism opens a possibility to eliminate (in a certain sense) overly rigid, logical and grammatical structures from the models of language and thought.

Some versions of naturalism are also clearly nonfoundational and antirealistic in their nature, and the later Heidegger might have found this attractive had he not been too dogmatic to recognize this and admit that there are nonnaive tendencies in naturalism too. As nonfoundational naturalism attempts to abolish the borderline which separates science and philosophy, it will leave science without the support of universally valid epistemic principles. This need not indicate that the end of philosophy is finally approaching us. Rather, it will point toward the ineradicable entanglement of philosophical and scientific questions, and, perhaps even toward their intertwinement with esthetic, political and practical questions too. According to nonfoundational and nondogmatic naturalism, the human mind is the soil where science, philosophy, art and politics are intertwined into an indivisible whole of human practice. In this entwinement, science is not allowed to assume any leading role. Nothing in science itself can legitimate such a role anyway. Scientific imperialism, as it is expressed for example in the doctrine of *scientia mensura*, belongs to dogmatic science, not to genuine naturalism. However, we may have to admit that *scientia mensura* factually reigns in the world because it is a fact that modern technology and its servile alliance, natural science, are the most powerful agents among the rivalling sovereigns who eventually decide what is real in the present-day world.

Nondogmatic naturalism may expose science to problems which are even harder than what standard science is used to facing. Questions which resemble traditional philosophical questions will now belong to the task field of nondogmatic scientists too. Typically, such problems of circularity which were sketched earlier in this chapter have to be addressed now within science itself. Let us consider another problem of a similar kind. A scholar, for example a linguist or psychologist, who is designing a theory of a particular field of language or perception decides to utilize standard connectionist notions, methods and models. If he takes seriously the overall view that language and perception are neural processing and believes that, at the level where he works, the best description of the particular phenomena of language and perception which he is interested in is to be expressed in connectionist terms, he should also think that *all* processes of language and perception, and ultimately, all processes of the human mind can and should be described in connectionist terms. Otherwise our linguist or psychologist is not designing a seriously *general* connectionist view of language and perception. In particular, he has to concede that the processes of language and perception which take place in his own brain and in the brains of the members of his research community are connectionist processes. And eventually, he has to admit that the research work done by the research community, all of the theories and models, including invention and development of the theories, are, especially as regards their language and perception, connectionist processing. In other words, connectionist processes have produced a theory which claims that the processes which have produced the theory are actually connectionist processes.

This reasoning should be almost self-evident. Yet it is not widely followed among the advocates of connectionism. Often this line of reasoning is rejected unwittingly when those who work with regular connectionist notions and models resort to mathematical, logical and philosophical notions which are way above the expressive power of the standard connectionist notions. If this happens then those who design connectionist models should not say that language and perception, and the human mind in general, consists of connectionist processing. It is known, for example, that every Turing machine can be simulated by a suitable connectionist network, and, assuming certain reasonable (though optional) constraints on connectionist models, every connectionist computation can be simulated by a Turing machine. Therefore, connectionist computability and Turing-computability are often defined to be mathematically equivalent characterizations of mechanical computability, and if any regular version of Church's thesis is accepted, both of them are equivalent with all other known versions of mechanical computability for that matter. Therefore, trivially, such notions as *truth* in any general philosophical (say, in the standard correspondence sense) or model-theoretical sense is *not* available within the connectionist sphere of notions. If connectionists need stronger notions, the definition of neural networks should not be tied to the constraint of Turing computability in the first place.

The situation is even more difficult if the scholar whom we are considering here claims that the human mind consists of, not connectionist, but neural processing in some strictly physiological and electrochemical sense. It is hard to understand how such perpetually changing electrochemical processes as those which are active in neural processes would be able to grasp such immutable structures as grammatical, logical and mathematical structures, including such relatively simple structures as those of the elementary syntax of natural language and those of permanent macrophysical objects of the so-called external world. And yet an average biologically oriented neuroscientist may unabashedly presume that regular mathematical structures, both enumerable and nonenumerable, are available; that external and nicely separable macrophysical objects are available; and that a correspondence notion of truth is available; and so on. If brain processes are really only electrochemical processes, then how can the brain ever create or even grasp such atemporal, immutable and infinite structures? Even the existence of a neural foundation for regular elementary syntax, let alone for nonenumerable mathematical objects, is far from obvious, to say the least. On the one hand, if we claim that the brain chemistry is purely classical and can be simulated as accurately as needed by Turing machines, then how is the human brain, say that of a mathematician or physicist, supposed to be able to handle, say, inseparable quantum phenomena or noncomputable mathematical structures, such as, for example, Gödel sentences? On the other hand, if we let brain processes be non-Turing-computable, then we will eventually be in conflict with the existing standard neuroscience which is purely classical and allows only mechanical processes to take place in the brain.

Hence, why would any scholar, be he a linguist, psychologist or neuroscientist, restrict the repertoire of his theoretical notions to connectionist notions if he doesn't actually believe that the human mind in general consists of connectionist processing in the first place, and if he is ready to abandon the restriction in the first situation in which he needs more powerful mathematical, logical and philosophical notions? It seems that dogmatic science is vitiated by unwitting dichotomies which were never consciously introduced to natural science but which were adopted in the sixteenth and seventeenth century along with the basic idea of mathematical modelling. One of the dichotomies is that of the mechanical and the nonmechanical, the idea being that a natural phenomenon which is rationally explainable must also be mechanically and feasibly computable. It was not, perhaps, understood during the early days of modern natural science that this would turn out to be a major constraint. It is far from obvious that nature itself is mechanical, that is, something that can be simulated by a Turing machine up to any desired degree of accuracy. In addition, against the original expectations, some of the numbers and functions which occur in the equations of classical natural science have turned out *not* to be mechanically computable (Pour-El and

Richards, 1981), suggesting again that nature is not easily domesticated and transformed into a servile mechanical device. Rather, standard science rests on the tacit policy to mechanize nature, to see nature as a potentially useful machine. One of the central tasks which holistic and anomalous naturalism has to face is how to deal with this and other similar problems, dichotomies and presuppositions. That nature is basically mechanical is a typical uncritical presupposition which is usually not addressed openly. The irreconcilable contrast of the microphysical and the macrophysical is just as embarrassing.

Prediscursiveness and pre-empiricalness

A nondogmatic naturalist may also want to say that human experience is neural processing. But what are the words *experience, is* and *neural processing* supposed to mean in the preceding sentence? The *is* is certainly not the *is* of regular logical identity because regular logical identity cannot be found in the world of empirical matters and isn't therefore a naturalistically acceptable notion in the first place. In genuine naturalism, the application of logical identity to the perpetually changing environment of neural processing can hardly be recommended.

Regardless of his reluctance to apply logical identity in the empirical context, the nondogmatic naturalist may be willing to admit that neuroscience provides an interesting road to the description of human experience. Therefore he is motivated to bring the discourse of neuroscience as close to the discourse of philosophy as possible and shed some light upon their mutual relations and interests. Perhaps the description of human experience as it is done, on the one hand, in philosophy, religion, history and poetry and, on the other hand, in neuroscience cannot satisfy any identity, equivalence, coding or reduction relation, but may, nevertheless, dwell in the same experiential region where they are related by the experience of neighborhood and nearness in Heidegger's sense (cf. Heidegger, 1957-58). Here *neighborhood* and *nearness* refer to distance of meaning and suggest some kind of mutual exchange, openness and assimilation. What they do not suggest is reduction or coding because that would require that the notion of logical identity is available, and such availability would bias the relationship of philosophy (or religion, history, poetry) and neuroscience to the advantage of neuroscience, which would make their mutual dialogue eventually impossible.

According to nondogmatic naturalism, no human discourse, including the discourse of the best future neuroscience, will ever reach a comprehensive description of human experience, and in order to reach even a satisfactory description, neuroscience must be open to *all* cultural and social influences. Due to many inherent limitations of the language of standard natural science, some aspect of the human experience, especially its aconceptual aspect, may always remain *transcendentally* inaccessible to the discourse of natural science. But, the less dogmatic the view of natural science is, the smaller the transcendental gap is.

This is a kind of Schopenhauerian view of the *inexhaustiveness of the human experience* with respect to the power of conceptualizations. *Der Wille* (Will) is and remains partly inaccessible to our conceptual representations (Vorstellungen), including the concepts of the best future neuroscience. In our vocabulary, *Wille* refers to the aconceptual regions of human experience. It is music that is able to express most immediately the life of the *Wille* in all its transcendental variety and abundance, and be quite comprehensive in its expressive ability, but even music may fail to catch it all. And with philosophy and poetry we are already much more closely tied to the constraints of conceptual representation than we are with music (see also Chapter 4).

Not only is human experience conceptually inexhaustible, but the discourses which are available to us for the description of the experience are not necessarily *intertranslatable.* Also this is one example of transcendental inaccessibility. Or, instead of transcendentality, we may speak of *predisc(o)ursiveness* or extradisc(o)ursiveness with respect to a given discourse, and, if the discourse is empirical, of *pre-empiricalness.* Part of our experience always remains ineffable, that is, predisc(o)ursive with respect to any given discourse. For example, musical experience may be partly ineffable in any empirical and rational terms.

The region of human experience which is and remains ineffable in terms of any neuroscience is pre-empirical with respect to the particular variety of empiricalness which is incorporated into the type of discourse which the language of neuroscience always represents. Yet there is no reason why we couldn't bring, say, music to the *neighborhood* of the discourse of neuroscience, assuming that our neuroscience is not too dogmatic for that purpose. Of course, the *nearness* here is not to be understood as a quantitative spatial notion because if we decide to speak about music in purely quantitative terms we have already, not only favored the discourse of neuroscience, but precluded beforehand some aspects of musical experience, and some of the precluded aspects are most probably those which cannot be captured by any discourse of neuroscience.

Even within the most dogmatic science, different discourses are not necessarily intertranslatable. Occasionally the untranslatability borders on contradictoriness and paradoxicalness, as is the case with the relationship between classical physics and quantum physics, no matter how dogmatically the latter is interpreted.

Reification

Pre-empirical and prediscursive questions can be raised within nondogmatic naturalism, but not within the dogmatic one. Dogmatic science is too dogged in its belief in the consistency and ultimate comprehensiveness of the scientific enterprise: all scientific puzzles are temporary epistemic puzzles and will be removed as science progresses. Therefore the problems with pre-empirical knowledge and transcendental untranslatability are never seriously addressed.

An advocate of nondogmatic naturalism doesn't believe that science, with the variety of its mutually conflicting discourses, is in the position to dictate to us what we should consider as *real*. For example, if a person is convinced that an intensive experience which he has had with Béla Bártok's music is, in some sense, as real as things which science deals with then it would not be wise for this person to restrict his language to such a primitive discourse as that of physics or neuroscience. Actually, that would in most cases be a disastrous mistake, and such a choice cannot be defended on any genuinely naturalistic grounds. The person has many naturalistically accept-able reasons to adopt the principle of *musical measure*: what accords with his musical experience determines what is real, and language must tolerate this choice.

Typically, reification and object formation are areas for which pre-empirical questions are vital. One part of our experience is experience of external things. External things are usually thought to be either "macro-physical objects" or some kind of "abstract objects." The impression which reification is able to produce is often so overwhelming that the modern Western man may be inclined to claim that he is unable to experience (as real) anything else but external things. For such a person, the world is simply a set of external objects, and perception and emotions are nothing crucially more than just different ways to relate the mind to the objects. In this triumph of externalization and reification, thinking appears to be concept manipulation, and concepts are internalized abstract objects with the help of which we individuate other objects.

In order to understand the mind of the modern Western man, the problem of reification or object formation has to be faced, but dogmatic naturalism is unable to do this. Reification processes *precede*, in one sense of *preceding*, our common sense knowledge and scientific knowledge of the so-called external world, and it seems that objectness, that is, what it takes to be an object, forms a kind of pre-empirical condition of regular empirical knowledge. Instead of resorting to the Kantian line of thinking with *synthetic a priori* structures, the nondogmatic naturalist has other options to choose. He may begin with aconceptual experience which is not yet organized into things and concepts. One way, but not the only way, to describe that experience is to say that the human brain, and the mammalian brain in general, tends to organize its experience into a form that creates a powerful impression that what is perceived consists of external objects. For example, certain neural arrangements in the mammalian visual system enhance contours and maintain color constancy. These neural arrangements contribute to the overall impression that our experience is caused by transtemporal, identity-preserving external objects. This impression is so powerful that we are inclined to say that our experience is *about* external objects which are independent of our mind. We must add, however, that the use of such words as "brain" and "visual system" above may be somewhat misleading. The words cannot, of course, be names of regular external things any more. In other words, the pre-empirical characterization of what it takes to be an object cannot be given in any standard discourse of empirical science (for more about this problem, see Chapter 3 and Chapter 4).

The reificational processes are partly innate, coded into our genetic heritage, partly caused by maturation and learning. It seems that mammalian evolution has endowed our brain with a solid tendency to adopt a thing-based ontology. At the same time, related neural mechanisms codify some other experiences into the internal furniture of the self. These internalized experiences form a kind of conceptual system, a hierarchy and perspective of interests which we attach to the experience of being a *subject*. However, this may not be the *only* tendency with which the evolution has endowed our brain. We could say that the natural prephysics with which our brain is endowed is not only or purely classical. In addition to classicalness, certain nonreificational or aconceptual tendencies have been effective in the evolution of the mammal brain too. Thus biological evolution may have equipped us with several, mutually incompatible, experiential capabilities. But here a reservation is in order again. Such words as *evolution* and *mammal* are not used above as theoretical terms of standard empirical science. We are not assuming that evolution, in some realistic sense of temporal order, preceded the human experience. Rather, the evolutionary story, if properly interpreted, provides one interesting way to understand and organize human experience.

Certainly, the experience of external things and internal subject is there, and, even more can be said, namely, that we experience their presence quite in an *a priori* way with respect to some other experiences. But this pre-empiricalness is *a priori* quite in another sense than that of Kant's. First of all, we have naturalistically acceptable knowledge also of the pre-empirical conditions of human experience, though it may be the case that a particular experience remains always pre-empirical, and therefore inaccessible, with respect to another empirical experience. So, instead of a strict hierarchy of discourses, like that of the philosophical and empirical discourses, we have several mutually untranslatable discourses in which philosophical and empirical interests are entangled. One kind of experience can mix with another, and one kind of discourse can be interpreted within another, as long as we do not expect to find translations and meaning identities.

Second, pre-empirical knowledge is not immutable or necessary but remains open for all sort of influences. For example, as regards object formation, pre-empirical knowledge is partly genetically supported, partly dependent on maturation and learning. Therefore, it is not pure and can be changed. Biological evolution, the environment of maturation, and learning can all change the conditions which shape our experience of thingness.

Thus we can claim that our experience is not *comprehensively* reificational. Our experience covers more that than just our experience of things. Even in quite a normal experience, the boundary of subject and object, which is never that absolute or crisp in the first place, can be dissolved. Dreams, extreme exhaustion, sexual ecstacy, anxiety, fear of dying during an acute lethal threat, falling in love, taking some mind-altering drugs, and so on, may help us to realize how fragile the interface between external things and the subject is. The reificational aspect of experience floats like a sloop on the high seas of aconceptual experience.

That biological evolution has endowed our brain with several rivalling, and not necessarily mutually compatible, ways to organize our experience may have had repercussions in the fragmentation of our culture. For example, the fact that we have several incompatible alternative frameworks of physics, such as classical physics, the theory of relativity and quantum physics, may reflect certain incompatible innate tendencies which our nervous system possesses for experience handling. Heidegger certainly had good reasons to remind us of that our Modern Western culture, which is dominated by the interests of technology, tends to overemphasize the reificational aspect of our experience. In general, we could say that each cultural environment chooses to support and enhance a certain innate inclination in our neural organization, and *vice versa*. During the last three hundred years in particular, such organization of human experience which tends to objectify the experience has been particularly dominant, and we could add: intolerantly so. It was this dominance that Heidegger wanted to challenge when he coined the notion of *onto-theo-logic*. However, there remains a question to be asked which was presumably *not* asked by Heidegger, at least not directly, and it is this: Can this self-complacent dominance actually be defended or justified in any naturalistically acceptable way?

Nature and *naturalism* in *Being and Time*

Had Heidegger asked this question, he, most probably, would have answered it with a definite "yes," meaning that naturalism isn't more than one attempt to justify the dominance of technology. In other words, he would have said that it is an intrinsic and incorrigible feature of modern natural science that it tends to reach cultural dominance; that the demand of the dominance is necessarily built into the scientific way of thinking; and, therefore, philosophical naturalism is bound, not only to scaffold an externally oriented, thing-based ontology, but to work as an errand boy for the veiled interests of modern Western technology in its pursuit of global cultural dominance. It seems that Heidegger never took seriously the prospects of *a*-onto-theo-logical, i.e. nondogmatic, naturalism; such naturalism where pre-empirical questions can be asked and where the difference of Being and entities can be addressed.

For example, *Being and Time* (1927/1992) contends that naturalism is necessarily dogmatic. It is somewhat confusing that, in *Being and Time*, when Heidegger analyzes *Dasein*'s existentials (Existenzialen) his own language is quite reificational. Even if at the outset he declares that Being is not to be confounded with entities (Seiende) (p. 4) and that the Being of entities is itself not an entity (p. 6), he doesn't hesitate to speak of *Dasein* as an entity (see, for example, pages 7, 11, 12, 37, 43, 52, 53 and 58, to mention only some of the first ones; p. 12: "Das Dasein ist ein Seiendes..."). Contrary to this, Emmanuel Levinas says it quite clearly: "L'exister n'existe pas. C'est l'existant qui exist." (Levinas, 1979, p. 25). Thus, in Levinas, there is (il y a) also being *without* entities, something that is difficult to envision in Heidegger. In Heideggerian English, Levinas seems to be saying that Being (Sein), especially the human *Dasein*, the Being of man, doesn't exist as an entity (als Seiende), whereas Heidegger says quite carelessly that Being is always the Being of an entity ("Sein ist jeweils das Sein eines Seienden." p. 9). But how could a *Dasein* face the Nothing and become authentic if it were *only* an entity? It seems as if the *Dasein* of "What is metaphysics?" (1929/1988) is already somewhat less entity-like than the *Dasein* of *Being and Time*. The *Dasein* of "Das Wesen der Sprache" (1957-58/1971) is almost a nonentity already.

But, in spite of this confusing feature, Heidegger's tendency is clear: "The existential analytic of *Dasein* comes *before* any psychology or anthropology, and certainly before any biology" (1927/1992, p. 71). (Die existenziale Analytik des Daseins liegt vor jeder Psychologie, Anthropologie und ernst recht Biologie) (Heidegger, 1927/1986, p. 45). This attitude is clearly antinaturalistic. The question of man's Being comes before any scientific attitude can be established, and the scientific attitude is *derivative* (in one sense of the word) with respect to the human experience of Being. Unlike what anomalous naturalism suggests, in Heidegger it doesn't seem possible that human experience of Being could become thoroughly intertwined with the scientific attitude. In other words, the early Heidegger rejects the possibility that the scientific attitude would, so to speak, color or corrupt the human experience throughout and would *not* at the same time demand and assume an intolerant stance of cultural dominance. Similarly, Heidegger thinks that it is impossible to describe all aspects of human experience from a scientific point of view. One reason for this position is that he assumes the scientific attitude to be so pure, naive and straightforward. It is understandable that a purely classical language cannot cover the human experience particularly comprehensively because the language of classical science represents a special reificational case of human language. According to Heidegger's line of thinking, it would, for example, be impossible to give an adequate description of the *Dasein* experience, let alone of the authentic *Dasein* experience, in the language of modern neuroscience.

The impossibility is of a strictly categorical nature, and no version of naturalism, no matter how nondogmatic, can escape it. It is not only that such a scientific description of the *Dasein* would miss some of the finest subtleties of our experience, as an advocate of nondogmatic naturalism might concede. It is not only that every naturalistic description is bound to remain somewhat limited and coarse. More seriously, the scientific attitude is derivative with respect to the *Dasein* and arises within the sphere of man's *Dasein* experience, and, therefore, a crucial part of any *Dasein* will necessarily remain inaccessible to the scientific approach. For example, all modern Western science presupposes a crisp and categorical contrast between the subject and the object, whereas in the authentic *Dasein* experience the contrast is violently challenged and eventually dismantled to some extent. Therefore, the dissolution has no description or explanation in the language of modern science.

Everyone who has given in to the temptations of naturalism should find this somewhat annoying. It is typical for a naturalistic approach that it views the prospects of a neural description of human experience with a considerable amount of optimism. A dogmatic naturalist would say the following. That which cannot be described in the language of (future) science must be irrelevant or nonexistent. For example, such aspects of the *Dasein* experience which cannot be captured by the language of neuroscience must be irrelevant or nonexistent. Contrary to this, a nondogmatic naturalist would say the following. Perhaps the language of the best future neuroscience will not be purely external and object-oriented and will not presuppose a crisp contrast between the subject and object. Such a language will, therefore, make a neural description of some aspects of the *Dasein* experience accessible and philosophically interesting. At least, we don't want to limit the possibilities of neuroscience in advance. Perhaps natural science of the future will show more inclination to self-reflection and willingness to overcome the crudest versions of naiveté, for example, by thinking of its own limitations and obsessions. It would not, perhaps, limit its consideration only to correct, normal and easily understandable areas of human experience (cf. Chapter 1).

Thus the future of science, including the prospects of neuroscience, remains genuinely open and unpredictable.

Though in *Being and Time* Heidegger's view of the possibilities of science are gloomy and he pictures science as an irremediably dogmatic enterprise, Heidegger's overall philosophy of science is, of course, neither that of common sense nor that of regular scientific realism which prevails in the academic world because Heidegger embeds scientific thinking and scientific attitude into the human *Being-in-the-World*. One can detect a strong inclination towards hermeneutic dualism (recall the contrast of *Angst* and *Furcht*, and its deconstruction in Chapter 1) in Heidegger's view, and this distances him from all forms of naturalism, including nondogmatic and holistic naturalism. One could say that it is the hermeneutic attitude that preserves a definite and quite dogmatic role for natural science within early Heidegger's philosophical framework.

Hubert L. Dreyfus (1991, pp. 251-265), not only assigns these views to Heidegger, but seems to accept them himself. According to the hermeneutic way of thinking, natural science needs a philosophical framework, but the kind of science which is hermeneutically embedded into the philosophical framework remains itself quite dogmatic. After the embedding, the hermeneutic attitude, so to speak, leaves science intact and unscathed, without muddying its clear waters by trying to deflect scientific thinking habits from their dogmatic course. The hermeneutic attitude leaves the practices and the self-image of science in peace.

But modern natural science doesn't deserve to be left in this kind of peace. Nondogmatic naturalism doesn't draw any categorical line between the human experience in general and the scientific experience in particular and demands that the human experience must saturate science throughout and question its apparent purity and isolation. At the same time, nondogmatic naturalism allows science to infiltrate the allegedly nonscientific mind, both the philosophical and common-sensical one. Scientific experience belongs inseparably to the spectrum of human experience as a rich, colorful and thoroughly confused ingredient. No intrinsic reason can prevent science from becoming philosophically reflective and conscious of its own limitations.

Perhaps we can illustrate the relationship between science and nonscientific experience with the help of a distributed network model where different discourses intertwine and become entangled into an indivisible whole. For example, the impact of scientific ideas upon the Western everyday experience is ineradicable and has lasted at least two or three thousand years. Therefore, the *Dasein* experience of practically every Western man has been incorrigibly corrupted by science from the very beginning. There is not much innocence left there, and there is no way back to the state of innocence either (cf. Chapter 5). We cannot separate the scientific ingredients of our culture from the nonscientific ones without destroying the culture itself.

On the other hand, science itself is unable to reach such a pure externality which has often been attributed to it, not only by scientists themselves, but also by the advocates of the hermeneutic tradition, recently, for example, by Deleuze and Guattari in their *Qu'est-ce que la philosophie?* This alleged purity and externality would elevate science into a position which cannot be defended in any naturalistically acceptable way. In genuine naturalism, natural science, too, is a human enterprise, ultimately a human science, namely, an attempt to understand the human experience of (or with) Nature. Heidegger certainly sees science as an inalienably human activity, but it seems that he separates the scientific aspect of human experience all to crisply from the nonscientific one. When Heidegger (1927/1992, p. 57) analyzes the *existentials* of the *Dasein*, especially the *Being-in-the-World* (In-der-Welt-Sein), he encounters the notion of *environment*. In the context of Being-in-the-World, environment is not just a set of independent external objects to which the knowing subject is said to maintain an epistemic relationship. Environment is part of Being-in-the-World, and, therefore, it cannot be understood comprehensively by any positive science alone, say by biology alone. It is only the analytic of *Dasein* that is able to reveal that biology has to take environment as something given, and that the environment of the biology arises through a special attitude which we adopt within the Being-in-the-World. This gives the impression that the Being-in-the-World is pure and innocent, not already corrupted by scientific attitudes and thinking habits. This purity may be hard to defend naturalistically.

Such a conception of knowledge which handles knowledge purely as a relation between a knowing subject and a set of objects and ignores the context of the human experience in which knowledge always arises is, according to Heidegger (1927/1992, p. 59-60), superficial and formal. It leads us to misconceive the essence of truth and consider truth only as a correspondence between the subject's representations and the world of entities. Nature is one of the entities but, in order to understand the essence of Nature and entities in general, we must notice that there is more to the human experience than the mind's correspondence with entities. Heidegger presents positive science as a superficial form of information gathering which has misunderstood its own essence because it lacks proper self-understanding. In order to understand its own essence, it should begin with the *Dasein*, analyze the Being-in-the-World, and, eventually, find the World and Nature through the analysis. One cannot move this route to the opposite direction: by analyzing or studying Nature with the concepts of positive science, one cannot reach the Being-in-the-World. This is a categorical one-way street.

Heidegger's ontological analysis in *Being and Time* reaches the objects of Nature only through the World, and the World can be reached only through the Being-in-the-World: "Nature is itself an entity which is encountered within the world and which can be discovered in various ways and at various stages" (1927/1992, p. 92). (Natur ist selbst ein Seiendes, das innerhalb der Welt begegnet und auf verschiedenen Wegen und Stufen entdeckbar ist.) (Heidegger, 1927/1986, p. 63). Because Being-in-the-World is one of the existentials of *Dasein*, we notice that the objects of Nature have no way of being which is independent of man and his experience (see especially Heidegger, 1927/1992, pp. 63-66). This line of thinking has a peculiar antirealistic (though not subject-centered) flair, assuming that *realistic* in the word *antirealistic* is used to designate the view that there are man-independent objects and that our concepts can represent their properties reliably without any peculiarly active interference of human experience. Heidegger is not suggesting that it is the subject with its consciousness that creates the objects of science. But Nature can be found and studied only through a certain special mode of *Dasein* by finding a proper reificational attitude toward Being: "Only in some definite mode of its own *Being-in-the-World* can *Dasein* discover entities as Nature." (Heidegger, 1927/1992, p. 94) (Das Seiende als Natur in diesem Sinne kann das Dasein nur in einem bestimmten Modus seines In-der-Welt-seins entdecken.) (Heidegger, 1927/1986, p. 65). The origin of this kind of *Dasein* antirealism is not the subjectivity of knowledge but the Being-in-the-world origin of knowledge. Neither does Heidegger's attitude as such, that is, without considerable reinterpretation, imply any *relativistic* views.

According to *Being and Time*, philosophical understanding, especially understanding of man and his relation to Being, cannot be based on any positive study of Nature alone because there is a categorical order of direction in Heidegger's philosophical approach, and studies of nature, as they are normally carried out, are never at the beginning of the order. If we mean by *naturalism* a view that all human knowledge has to be based on representative knowledge of natural things, and we understand "natural things" as Heidegger did, then philosophical naturalism can never come even close to the genuine understanding of the human experience and, therefore, philosophical naturalism is bound to remain dogmatic and naive.

Heidegger and atomic physics

But how well do Heidegger's views reveal to us the essence of modern natural science? Is it obvious, for example, that recent physical science must be interpreted as Heidegger does, namely, in a way which makes science automatically naive and dogmatic? Do all tenable interpretations present modern physics as a study of external objects, such that the context of human experience is ignored? Does the scientific attitude automatically forget its experiential origin and the inseparable, dependent and impure role which science plays within the human experience? What Heidegger did was paint quite a regular picture of science and then frame this picture with a philosophy which, by revealing the limited self-understanding of science, presents science as naive and dogmatic. He abandoned the alternative possibility of making science itself philosophically self-reflective and mature; and, at the same time, the possibility that science itself, through its own effort, might think of its own limitations and origins, without philosophical help from the outside. He didn't take seriously the possibility that science itself, or related nondogmatic philosophical naturalism, may have already been able to abandon the view which presents nature simply as a collection of external objects and science as a project which attempts to find out the universal laws which govern the behavior of external objects.

Heidegger wrote extensively on science and technology already from the late thirties onward. At that time he was distancing himself from the rather bullheaded, if not pompous, application of the phenomenological and hermeneutic method and vocabulary, turning more aggressively against subject-centered metaphysics and focusing on the difference, or even struggle, between Being (Sein) and entities (Seiende). In this light, one might expect that he would have been willing to deliberate, without the hermeneutical bias, the essence of modern physics and consider modern philosophical naturalism as a serious philosophical alternative and perhaps even would have been ready to recognize some similarities between his own work and that of, say, American pragmatists like James, Peirce, Mead and Dewey. Such similarities between the American pragmatists and continental thinkers are often surprisingly strong though far from clear and unproblematic as we have seen above (for an interesting comparison, see Rosenthal & Bourgeois, 1991). Eliminative and holistic naturalism shouldn't be too far from the asubjective and experiential line of thinking which is characteristic of the not-too-early Heidegger and other postphenomenological thinkers. But no indication of any interest, let alone reconciliation, of this kind can be discerned in Heidegger's work. One of the reasons for this may have been that the later Heidegger associates the recent natural science with the naiveté of externalism and reificationism.

Heidegger seems to have thought that classical, Newtonian science is the irremediable core of all modern Western natural science, and that the philosophical presuppositions of classical science cannot be overcome within natural science itself. Therefore, natural science is necessarily tied to a Cartesian or, alternatively, to a materialistic, pragmatic or empiricist view of man and the world. Surprisingly, he seems to have also believed in a cumulative view of the growth of scientific knowledge because he presents modern atomic physics as an immediate continuation of classical science (see, for example, Heidegger, 1938/1977; and Heidegger, 1957-58/1971). However, it is far from obvious that quantum physics, the greatest upheaval in the twentieth century science, perhaps of all modern science so far, actually continues or smoothly extends the classical picture of nature and man. In other words, it is not clear that classical physics is the limiting core of all subsequent natural science. Even though Heidegger wrote *Being and Time* almost at the same time as quantum theory was conceived, and the great universities of southern Germany played a central part in the process of conceiving it (of German physics of that era, see, Cassidy, 1992; Olff-Nathan, 1993), the revolution in physics seems to have left no deep trace in Heidegger's work. This lack of influence may have been one of the reasons why Heidegger's notion of science remained all too deeply attached to the classical science and to its background assumptions, especially to the classical individuation, separation, determinacy and accuracy conditions.

Equating classical and modern physics was unfortunate. It was particularly unfortunate because some of the results of Heidegger's later thinking might have been able to shed new light upon the problems of quantum philosophy. The later Heidegger's view of language as preconceptual experience might be used to illustrate the peculiar way in which quantum physicists are forced to use language when they speak of microphysical phenomena which are in the mode of superposition. In superposition, the values of the properties of a quantum phenomenon, say, an electron, are inseparable in a way which cannot be described in terms of classical physics or classical logic alone. Yet it seems natural to say that they can be and actually are spoken of. But, had Heidegger decided to deliberate the problems of quantum physics in terms of his own philosophy, he would have had to revise some of his earlier views of science, technology and naturalism. For example, if natural science is a kind of application of technology (Technik) or of the technological principle, as Heidegger seems to have thought (Heidegger, 1954/1977a), then how are we supposed to understand such antireificationism, dissolution of the boundary of subject and object and the destruction of ontology which characterizes the Copenhagen interpretation of quantum theory? According to Aage Petersen (1963) who worked for many years as Niels Bohr's personal secretary, Bohr had no ontology whatsoever. For Bohr, there is no microphysical reality behind the quantum phenomena. Instead of speaking of how the quantum reality should be researched, Bohr preferred to speak of how quantum phenomena are to be described, and he shifted the focus of his interest from the alleged physical reality to the language of quantum physics (see also, Pylkkö, 1996a). But in the light of this shift of emphasis toward antirealism, how is it possible that technology, which expresses its essence or *Gestell* by transforming our thinking habits into a reificational and mechanical mode, suddenly produces a theory, namely the quantum theory, which, according to some interpretations, destroyed the last remnants of thing ontology? If quantum theory annihilates external microphysical objects and questions mechanical thinking habits, including the contrast of subject and object and, hence, so obviously challenges the intellectual authority of its alleged master, the Western technology, how can the power of *Gestell* be so overwhelming as Heidegger claims it to be?

Heidegger deals briefly with atomic physics in some of his writings (see for example, Heidegger, 1935-36/1977; 1941/1993; 1954/1977a; 1954/1977b; 1955/1958; and 1957-58/1971), but we cannot find any satisfactory answer to this question. In a lecture, "Science and reflection" (1954/1977b), Heidegger describes modern atomic physics and acknowledges Heisenberg's indeterminacy principle; the unsurmounting difficulties which atomic physics has had in retaining the classical notions of causality and object; and the problematic relationship of the subject and the object in atomic physics. He notes that actually the notion of physical object is destroyed in modern atomic physics but adds that he will not deal with the problem in this context. It is obvious that the destruction of the microphysical object in the Copenhagen interpretation fits neither Heidegger's picture of science nor what the self-image of science should be in Heidegger's opinion. No wonder, therefore, that Heidegger hurries onwards to other problems.

After the list of all these qualitatively new features, the reader expects Heidegger to give some credit to the obviously ametaphysical inclinations of quantum physics. This is not what happens. According to Heidegger, quantum physics deals with nature only as an object-area. This object area is new but is determined by a notion of identity which is basically classical. This commitment to objectification makes it impossible for quantum physics to approach the *physis* aspect of Being. The *physis* aspect of Being (Heidegger, 1935-36/1977) had originally a vital access to human experience until reification and objectification took over the experiential scene and shaped man's experience into external, identity-preserving objects. The objectifying attitude transforms Being into entities and blocks man's way to the original *physis*. Hence, Being appears to us as Nature, as a collection of objects to be utilized. Heidegger (1954/1977b) adds without further deliberation that he doesn't believe that the new atomic physics will eventually be able to break the classical subject-object boundary, but this comment carries already the flair of suppression around it, as if he had found the situation in quantum physics somewhat alarming and, perhaps, even embarrassing to the views which he had held since his youth.

In his article, "The question of Being", Heidegger (1955/1958) repeats his stance. It is clear that here he addresses again the realistic *doxa* of average scientists who are accustomed to cherish their classical thinking habits and retain the traditional subject-object contrast. What he doesn't address is the problem of whether the classical thinking habits can still be retained after the qualitatively new vista of nature which quantum theory opens for us has been properly understood. It seems that he was not prepared to *see* that the essence of technology, the overwhelming *Gestell* which forces us to adopt a control-ling and externalizing attitude toward nature, has begun falling into pieces. And what is so surprising is that this happens, not as a result of the work of a great German master thinker, but as an earthquake the epicenter of which lies at the very heart of modern Western technology itself, in the most advanced department of natural science.

In his lectures on language, "The nature of language," Heidegger (1957-58) says again that the antireificational trends of modern atomic physics are only apparent. This view is presented in a context where he himself attempts to deconstruct the notion of space-time with the help of the notions *nearness* (die Nähe) and *neighborhood* (die Nachbarschaft). Heidegger's intention is to present these alternative notions, not as measurable spatio-temporal concepts, but as expressions of a more primordial *nearness of meaning and experience*: "Nearness, then, is by its nature outside and independent of space and time." (Also hat die Nähe ihr Wesen ausserhalb und unabhängig von Raum und Zeit.) Nearness doesn't rest on space and time considered as quantitative physical parameters. But here again, he is not willing to acknowledge that a similar destruction of causal and spatio-temporal concepts had already been carried out in quantum theory and quantum philosophy. Already Bohr used to say frequently that the notion of causality and the notion of space-time are mutually complementary. Today, the problem of *nonlocality* is a common-place in physics, and the examination of different *pre-space* notions comprises a vital branch of the latest quantum physics (see for example, Hiley, 1991).

Identity with Parmenides and Leibniz

Heidegger's unwillingness and inability to give any credit to the anti-onto-logical trends of twentieth century natural science can be traced back to his rather dogmatic conviction that science is an enterprise which is based on reification, externalism and classical individuation of objects. In this individuation, the classical notion of identity plays a central role. In *Identity and Difference*, Heidegger (1957/1969) studies the history of identity and the history of different identity notions. We can summarize Heidegger's overall view by saying that there are two different and rivalling notions of identity, namely *Leibniz's identity* and *Parmenides's identity*, and that it is the Leibniz identity which was adopted by modern natural science in the seventeenth century. The inevitable consequence was that Parmenides's notion was pushed aside and forgotten.

Leibniz's identity is the identity with which we are familiar through modern text books of logic. It satisfies the identity laws of predicate logic plus the so-called Leibniz laws. The first-order law, or the *Indiscernibility of the Identicals*, tells us that identicals cannot be discerned by any property. In other words, if x and y are identical then, if x has the property P, then y has it too. The second-order law, or the *Identity of the Indiscernibles*, says that what is not discerned by any property must be identical. In other words, if it holds of every property P which x has that y has it too, and other way round, then x and y are identical.

It is fair to say that it was and still is widely believed that the individuals or objects of classical physics satisfy the principles of the Leibniz identity, especially the Leibniz laws. The idea that physical identity satisfies the Leibniz identity is not, however, particularly hard to deny, but usually such attempts remain only apparent in that sense that they just switch the application of the Leibniz identity from one region or level onto another, for example, from the macrophysical body itself to some of its constituents. One way to characterize physical identity would be to say that x is physically identical with y if and only if x and y fill up exactly the same area of space at exactly the same time. Thus x and y are identical if and only if they fill up exactly the same four-dimensional "slot" of the space-time. In addition, it is usually thought that each body has a continuous surface which separates it from other bodies.

However, this definition may conflict with some of our basic intuitions about physical sameness. We are inclined to think that position, time and relational properties should not count in the determination of physical sameness. Even minor changes in inessential or secondary properties are often thought to be acceptable without the loss of identity. Thus we are inclined to think that in the individuation of a body at least locational, temporal and relational properties of the body should be exempted from the set of properties to which the Leibniz identity applies. If this is not accepted, any two moments of time would always differentiate all physical individuals, and no individual would continue its existence at the next moment. Therefore, natural characterizations of physical identity do not usually refer explicitly to the temporal properties of the body but assume instead that we can reindividuate 'one and same individual' at different moments by 'following' its life through the course of time. It is thought that some kind of physical continuity which doesn't prohibit inessential changes helps the physical individual to extend itself from one moment to another. Thus a physical body would occupy a certain closed area of a three-dimensional space and, at the next moment, the same body could occupy either the same area or move around to another area.

These characterizations of physical identity require, of course, that we can tell *without* physical identity what we mean by the "same area" and by the "same time." Whether or not this can actually be done is one question. But nevertheless, our intuition seems to say that the individuals of classical physics satisfy, one way or another, the Leibniz identity, and classical science seems to rely on this intuition. Which properties of the body are supposed to satisfy the Leibniz identity may vary considerably. Even in those interpretations in which inessential changes in the body are said not to destroy its identity, the essential core of the individual is usually supposed to satisfy the Leibniz identity. This intuition holds even if we decide to adopt an interpretation which deviates from the standard realistic interpretation. Also such substantiality which arises from some synthetic *a priori* intuition would satisfy the same Leibniz identity. And even if we want to say that the foundation of physical identity lies in abstract mass points, whereas the body itself may go through considerable changes of size and shape, the mass points are assumed to satisfy the Leibniz identity. Analogously, even if identity through time is denied completely and replaced by a similarity measure, the evaluation of similarities require that there exist permanent units of measurement which remain constant over time and satisfy the Leibniz identity. As a summary, we could say that classical thinking habits, especially those of classical physical science, rest on the Leibniz notion of identity, though it is possible that the identity is incorporated, not into the body as a whole, but into some of its spatial or temporal parts, mass points, essences, substances, monads, primary qualities, similarity units, or to some other kind of individuative functions. They all presuppose classical identity, even when they seem to be characterizing what identity and individuation is.

According to Heidegger (1957/1969), the Leibniz identity holds among entities (Seiende) and each natural science has to assume that the things which constitute its subject matter (object-area, as Heidegger also says) preserve their identity over time, that they are "transtemporally identity-preserving" as the matter is sometimes expressed. Without this assumption, says Heidegger, natural science as an enterprise is impossible. Thus the Leibniz identity is the core of modern onto-logic.

One part of the Leibniz identity is the law of self-identity which is often expressed by the formula $A = A$. Heidegger says that we are not dealing here with an empty tautology with the help of which we can tell such eternal truths as *John is John* or *a cat is a cat*. According to Heidegger, $A = A$ means that every A is itself the same with itself (Mit ihm selbst ist jedes A selber dasselbe). Identity has something to do with "a mediation, a connection, a synthesis: a unification into a unity." This is active unity which is incorporated into the word *with* (mit). Something which is originally chaotic is unified into something which, after the unification, can be called *one*, and, as soon as this has happened, a connection runs from what is now one back to itself. Therefore, also some kind of selfness arises from the action of identity.

We could add here that there is something atemporal in the Leibniz identity, as if it tried to reconcile two incompatible views, namely, that the world keeps changing all the time everywhere but that there nevertheless is a department within the world which doesn't change after all. That which doesn't change is called an *individual* (with Leibniz, *substance* or *monad*), or the essence of an individual, and it is the individual which has reached self-identity. Individuation creates, so to speak, immutable regions in the world, such that these regions are saved from the corrupting touch of the time. According to the normal interpretation of classical physics (not that of Leibniz's himself), these regions are what common sense calls *physical objects*, *bodies* or *things*.

In every regular physical interpretation, the Leibniz laws require that what is *one and the same* doesn't lose its identity and remains the same from one moment to another. The laws require also that different spatial or temporal parts of a given object themselves preserve their identity and belong to the *same* object. Also in this latter case, the laws attempt to annihilate the effect of time because the parts of one and the same thing are said to belong together without assuming that there is a natural process which connects them. No natural process can create identity because natural processes need time to take place, and where there is time there is change, too, no matter how small the interval. And where there is change there is no identity. Analogously, the so-called *temporal parts* need first to establish their own identity before they can be used to scaffold the identity of the individual in which they are temporal parts. In order to arise, sameness has to overcome time and change metaphysically. In this overcoming, where change is nullified and time ceases to go forward, unity and selfness is created under the metaphysical gaze of the Leibniz identity.

Leibniz himself was intensively aware of the difficulties which the reconciliation of change and identity creates (see *Noveaux Essais*, 1704/1985, for example, Book II, Chapter xxvii, pp. 229-248; but see also the collection of essays and letters, Leibniz, 1989). On the one hand, no two physical bodies are numerically identical with one another. This makes change possible. But, on the other hand, both physical science (dynamics, mechanics) and moral theory need identity in order to induce general laws and moral responsibility. This *dilemma* led Leibniz eventually to introduce spiritually guided substances, monads, who received their unity from divine sources - a solution which has often been ridiculed even by those who are completely unable to provide any alternative solution.

But there is another notion of identity, too, and it is much older than the Leibniz identity. Heidegger's reminds us that there is also the word *is* in the sentence "A is identical with A". A also *is*. He says that we have to cast some light upon this existential aspect of identity, too. In one of his fragments, Parmenides says, through Heidegger's mouth of course, something like this: "For the same (is) perceiving (thinking) as well as Being." And this is something different. Heidegger's translation is: "Das selbe nämlich ist Vernehmen (Denken) sowohl als auch Sein." (For more about the interpretation of this fragment, see also Heidegger's Parmenides essay, *Moira*, Heidegger, 1954/1975).

At first sight, this doesn't seem to be an attempt to characterize *sameness* in any general terms at all. However, according to Heidegger, Parmenides tries to say that Being (Sein) belongs to identity, or that Being is in identity. Heidegger seems to think that if perceiving (thinking) is identical with Being, and identity, in some sense, arises through perceiving and thinking, then Being has to belong to identity. Identity is primary with respect to Being, something that Being needs in order to become effective. Being is determined by identity, not vice versa. Thinking and Being belong together in the same or by virtue of the same. We could even say that sameness forces thinking to reach Being and Being to become thinking or thinkable.

Sameness in this primordial sense is *belonging together* (Zusammengehören). But of course, here *identity* or *sameness* doesn't refer to the Leibniz identity. What is same belongs together and to each other. With Parmenides, Being is determined by sameness, whereas in modern metaphysics sameness is a characteristic of Being. Heidegger wants to emphasize the *belonging* (gehören) aspect of *belonging together*. If the *together* (zusammen) is underlined, we will eventually end up at the Leibniz identity where identity is a unifying relation from a thing back to itself and where Being comes before identity. By underlining the aspect of *belonging*, Heidegger reaches up to what he is looking for, namely to the authentic notion of identity. Because perceiving-thinking is a characteristic of man, in order to understand what *belonging* is, we have to think it in the context of man and his Being. And what is characteristic of man is that, in thinking, he can be open to Being. To be open to Being means a peculiar asubjective kind of experience where the future is genuinely open and unpredictable. One characteristic of it is that it is neither representational thinking nor a relation between two entities or terms. It is a jump to the experience of sameness. This is an experience of disclosure toward that with which one is the same, a kind of assimilation with, or surrendering to, that to which one belongs.

Sameness in quantum phenomena

Now, our original question, whether modern science is necessarily onto-theo-logical, and its parallel question, whether nondogmatic naturalism is possible, have reached a new turn. They have been transformed into the following, new question: Is the notion of sameness which prevails in modern Western natural science really the Leibniz identity? The point is, of course, that if this is not the case, then, perhaps, modern science isn't necessarily onto-theo-logical. This reasoning is based on the assumption that the Leibniz identity is the core of onto-theo-logic.

The negative answer, namely that the notion of sameness which prevails in modern science is not the Leibniz identity, will again raise a new question. This is the question whether the rivalling identity notion which we called Parmenides's identity is applicable in modern science. Perhaps the notion of sameness which we need in the philosophy of modern physics, say in quantum philosophy, resembles Heidegger's notion of sameness as "belonging together," sameness as disclosure and surrendering to that with which one is the same.

Many quantum philosophers have claimed that quantum phenomena do not satisfy the Leibniz laws. According to Alberto Cortes (1976), photons violate the law of the *Identity of the Indiscernibles* and cannot, therefore, be genuine individuals at all. For example, we cannot quantify over them and they do not exist in the sense of *existing* which was made popular by Quine (that is, by serving as values of bound variables, see Quine, 1953, pp. 12-13). Of genuine or classical individuals, but not of photons, we can say that if "two" individuals (or something that gives the impression that it consists of two individuals) have exactly the same properties, then the individuals are actually one and the same, that is, they are identical.

In order to deny this principle, Cortes has presented the following thought experiment. Let us fill a small box with electromagnetic radiation of frequency í such that the amount of energy of that frequency inside the box is 2hí where h is Planck's constant. From this we can infer that there are two photons of frequency í in the box, such that they are exactly in the same state. Two photons, which are bosons, may, according to the standard interpretation, simultaneously occupy exactly the same position and have all physical properties in common. Because the photons have all properties in common, they should, according to the law of the *Identity of the Indiscernibles*, be identical. But they are not. Therefore, says Cortes, the law is violated.

Also the law of the *Indiscernibility of the Identicals* is threatened if we try to apply it to quantum phenomena. For example, in the EPR thought experiments we have to deal with a "single" electron of which it is possible to say that it is in two different places simultaneously.

The overall conclusion is that the Leibniz laws are not universally valid because they do not apply to all quantum phenomena. It is possible to design at least two kinds of counterexample. Either we suggest that two "particles" are in one place at the same moment (Cortes); or we claim that one "particle" is in more than one place at one moment (EPR-type of examples). (Of course, we use here the word "particle" only for the sake of argument. The whole point of these counterexamples is that there actually are no particles or any other classical individuals, not, at least, among quantum phenomena.) Such restrictions which require that there is only one thing in one place at a given moment, and that one thing cannot be in several places at one moment, are typically thought to characterize classical individuals, for example such individuals or material substances which are studied by classical physics. (See, for example, Russell's attempts to characterize the notion of *materia* of classical physics, in Russell, 1903, Section 440, pp. 467-8).

Quantum phenomena violate classical individuation and separability conditions. It doesn't seem that science, in order to able to speak of a phenomenon, necessarily utilizes Leibniz's notion of "identity as unification." Here Niels Bohr would have disagreed because he thought that, in order to be meaningful at all, natural language must be understood as a medium in which we speak of external common sense things. He thought that classical science studies these same things from a scientific point of view (see Pylkkö, 1996a). An unfortunate consequence of this view is that quantum physicists cannot really speak of what they are studying! If Heidegger thought that the Leibniz identity is one of the core principles of scientific thinking, and scientific thinking represents what he calls *onto-theo-logic*, then we would expect quantum theory, the very core of modern natural science, not to violate the Leibniz laws and related classical individuation and separation principles. But it *does* violate them. Isn't this a counterexample for Heidegger's thesis that modern science is onto-theo-logical? It seems that the answer is *yes*.

How to speak of quantum phenomena?

This is especially so because the massive holism of quantum phenomena forces us to modify our conception of language and mind in general and distance it from common sense, and the overall direction of this modification and distancing seems to go against onto-theo-logic (For more about quantum theory and language, see Pylkkö, 1994b). It is ironic that the later Heidegger's *a*-onto-logical view of language, especially his notions *nearness, neighbor-hood* and *Parmenides's sameness*, might be more appropriate for speaking of quantum phenomena than the Leibniz identity and related onto-theo-logical notions of dogmatic science. If we consider the electron of the two-path thought experiment which David Albert has presented and discussed (Albert, 1992), we must conclude that, whatever runs through the paths, it is not a classical individual. Therefore, if we want to explain what speaking of electrons and other quantum phenomena is, we cannot resort to any such theory of naming which attaches names to classical individuals. Yet practically every theory of naming seems to be a theory of how to name classical individuals. An electron which is in the mode of superposition and whose properties are therefore indeterminate and inseparable is something *less* than an individual. If we try to handle it as if it were an individual of classical physics or classical logic we will end up with paradoxes because we are forced to say that an individual both has a property P and that it hasn't it, that it is in two places simultaneously, and so on.

In order to avoid these paradoxes, nondogmatic naturalism might suggest, among other things, that natural language and the human mind are primarily aconceptual and asubjective experience. In order to produce things, concepts and subjects, the experience has to be reified by repeated associations which eventually shape the experience into what creates the impression that some internal objects (concepts) and external objects (things) are present. But even after the reifying polarization, the internal and the external always remain partly entangled.

When we are dealing with electrons, we are dealing with this kind of collective, originally aconceptual experience of physics research communities which are embedded into Western societies. In special social and historical circumstances, the experience can become articulated by repeated cycles of association and eventually create the impression that some kind of things, electrons as things, are present. For example, quantum-physical measurements are situations in which electrons appear to behave almost as if they were classical things. But it is better here, too, to speak only of *surrogate or apparent individuals* (simulacra), not of genuine ones. As soon as we try to determine two suitably chosen properties simultaneously (say position and momentum), we notice that their classicalness is illusory. It seems that we cherish the classicalness assumption in order to make understanding easier for us. Actually, we cannot strictly separate ourselves as observers from the observation situation in which we decide which one of the properties will assume an accurate value and which will remain indeterminate.

Along with this act of reification, we bring our mind, beliefs and language onto the scene where our aconceptual experience is articulated into theoretical concepts and objects. For example, the idea of measurement has a long history which ties the notion ineradicably to the history of Western technology. Without this history we wouldn't know how to interpret measurements. Moreover, modern technology would not have evolved without the older background of Western mathematics, logic and grammar. These disciplines cannot be understood without relating them to the history of Western metaphysics. Eventually, the roots of Western metaphysics and technological attitude which dominates the Western mind today date back to pre-historical Indo-European conceptions of thing, man and God.

Thus, when reified by repeated associations and surrounded by a history of proper thing-enhancing beliefs, the aconceptual experience may create the impression that we are dealing with permanent things. For example, measuring instruments look as if they were either common sense objects or classical individuals; analogously, the symbols (formal or typographical signs) which we use in the quantum formalism behave almost like macrophysical individuals. But, if taken too literally, both sorts of classicalness are illusory and leads us to absurdities. No classical law is able to predict to an arbitrary degree of desired accuracy how a measuring instrument behaves if the instrument is arranged to indicate the values of suitably chosen properties of a singular quantum phenomenon. It is exactly the non-classical behavior of the quantum-physical measuring instruments which forced Max Planck to adopt the original *quantum of action* hypothesis as he pondered over the black body experiment (for which see Jammer, 1966, pp. 10-28). Thus it is literally false to claim that measuring instruments are classical objects. If they were purely classical, man would never have invented the quantum theory in the first place. Nevertheless, it is possible to assume conditionally, counterfactually and tentatively that they are classical. This assumption may have been important for the invention of quantum theory. But as soon as we reach the quantum theory proper, the condition must be abandoned. Hence, strictly speaking, there exist no classical objects, and *quantum-physical influences are effective also at the so-called macrophysical level* (cf. Sharp, 1961; Putnam, 1961; Putnam, 1964; see also Pylkkö, 1996a). We just decide to ignore the influences in certain contexts.

It is typical of collective aconceptual experience, including the kind of experience from which scientific knowledge arises, that it doesn't satisfy Evans's generality constraint (Evans, 1982, pp. 100-105) or Fodor and Pylyshyn's (1988) systematicity constraint. It is neither separable nor decompositional. Names cannot be taken to be constituents which mean the same thing in different verbal and behavioral contexts. We cannot predict the meaning of a whole, say the meaning of a whole sentence, from its alleged parts, say from the so-called words. Aconceptual experience is not systematic or systemic in the sense which requires that the behavior of a whole can be predicted from the behavior of its alleged constituents.

Aconceptual experience is holistic or inseparable (in the sense of *inseparable* which has been recommended, for example, by Howard, 1989, which says that an inseparable phenomenon is not a system because its behavior cannot be explained in terms of any subsystems). The human mind, language and environment encompass an indivisible flow of perpetually changing experience. And, as with quantum-physical effects, we just decide to ignore the overall holism of the human mind in certain contexts. For example, we may decide to do common sense reasoning in some contexts or we may decide to do a classical kind of science of the human mind. Standard artificial intelligence and cognitive science are typical examples of the latter possibility.

In the kind of holistic naturalism which has been sketched here, the human mind is not primarily a representational system, and the boundary of the subject and the object cannot be drawn in any unambiguous or permanent sense. The boundary is always conventional and relative to the interests of the community which draws it. For example, the pretheoretical beliefs which a research community holds are inseparably entangled with the theoretical ones. Ancient and partly unconscious associations which have hardly been submitted to critical discussion saturate the meanings of the theoretical terms. Language, observations, imagination, thought experiments and mental models form an indivisible whole from which the external objects of research cannot be cut apart in any absolute, independent, universal or definite sense. Electrons are not external objects but part of human experience which can be individuated and objectified into surrogate individuals. This happens under the pressure of many practical purposes and succeeds only in proper social and historical circumstances.

Is this kind of holistic naturalism onto-theo-logical? If it is, it isn't necessarily or fatally so. The difference between Being (Sein) and entities (Seiende) can be understood and discussed within it. Entities belong to experience which is originally asubjective and lacks thing structure but which, in special circumstances, appears as if it consisted of permanent individuals. For example, regular modern Western common sense and classical science require such experiential circumstances in which permanent, identity-preserving entities can be established. Such circumstances require that the evolving center of experience which may become a subject, or better, a surrogate subject, is stabilized as a conceptual organization to such an extent and in such a way that it is able to deal with the so-called external entities. The Being of electrons is determined by their sameness (cf. Parmenides's sameness as it was discussed earlier), that is, they are (appear in the world, so to speak) in and through the sameness that is provided to them by the community of Western quantum physicists. As we have seen, the sameness is not, however, completely free of the assumptions of the surrounding nonscientific community, and therefore the sameness is constantly threatened by the reification and trivialization tendencies of common sense.

In order to attain their Being, electrons need the sameness which only the human perceiving and thinking processes can provide. Thus perceiving and thinking are not representational but actively constructive processes which are ineradicably entangled with many Western scientific beliefs. It is by going through such active human construction processes that electrons appear in the world, and it is with the help of such processes that man is able to belong together with Being. Those processes are constantly under the pressure which the common sense of the surrounding society exercises. Common sense serves as a kind of inertia of meaning which intends that the quantum-philosophical views do not depart too radically from their nontheoretical background. In order to let the distance from common sense grow more freely, research communities should develop peculiar social arrangements of their own which are less vulnerable under the metaphysical pressure from the outside.

Has the forgetfulness of Being poisoned Western culture?

If nondogmatic naturalism is possible, then Heidegger's famous vision of the Western culture as a history of *Seinsvergessenheit*, some ingredients of which he seems to have adopted from Emil Lask's thinking already in the early twenties (for which see, Nolte, 1992, p. 38), has to be questioned, too. It seems that the problem of Being has been forgotten far less completely than what Heidegger has suggested, or that the nature of the forgetfulness is not quite what he thought.

Let us consider, for example, David Hume's work, especially his early *A Treatise of Human Nature* (Hume 1739-40/1987). The young Hume questioned the reality of internal meaning entities, as well as external objects. He also abolished the borderline which allegedly separates perception from thinking by saying that thoughts are impressions which have lost something of their original vividness. In addition, Hume intended that there is no permanent, identity-preserving Self which controls the flow of experience, and that human behavior is guided, not by reason, but by passions. Now, assume that the intensity of this kind of experience is increased. Why wouldn't we say that we are approaching here a pre-Heideggerian description of the authentic *Dasein* experience?

Of course, for Hume all experience originates from the senses, and it is not clear how much thoughts are able to influence impressions in Hume's view of the mind. But if there is no sharp borderline which can be said to separate perception from thinking, and experience in Hume is neither organized by referential concepts nor caused by external things, then perhaps some kind of holism can be said to characterize also that part of experience which is often called "inner experience," and, eventually, we can say that thoughts may somehow exercise their influence on perception too. Therefore, the issue of direction, that is, the idea that impressions are somehow prior to thoughts, loses some of its edge. Perhaps there is an overall direction in the flow of experience; but, at the same time, if the flow is holistic enough, its causal organization may become distorted and the past and future could become entangled with one another.

Also Wilhelm Ostwald's philosophy of nature (Ostwald, 1901) and Ernst Mach's neutral monism (Mach, 1897) deconstructs the boundary of the internal and the external. Mach's naturalism was antidogmatic in the sense that, in his thinking, both the physical and the psychical are derived from neutral elements. Therefore, the absolute borderline of the subject and object is dissolved. In addition, the physical and the psychical interact perpetually, and whatever we learn about the physical, in physics for example, is controlled, edited and restricted by the activities of the human mind. Respectively, Mach thought that the principles which govern the human mind are restricted by what is physically possible.

But what is crucial for our questions here is that the difference between Being and entities can be addressed and understood in many philosophical traditions in which natural science has played an active role. Hume's *flow of experience*, Ostwald's *unstructured experience* and Mach's *neutral elements* are not yet entities but belong to the experience of Being which precedes the emergence of entities. Therefore, contrary to what Heidegger suggested, we should not claim without qualifications that the problem of Being cannot be discussed in any such tradition which has been dominated by the thinking habits and presuppositions of natural science. What we *can* say is that the problem cannot be discussed within dogmatic natural science and that, even in less dogmatic science, it hasn't, perhaps, been discussed as much as it deserves to be discussed. And perhaps we should add that the Hume-Ostwald-Mach-Bohr tradition is not particularly popular today. In a sense it has been "forgotten," and this sense may come quite close to the kind of forgetfulness of Being that Heidegger had in mind (see also Pylkkö, 1996b).

But even in the obscurity of this forgetfulness, Heidegger's bleak view of the possibilities of empiricism which he expressed, for example, in *Moira* (1945/1975) isn't quite fair. Perhaps it was never intended to be so. Be that as it may, to claim straightforwardly that the modern statement (Berkeley's *esse* = *percipi*) asserts something about Being "understood as objectivity for a thoroughgoing representation" is an oversimplification of the condition of modern thinking. Berkeley's famous dictum doesn't mean only that *being is representation* but carries possibilities of many other interpretations too. We could easily suggest that Hume showed, not only that the concept of the external object is unable to face the challenge of a skeptical analysis, but also that any object-like element of perception is equally ill-founded. Thus Heidegger's critique of empiricism as unwitting representationalism doesn't apply directly and without qualifications to Hume, Mach, Ostwald, Pauli and Bohr.

So, we don't have to resort to the Schelling-Schopenhauer-Nietzsche tradition in order to claim that, already before Heidegger's influence began to spread, *Seinsvergessenheit* hadn't been able to overwhelm the European culture. Besides the antirealistic empiricism discussed above, the question of Being and human experience was also central in the German *Lebensphilosophie*, Existentialism and Expressionism in the 1920s and 1930s. For example, Ludwig Klages (1921) taught that we should not let the human Soul (Seele) be dominated by the *logocentric Spirit* (Geist). The soul lives naturally close to the Body (Leib) and its sexual resources, whereas the Spirit tries to pull them apart. In this pulling apart, the Spirit tends to make an alliance with Consciousness and Reason. The Spirit, now controlled by Consciousness and Reason, reifies and corrupts the human experience. Eventually, in an inauthentic culture, or in "logocentric culture" as Klages used to say, the Logos may saturate the whole of the human experience. Klages is one of those thinkers whose work hasn't deserved the almost complete oblivion which its connection with Nazism has inflicted.

Also Heidegger's contemporaries, Emil Lask, Hans Heyse, Franz Böhm and Alfred Bäumler, were academic *Dasein* philosophers of whom we cannot say that their work was dominated by *Seinsvergessenheit*, *Gestell* or *onto-theo-logy*. And if we choose to consider the wider perspective of *German Expressionism*, with which Heidegger's work should be closely associated, we cannot say that the power of the *Gestell* was particularly dominant there.

The masters of German movie Expressionism, Leni Riefenstahl, Fritz Lang and Thea von Harbou, or the expressionist poet Gottfried Benn and the painter Emil Nolde, tried to penetrate down to the roots of human experience and succeeded in casting light upon its aconceptual and asubjective origin.

Conclusion: Answer to the title's question

The answer to the question of our title, whether modern science is necessarily onto-theo-logical, is negative. The difference between Being and entities can be discussed within science itself, assuming that the self-image of science is not too naive and science is ambitious enough to raise such questions. Quantum philosophy comprises a good example of this kind of avoidance of naiveté. This makes the prospects of nondogmatic philosophical naturalism look much better than what Heidegger thought. However, holistic and antirealistic naturalism seems to be quite unpopular among scientists and philosophers, and one of the reasons for this is that it offends our common sense. A perpetually changing flux of experience in which subject and object cannot be kept separate is not a place where we want to live. We need the protection which only an identity-preserving Self and its rationality can provide. Therefore, there are a lot of reasons to abandon and even suppress nondogmatic philosophical naturalism. Similarly, Wolfgang Pauli's view, according to which there is an irrational component in physical reality, is not an issue which has been widely discussed within the scientific and philosophical community.

As regards the question of suppressing the prospects of holistic naturalism, we cannot quite absolve Heidegger either. Heidegger was bold enough to remind us of the philosophical importance of the most violent asubjective experience in which the subject is almost destroyed by the nearness of the Nothing (see Heidegger, 1929/1988). He even suggested that the experience may be too powerful to be endured by modern man who lives in the artificial environment of a welfare state. But also Heidegger seems to have suppressed something. He was not willing to admit, or even to see, that the weakest link in the essence of technology, where the dominance of technology may begin to break down, lies within the most advanced department of modern science itself, namely in quantum theory and in its aconceptual and holistic nature. In the *Der Spiegel Interview* (1966/1988) Heidegger resigned to the mercy of divine help and proclaimed that only God can save us. But perhaps the salvation, or the end of onto-theo-logic and the dominance of *Gestell*, needs no God to be accomplished. Maybe the *Gestell* itself is able to do it.

CHAPTER THREE

What is *noncomputational* in recent consciousness studies?

Back to experience

That human experience is not comprehensively describable in purely factual, realistic and objective terms is a view which we are accustomed to relate to Continental Philosophy, especially to phenomenology, that is, to the work of such philosophers as, for example, Edmund Husserl (1913/1976; 1937/1989) and Martin Heidegger (1927/1992), to mention some of the most famous names. Classical phenomenology, especially that of Husserl's, used to pay much attention to such notions as *intuition* and *intention*, and it was the activities of the subject's consciousness upon which the study of human mind and knowledge was supposed to concentrate. Yet it can be said that one of the main directions which the phenomenological movement has taken after the prime of Husserl's work has gone against the view that the subject is the centerboard of human experience and that consciousness and rationality comprise the most central subject matter and focus of philosophical work in general.

Let us call *asubjectivism* such a view which emphasizes that the understanding of human experience and behavior remains inadequate if the understanding is based only on the subject's consciousness and rationality. This holds for self-understanding, too. According to asubjectivism, human experience is crucially broader than just a setting for the conscious manipulation of representative concepts; similarly, human behavior cannot be reduced to rational decision making. Man isn't only a goal-directed achiever who stands in front of well-articulated alternatives of the future course of events calculating the best possible course of action. Any adequate view of the human mind, language and behavior has to begin with such experience which precedes the emergence of the subject, consciousness and rationality. The outgrowth of phenomenology which has realized this and appreciates the asubjective view of the human mind might be called *postphenomenology*. One may associate postphenomenology at least, to the work of the later Heidegger (1947/1977; 1957/1969; 1959/1969), Maurice Merleau-Ponty (1945/1971), Jan Patocka (1988) and Georges Bataille (1943/1988).

From the postphenomenological perspective, human mind and language are originally less structured and more holistic than what any purely representative mechanism can be. The primary state of the human mind may be so primitive or primordial that even the dichotomy of the internal and the external is not yet fully present there. Such experiential primitivity is not organized into concepts and it lacks such hierarchy and perspectivity which characterize full subjectivity. Therefore *experiential centers* which are not yet full-fledged subjects cannot be separated from one another by a crisp conceptual cut. The experience in which they float is *aconceptual*, and because aconceptual experience doesn't yet recognize separate individuals, it has a peculiar collective nature. This kind of preindividually collective experience need not, and in practice cannot, be completely free of all conceptual ingredients, but it is not individuated, consolidated and dominated by them.

Any attempt to describe aconceptual and asubjective experience is bound to encounter the following obstacle. Both normal modern Western common sense and any standard scientific attitude (cf. Chapter 2) presuppose a conscious and rational subject who has access to a conceptually structured language. With the help of the conceptual language, objects and things can be referred to and propositions and ideas can be communicated to other speakers, i.e., to other subjects. For a subject, but not for an experiential center in general, large and central areas of meaning rest always on referential abilities. But now, if we want to describe such experience and meaning which precedes conceptuality and the emergence of a solid subject-object dichotomy, it seems that we shouldn't attempt to do it in colloquial language or in standard scientific language. In order to avoid the absurdities which such an attempt would inevitably bring about, we should, from the very beginning, have access to a language and view of language which is not committed to the philosophical priority of conceptuality, reference and representativeness (cf. Pylkkö, 1996a). This view must, in a sense, be *atheoretical*.

From the aconceptual point of view, what is called *consciousness* is just one special case of human experience, namely, such a case in which the aforementioned dichotomies (subject-object; internal-external; concept-reference) are, to a considerable extent, effective. Asubjectivism tells us that, regardless of the limited and special perspective and derivative nature of consciousness, there is an obvious danger that it is exactly consciousness that will dominate our view of what the human mind is. This danger is particularly strong if we work within the Western scientific and academic world. Though *standard science* may be unable to explain consciousness and may even avoid the whole word, it nevertheless presupposes it one way or another. This presupposition, especially if it is accepted uncritically, may bias and even distort our view of what the human mind is.

It was, in particular, the rise of modern technology and science which encouraged such thinking habits which forcefully reduced the human mind and language into a representative mechanism and suppressed its originally experiential nature. Because scientific and technological representations are, at least seemingly, conscious and rational, scientific culture, with all the self-confidence which its success has conferred to it, tends to overdo the role which consciousness and rationality play in human experience in general, and this bias all too easily pushes the rest of human experience into a cultural periphery. Because of this 'forgetfulness,' which may happen unwittingly too, the human mind and its language no longer appears to us as such open-ended experience in which man could dwell and through the unfolding of which he could move toward something genuinely new and unpredictable. Surprisingly perhaps, this forgetfulness doesn't imply that standard science would be particularly good in explaining what normal consciousness is.

Search for a noncomputational view of mind

Such postphenomenological views which were sketched above are usually seen as a continuation or modification of a philosophical tradition which is critical of, and sometimes even hostile toward, modern natural science and technology. And indeed, postphenomenological asubjectivism tends to be highly critical of the standard theoretical-technological attitude and its prevailing dichotomies. Postphenomenological thinking endeavors to approach the human mind and language from a point of view which would not ignore or 'forget' the originally aconceptual nature of human experience, whereas, according to standard science and its self-image, such experience has no place in the world of science and technology and must be either ignored as irrelevant and marginal, or occasionally even classified as nonexistent. The latter choice is particularly tempting if the experience cannot, even in principle, be given a consistent conceptual description.

Contrary to postphenomenological thinking, classical phenomenology (say, as it is developed in Husserl's *Ideen*, 1913/1976) is not free of the intellectualist bias of the scientific-technological attitude because classical phenomenology clearly sides with the conscious subject and its allegedly autonomous rationality and quite openly acknowledges the rational subject's right to dominate the rest of the mind. But even classical phenomenology with its ratio-oriented bias has always considered the standard, in Husserl's terms, *factual* or *empirical*, scientific attitude mainly as a *derivative* of human consciousness. Yet from the point of view which is opened by asubjectivism, the problem here is, not that factual knowledge is seen as secondary with respect to consciousness and intuition, but that mind and intuition, and eventually consciousness too, are often characterized in a way which is so purely rational and conceptual that even the famous *Lebenswelt* of the later Husserl (1937/1989) appears to be, not a world with historical, social and cultural variety, but, quite the opposite, namely, something almost *a priori*-like, immutable and purely essential in its nature.

Also quantum theory presents a serious challenge to classical phenomenology because, according to classical phenomenology, the intuitive capabilities of the human consciousness are realized by logical principles which are so purely classical that the holistic aspects of microphysical phenomena can hardly be expressed in them. Actually, Husserl's view of logic in *Ideas* seems to be, not only purely classical, but even formal because he seems to equate logical truth and formal provability (Husserl, 1913/1976, see especially section 72, p. 205). But if factual or empirical knowledge, in the context of classical phenomenology, always appears as a derivative of human conscious intuition, and it is the case that human consciousness is realized by purely classical or even formal principles, then it becomes impossible to understand how factual or empirical understanding has been able to beget something, namely knowledge of quantum superpositions, which is genuinely holistic and violates explicitly the principles of classical logic.

From the point of view of classical phenomenology and hermeneutic thinking, it must seem quite surprising that some of the most recent attempts to elevate human experience back to a central position in the study of man (be it the study of mind, brain or language) and nature, and address the peculiar difficulties which human experience presents as a subject matter of research, have come from within the scientific world itself. This rethroning of human experience, or, at least, of consciousness, in the study of man, has eventually forced its advocates to recast and occasionally even reject some of the most central notions of standard modern physical and biological science. Most notably, such notions as *computation, causality* and *physical object* have been probed and modifications of their traditional meanings have been called for.

The discoveries of recent natural science and the related remolding of classical thinking habits have not usually been inspired by continental philosophy or phenomenology. Neither have such discoveries been particularly successful in spreading their influence among those who have traditionally studied the human mind and language. Quantum theory did inspire physicists, Niels Bohr and Wolfgang Pauli as the first among them, to rethink the role which human action, measurement, perception and language play in the interpretation and understanding of physical phenomena. Therefore one might expect that repercussions of such rethinking could have found their way into the sphere of humanistic studies, too. For example, one might expect that purely externalist, deterministic or mechanical notions would have become less popular. Yet it is far from obvious that this has happened. Ironically, humanistic studies, for example modern psychology, linguistic and semiotic theory, are often more mechanical, formal and externalist than recent physical science! But, on the other hand, Niels Bohr and Wolfgang Pauli were hardly aware of the similarities which their philosophy bears with postphenomenological thinking. These similarities have been studied recently, among others, by Plotnitsky (1994).

One of the main targets of the new antireificational and holistic tendencies of recent natural science has been the view that the human mind or brain can be described comprehensively in *computational terms.* In what follows, I will review some of these new *noncomputational* approaches to the human mind, deliberate upon what they actually mean by *noncomputability,* criticize them and, eventually, suggest an alternative noncomputational view. The crux of this alternative view will be that some human experiences are genuinely aconceptual, and the origin of this aconceptuality may lie in the *randomness* of the underlying physical, chemical and biological phenomena which are effective in the human brain, body and environment during such experiences. Strictly speaking, it is not even necessary to assume that genuine randomness and inseparability reign in the human brain. It is sufficient if we assume that the human brain is immediately *related* to such a physical environment where random and inseparable phenomena occur. This suggests, among other things, that the so-called *freedom of will* should be associated, not directly with the results of the choices which we allegedly make in conscious thinking, speaking and planning, but with such genuinely aconceptual ingredients of our experience which, in some sense, precede conscious thinking, speaking and planning (for more about this topic, see Pylkkö, 1995a; 1996b). The philosophical point is that this view, *freedom as asubjective randomness*, which is inspired by certain interpretations of quantum theory, conforms, not with classical phenomenology, let alone with regular analytical philosophy, but with postphenomenological thinking (cf. Chapter 1).

Roger Penrose (1994) has recently advocated a noncomputational view of human consciousness. Penrose doesn't resort to continental philosophy and prefers to introduce himself as a representative of the venerable tradition of modern Western science. Yet some of his ideas point, perhaps unwittingly, not only to new, and presently nonexisting, scientific theories, but also to a slightly modified view of what science actually is. Nevertheless, his theory of consciousness is riddled with difficulties. For example, Gödel's proof of the incompleteness of axiomatic arithmetic doesn't necessarily or directly support the view that the human mind is not a computer. More is needed to support such a belief: a strong Platonic conviction. Penrose's work bears also a strong Western bias and approaches consciousness mainly from an academic point of view, ignoring thereby certain serious problems which are related to circularity, self-reference, relativism and scientific realism.

In addition to Penrose's famous work, several scholars working under the broad umbrella of neuroscience have recently been searching for new noncomputational alternatives to regular cognitive science, and, unlike Penrose, some of these scholars have explicitly resorted to continental philosophy. One of them is Gordon Globus (1990; 1992a; 1992b; 1995) who has found help both from Heidegger and from Derrida in his attempts to go beyond the regular 'information processing' view of the human mind. I will review some of his work and criticize his conception of *noncomputational neuroscience*.

But there are others, too. Skarda and Freeman (1987; 1990) who have introduced chaos theory in their neural models have also recommended Merleau-Ponty's philosophy as a proper, and perhaps even anticipatory, background of their own work. Also Engel and König (1992) resort to Heidegger and Merleau-Ponty. However, this alliance of neuroscience and continental thinking is much older than what these recent examples might suggest. Already in the fifties and sixties, the Finnish physiologist and philosopher, Yrjö Reenpää (1959; 1967), a specialist in physiology of the sense organs, used Husserl and Heidegger as his philosophical guides. His main goal was to understand how empirical sciences, especially physiology, and the exactness which they attained, gradually evolved within the tradition of Western metaphysics.

Penrose and the *noncomputational*

The reader of Roger Penrose's book *Shadows of the Mind. A Search for the Missing Science of the Consciousness* (1994) is frequently reminded that the author wants to work within the tradition of modern physical and mathematical science and that he will, at most, extend and improve some of the existing theories in order to carry on the very idea of scientific research into new virgin regions. There is no room for problems of asubjectivism or other themes of continental philosophy in Penrose's world, and indeed, in this sense, Penrose works within the boundaries of standard Western science. If new theories are needed in the explanation of human consciousness it is obvious that, in Penrose's opinion, there are no good reasons to go beyond the boundaries of Western science.

Penrose develops further an argument which is usually associated with J.R. Lucas (1961). The main idea is that because man himself is able to ascertain the truth of the so-called Gödel sentences (how to construct such sentences, see Nagel & Newman, 1957), and because, at the same time, he can write for any computer, abstract or concrete, a specially tailored Gödel sentence which the computer cannot formally prove, the human mind must somehow be essentially more powerful than any mechanical or formal device. Therefore, human understanding cannot be comprehensively simulated by computational (mechanical, formal) procedures. The human mind is *noncomputational* in the standard mathematical sense of being *non-Turing-computable* or *not-finitely-formalizable*.

The argument can be rephrased in an obvious way by referring to *consistency* instead of *truth*. According to this variant, no theorem-proving computer can simulate the full power of man's mathematical knowledge, because no computer, if it is consistent and powerful enough to deal with axiomatic arithmetic, can prove its own consistency, whereas man allegedly is able to prove the consistency of his own mathematical intuition.

One of the difficulties which this view is known to imply is that we are accustomed to think that our brains belong to the physical reality, the received view being that the physical reality *can* be described comprehensively in mechanical or Turing-computable concepts (numbers, functions, and so on). Regular physical, chemical and biological laws which are believed to hold in neuroscience and other special sciences, too, are supposed to be mechanically computable, even trivially so. Therefore, it seems that we can simulate the full capabilities of the human brain in Turing-computable concepts. But, if this is so, how are our brains, as part of the physical and biological reality, supposed to have access to noncomputable truths, including the truth of Gödel sentences, and understand them? How can a mechanical device understand nonmechanical truths, assuming that it can understand anything? If we believe that we actually are able to understand Gödel-sentences, it seems that our mind is able to surpass the boundary of the mechanical whereas our brain is not. Therefore, we end up claiming that our minds can do something that our brains are unable to realize, and that sounds dangerously dualistic.

Therefore, there is an obvious reason for Penrose and others who want to avoid this kind of psycho-physical dualism to hope that the physical reality, and along with it the human brain, would turn out to be noncomputable (not mechanically computable; not-Turing-computable). And this is where Penrose's own theme emerges and he contributes something original to the old Lucas-type argument of the noncomputability of the human understanding. Penrose doesn't take the mechanical computability of the physical for granted and, after having looked for examples of the noncomputability in the physical sphere, he thinks that he has found it in the strange world of quantum gravity.

The idea that physical theories are not necessarily mechanical (Turing-computable) is by no means new. Kreisel (1974) discussed the issue already more than two decades ago (for further developments, see Pour-El & Richards, 1981; and Geroch & Hartle, 1986). Also the idea that quantum-theoretical indeterminacy may be a repercussion of the logical incompleteness of the quantum-theoretical formalism is not a new idea but belongs to old philosophical folklore. In several private discussions, professor Jaakko Hintikka used to speculate about this topic already during the 1980's. Also Quine (1969, pp. 70-71) has found parallels between, on the one hand, the formalist program which attempts to reduce mathematics to elementary logic and, on the other hand, logical empiricism which attempted to reduce physical knowledge to sense data. Quine's philosophical point was that if the former program, due to Gödel's incompleteness results, is impossible then the latter one should be impossible too. Only a small modification of the analogy is needed for drawing the conclusion that our observations of microphysical phenomena are not, perhaps, finitely formalizable or axiomatizable, and it is this incompleteness that physicists call *indeterminacy* (see Quine, 1953, p. 19).

Gödel himself seems to have believed that the physical reality and the human brain as part of it *is* classically closed, that is, comprehensively describable in terms of classical physical science and that classical physical science is formal or mechanical. (At least Gödel, 1944, points to this direction, and Hao Wang confirms that this was Gödel's opinion, Wang, 1987, p. 198). But because some mathematical objects, according to Gödel, clearly are not mechanically computable, and the human mind obviously has a good grasp of their nature, Gödel had to give up the view that human mind and the physical brain are identical or equally powerful. According to him, the human mind is not tied to the classical and mechanical constraints which the physical brain has to obey.

Penrose thinks that such dualism which Gödel's views implies is untenable and suggests that we should not take the mechanicalness of physical nature for granted. Therefore, we should search for noncomputable processes in the physical world. In this respect, it is quantum phenomena which comprise the most promising area (though not the only one), and several alternatives are available there. The first of them is provided by the randomness which characterizes single quantum phenomena. In the light of the standard interpretations, the deterministic dynamics of the state vector (the Schrödinger equation) is unable to *explain* its own probabilistic *collapse*. Here the rationality of explanation would require that we could *deduce* the collapse from the Schrödinger equation (as, for example, David Albert, 1992, on pages 37 and 73 demands). But this cannot be done. A single event which is observable at the macrophysical level, for example, as the output of a measuring instrument is, to some extent, random and even unpredictable in the sense that quantum theory seems to be unable to provide us with a *theoretical explanation* of how something apparently purely deterministic ends up producing random events. As Wolfgang Pauli (1954) used to put it, there seems to be an *irrational aspect* in quantum phenomena, and that aspect is the unexplainable step from determinism to randomness (see also Laurikainen, 1988; Pylkkö, 1996b). One way out of this quandary holds that physical phenomena are irreducibly indeterminate and inseparable, and it is already the formalism of the quantum theory and related measurements which attempt to impose upon these holistic phenomena a formal and mechanical frame which never really fits and thus generates a bunch of paradoxes. It is the frame of formal and mechanical thinking habits that gives rise to fictitious constructs which we know as macrophysical entities.

In other words, our knowledge about quantum phenomena seems to acknowledge a limit. In the standard interpretation, this limit is drawn by the statistical nature of the theory itself. Therefore the limit is not contingent, and the necessary lack of knowledge (Pauli's 'irrationality') concerning the exact behavior of single microphysical phenomena, which the theory implies, cannot be eliminated by providing new explanatory information (which would, say, reduce the indeterminacy of single events to some underlying deterministic principles). In this respect, the situation in quantum theory is quite different from classical physics where our possible ignorance of physical details may force us to adopt statistical methods but doesn't force us to abandon the view that the physical nature is ultimately systemic and deterministic.

Now, the first possibility for Penrose and all of those who are looking for the noncomputable in the physical sphere would be to equate the noncomputable and randomness. Let us call this the *randomness view of noncomputability*. This alternative could be developed further in an obvious way by claiming that the unpredictability of human thinking and experience originates from the quantum-physical randomness in the brain processes which are effective during thinking and experience. If the description of the human brain actually requires quantum-level notions, then this view would accord even with the standard Copenhagen-style of interpretations.

Penrose rejects the randomness view because he believes that it is not randomness that is characteristic of human consciousness and understanding. All of his examples of noncomputable understanding which are at all credible come from mathematics and other related academic and intellectualist fields, Gödel's famous sentences being the foremost among them. And, indeed, the understanding of Gödel sentences (or, the incompleteness of every formal characterization of arithmetic truth) doesn't seem to be a particularly random event at all. On the contrary, ascertaining oneself of the nonformalizability of certain arithmetic truths seems to bear a highly determinate character because, in an obvious sense, Gödel sentences are well defined sentences which have a correct syntactical structure and, assuming certain philosophical views of mathematical truth, semantical content (meaning) too.

Penrose tries to make his idea of the nature of noncomputability clear with the help of another noncomputable problem. The so-called tiling problem is not mechanically decidable. Whether some definite geometrical figures will fill up an Euclidian plane without gaps and overlappings is a matter for which there doesn't always exist a Turing-computable solution. Yet the geometrical shapes of the tiles may be quite simple and they look perfectly well defined. Nonetheless, we can give examples of such cases of which we know that the figures will continue filling the plane indefinitely though this cannot be ascertained by any computer. Even if the tiles do not repeat any finite pattern, we can say that, in quite a definite sense, the way in which they fill out the plane is well-defined, determined, or even deterministic, though here 'determinism' cannot, of course, be equated with 'mechanical determinism.'

So, we might say that this is Penrose's picture of what the noncomputability of human understanding is: it is something well-defined in the standard mathematical sense and, in one obvious sense, deterministic, that is, something that is defined in advance, too, and, yet, it cannot be simulated by any computer. The main problem now is that the physical sciences do not seem to support such a determined or 'noncomputationally deterministic' picture of the physical reality, at least not at first glance. Present-day physics does allow noncomputable phenomena, namely single quantum phenomena, but their noncomputability is of the random type which Penrose detests and doesn't want to associate with consciousness. Therefore, something new is needed. This is nothing less than a brand new physical theory, Penrose's OR-theory. The problem is, as one may almost guess, that such a theory doesn't yet actually exist.

The OR-theory would fill nicely a gap in Penrose's argument. It would explain in gravitational terms what we now call the "collapse" of the wave function, and the explanation would consist of functions and numbers which are known to be *non-Turing-computable*. This would give him what he needs: well defined, deterministic and noncomputable physical processes which would be effective in the human brain when a mathematician happens to be thinking some token of the Gödel sentences.

No matter how probable or improbable it is that such a theory will appear one day, there are several difficulties which the theory would have to address at the very beginning of its existence. At first glance, Penrose's view of scientific work appears to be quite normal. Because the existence of non-Turing-computable structures is a commonplace in standard mathematics, it doesn't sound particularly shocking when someone suggests that also some theories of natural science might be non-Turing-computable. But contrary to mathematical realism, realism with respect to physical structures has assumed, implicitly at least, that physical laws must be, not only Turing-computable, but feasibly so. In the context of physical science, non-Turing-computable numbers or functions would conflict with the conditions of simplicity, perspicuity and, eventually, testability and repeatability, which all regular laws of physical science are intended to satisfy. Therefore, Penrose's vision of future physical science is not quite the ordinary one.

Anyway, at the present phase of physical science, Penrose's solution is quite far-fetched and it has an obvious arbitrary feature. The reader has the impression that Penrose guides the physical science in a certain direction just in order to bring home his Gödelian view of the creativity of mathematical thinking. His strategy is to sketch a theory which, if it existed, would satisfy his need for deterministic-cum-noncomputable physical processes; these processes are allegedly effective in the human brain during mathematical understanding. This whole schema of filling gaps with nonexistent future theories is particularly unattractive if the reader is, for independent reasons, unable to take the Lucas-type of argument fully seriously. In other words, if he is unwilling to believe that the ability of man to ascertain himself of the existence of noncomputable truths provides evidence for the claim that the human mind is superior to computers, then the whole motivation for the arbitrary strategy is lost.

It is not completely out of the question that a mechanical device is able to 'produce' a Gödel sentence and a demonstration of its nonprovable truth value if this sentence is designed to characterize the computational capabilities of another mechanical device (or a genuine subsystem of the device itself). After all, a mechanist also has to explain how Gödel-sentences appeared in the world. But here 'producing' would not mean that what is produced, a Gödel-sentence, would result step by step from a set of simple and perspicuous sentences which describe some self-evidently true and primitive properties of the system. What is usually admitted is that no mechanical device is able to formally demonstrate the truth of a Gödel sentence if this sentence has been designed purposefully (malevolently) to characterize the full computational capabilities of the device itself. Most people seem also to think that nonformal demonstration requires understanding, and mechanical systems which produce Gödel-sentences to other mechanical systems do not really understand what they are doing, let alone what the Gödel-sentences are about. For example, when a printing machine prints a Gödel-sentence for an axiom system of arithmetics we don't count that as a 'proof,' though it is a mechanical procedure. This seems to indicate that for a mechanist the fact that there are Gödel-sentences around and that they describe the properties of some formal systems must be a matter of chance or randomness.

But what hasn't yet been shown, says the mechanist here, is that Gödel-sentences are really meaningful and that the human mind is somehow more powerful than a computer, and that exactly the same limitations which we supposedly impose upon machines would not apply also to the human mind itself. It is possible that no human mind is able to design a Gödel sentence for a particularly complex machine, especially if the machine is intended to approximate as closely as possible the mathematical intuition of the human mind. A similar argument can be designed against the consistency version of the Lucas argument. Even Gödel himself (in the Gibbs lecture, 1951) admitted that it is logically possible, i.e., accords with the second incompleteness result, that there exists a theorem-proving machine which is equivalent to human mathematical intuition. If such a machine exists its equivalence with mathematical intuition cannot be proved, and it may turn out to be unsound or inconsistent (see Wang, 1974, p. 324).

Combined with this kind of standard counterargument to the Lucas argument, Penrose's rather arbitrary and almost *ad hoc* strategy doesn't give us a credible insight into what the alleged noncomputability of the human thinking and experience actually is. Penrose's strategy seems quite arbitrary because he sketches a future theory of quantum gravitation just in order to make the human brain noncomputable. But perhaps we should add that major scientific inventions have often been inspired by purely *ad hoc* ideas, and the reasons and motives which inspire and guide ingenious scientists when they feel the urge to invent a new theory almost have to be arbitrary because new theories are often designed *before* the proper facts and observations which will later fit the theory have been invented (cf. Feyerabend, 1988, especially pp. 39-67).

Yet Penrose's theory comprises a major step forward in the Gödelian type of argumentation for the noncomputability of the human mind. A noncomputational and gravitational theory of what is now called "collapse of the wave function," if it turns out to be possible, would solve elegantly the difficulty with psycho-physical dualism which Gödel's original position implies. But it seems that Penrose's solution would not be completely free of quantum paradoxes either. Not only will the collapse of the wave function remain practically unpredictable and, through that, the theory nontestable, but Penrose is unable to explain how something noncomputable in the brain, namely quantum coherence which is allegedly brought about by the microtubules of the neurons, can produce something which is said to be purely mechanical and computable, namely the regular action potential of the neuron membrane. It seems that the paradoxical relation of the microphysical and macrophysical (the deterministic and the indeterministic) is still there with Penrose, though now in a new disguise, namely, as the paradox of how something which is not mechanically computable is able to give rise to something which is mechanically computable. In the beautiful world of tiles and numbers we may be able to discern the mechanical from the nonmechanical. But to do the same with living cells may force us to cut the biological world into two unrelated universes.

The intellectualist fallacy

From the point of view of postphenomenological thinking, Penrose's view of consciousness is undermined by another negligence, and that may also turn out to be fatal: Penrose's straightforwardly realistic approach to the philosophical problem of consciousness is incorrigibly naive. If the physical and biological sciences are purely external and objectivistic, it remains questionable whether the holistic and aconceptual aspects of human experience can ever be handled in a scientific theory, including Penrose's theory. We are reminded of this danger by Bohr (1933): ".. an analysis of the very concept of explanation would, naturally, begin and end with a renunciation as to explaining our own conscious activity."

Penrose is not concerned even with the most common type of philosophical problems, like self-referentiality and circularity, which every study of consciousness is supposed to address (see Chapter 2). This is the problem type which arises from the fact that the study of consciousness itself is a conscious phenomenon, and therefore the study itself and its background culture are bound to shape consciousness in a particular direction. As a conscious phenomenon, the study itself and its academic background culture belong to the subject matter of the study. But the scientific study of consciousness belongs to a very special and limited branch of consciousness. Therefore it is possible that also the subject matter of the study of consciousness, and eventually also the point of view and results, is somehow constrained by the special, limited kind of consciousness to which the study belongs.

For example, mathematical understanding is not possible without a complex cultural setting which requires access to the cultivation of natural language, certain social and economic arrangements, including the academic training during which an almost endless variety of scientific beliefs is acquired, and so on. Full consciousness, including Penrose's examples of mathematical understanding and the scientific study of consciousness itself, is not possible if complex linguistic, cultural and social conditions are not satisfied. Now, one of the most intriguing problems which Penrose has neglected to consider is how these conditions have shaped our consciousness, our view of consciousness and, eventually, our scientific studies of consciousness, and how the conditions, including the scientific study of consciousness itself, eventually influence our experience of consciousness.

For example, the origins of the modern technological and scientific attitude itself, especially after the seventeenth century, are deeply rooted in the soil of the European culture and, therefore, modern technology and science are, in a peculiar way, tied to the European social and economic life forms, technical know-how, linguistic context and philosophical problem sphere. Now, it is far from obvious that any so conspicuously European enterprise can provide us with a comprehensive and unbiased picture of non-European experience and consciousness.

Penrose's study of consciousness is biased also in the sense that it allows intellect to dominate the study, and this domination is accepted in quite an uncritical way. Penrose's point of view on conscious experience is that of a European scientist's who is overly rational and, up to the point of an obsession, theoretically, technically, conceptually and objectively oriented. This is not just an irrelevant question of taste. The restricted point of view determines

what Penrose thinks is relevant in the human experience, including consciousness. First of all, Penrose seems to think that almost all that there is to
human experience is conscious experience. And, furthermore, the conscious
experience, in Penrose's opinion, is dominated by conceptual activities, not,
say, by sexual desire, religious ecstacy or suicidal obsession.

That Penrose doesn't equate conceptual activities and mechanical computations represents an obvious step toward a nontrivial view of consciousness, but this step is undermined by Penrose's uncritical conviction that the
human mind consists primarily or mainly of conceptual activities which are
controlled by a rational and autonomous subject. Perception and feeling are
mentioned, but here, too, the impression is that also they are *about* something,
namely that they are representations of something which happens outside of
the perceiving and feeling subject. Basically the big picture is this: There is a
rational, autonomous and thinking subject who, with the help of his representations, perceives how things are in the world, thinks of its state of affairs,
feels something during these conscious experiences and attempts to carry out
some acts which change the state of the world. All this accords with common
sense, and the scientific study of consciousness can be seen as a refined
version and continuation of this common sense picture. It is obvious that in
this picture modern Western natural science represents the best available
knowledge.

Penrose doesn't seem to think that common sense realism as an attitude
needs to be defended. Analogously, he doesn't seem to think that modern
natural science is biased toward adopting and promoting the modern Western
view of consciousness. He doesn't think that the scientific attitude, as a
special department of consciousness, might be somewhat selective, discrimi-
nate and, perhaps, biased in its dealing with the rest of consciousness and
human experience. Both the present-day Western common sense and the
scientific attitude are special cases of human consciousness and experience,
and the problem is that if there is something else in human consciousness and
experience than common sense and the scientific attitude, then common sense
and the scientific attitude may suppress or misrepresent this 'something else.'
Occasionally this suppression may be so effective that those who are convinced of the comprehensiveness of common sense and the scientific attitude
may actually not experience anything which would violate this conviction.
Penrose doesn't discuss even the most obvious danger involved in his explanatory strategy: because common sense and the scientific attitude are part

of the subject matter of the study, namely, consciousness, it may happen that common sense and the scientific attitude are, perhaps, not completely impartial as regards the problem of what the mind, human experience and consciousness are. This philosophical naiveté might be called the *intellectualist fallacy.*

Consciousness, especially modern Western consciousness which is shaped by modern Western common sense thinking, is biased to encourage such an approach to the study of the human mind which emphasizes its conceptual organization, and, therefore, consciousness almost necessarily sides with concepts in the struggle between the conceptual and the aconceptual in the human experience. Especially this holds for the scientific consciousness. It is plausible that consciousness, as it is equipped with concepts, especially with those of recent science, either ignores aconceptual experience as something irrelevant, perverse and crazy, or fails completely to observe the aconceptual in our experience.

Globus and the *noncomputational*

When Gordon Globus (1992a) uses the word *noncomputational*, it is not intended to mean the same as *non-Turing-computable*, though this possibility isn't necessarily excluded. Fractal systems or nonlinear dynamic systems are usually Turing-computable even if not always in a practically feasible way. The basic idea of chaotic dynamics, namely that small differences in initial conditions may have large and *practically unpredictable* consequences in the output, doesn't require that such systems are non-Turing-computable. Almost always they are Turing-computable, and this implies that the word *chaos* is ambiguous in a similar way as, for example, the word *connectionism*. In regular use both words refer to Turing-computable processes, but this limitation is not a logical necessity built into the meaning of these notions. Rather, in this field of inquiry, Turing-computability is a convenient constraint, though, at least occasionally, an unwitting one. Nothing as such precludes the possibility of using the words *connectionism* and *chaos* in a way which allows a reference to functions or numbers which are not Turing-computable.

Globus prefers to use *noncomputable* to refer to modelling which is not *representational*. It seems that what Globus has in mind is the contrast between rule-governed symbol representation systems of classical AI and connectionist models which are distributed and self-organizing (for the contrast and related controversy, see, for example, Smolensky, 1987; Smolensky, 1988; Fodor & Pylyshyn, 1988). According to Globus, nonlinear dynamic and self-organizing systems use no representational symbols and are therefore noncomputational. For Globus something should be called *computational* if it can be represented in a symbol system.

Because standard nonlinear dynamic systems are Turing-computable, though not always realizable in existing digital machines, there is an obvious danger that Globus's *noncomputable* and *non-Turing-computable* will be confounded. For example, if Globus intends that *computable* means something like *representable in a symbol system* the following problem may arise. *Representable in a symbol system* doesn't as such prevent us from going beyond the boundary of Turing-computability. Gödel-sentences are representational and have a definite syntactic form though their truth cannot be ascertained only by syntactical or formal means. The situation is not clarified by saying that chaotic systems are *deterministic*. Certainly all regular Turing machines are, in an obvious sense, deterministic, but, as we have seen, also non-Turing-computable structures can be perfectly determined in advance and, in a sense, deterministic too.

One of the problems seems to be that Globus ignores the well known fact that every Turing computation is connectionistically computable (Franklin and Garzon, 1991) and that, most probably, also all of the connectionist and chaotic processes which he has in mind are Turing-computable (or can be approximated by a Turing machine to any desired level of accuracy). Of course it is possible to design purely theoretical or abstract neural nets with units whose functions and numbers are non-Turing-computable. But, most probably, all existing artificial neural networks and artificial models of chaotic systems are Turing-computable and, therefore, *mechanical* in the obvious sense of the word (as it is used, for example, by Kreisal, 1974). Therefore, in all normal cases there exists a mechanical coding from a neural-cum-chaotic dynamic system into some Turing machine, and *vice versa*. This establishes the mathematical equivalence between all regular connectionist-cum-chaotic systems and Turing machines. But if this is the case we may ask: Where is the big philosophical difference between modelling in standard computational style and in Globus's 'noncomputational' style.

The difference may be the following. Suppose that a mathematical equivalence between normal connectionist-plus-chaotic systems and Turing machines can be established. It may still be the case that if an actual nonlinear dynamic neural system is coded into a Turing machine (or any other symbol representation system for that matter) *all* of the symbols of *any* resulting Turing machine (or other symbol representation system) will lack *intuitive content*. The symbols may also turn out to be empirically, practically and scientifically useless. In other words, they all are purely theoretical symbols used mainly for coding purposes, lacking explanatory, causal or intuitive power. If they are representative at all their representativeness may prove to be quite uninteresting from any scientific point of view, including empirical neuroscience.

This is a plausible view but it doesn't make symbol representation systems (Globus's 'computable systems') *theoretically* impossible as models of the human brain. For example, in a mathematical sense, Penrose's attack on mechanical computability is more compelling than that of Globus's because Penrose's view makes all Turing-computable models of the human mind clearly inadequate and incomplete.

Does Globus really question the metaphysics of subjectivity?

Penrose's straightforwardly realistic view of scientific research accords with his representative view of the human mind in general. It seems unlikely, for example, that the Heideggerian difference of *Being* (Sein) and *entities* (Seiende) (see, for example, Heidegger, 1957/1969) could ever be addressed in Penrose's framework. For Penrose, physical and mathematical structures are purely external and independent of our mind, language and culture. There is no room for any such considerations which *precede* the existence of physical and mathematical structures. Therefore, it is somewhat surprising that Globus, who doesn't tell us that he is interested in going beyond the boundary of mechanical computability, is willing, unlike Penrose, to question metaphysical realism and the strictly representative role which such realism has reserved for the human mind.

In an article where he compares Derrida's thinking to certain antimetaphysical tendencies in neuroscience (radical connectionism; chaos theory), Globus (1992b) tries to interpret Derrida's *différance* (notice the nonstandard spelling) in connectionist terms. The *difference aspect of différance* can, according to Globus, be understood as distinctions which neural networks are able to produce due to the weight values on their connections. Connection weights provide a mechanism to deal with possible (Saussurian) meaning distinctions in neural nets, and, in some sense, they do, in the connectionist context, what Derrida's difference does in the context of *différance*, namely provide the possibility to produce meaningful opposites.

Similarly, the *deferral aspect of Derrida's différance* which is inspired by Freud, is supposed to be realized by the thermodynamic and economic properties of neural networks. Defences, delays, postponements and logocentric repression arise as *tunings* of the constraints on the weights of network connections, such that the network is either postponed in, or prevented from, taking a path toward a low energy state. Globus suggests that an instinctually pleasurable memory trace is a powerful attractor into which a wide range of initial network states tend to settle. In tuning, connection weights are altered so that the most probable paths through the state space are blocked and the network is prevented from settling into the state which corresponds to the pleasurable memory trace.

No matter how interesting the idea of deferral as network tuning is, Globus's approach raises the following question: Isn't the standard vocabulary of connectionism, thermodynamics and harmony theory incorrigibly metaphysical in Heidegger's (1957/1969) sense? *Weight value, energy state* and *tuning* seem to be purely external, strongly reificational, completely mechanical and even technologically oriented notions. It seems impossible to discuss the difference of *Being* (Sein) and *entities* (Seiende) in this kind of vocabulary because we are already moving fully within the realm of entities. Even if such notions would allow us to eliminate some representational macro-sized entities, mental as well as physical, and replace them by connectionist and chaos-theoretical notions, it still seems that the connectionist and chaos-theoretical notions themselves are not properly antireificational, a(nti)-mechanical or holistic. Therefore, it seems that Globus's vocabulary forces every description of connectionist and chaotic processes to be what Heidegger would have called *onto-theo-logical*.

In addition, *différance* is not supposed to be a concept, let alone a scientific concept, whereas theorizing about nonlinear self-organizing systems is clearly a conceptual enterprise. One may even claim that all regular nonlinear self-organizing systems are classically Newtonian and therefore separable in a sense which will eventually exclude genuine holism. Let us say that a genuinely holistic phenomenon (alleged system) cannot be explained comprehensively by reducing it to its alleged subsystems (cf. Howard, 1989; d'Espagnat, 1984; d'Espagnat, 1981, pp. 48-85). In other words, holistic phenomena do not consist of constituents which can be explained comprehensively with the help of smaller constituents. In this sense regular non-linear self-organizing systems are not holistic. In addition, the concept of identity which is used in the theory of nonlinear self-organizing systems is the regular Leibnizian identity which, according to Heidegger (1957/1969), characterizes every onto-theo-logical thinking enterprise (see also Chapter 2).

In order to address the difference between *Being* and *entities* in network vocabulary, Globus writes: "It is admittedly difficult to find such an obscurely rendered anterior enfolding process in neural nets but perhaps it is akin to chaos..." But every regular theory of chaos is purely mechanical and can be simulated by some Turing machine. And even in those non-Turing-computable cases where the simulation cannot be done, the power of determinism and the classical Leibnizian identity is not seriously threatened. It seems that Globus is not, after all, willing to take the ultimate jump (Sprung) away from onto-theo-logical thinking toward something genuinely unpredictable, not even toward such unpredictability which cannot be approximated, up to an arbitrary or desired degree of accuracy, by a Turing machine.

Or perhaps we should say that Globus's theoretical framework deprives him of such a jump. Globus's work doesn't suggest that he is interested in modifying neuroscience, say connectionism and chaos-theoretically oriented neuroscience, toward a seriously less onto-theo-logical direction. For example, he seems to have abandoned the possibility that we could weaken or undermine the subject-object dichotomy within neuroscience itself. In this sense his view of science is just as dogmatic as that of Heidegger's (cf. Chapter 2): modern natural science is what it is, for example, it is, by some kind of necessity, committed to the subject-object dichotomy, and the only thing that we, as philosophers, are expected to do is to see science in the proper light or perspective. We are not expected to actively change science to new directions which would alter its identity.

In an earlier article (Globus, 1990), this difficulty is incorporated into the following slogan: *No brain, no Dasein.* Globus asks rhetorically who would deny this. This is, according to him, an unassailable truth which cannot be violated. Or, as he proclaims: "No future scientific revolution will change this fact's significance." Well, I wouldn't bet on that. Rather, I would say that it is exactly this statement which any future neuroscience *should* challenge in order to attempt a jump away from dogmatism toward thinking which is not committed to onto-theo-logical attitudes. What we say about the thing which is in present-day neuroscience called the *brain* may, in light of the future research, turn out to be based on a ridiculous misconception; or, if the future science is tolerant enough, it will honor the old conception by calling it 'another alternative.' Perhaps some part of the present picture can be included also in the future picture, but which part it is and how large it is remains to be seen. What we today happen to be denoting by the word *brain* may, according to future conceptions, simply turn out to be nonexistent. What we cannot guarantee is that one word, for example the word *brain*, to which we associate two, radically differing clusters of beliefs, for example the beliefs of the present and future neuroscience, is nevertheless able to refer to one and the same thing. Even the most straightforward-looking natural kind words, like *water* and *air*, let alone such obviously belief-laden theoretical words as *brain*, *person*, *thing*, or *number*, refer to different phenomena in different historical, cultural and other experiential contexts.

For example, it may turn out that the future neuroscience, or some interpretation of it, will be unwilling to separate the brain from its alleged environment with such a dogmatic cut as happens today. Or, perhaps, the brain will not, in the future science, belong to the so-called external world any more. Or, perhaps the utmost boundary of the human brain will be situated in the most distant galaxies. Perhaps the brain will be understood, not as an external organism in its own terms, but, rather, as a philosophical and conceptual construction which can be used, say, for the purpose of deriving physical laws, as actually happens in Reenpää's philosophy. Reenpää's *Aufbau des Sinnesphysiologie* (1959) doesn't just sketch how the empirical sciences emerge within the tradition of Western metaphysics; it also shows how physical knowledge, and eventually scientific physics, can be derived from perceptual intuition. One of his ingenious ideas was to derive quantum-theoretical indeterminacy relations from perceptual indeterminacy. In Reenpää's thinking, such notions as *brain* or *neuron* are derivative or secondary with respect to perceptual experience, and it is far from clear that their meaning accords with the meaning which Globus has in mind. In accordance with Reenpää's way of thinking, we could suggest that the future neural networks will consist of some kind of experiential or atheoretical units, not of external and theoretical 'processing units.' Or something in that direction. Therefore the slogan *No brain, no Dasein*, in which the use of the word *brain* is understood to accord with the *doxa* of the present-day neuroscience, may simply be untenable in the future neuroscience or in some of its interpretations.

Whether any theory of natural science, let alone of neuroscience, has been able to attain unassailable or immutable truths is questionable for the obvious reason that we have no reliable way to control that our theoretical terms, such as *brain* or *neuron*, have meant and will mean the same thing in different experiential and historical contexts. Therefore, it is also possible that future neuroscience will guide the meaning of the word *brain* to such areas which would have also been inaccessible to Heidegger and which will not comply with Heidegger's overall picture of what science is able to accomplish. It is even possible that one of the roads to less onto-theo-logical thinking goes through future neuroscience. But the question is now whether Globus's radical and chaotic connectionism is radical enough to take us down that road.

How to take Heidegger seriously in neuroscience

In order to take Heidegger seriously in the context of neuroscience, we must have access to something which is genuinely *aconceptual*, something that is even in principle inaccessible within a single consistent conceptual system. We should try to question the metaphysics of subjectivity, undermine the dichotomy of subject and object, and plunge deeply into their holistic entanglement; we must deal with something that is unpredictable, not only due to accidental technical limitations, but also due to philosophical reasons; we must not equal meaning and reference, for example, meaning as arising from the reference of allegedly universal natural kind words; we must challenge the entity-based and class-based notion of scientific knowledge and the related idea of scientific realism; and, we must get rid of the Leibnizian identity.

It seems that Globus's thinking doesn't open for us any access to genuinely aconceptual experience in this sense. The aconceptual is unpredictable in principle and differs crucially from ordinary chaos. Ordinary chaos is indeed intended to represent unpredictability but remains basically mechanical, fully conceptualizable and therefore ultimately predictable too, at least in principle though not always in practice. One could say that chaos comes as close to being unpredictable as a mechanical notion can. But that is not enough.

One way toward aconceptuality goes through the attempt to deconstruct the boundary of the mechanical and the nonmechanical. According to this way, something is *amechanical*, and thus illuminates one aspect of aconceptuality, if and only if it is neither mechanical (Turing-computable) nor nonmechanical (non-Turing-computable). This characterization complies with the view according to which nothing in the natural or experiential world is really and thoroughly mechanical (cf. Pylkkö, 1996a; 1996b), though in certain circumstances some experiences give the impression of being highly object-like. If this alternative is chosen, the boundary of the mechanical and nonmechanical will evaporate, leaving us with physical phenomena which can help us to understand aconceptual experience from a naturalistic point of view. In a naturalistic and experiential context, this must be interpreted neither as an invitation to reductionism nor as a recommendation to adopt non-Turing-computable structures and theories in the standard mathematical sense. Rather, it is an attempt to destruct the foundation of the mechanical-nonmechanical dichotomy.

If the natural world is amechanical in the foregoing sense, and if human experience, and, through that, the human mind and language, are originally aconceptual, the prospects of the realistic attitude of standard science are not encouraging. There are many reasons for this. First of all, if the human experience cannot be described without resorting to aconceptuality, we cannot keep the human mind (or brain) separated from its environment in such a way which every standard scientific attitude presupposes. In other words, the subject-object boundary tends to dissolve. This is not what happens in Globus's work. In his framework, neuroscience, regardless of its resort to radical connectionism and chaos theory, remains basically external and objectivist and, therefore, the subject-object boundary is not seriously questioned. Thinking which is based on the acceptance of the subject-object boundary is, according to Heidegger, bound to remain onto-theo-logical and will, as such, be unable to handle the difference between Being and entities.

We cannot do neuroscience along lines which depart from onto-theo-logic if we just leave science to dogmatic scientists. We may, however, wonder whether nondogmatic science, that is science which is amechanical in the above sketched sense, should be called *science* any more. Whatever the amechanical interpretation of man's experience of nature is called, it cannot provide us with a comprehensive mathematical law-like characterization of all natural phenomena within a single consistent theory. But if natural science cannot be radically a-onto-theo-logized, we are forced to adopt Heidegger's gloomy view of the prospects of science. In *this* respect Globus is quite Heideggerian, of course: Heidegger, too, wanted to leave science in peace. According to Heidegger's view, as it appears, for example, in *Being and Time* (1927/1992), natural science is doomed to remain dogmatic and philosophically naive (see Chapter 2). Natural science is essentially tied to the metaphysics of subjectivity and this view reduces the human mind and language into a representational mechanism.

However, it is quite obvious that what Heidegger is addressing here is the classical, Newtonian natural science. Therefore, we may ask if the emergence of quantum physics changed the situation. Is also quantum theory, for example according to Bohr's and Pauli's interpretation, an onto-theo-logical enterprise? Not necessarily. Indeterminacy, complementarity and the evaporation of the classical subject-object boundary make it possible to address the difference between Being and entities in the quantum-philosophical context (see Chapter 2 for details). Also some recent inseparability interpretations (see Howard, 1989) seem to be much less onto-theo-logical than what classical science ever was. But if this is the case, then, obviously, what neuroscience needs, in order to free itself from the metaphysics of subjectivity, is a holistic, if not directly quantum-philosophical, point of view. We need such a philosophical approach to neuroscience which allows inseparability and indeterminacy to flourish, and it seems that Bohr's and Pauli's interpretation and its proper modifications can be used for this edifying purpose (see Pylkkö, 1996a; 1996b). It is not just a question of whether or not quantum-sized processes are effective in the human brain when we think and experience, and whether or not quantum-theoretical notions are necessary in neurosciences; neuroscience and cognitive science must be reconciled with the fact that physicists, not only invented the quantum theory, but actually seem to be speaking of superposed quantum properties, and that all of us live in an environment which is not classically closed. Even if it is preferable and feasible for practical reasons to consider the brain as a classical system, the brain is immediately related to an environment which is not classical. Thus, a purely classical explanation of human behavior, cognition and experience is not possible any more.

Inseparability, indeterminacy and experience

Let us assume that we don't preclude the possibility that quantum-sized phenomena are effective in the human brain during thinking and experiencing (see especially Beck & Eccles, 1992; Eccles, 1989, pp. 187-193; but see also the more adventurous suggestions by Hameroff, 1993). Then the inseparable and indeterminate properties of quantum phenomena allow us to modify neuroscience and adjust it to satisfy some of the requirements which any adequate description of aconceptual experience has to satisfy. Purely formal or mechanical models, including connectionist models which include chaotic ingredients, cannot adequately represent the aconceptual aspects of human experience. Neither is Penrose's approach sufficient because it associates consciousness with noncomputability in the standard mathematical sense, and this sense of noncomputability doesn't really comply with aconceptuality. But genuinely random single quantum phenomena and their inseparable properties seem to give us what we need, namely access to a naturalistic description of aconceptual experience. This is not to exclude the possibility that also quantum coherence is involved in some types of conscious experience. Neither does this mean that *every* adequate description of aconceptual experience necessarily rests on the hypothesis that neural phenomena cannot be described properly without quantum theory. But clearly, the spirit of all standard interpretations of classical physics precludes holism, indeterminacy and inseparability, and this preclusion seems to block the way to any proper naturalistic understanding of aconceptual experience.

Single quantum phenomena reveal an aspect of nature which Pauli characterized as *irrational* (Pauli, 1954; Pylkkö, 1996b). They are, to a certain extent, unexplainable in purely rational terms, and, in one sense, unpredictable. Neither do single quantum phenomena have any constituent structure or substructure. This means that they neither serve as subsystems of any larger system nor consist themselves of any subsystems. For example, macrophysical objects cannot be composed of microphysical phenomena in any *systematic* way. If we assumed such systematicity we would eventually violate the inseparability condition of microphysical phenomena and we would have to conclude that quantum theory doesn't apply at the macrophysical level. This conclusion would violate, not only quantum theory itself, but would lead us to untenable dualism because it would divide the universe into two alien subdepartments. We may, of course, find it reasonable or feasible to *ignore* quantum-physical inseparability at the macrophysical level, and many practical reasons encourage such voluntary 'oblivion.' For example, at a certain point, quantum effects become too small to be measured with available measuring techniques, or their impact at the macrophysical level becomes too small to have any measurable consequences.

But if we decide to accept that quantum-sized phenomena cannot be ignored in the proper description of cognition and experience, the next step is that we assume that single quantum phenomena are indeed effective during some of our aconceptual experiences, and that also experiences which give the impression of being conceptually organized, like logical thinking and intentional planning, say in a macrophysical context, are unavoidably influenced by the randomness of single quantum phenomena. For example, the initiation or appearance of such experiences may remain indeterminate and unpredictable.

Due to the collapse of their wave function, single quantum phenomena are amechanical. In other words, they are neither mechanical (Turing-computable) nor nonmechanical (non-Turing-computable in the regular mathematical sense), and we must concede that there exists no kind of law which would explain the collapse itself. The indeterminacy and inseparability of single quantum phenomena evades the dichotomy of the mechanical and nonmechanical, and destroys its metaphysical status. This view takes the origin of noncomputability to lie in amechanical randomness, whereas the standard mathematical dichotomy of the mechanical and the nonmechanical presupposes that, at least, something is strictly and purely mechanical. Typically macrophysical objects and syntax are thought to be mechanical. But if nothing in the physical or experiential nature is purely mechanical in the first place, then the dichotomy is not really tenable.

Here we have to depart also from Bohr's and Pauli's interpretation which confers an ambiguous but highly significant role also for the classical world and for the related classical language. This concession to classical thinking led Bohr eventually to design the notion of *complementarity*. But if, contrary to Bohr's and Pauli's intention, the reality of classical objects, including syntactic objects, is undermined by an interpretation which accepts them only as useful fictions (as happens in Pylkkö, 1996a; see also Chapter 2), then also all standard mathematical proofs of such statements which say that something is nonmechanical (nonformal) become much less compelling because all such demonstrations rest, of course, on the assumption that at least something is classical and that some classical objects exist (typically, say, syntactic objects or measuring instruments). Analogously, already the status of the quantum formalism as a macrophysical entity is fictional, and, therefore, there is not much point to insist that the Schrödinger equation and other related formalisms provide realistic descriptions of some microphysical processes. We end up with indivisible human experience which is thoroughly amechanical and holistic but which can, under certain circumstances, appear to us as almost mechanical, that is, mechanical for some practical purposes.

Freedom as randomness

It is now possible to see indeterminate and unpredictable neural events as one of the sources of human freedom. If chance is an irreducible aspect of microphysical phenomena, and it turns out that quantumphysical terms are necessary in the proper description of the human brain, then we have found some ingredients for a naturalistically credible view of the origin of human freedom. Assuming that we want to adopt a neural point of view, freedom in experience originates from the randomness of some neural events, and it is this kind of randomness which is sometimes experienced as aconceptual. At the moment of an aconceptual experience, the future lies open and unpredictable in us, waiting to be unfolded and evading the controlling grasp of reason. Some part of the future always remains irreducible to past events, and no conceptual or rational means, let alone mechanical means, can help us to predict its course with comprehensive accuracy.

This view isn't necessarily in conflict with the postphenomenological view of the human mind, but it may be hard to reconcile it with that kind of classical phenomenology which Husserl developed in his *Ideas* (1913/1976). Analogously, standard Anglo-American analytical philosophy may be unable to deal with it. Thus the view of freedom as aconceptual experiential randomness is in conflict with many renowned theories of human freedom. The problem of human freedom, for example with Kant, is often understood as the problem of how rational thinking can be autonomous, that is, free of external influence, and therefore nature, for example the human body and its natural demands, is seen as a hindrance of freedom. This view rests on the idea that nature is mechanical and deterministic, whereas the human mind is free exactly because it is able to wrench itself above and away from its low natural origins. This version of antinaturalism is so popular that even such thinkers who would otherwise like to distance freedom from rational thinking and associate it with unconscious creativity, negativity, deviation from norms, and so on, still see nature as the enemy of freedom, as if the rationally graspable law-likeness were the ultimate essence of nature. (More of this problem area, see Ferry & Renaut, 1990, pp. 98-99; and Descombes, 1988, pp. 33-49.) Assuming that we don't take the level metaphor too literally, we can say that the view of freedom as randomness finds one of the sources of freedom, not only in nature, but in the 'lowest level' of natural phenomena, that is, among microphysical phenomena. This would be so even if it were practically feasible or almost necessary to consider the human brain as a classical system. If we want to attain proper understanding of the behavior of living organisms in the natural environment, we cannot ignore all of the influences which random microphysical phenomena exercise upon the organism.

In a sense which comes quite close to the original Heideggerian sense of 'forgetfulness' (vergessen; Vergessenheit), we may even express in quantum-philosophical terms what the *forgetting of aconceptuality* means: It is the misconception that quantum randomness and inseparability can be reduced to or made to comply with deterministic, classical and mechanical principles, and that deterministic, classical and mechanical notions are sufficient for the understanding of human behavior. This tendency which has inspired, among others, the original *hidden variable interpretation* (see Bohm, 1952; 1957), has also had advocates who work within the Copenhagen-style interpretations (for example, Omnès, 1992; for critical views, see also Albert, 1992, p. 92). Experience of *thingness*, our tendency to reify experience into external objects and internal concepts, can be so overwhelming that, in suitable social and historical circumstances, the original aconceptuality of our experience may be pushed aside into the experiential forgetfulness to such an extent that everything that we experience eventually seems to consist of external objects and internal concepts. Quantum theory may teach us that this experiential forgetfulness is not really naturalistically acceptable. As Laurikainen has frequently pointed out (see for example, Laurikainen, 1988), regardless of the fact that there is no serious alternative to the Copenhagen interpretation today, the new generation of quantum physicists has ignored or forgotten Bohr's and Pauli's philosophical teachings and tried to dispense with such notions as *complementarity, indeterminacy* and *irrationality*. It is not correct to say that microphysical phenomena behave mechanically and deterministically and that it is the measurement which brings indeterminacy onto the scene. Microphysical phenomena as such, that is, as human experience, are indeterminate and inseparable, and it is the measurement and the quantum formalism which attempt to render indeterminate and inseparable phenomena as determinate and separable and which thereby yield paradoxes into the interpretation of quantum theory. The measurement and the formalism belong to the mechanical and fictitious aspects of the phenomenal.

Assuming that our dogmatism doesn't lure us into ignoring it, aconceptual experience lies, though perhaps somewhat hidden, near to our everyday, nonscientific experience, too, waiting to be encountered (cf. Chapter 1). It appears to us in the unity of our perceptual experience; we meet it in the feeling that the future is, not only hidden, but genuinely open and indeterminate in us, so that it is not contained in the past and cannot be rationally derived from it either; it is in our passions which may destroy the subject-object boundary; it reminds us of itself in the ultimate state of horror when we come close to lethal danger; it comes to us in moods of familiarity and strangeness which color our experience of places and people; one can become familiar with it in experimenting with certain drugs, and so on. And what is one of the most important cases, its evasive presence can be sensed almost everywhere in a non-Western cultural environment, in language, art and habits which are not yet fully corrupted by the Western obsession for mechanicalness. Here, too, the experience may lie hidden and be difficult to disclose and capture by concepts, especially by Western concepts (see Chapter 8).

Within the Western world, both in the colloquial and scientific context, we tend to say that all of these experiences are realized by 'brain processes.' But what we mean by 'brain processing' is not independent of our experiences which, in this case, are shaped by the Western civilization, its institutions, social and economic arrangements and cultural traditions, including scientific traditions. This civilization and its institutions and traditions are, however, thoroughly saturated by conceptual thinking, externalism and objectivism. Yet experience is a broader notion than the notion of present-day Western consciousness, and it is experience which ultimately makes both concepts and objects possible. Even if modern science would always remain Western in its character, Western science would still have such amechanical and ametaphysical aspects (see Chapter 2) which may make it more receptive and sensitive to aconceptual experience. This may also make it culturally more tolerant.

Subjectivity as the domesticated region of experience

Even such a first person perspective to experience which is sometimes called *transcendental subjectivity* (for the characterization of which, see Frank, 1995) originates from aconceptual experience. The separateness and perspectivity, as well as the irreducible feeling of the presence of the self which we attach to a subject's point of view, would be incomprehensible without the aconceptual origin from which the subject ascends. This is so because the subject as a conceptual organization of experience always remains partly entangled with its low origin, and we tend to confound the volatileness, temporariness and unpredictability of the origin of subjectivity with subjectivity *simpliciter*.

However, because the gradual articulation of the subject's point of view decreases the degree of aconceptuality in experience, there is almost nothing genuinely unique in subjects or subjectivity, unlike what the modern enlightened *doxa* seem to suggest. Actually, concepts are assumed to provide something that is common to all men. It is the aconceptual that is genuinely unique, irrepeatable and untractable, whereas subjectivity comprises the particular aspect of experience which is open to communication and thus prone to the organizing influence of cultural unification. Cultural unification tends to diminish experiential intensity by shaping aconceptual experience into a conceptual framework which is easily communicable.

This doesn't mean that the aconceptual experience is 'pure' or closed to cultural influence. It is closed only as long as the influence is conceptually organized or conceptually expressible. The subject, the domesticated and cultivated region of experience, is always entangled with its wild and low origin and remains, to some extent, open to conceptually uncontrollable influence. This entanglement receives its special character through the oppositional role which the organization of the subject plays as a lion tamer of the underlying aconceptuality. But the entanglement serves also as a channel of influence from the subject down to the aconceptual and back. The aconceptual experience is transcendentally inaccessible to concepts as such, that is, to concepts which work as concepts and try to represent something which lies outside of them, and the purer the concepts are the more inaccessible the experience is. This holds the other way round too, and we must say that the conceptual organization of the subject which serves the purpose of representation remains transcendentally inaccessible to aconceptual experience as such. But, at the same time concepts are also alive, and need nutriment from within, and this doesn't come from their representative role. This means that aconceptual experience seldom influences the representative work of concepts directly. We just notice the influence indirectly. For example, it can be experienced as anxiety, the feeling of marginality, misbehavior of the subject, disfunction of representation, and perhaps we may experience it ocassionally as irrational joy. These experiences may indirectly alter something in the subject and its conceptual organization too. There is a low-level influence which is technologically useless and which never ascends to the level of representation, communicability and conceptuality. We hardly have language to describe this influence and separate it from aconceptual experience *simpliciter*. This influence arising from aconceptual experience flows below the consciousness and rationality of the subject. The mutual uncommunicability of the subject and its aconceptual origin which can be transcended only by this nameless and useless flow of aconceptual experience is what we experience as the transcendentality of the subject, as the irreducible feeling of being a self who is separated from other selves and whose fragility and vulnerability in front of possible destruction makes us particularly concerned.

Of course, there is a special kind of 'uniqueness' also in a subject's conceptual organization. This is conceptual, often combinatoric or syntactic of its character. But this sense of 'uniqueness' is perverse and much less genuine than the aconceptual one because the conceptual organization of a subject is based on the assumption that at least some elements or primitive features of human experience are permanent and universal, that is, common to all men, regardless of their cultural and historical background. Because this assumption may be mistaken, the whole conception of the present-day Western subjectivity may rest on an illusion.

Though it is fair to say that there is 'uniqueness' both in the conceptual aspect of experience (the subject) and in the aconceptual one, they are quite different from one another, and it may be preferable to speak only of aconceptuality as genuinely unique (irrepeatable). Unfortunately we lack a proper language to describe the difference. The conceptual and communicative bond between men works on the level of subjects and is based on the belief that at least some of our experiences have found a common ground in elementary and repeatable units of experience; the aconceptual commonality originates from the inseparability of primitive experience: we live also within the sphere of collective human experience which doesn't yet recognize persons or individuals. These two modes of uniqueness are easily confounded with one another, and therefore only the latter is here called genuinely unique. There is, of course, also an aconceptual influence running between men. This doesn't ascend to the level of subjects, and is thus never communicative or representative.

Thus, if Nagel's famous question (Nagel, 1974), 'what is it like to be a bat?' is read as 'what is it like to be a subject?', the answer is: almost nothing! This is so because the subject aspect of experience is, due to its conceptual organization (causation; space; time; identity), the weakest aspect of experience as regards the degree of intensity. It is exactly that aspect of our experience which is standardized and unified and which is thus relatively easily communicated to others with the help of concepts and ideas. The aspect of experience which is conceptually inaccessible tends to be experientially more intensive and often impossible to communicate, though it may be possible to express it in such language which is not conceptually organized and doesn't serve the interests of communication. Thus Nagel's question is ambiguous because we don't know which aspect of experience he is addressing with his question. It is plausible that *some* aspects of the experience of being a bat are inaccessible to human concepts; analogously, some aspects of human experience may remain inaccessible to human concepts. But the aspect of being a 'bat subject' (in the above sketched sense of 'subject' as the conceptual organization of experience) is not the hardest part of the story of understanding bats. In order to envision a bat's subjective world in human imagination we need to replace the form of humanly experienced causation, space, time and identity by a bat's respective perspectivities and hierarchies. Even a person who is not blind may occasionally orientate in the dark by utilizing echoes and have a vague impression of bat life. Nagel must be credited with stressing the hardness of this task. However, that the bat's conceptual world, the system which creates its perspectivity and hierarchy, is extremely difficult to model in human concepts doesn't make the task impossible. After all, simplification and idealization is widely believed to be a necessary by-product of all conceptual work which aims at modelling and generalizing.

But *being something* is a different matter, not just a matter of modelling and generalizing. Thus the difficulty of modelling bat's and man's subjective experience is accompanied by a straight impossibility: certain aspects of man's and bat's asubjective experience are inaccessible to *any* concepts whatsoever, assuming that conceptual access requires, at least in principle, a comprehensive and consistent description. This problem is not addressed by Nagel whose choice of words ('facts,' 'structure of mind,' 'exact nature,' and so on) suggests that he thinks that facts which lie beyond the reach of human concepts are nevertheless accessible by *some* (nonhuman) concepts, in other words, that such facts have a humanly inaccessible conceptual structure. Therefore, there is only very little he can tell us about the reasons why being some other type of a creature creates a barrier to our concepts. Nagel's final explanation, that the creature is not sufficiently similar to us in order to make its experience accessible to our concepts, is a disappointment. We would expect a conceptual structure, even a humanly inaccessible one, to be somehow partly translatable into respective human concepts. It is the aconceptual randomness in bat's experience, bat's freedom so to speak, which is impossible for us to deal with.

Are all preconditions of the scientific attitude scientifically accessible?

We should not let our overall view of experience be dominated and constrained by the Western perspective, let alone by the concept-oriented and objectivist (or, which amounts to the same, subject-centered) point of view. Therefore it is not sufficient to require, as Engel and König (1993) do, that neuroscience adopts a phenomenological perspective, because this doesn't necessarily make neuroscience receptive to aconceptual experience. The need for a phenomenologically framed point of view in the physiology of sense organs was discussed systematically and extensively already by Yrjö Reenpää (1959; 1967) but, unfortunately, adopting a phenomenological framework doesn't make neuroscience capable of dealing with experiential holism. In order to do that, we have to make room for the aconceptual and extend the basically concept-oriented framework in which standard neuroscience is carried out.

This difficulty is seen even more clearly with Skarda and Freeman (1990) who, quite correctly, proclaim that antireductionism is what neuroscience has to opt for. Explanation in neuroscience should not and can not be provided by resorting to such system properties which can be reduced to a sum of the properties of the system's parts. And, as Skarda and Freeman point out, Maurice Merleau-Ponty also made similar suggestions. But what is not obvious is that Skarda and Freeman's own notions, such as *self-organization* and *chaos*, can provide all they need in order to get rid of reductionist system-thinking. In Kreisal's (1974) sense of *mechanical*, self-organized and chaotic neural processes remain mechanical, and, therefore, also their system properties remain reducible to the properties of the parts of the system. What Merleau-Ponty (1945/1971) had in mind comprised a much more radical departure from reductionism: that neuroscience itself must be seen as an outgrowth of *presubjective* body experience which precedes, not only conceptual thinking, but the emergence of the space-time itself. Nothing in Skarda and Freeman's work indicates that they are willing to follow Merleau-Ponty along this path toward radically prelogical antireductionism.

Not only should the scientific attitude be seen as emerging from human consciousness, as classical phenomenology already suggested; consciousness, and the scientific attitude along with it, must be embedded in prelogical and preconscious experience. Some recent results of neuroscience may help us to understand what this could mean, assuming that we want to express this - rather paradoxically, perhaps - in quite a standard scientific vocabulary. For Edelman, *higher-order consciousness* of language and planning rests on *primary consciousness* which combines the categorization of perceptual signals with signals coming from limbic and neuroendocrine systems (Edelman, 1989). MacLean's (1973) studies of the evolution of the human nervous system show that below the neomammalian and limbic system lies an even more primitive, reptilian system which affects such aspects of our behavior as mating, breeding, finding the homesite and selecting leaders. Benjamin Libet's studies of the readiness potential (Libet, 1985) indicate that the conscious decision to act is preceded by unconscious neural activities. Yet none of these three scholars deliberate on what these obvious attacks on the supremacy of human rationality imply as regards the prospects of the standard, conceptually and realistically oriented scientific attitude. Can science as a conscious activity penetrate those regions of human experience which precede the emergence of full-fledged consciousness? In light of the dogmatic attitudes of standard science, the positive answer sounds almost impossible or paradoxical. For example, if conceptually regimented language and logical reasoning are necessary preconditions of every standard scientific attitude, and language and reasoning belong to the higher-order consciousness, then the least we can say is that the attitude of the standard science toward primary consciousness must be somewhat biased and selective.

Originally the above-mentioned studies are, of course, intended to solve regular scientific problems. Yet their results suggest that conscious human experience is preceded (phylogenetically; ontogenetically; in temporal or causal order of brain processing, and so on) by less than conscious and less than conceptually organized neural activities. But is the problem of *preceding* here only a standard scientific problem? This is a vital question because regular science itself belongs to the conceptual sphere of human life. If we have to derive the conceptual from something that is less than conceptual, we have to derive the scientific attitude from something that is not yet scientifically understandable and accessible. It seems that this derivation cannot be carried out within the conceptual and theoretical realm of standard science alone. Or, if we attempt to do something like that, we will encounter serious philosophical difficulties because, from the conceptual point of view, all experience which is less than conceptual appears either as incomprehensible, marginal or simply nonexistent. However, pondering over the difficulties, which already quite regular science necessarily encounters in its attempts to reveal to us the preconceptual origin of human experience and consciousness, may help us to appreciate the importance of a philosophically motivated *atheoretical* view to the study of human experience and consciousness.

The problem of the freedom of the human mind is, among other things, the problem of how standard natural science is able to attribute to the physical such properties which we expect the human mind to possess. For example, if the relationship between the human body/brain and mind proves seriously problematic, we have good reasons to suspect that our conception of the body is designed to satisfy the separation and individuation conditions of classical natural science. Only the classical notions of thing and body, not human experience as a whole, satisfy the classical separation and individuation principles. As long as our conception of science conforms with the most dogmatic aspects of standard classical science, the freedom of the human mind either escapes our explanation or appears as a paradoxical anomaly.

This situation inspired Heidegger to speak of the history of Western thinking as a history of forgetfulness of Being (Seinsvergessenheit). According to this vision, the essence of technology (Technik), the *Gestell*, is an overwhelming frame of mind which forces us to think and experience in terms of external objects and internal concepts. This frame of mind leads us to a kind of experiential desert or waste land, and the force of the frame can be overcome only after our thinking has adopted a crucial turn. Heidegger seems to have thought that we cannot take the turn without God's help (Heidegger, 1966/1988). Now, in the light of Pauli's view of the irrational aspect of statistical causality, it seems that the *Gestell* needs no divine help in preparing its way down: the Gestell, the core of technology, contains the seeds of its own destruction (see the end of Chapter 2). The primordially physical, or *physis*, as Heidegger would have put it, is not exhausted by the notion of bodyhood and thingness. Rather, our habit to think of the physical in terms of bodies and things is an attempt to domesticate the *physis*, tame it in order to make it serve certain technological purposes. Quantum theory and some of its interpretations remind us that this taming process can never be perfect, and the physis aspect of nature always remains partly unreliable. If this is so, at least one of the ingredients which has contributed to the rise of the so-called body-mind problem is dissolved. The physical is not reducible to the behavior of classical bodies.

That the core of modern Western technology is hollow and possibly contains the seeds of its own destruction is by no means a short term prediction of the prospects of modern Western technology. It is not only possible but even plausible that the a-onto-theo-logical (ametaphysical) aspects of recent natural science will never be widely acknowledged (see Pylkkö, 1996b). For example, it is plausible that the holistic and even irrational aspects of quantum theory will be suppressed, and the theory will be used mainly as a device for promoting misguided technological purposes, as happens widely today. Analogously, subjectivity, conceptuality and consciousness do not exhaust experience, and our habit to think of ourselves in terms of subjectivity, rationality and consciousness is an attempt to domesticate the aconceptual in our experience. Therefore, it is highly plausible that the varieties and intensities of aconceptual experience, due to its futility for modern technological purposes, will never find full cultural expression in the globally Westernized and unified future world but will be pushed to marginality and forgetfulness.

CHAPTER FOUR

On surprise

The gap

Intensive pleasure and horror arise from violated expectations, and the degree of the intensity depends, among other things, on how firmly the expectations have been conditioned. For example, the pleasure of artistic surprise cannot entrance us if we haven't learned some firm artistic reception habits which are questioned by some new and challenging stimuli. In general, a course of events which too slavishly satisfies our expectations saves us from horror but also deprives us of intensive pleasure. As Karl Groos already pointed out (1899, p. 153-6), repetition and recognition alone are able to promise us only mild pleasure. Obstacles, conflicts, opponents, and attempts to overcome them are needed to intensify our experience. What we experience as a surprise betrays a *gap*, or *incongruity*, between expectations and what is actually encountered, and the surprise exploits the energy which is released by the incongruity. The gap wouldn't be there without a conflict, without opponents who have worked against our goals and interests. From the point of view of the person who experiences the surprise, the gap appears to bear a special aconceptual character with respect to expectations. Had the stimuli which violated our expectations been fully conceptualized and well-structured with respect to the expectations no room would have been left for genuine surprise. Neither have pleasure and horror a well defined structure (cf. what was said of the intensity of experience in Chapter 1). It is this gap on which we will focus, its relatively aconceptual nature with respect to expectations, and the role it plays in connecting game institutions to experience.

Games are institutions which provide an organized environment where pleasure, horror and other experiences can occasionally find expression and become released. Games do not directly produce experience; rather, the intensity of experience lies latently in us waiting to be ignited and released. For example, a work of art, or, say, a person whom we love, doesn't directly cause our experiences and sometimes doesn't even deserve them. This kind of autonomy is typical for experiential signification in general. In case of surprise, what triggers the eruption of our energy and becomes experienced as surprise must somehow be deviant or even perverse with respect to the conceptions which our expectations consist of. It must be something in front of which our semiotic habits turn out to be helpless. (The word *semiotic* is here used in the holistic and naturalistic sense sketched in Pylkkö, 1993b, which deviates from the standard structural use; as regards the semiotics of natural language, see Chapter 5). Surprise disarms our semiotic intelligence temporarily and reveals the uncertainty on which its concepts lie. Surprise comes out of this temporary helplessness or disorientation during which intelligence is not fully in control.

The incongruity cannot be understood properly if our descriptions of surprise are based only on the structural properties which characterize, or are said to characterize, conceptual expectations and semiotic stimuli. The incongruity creates an amorphous and asemiotic zone around itself and this zone is favorable for surprise because it allows the intensity of aconceptual experience to grow relatively freely (cf. Chapter 1). Here chance enters the scene. The asemiotic zone cannot protect us against the impression that, during the experience of surprise, *chance* (cf. *randomness* of Chapter 3) is able to take us over for a while. The zone of surprise remains transcendentally inaccessible for any well-structured semiotic concepts which the receiver might apply in the situation. In other words, surprise as an experience is, in a certain sense, inaccessible for anyone who has experienced it and tries to approach it in terms of a well-defined network of signs, concepts or rules (cf. *irrationality* of Chapter 3). If the person who experienced the surprise had access to semiotic concepts which could smooth the incongruity away the person wouldn't have experienced the surprise in the first place. Intensive pleasure and horror remain always partly accidental (that is *free* in the sense which was introduced in Chapter 3 and will be developed further in Chapter 8), and it is the main role of conceptual expectations to protect us against the excesses that accidents may expose us to.

Pleasure and horror, as results of genuine accidents, are not something predictable that we can keep fully under the control of habit and repetition.

Even in watching a tennis match, what excites us most is, perhaps, not the uncertainty about who will eventually win the match, but such breathtaking events where skills of the players intertwine with what is, or looks like, chance. As to the most exciting events, we experience pleasure and fear when we notice that a player survived an accident with the help of his skills. In the sense intended by Schopenhauer, accidents are *transcendental* with respect to habits which are controlled by firm schemes or concepts. Yet certain game-like semiotic activities, if they are not too strictly structured, may provide the only organized environment where we can expect (in one sense of 'expecting') to encounter such transcendental accidents. Gaming is not *only* rule-following, but also an experiential environment in which we can excounter the remnants of our freedom.

'Surprise me!'

According to a literary legend (retold for example in Steegmuller, 1970, p. 82) the truth of which doesn't concern us here, Sergei Diaghilev, the impresario of the famous Russian Ballet, advised the young Jean Cocteau with these surprising little words: 'Surprise me!' This was supposed to suggest that so far Cocteau hadn't been able to do quite that much and, in order to be accepted as a professional artist, he should be able to produce something that surpasses the expectations of a person like Diaghilev whose sensitivity and taste have been shaped by most qualified experiences. This small phrase, 'Surprise me!' conceals an abundance of possibilities for further elaboration.

As a contribution toward the elaboration, let us say that an artist, by doing art, takes part in a game in which his opponent is any person who is equipped with adequate reception skills and who happens to receive the artist's contribution (cf. Pylkkö, 1991). Here the opponent can be either a living person or, depending on our interests, a more or less theoretical, or fictitious, construction. After all, Cocteau knew Diaghilev in a manner that is unavailable for most of us who, therefore, can only imagine such a blasé opponent for our own purposes. But let us not overdo here the fictitious-nonfictitious contrast either because both fictitious and nonfictitious persons alike are, after all, constructions which arise as results of certain gamelike activities. Anyway, in the game-theoretical framework, and in any game-metaphorical elaboration, the goal of the artist is to surprise the opponent, the receiver of the artist's contribution, and the goal of the receiver is to remain as unimpressed as possible. The artist designs his contribution to be as surprising as possible with respect to what he believes the receiver's expectations to be. The receiver tries to educate his expectations as well as possible in order to remain unimpressed by what he expects the artistic move to be. In brief, the artist wins if he is able to surprise his opponent; otherwise the receiver wins.

The more surprising a work of art succeeds in being with respect to a given frame of expectations, the more intensively the work of art is experienced. Here we associate *intensity* to the ability to elicit surprise, that is, to break the protective structure of our expectations. Therefore, surprise and its intensity are relativized with respect to the receiver and his expectations, and the conditions of successful reception do not require that expectations in some realistic sense represent or misrepresent the properties of the message. As to art, we, as receivers, tend to say to ourselves, perhaps somewhat pretentiously, that we play to win, that is, to remain unsurprised, but actually it is only a loss, not a victory, that can shake us experientially. Only a loss may drastically change us to something that we were not before. This is so because only a loss can force us to face the inadequacies of our reception habits, and only this may lead us to modify the reception habits in a manner which makes future loss in similar situations less probable. Thus, gaming is more about losing than about winning, and our eagerness to win is just an indication of our inability to encounter the pain of knowledge.

As the artist's contribution takes us by surprise, we surrender to the work of art and this experience may ignite new sources of vitalizing energy in us. We can utilize the energy if we are willing to change our thinking, feeling and reception habits. As in erotic love, this affair has some air of paradox around it because no one really wants to lose a game, to be outsmarted by someone else. We would like to remain fully in control of our experiences and preserve the illusion that our dignity has remained intact. And yet we play even if the risk of losing is considerable because uncertainty and danger excites us, keeps us close to the possibility of change and open-ended future, and because no one fully in control of the course of his experiences is able to learn anything genuinely new. Similarly, we don't necessarily love to love. Actually, we may occasionally even hate to love. And yet we get involved in erotic love because uncertainty, chance, change and danger excite us. They excite us because we know that there is no great pleasure, not even pleasures of knowledge, without risks, and no ultimate pleasure without the risk of horror and destruction.

Subjects: growing perspectivity and hierarchy

In esthetic and erotic surrender we expose ourselves to the powers of chance. The grasp of the controlling subject is temporarily loosened as we approach the gap of incongruity where surprise takes hold of us. In the regular ways of life, the subject is or appears as the organizing principle of the mind, and it is the associative habits of *perspectivity* and *hierarchy* through which the subject emerges. The perspective creates an illusion of a spatio-temporal center which organizes perceptions, memories and movements, and reconciles their conflicting interests with one another. The hierarchy orders events of the perspective to flow as much as possible according to expectations, beliefs and preferences, and, in case of conflict, reconciles them with each other. The activation of this hierarchy during action is what is experienced as the presence of intention. For example, we intend to win. We focus our attention and activate our imagination in order to predict our opponent's movements and to reach full control over the situation of the game. Sometimes we are able to remain in control, and score a victory; sometimes not, and surprise pushes us toward a loss and even over the edge of catastrophe. The intention to remain in control is seriously frustrated as the surprise shatters the habits which have generated the perspective and hierarchy of the subject. In extreme cases, we may experience surprise even as the dissolution of the subject. Ludwig Klages (1922, pp. 43-73) describes how intensive erotic experience questions the coherence of the subject: 'Ist nun Ekstase Seelenentgeistung, so muss sie auch sein: Seelenentselbstung' (p. 46). The point is that the logocentric spirit (Geist) pulls the soul (Seele) and body (Leib) apart by making a questionable alliance with the self and its consciousness. Only ecstasy can break this unholy alliance by shattering the status of the self.

Thus, the *presubjective center of experience* is not an object. It is a way to articulate experience, such that objects are eventually able to emerge. During the temporary dissolution of the subject, that is, during the dissolution of the perspectivity and hierarchy of which the subject is composed, beliefs and preferences may become more or less permanently disorganized, and even perceptions and movements may become disoriented. But this wouldn't be possible if there hadn't been regular games during which the subject had been organized. No subject could reign over the flux of our experience had men not become involved in playing with and against one another. It is through games that the perspective and hierarchy of the subject are established. Ultimately, the subject is a system of conceptual expectations which protects us against the attacks of extreme surprise, that is, against too threatening pleasure and horror which skillful opponents may inflict. The extent to which we experience our subject as real is directly proportional to the extent to which we experience our opponents as real.

The frequency of surprise can be made smaller and the impact of surprise can be domesticated to some extent by reifying the flux of experiences into suitable objects, the most important ones of which are 'other persons.' According to Wilhelm Ostwald (1901), we divide our experience (Erlebnisse) into distinguishable things (Dinge) in order to make experience manageable. More recently, Adrian Cussins (1992) has emphasized the interdependency of the constitution of objects and the constitution of subjects: no subjects without objects, and *vice versa*. Both Ostwald and Cussins see the reification of experience into common objects as a beneficial step forward in the development of the human individual and in the evolution of the human species. Especially Cussins hopes that the notions of truth and reference would eventually be established if the reification of experience is continued long enough.

The reification of experience makes experience behaviorally manageable and less susceptible to extreme surprise, and as a result, experience becomes gradually more and more object-like and objective-looking. Objects, or should we say *surrogate objects* (objects whose life depends on the subject), make it possible for us to believe in the common world, but this belief is partly a social and political convenience, not a physical or biological necessity. A great deal of the reification is culturally and politically relative. In other words, the store of objects is always partly a cultural product, a convention. A social unanimity can often be reached quite easily because what is common is not usually too threatening and is likely to be predictable. And we want to be predictable, and, in particular, we want to be accepted as full members of a community of shared predictability. In addition, the one who is able to dictate a frame of reification upon a community exercises a great power over the the members of the community.

After objects have been constituted in the games of a community, only a short step separates us from assuming that our thoughts, desires and beliefs are some kind of objects, and that a common world can be built of them, too. This assumption says that we can share common beliefs, that our beliefs are directed toward common objects, and there is someone, the subject, who entertains the thoughts, desires and beliefs, and shares them with other subjects. Most games take the prevailing frame of reification for granted. However, there are games, in religion, politics and art, which have always appreciated surprise to some extent and preserved a prominent role for it in their institutions. These games provide an institutional environment to which unpredictability is thought to belong. Here a confrontation with challenging new opponents can still be arranged, and some prevailing frames of reification can still be questioned. Occasionally games with skillful opponents may force us to dissolve too established habits of ours and create room for genuinely new experiences, which may even turn out to be threatening to the organization of the subject.

The increasing perspectivity and hierarchy create an illusion of a gradually evolving center. This wouldn't be possible without a presubjective center of experience upon which the subject is organized; neither would it be possible without *other* experiential centers of experience, because subjectness is constituted in the perpetually changing game relationships in which 'my own' center confronts 'other' centers. It is exactly because centers are not objects that the irreducible and paradoxical experience of being *I*, *my-owness*, can emerge. It is paradoxical because it combines uniqueness with the conceptual organization of the subject. The experience presupposes that the experience of objects has also emerged. Thus, we are not dealing here with the traditional transcendental subject (say, in Frank's, sense, for which, see Frank, 1995) which would be independent of objects. But it is equally incorrect to say that the subject is an object among other objects or that it consists of objects. Both the subject and object are derived from the aconceptual experience. The subjectivity experience requires the objectivity experience, and *vice versa*, because they arise in parallel. Subjectivity is always about objects, a conceptual attitude of grasping objects which are constituted with the help of the very subjectivity. Thus the *appearance* of irreducibility which we attach to the self is just as strong as the feeling of objectivity is. But the irreducibility is not absolute (as it is, for example, with the transcendental subjectivity or with things of corpuscular materialism) because they both, the subject and object, can be dissolved back into their aconceptual origin. The upmost layer of subjectivity, the self-consciousness, which is clearly a historically and socially conditioned experience, arises from the perpetual nostagia of separateness with which the subject encounters the aconceptual mind.

The agonic and confrontational relations through which the self emerges cannot guarantee any strong personal persistence for a center, let alone personal identity. What they promise is something much weaker: a temporary personal survival as a coalition of distributed and conflicting subcenters (subsubjects, so to speak) which do not preserve their identity either but may compete and negotiate with each other in order to reach a temporary equilibrium. There is something in this coalition making which we experience as perspectival order of external things; as relatively coherent interaction of perceptions, memory and behavior; as our bodily presence within the actuality of the present place and moment; as selective attention which picks out thoughts, beliefs and desires one by one, just as perceptual attention focuses selectively onto one part of a perceptual field at a time; and as hierarchy of interests among alternatives. That something which binds the coalition of subcenters together, such that the coalition emerges as a unity, is energized by the urge of the coalition to play successfully and survive as a behavioral unit.

The subject is a coalition of subsubjects which has reached a temporary equilibrium of conflicting interests. Its survival possibilities in the cultural environment of the West are better than that of a presubjective experiential center alone. The coalition, the resulting unit, can play, that is, organize its perceptions, memories and behavior in such a way that it can be taken as an opponent. Opponents are what we usually call 'persons.' What survives well and, at least seemingly, preserves its identity in time is the subject, not the aconceptual experience. This is somewhat paradoxical because there is almost nothing unique in the subject: the subject is what is common in people, that is, the conceptual organization of their mind. *All that is unique in our experience originates from the presubjective and collective aconceptual experience.* In terms of a geographical metaphor, we could say that a person is like an archipelago, a distributed network of local centers, linked together by ferry connections such that the coherence and compactness of the connections, the amount and quality of the ferry connections, varies considerably from case to case, and within one case from moment to another. Assume also that the archipelago is at war with another archipelago struggling over the domination of some pleasures. What we experience as 'consciousness' is a collective attempt of the subcenters to reach stability, prevent threatening change, and make the chaotic variation of our impressions, if not to something which is not experienced at all, at least to something as nice, small and manageable as possible. The overall goal is to make war successfully. But, in order to do that, a battle field, an area of communality, is needed.

Consciousness is an illusion of permanent actuality which is created as perceptions of different modalities of the subject become unified with each other, and with emotions and other experiences. The full human consciousness is based on a more primitive form of consciousness which may be called *mammalian consciousness* and which is an illusion of perceptual actuality and bodily presence. It is in the mammalian consciousness upon which other, more sophisticated experiences, complex emotions and thoughts, may enter, the characteristic feature of them being that they appear only one by one, selectively and consecutively (cf. Edelman, 1989). The 'here and now' of consciousness is a temporal and perspectival illusion which is created by unification of nonsimultaneous neural events. Among other things, this unification makes chaotic impressions look objectlike and immutable.

Consciousness and objectivity (objective representation) go hand in hand. Both are gradual evolutionary tendencies to produce illusions which organize our experience into permanent macro-sized units. This tendency has a genetic foundation which has been strongly fortified by the Western object-oriented culture. This fortification, which Ludwig Klages would have called *logocentric*, has become a cultural obsession, and it has tried to illegitimate other, less objectual, views of what experience is. Less object-centered (and, therefore, less subject-centered) views of experience have frequently tried to dethrone consciousness and deny that consciousness is all that experience is about. For example, Klages (1921) disapproved the frequency with which *consciousness* (Bewusstsein) is equalled with *experience* (Erlebnis). Thus, contrary to a common belief, there is nothing particularly 'subjective' or unique in the subject. Though it always remains partly entangled with its unique aconceptual origin, the whole tendency toward the emergence of subjectivity goes against uniqueness because it is habit and repetition from which the perspectivity and hierarchy of the subject emerges. Therefore, whatever the nature of the experiential coherence that we call *subject* actually is, it may be destroyed by intensive pleasure and horror.

We can see that the human experience is saturated, at least, with three very different kinds of isolation: the isolation of subjects from one another; the isolation of presubjective experiential centers from one another (before the emergence of full subjectivity); and, finally, the isolation of the subject from its aconceptual origin. The isolation of a subject from other subjects resembles the isolation of external things from each other. Subjects resemble one another almost like things do. This provides also the ground for the communicative connection between them. As soon as our experience has attained the separateness of subjectivity, communication is needed to serve as a channel between subjects. This makes it impossible for us to express anything *unique* with the help of a communicative channel. For example, if language is reduced into communication, then language is unable to be or describe anything unique in our experience.

The isolation of the presubjective experiential centers from one another allows influence but denies communication. This is the human condition before the emergence of subjectivity. Of course, it holds also for the asubjective remainder of the human mind after the emergence of subjectivity. The unique asubjective experience is open to the influence coming from other centers, and this is sufficient to break down the wall of privacy. But, obviously, if it happens to be language that serves this influence then language is not primarily a communicative medium.

The isolation of the subject from its aconceptual origin serves as a perpetual source of nostagia for the subject. At the highest level of its development, the consciousness of the subject recognizes its isolation and longs for returning to the experiential continuity which precedes the emergence of subjectivity.

A brief history of surprise

Let us consider some earlier views about surprise. Novalis thought that all chance and accident is miraculous (here I am indebted to Pfefferkorn's Novalis interpretation, Pfefferkorn, 1988). In a miracle we may sense the presence of an evading higher being. Games organize human experience and provide an environment where we may expose ourselves to chance. Novalis applied elementary game-theoretical notions in order to relate art to experience and said that one of the games in which we may experience miracles of chance is poetry. It is due to game-theoretical notions that Novalis's thinking anticipates present-day semiotics. We could say that his *miracle* is an early counterpart of what we have called *incongruity* of semiotic experience. Unlike most of the modern semioticians, Novalis didn't neglect the role of human experience in semiotic theory, and I think that it is exactly his ability to connect games with experience that makes his thinking, regardless of its fragmentary and apparently unrefined character, superior to standard modern semiotics.

Modern semiotics might learn something from Schopenhauer, too. Concepts or signs alone, as part of representations (Vorstellungen), cannot explain where concepts or signs come from. They come from something that is less than conceptual, less than structurally and systematically organized, something where the contrast of the subject and object is still weak. Concepts arise from aconceptual experience, from the raw experience of being alive in which the the full-fledged contrast of the external (physical) and the internal (spiritual) is not yet present. This is experience which precedes the phase during which experience is articulated into objects, and, therefore, it is experience from which objects arise. It is experience without subjects too, before Me and You became articulated as individuals. Schopenhauer coined a special notion to describe this primordial experience. He called it *Wille* (Will). Assuming that the comparison makes sense, *Wille* may be even more primitive than the nonverbal mammalian consciousness because *Wille* doesn't recognize temporal and spatial order. But *Wille* is definitely not an empirical notion, and the comparison is a bit questionable. Schopenhauer's message to modern semioticians might be that they have forgotten that there is no meaning or signification without experience, and there is no experience without *Wille*, namely, without the holistic, aconceptual and nonintentional experience of being.

In the third book of his *The World as Will and Representation* (1819/ 1969, see especially section 49), Schopenhauer contrasts concepts and Ideas, and we could say that, from the Schopenhauerian point of view, the pitfall of modern semiotics is that it deals only with concepts. The misguided presupposition that it is concepts (differences, dichotomies, opposites) or propositions of which the human mind consists has driven semiotics to overestimate the role of abstractions and representations in the life of the mind. This critique applies to many fields, including cognitive science and logical studies of language and mind. In these fields, if experience is allowed to play any role, the role is usually limited to perceptual experience. It has been claimed (see for example, Crane, 1992) that perceptual knowledge is nonconceptual indeed but that it still is contentful and representational. Every view which sees the human mind mainly as conceptual or propositional activity tends to separate perception all too categorically from thinking, believing, desiring and other cognitive operations, or, what is even worse, tries to make perception a conceptual activity too. The tendency to separate perception and cognition seems to be based on the underlying assumption that thinking, believing and desiring are nonexperiential, whereas perception, due to the lack of cognitive or propositional structure, is the only genuine experiential channel of the mind.

Contrary to this, Schopenhauer thought that an experience which is not immediately perceptual but which is not conceptual either should have a central position in our view of the human mind. The division of mind into the perceptual and nonperceptual departments is artificial because the aconceptuality which is characteristic of perception is able to permeate also those parts of the mind which are traditionally not considered to be immediately perceptual. According to Schopenhauer, our thinking and memory, especially if it is authentic, can remain faithful to its perceptual and aconceptual origin. Conceptual knowledge which is abstract in the sense that it presupposes the contrast of subject and object (see sections 33 through 35) is not authentic in this sense. Concepts are purified of their perceptual origin, and this purity, namely the all too crisp borderline between perception and thinking, undermines the quality of conceptual knowledge. But if this borderline is abolished, we may surrender to genuine Ideas. At that moment, our individuality is temporarily lost. Ideas are perceptive (indirectly perceptual of their origin), nonintentional and live holistically like organisms. According to Schopenhauer, Ideas, unlike concepts, are something which we are able to genuinely experience.

The relation of Ideas to the Will is problematic, to say the least. (Some of the problems have been discussed in Hamlyn, 1980, pp. 103-122). The main problem is that, in Schopenhauer's view, Ideas somehow pacify or domesticate the Will by rendering the person who entertains Ideas into a Will-less (willenlose) contemplative state of mind. This is almost paradoxical but we will here not enter into a detailed critique. Anyway, Schopenhauer goes on by asking what kind of knowledge can lead us to encountering the Will (section 36). His answer is that it is art, or artistic knowledge, which reveals Ideas most perspicuously. Here music has a special role to play. Music, unlike other arts, is able to copy the Will directly without the objectivizing mediation of Ideas. In good music, neither Ideas nor concepts control or diminish the impact of the Will in our experience. Music transforms desire into satisfaction. Melody expresses the movements of the Will from the expectation of desire, through surprises of digressions and delays, to the satisfaction of returning to the tonic of the key. Though music is a universal language, it is neither an external language of abstractions nor a language of conceptual structures; it is expression of the Will.

It is quite obvious that this kind of view of music is inaccessible to practically every branch of modern semiotics because modern semiotics has no genuine connection to aconceptuality. But, in the light of the foregoing view of surprise, especially if it is expressed with the help of the game metaphor, we can say that a listener who has experienced a surprise during a course of a musical game is, as he encounters the surprise, exposed to what Schopenhauer called *Wille*.

Experience and modern semiotics

Modern semiotics has tried to theorize about signification without rendering human experience the role it deserves (cf. Pylkkö, 1993b). It remains quite incomprehensible how meaning can ever enter such blatantly mechanical, separable and isolated systems as those of, say, Saussure, Greimas, Goodman and Lévi-Strauss. It doesn't help too much to proclaim that sign systems are abstract systems because it is equally unclear how meaning can enter abstract systems, especially if the systems which are said to be abstract nevertheless remain tacitly mechanical and separable. If human experience is taken seriously as the site of signification production, it must be taken into account that human experience is massively holistic and consists of inseparably super-posed and schematic fields of experience. Experiential holism means that the whole of our experience cannot be explained in terms of its alleged parts because the whole perpetually exercises an influence upon the alleged parts. Experience doesn't consist primarily of objects or anything object-like, either abstract or concrete. In particular, human experience doesn't consist primarily of systems which can be explained in terms of their alleged subsystems. Very little, if anything, is mechanical in the human experience, and if something is mechanical there, or, rather, mechanical-looking, we should suspect that it originates from Western academic institutions which, in order to make our experience seem more disciplined, have, already for centuries, endeavoured to shape our experience into something external and objectlike.

Permanent, nicely separable and mind-independent objects can be found nowhere in nature. We assume here that the best interpretation of the quantum theory allows us to eliminate macrophysical objects and handle them as handy fictions (see Pylkkö, 1996b). Because what applies to nature must also apply to human nature, such objects cannot be found in the human experience either, except as illusions and fictions. That mechanical structures are real is a popular but nevertheless questionable view which has been postulated by obsolete theories about the human experience, that is, by fictions which have been scaffolded by the tradition of grammatical and logical theorizing. Therefore, semiotics, as a general view of signification, should not resort to the assumption that nature, human mind, and language, or experience in general, consist of separable classical objects.

Unfortunately, modern semiotics has widely, if not always consciously, resorted to unabashedly classical thinking habits which take the reification and separability conditions for granted. For example, code systems, production systems and transformation systems are widely used in modern semiotics. Yet their underlying conception of nature and experience is mechanical and originates from a particular interpretation of Newtonian physics. This holds also for those views which claim that the mechanical structures of the mind and language are abstract or hold *a priori*. For example, Kant's philosophy can be seen as an attempt to provide a solid foundation for Newtonian mechanics. Thus, no room for inseparability and indeterminism can be found there, though, at the same time, it is questionable whether Newtonian physics itself was ever really able to reach the mechanical ideal which underlies its conception of nature. Regardless of the original ideal, nonmechanical (noncomputational) structures seem to have found their way to the core of Newtonian physics anyway. This seems to have happened unwittingly, in spite of the ultimately mechanical endeavor of classical physicists.

As to modern semiotics, Hjelmslev (1961), among many others, advocated the use of mechanical methods in linguistics and other human sciences because he mistakenly thought that it is mechanicalness that characterizes genuine science. According to Hjelmslev, the human sciences can become genuinely scientific only by becoming mechanical, and the ideal of mechanicalness could be reached mainly through the application of production systems. Unfortunately, the rise of quantum theory made the mechanical ideal obsolete, and it was obvious already thirty years before the publication of Hjelmslev's work that singular microphysical phenomena cannot be explained comprehensively in terms of any purely mechanical notions.

In addition, I wouldn't hesitate to associate Freud to this tradition of mechanical thinking. Freud's basic endeavour was to reduce dreams, jokes and other partly unconscious experiences to a mechanical code which could be interpreted with the help of an objective and universal method. In his theory of jokes, Freud (1905/1976) puts forward a mechanism which generates sequential, manifest and incomplete jokes, 'surface jokes' so to speak, from simultaneous, latent and complete joke thoughts. This is basically a mechanical enterprise. However, Freud surpasses regular semiotics in one respect, namely by not limiting the description of jokes and dreams to a mechanical generation technique. Instead, he proceeds to explaining why the technique of jokes is able to produce pleasure. And here he surpasses, perhaps unwittingly, the mechanical ideal that dominates his thinking. In spite of the role which the notion of pleasure plays in Freud's thinking, Freud's ideal of the scientific method is overwhelmed by undue rationalism because, for Freud, the unconscious is something that has to be revealed, tamed, codified, regimented and finally reduced into what look almost like logical or grammatical structures.

Mechanical, nonmechanical, amechanical

The popularity of mechanical explanations notwithstanding, human experience and the organization of the human brain cannot be explained in terms of code systems or any sort of syntax alone. If Church's thesis is accepted, standard connectionism cannot help us to transcend mechanicalness either because standard connectionism is just one computational formalism among many others. Assuming certain widely accepted constraints on the nature and size of neural networks, standard connectionism, as a computational formalism, is mathematically equivalent with Turing-computability (cf. Minsky and Papert, 1969, pp. 321-2; for a proof that all Turing computations are neurally computable, see Franklin & Garzon, 1991) and, due to Church's thesis, with any other characterization of mechanical computability. Therefore, whatever can be expressed with the help of Turing machines is connectionistically computable; and, under certain widely accepted, but by no means necessary constraints into which we will not enter here, whatever can be expressed in any connectionist formalism is Turing-computable.

Human signification, both what carries meaning and what is meant, assuming that we want to adopt the dichotomy, consists of perpetually changing, inseparably superposed and schematically incomplete experiences. The experiences from which signification arises, surprise among them, can be described adequately in suitable holistic terms but not in terms of any formalism which satisfies the classical separability conditions. The philosophical choice is not between formalisms but between genuine aconceptuality and conceptuality. Conceptuality comprises here both the mechanical (formal; Turing-computable; connectionistically computable; and so on) and what is not mechanical (not formalizable; non-Turing-computable; non-connectionistically-computable; and so on). What is not mechanical (in the sense of being non-Turing-computable) is still conceptual because it cannot be defined without commitment to the existence of mechanicalness (syntax; formalizability; Turing computability) and because nonmechanical (noncomputational) structures can be perfectly well defined and well structured in the normal mathematical sense. But what is genuinely aconceptual is neither mechanical nor nonmechanical but *amechanical*, that is, something where the dichotomy hasn't yet arisen. Thus, the thesis is this: without access to genuine aconceptuality, the naturalistic description of human experience, especially that of surprise, will remain inadequate.

Suppose, for example, that we relate a production system to a subject whose experience we want to describe. With respect to this kind of framework, it has often been suggested that something, say a string of symbols, surprises the subject if it is logically possible for the production system which is related to the subject to generate the string but, for some accidental reasons, for example because of time and space restrictions, the system isn't actually able to produce it. It is typical for this kind of mechanical explanation that surprise is said to come out of the subject's inability to foresee or foretell what is potentially generable by its production system. For example, it can be suggested that a subject experiences a theorem of sentential logic as surprising if the subject is familiar with, for example, a complete set of axioms and inference rules for sentential logic but still cannot produce a proof for the theorem. And analogously with any other Turing-computable task, connectionistically computable tasks included.

However, anyone who attempts to explain surprise along these lines has to decide where the border line between familiarity and what is experienced as surprise is to be drawn, and that decision is hard, if not impossible, to make. This is so because even the most simple axioms and production rules may themselves be quite surprising, and any candidate for the limit will most probably be very arbitrary. For example, it has been claimed in relevance logic that already some of the axioms and most well-known theorems of the regular sentential logic are intuitively paradoxical. Furthermore, psychological tests on sentential reasoning show that already reasoning which requires the application of one implication symbol to a real life situation goes beyond the capabilities of the vast majority (practically all) of academicly trained people (Johnson-Laird & Byrne, 1991). Therefore, most people, including practically all of those who have received formal training in elementary logic, should find some of the most obvious truths of sentential logic quite surprising. This alone calls into question the whole approach which is based on the assumption that mental representation or human reasoning has much to do with elementary logic. But it also questions the line of thinking which tries to explain surprise and creativity in terms of mechanical production systems without any reference to experience.

The problem of understanding surprise is not solved by introducing non-Turing-computable structures or concepts, and by defining surprise in terms of them. Though this alternative is clearly less trivial than the purely mechanical way, it may still fall short of dealing with genuine surprise which tends to be aconceptual and thus inaccessible to all structural approaches, including such which applies non-Turing-computable concepts. It seems that, though mechanical processes are clearly not holistic, not all nonmechanical (non-computable in the standard mathemetical sense of the word) structures are genuinely holistic either.

Nietzsche's *Wille*

Holism as such is not something new in the history of Western philosophy. For example, according to Nietzsche's *Will to Power* (1884-88), human signification production is dominated by inseparability, perpetual change and contextuality. Meaning processes are in a perpetual flux and do not consist of permanent separable parts. They are made to serve the interests of a speaker who always works in a changing historical and social situation. Meanings are delays between perception and action, and because perception and action vary perpetually from one moment to another, meaning is bound to do that too. Meanings cannot be experienced abstractly, out of the human context of interests, beliefs, perceptions, goals, dreams, emotions, drives and games. What energizes the context and keeps it moving is what the later Nietzsche called *Wille*. *Wille* is nonintentional, conceptually unorganized, partly unconscious, but interest-driven experiential energy which vitalizes and intensifies signification processes and keeps human games going on. The intensity has a distinctively sexual nature, and its presence in games, plays and art makes them compelling and appealing. In this respect Nietzsche followed Giordano Bruno. Already Bruno had studied the role of sexuality in human imagination and power relations (Couliano, 1984). According to Eugen Fink (1960, pp. 179-89), Nietzsche was able to liberate himself from the spell of Western metaphysics by assuming that signification always arises from power relations which are realized by human game and play. Meaning as sex-driven power is certainly an experiential notion which precedes the concepts of the regular empirical science, though some aspects of the intensity and energy of meaning can be studied also by the methods of science. Surprisingly, Nietzsche's and Schopenhauer's conception of the mind, according to which the initiation for meaning and action comes from the unconscious and aconceptual layers of the mind, has received new evidence from recent neuropsychological research. For example, Benjamin Libet's (1985) experiments with readiness potential seem to indicate that the so-called conscious will to act is preceded by unconscious cerebral activities.

For Nietzsche, the human Subject or Self is a social illusion which can never establish a permanent identity. But he went further. The subject as a grammatical, logical and metaphysical category is an illusion, too, and not necessarily fully separable from the illusion of the Self as the initiator of action. The logico-grammatical illusion has been enhanced by the traditional view of the structure of the Indo-European languages. This view reifies language and its content into permanent units. The folk-psychological view according to which human beings are intentional or means-end-rational subjects has a counterpart in folk linguistics which sees language as a collection of sentences, such that each sentence is or represents a predication. In predication, a grammatical subject is concatenated with a grammatical predicate. The underlying assumption is that the grammatical subject is a name for a person, and the predicate tells what the person is doing.

The assumption can be extended to cover nonhuman things, too, but the price is that we make them tacitly subject-like and intentional. Respectively, in logical analysis, the name of a logical subject is concatenated to a logical predicate which is assumed to be a name for a property. According to Nietzsche, the underlying folk-linguistic view of language which has been adopted in traditional grammatical and logical analysis makes all sentences unwittingly look like descriptions of intentional action. Not surprisingly are logical substances often called 'logical individuals' or 'logical subjects.' This basic Indo-European mythology forces us to see the universe as a set of individuals and sentences as predications which tell us what the individuals are or what they are doing. We understand the meaning of a sentence if we grasp, not only the intention of the speaker, but the intention of the individual whose action the sentence describes. No wonder therefore that descriptions of the so-called nonhuman nature have for so long presented the nature as a site which is populated by humanlike spirits, gods and other intentional agents.

But we may ask whether the introduction of causality and the need to describe the nonhuman nature as something which is genuinely independent of human action was really able to free the descriptions of the nature from all anthropomorphism. At least in folk physics, causality still seems to express nature's intentions. And in general, opposites, like that of the intentional and causal, presuppose each other. Therefore, when causality was introduced as the main nonintentional principle, a tacit motivation, or at least an unwitting implication, may have been the desire to make the human mind look less causally determined. But this endeavor is somewhat paradoxical because causality had to be defined as something nonintentional in the first place. Thus it seems that the intentional and the causal are interdependent, and only an intentional mind can find its environment as consisting of causal relations. The human mind which tries to understand the physical nature remains necessarily inseparably entangled with it. Thus causality is just an external aspect of intentionality.

An intention-free causality is not a coherent notion because it would be impossible to explain how any purely causal structure of the world, say, as it was allegedly revealed by the mathematics of classical physics, could be reflected by the corresponding structure of the intentional mind: either a miracle is needed to project the mathematical structure onto the world, or it is the human mind that does it. Of a pure (intention-free) causality, nothing could be known. As soon as we claim to know something, the purity is lost. Fortunately we are free of the burden of explaining what pure causality is because modern physics, especially in the twentieth century, is too inconsistent to make this task properly motivated in the first place. If there existed only one consistent theory of physical reality which could explain everything, scientific realism would be a much more plausible philosophical position. That no such theory exists doesn't make physics useless but casts a dubious light upon realism. Though philosophers, especially outside of the Western cultural sphere, have argued for centuries that there are holistic features in the human experience, it wasn't until the emergence of the quantum theory that the idea of inseparability has received respectability in the scientific quarters of the West. It seems that in the modern West we have to find a feature first in so-called external nature, hopefully with the help of a scientific-looking method, before we can appreciate it as a feature of our mind.

Change, and meaning change

The picture of language as a predication mechanism has fatal disadvantages, the most striking one of which is that the picture cannot deal adequately with change in general, and with surprise and meaning change in particular. Because the description of action was privileged to the predicate, the Indo-European mythology about what sentences are, and the predication picture based on the mythology, unwittingly overemphasized the contrast of subject and predicate, and therefore made subjects (and denotations of names in general) look immutable. This is a repercussion of the aforementioned contrast of the causal and the intentional. Already Hume, in his *Treatise of Human Nature*, (1739-40/1987), noticed that either there are identity-preserving, external and transtemporal individuals, and change is impossible; or that there actually is change around, and identity-preserving, external and transtemporal individuals are impossible. Hume found this quite alarming because perception, and thinking habits which do not exceed the degree of regularity which perceptions legitimate, speak strongly in favor for change, even for perpetual change.

The picture of language as a mechanism of predication encounters great difficulties when it has to deal with change because grammatical, logical and metaphysical subjects make change look impossible. It is not a healthy policy to partition what exists into two separable universes, namely, into the universe where nothing changes (immutable substances) and into the one where everything changes (relations among substances). The need to avoid this led Hume to question the existence of substances, or subjects, external objects, individuals, or whatever substances happended to be called. Change rules everywhere, also in what is misleadingly called 'substances.' Internal objects and their law-like relations are just as illusory as their external counterparts. The internal (intentional) and the external (causal) are confluent, tend to lose their independence, and the border line which is said to separate perceptions from thoughts, beliefs and desires becomes vague and should eventually be abolished. Therefore, thinking and speaking do not consist of predications.

The predication picture of language cannot deal nicely with meaning change either. A surprise which is induced, say, by a poem doesn't only lead us to recognize an incongruity in the flow of our experience; it may also teach us to modify the processes through which we give signification to poems. If these modifications happen to be properly designed they may help us to protect ourselves against such future surprise attempts which are similar with the one that triggered the original surprise. Typically, modifications amount to changing some of the reception strategies which the reader has adopted. But if two different reception strategies are fed with what looks like one and the same message, the strategies will output the message attached to two nonidentical meanings. In other words, there are no reception-independent (or strategy-independent) meanings. A surprise experience with a poetical metaphor or symbol may educate our reading skills to deal successfully with similar or even with more sophisticated metaphors and symbols in the future reading situations. But the revised reading skills end up changing the meanings of the terms of which the symbols and metaphors consist. This kind of interdependence cannot be modelled within any framework in which language is a predication mechanism and in which predications consist of constituents with permanent meanings. If, for example, a proper name picks out an individual, every modification of the speaker's reading skills would force the name to pick out a new individual (when the name is reinterpreted with respect to the new reception skills), and that sounds absurd.

Even a relatively unsurprising reading process may be able to change the meanings of such terms which are central for the understanding of the text. That word meaning must be open to the contextual effect of the sentence where the word occurs was noticed and studied already by Jan Mukařovský (1940) who said that the utterance where a word occurs pulls the word into a continuous semantic flux. Perpetual accumulation and change of meaning (of a word, for example) becomes even more prominent if the meaning is, unlike what Mukařovský intended, relativized, not only with respect to one sentence, but with respect to the gradually unfolding understanding of the whole text. This kind of perpetual semantic change, feedback and interdependence where the word meaning affects textual meaning, textual changes of meaning modify reading skills, and textual meanings and modified reading skills affect word meanings, and so on, cannot be modelled in any language theory which takes predication as its primary notion. If a proper name picks out an individual, and the name happens to be central for the understanding of the text, in the predication framework the name would have to pick out a new individual practically in every sentence where the name occurs!

And we may go even further and say that any reading process may have a modifying impact on the reader's expectations and preferences, that is, on all that which is called his 'system of beliefs.' But changes in beliefs, especially large changes, may change the meaning of practically any word the reader will encounter in a future reading process. In other words, a text which is read after the changes of belief took place in the reader doesn't mean the same as what the (allegedly same) text used to mean before the changes. Of course, we use the expression 'same text' here only conditionally for the sake of argument, that is, we assume that it makes sense (which it doesn't!) to speak of one and the same text (word, expression, message) under different reception processes (or with respect to different beliefs systems).

Naturalism, holism, associationism

A view of language which takes association and experience as its basic notions (for example, Pylkkö, 1993a; 1993b; see also Chapter 5) is much better equipped to deal with surprise and meaning change than the predication picture. A picture of language which doesn't see language mainly as a mechanism of predication, and which rejects such traditional notions as (grammatical, logical and metaphysical) subject and predicate, may, for example, handle speech as a flow of associative experiences which lack definite structure. From this kind of point of view, language is seen as a spectrum of discourses in which human experience finds home and expression for itself. The discourse of philosophy, in particular, is an activity in which restrictions are cast upon other discourses, and discourses are compared with one another in the light of the restrictions. Philosophical work tries to illuminate how discourses of different backgrounds mix and converse with each other, and under which conditions they are commensurable or compatible with one another. A philosophical result may tell us, for example, that a discourse, under such and such conditions, cannot be reconciled with another discourse. Thus, philosophical work and results can be negative in the sense that they show how some distinctions and dichotomies lead to absurdities (with respect to some contextual conditions of absurdity) and how the distinctions and dichotomies can be abolished if someone doesn't like to live with the absurdities.

One group of discourses in which human experience has found expression consists of the discourses of neuroscience, and one particular discourse of that group is the discourse which has been inspired by eliminative, non-implementative and holistic connectionism. Clearly, this is not standard connectionism which is just a computational formalism and, as such, mathematically equivalent with the Turing machine formalism. One of the philosophical restrictions which the discourse of the anomalous connectionism has to satisfy is that its language, as well as any theoretical language which is used to describe the language, doesn't rest on the predication picture of language at any phase or level of the theoretical elaboration. Actually, this restriction is a consequence of strictly interpreted naturalism. If the restriction is not accepted, any attempt to avoid reificationism elsewhere would be pointless. Hence, the following kind of circularity must be accepted: the theoretical language in which natural language is described is itself a part of natural language. For example, the language of the associative, experiential and neural theory which describes how naming and meaning arises in natural language is itself an example of how neural associations work in language. Naturalism is deprived of the Tarskian resolution to the semantical and other classical paradoxes because the contrast of object language and metalanguage cannot be defended in any naturalistically understandable way. Fortunately there are better ways to deal with the semantical paradoxes than those suggested by Tarski but we will not consider them here.

In general, we may say that a term is *naturalistically understandable* if it can be interpreted in neural, behavioral and experiential terms. Here *interpretation* must be a notion which differs crucially from the standard notion of reduction because interpretations cannot resort to logical identities and equivalences. *Interpretation* itself must be a naturalistically understandable notion, and, therefore, it cannot be characterized or justified without circularity. Here *interpretation* is basically a philosophical term whose conditions of success require that certain philosophical feasibility (ability to solve experiential problems) and elegance conditions are satisfied. The terms of an old discourse cannot be interpretable and understandable in a new discourse if the languages in which the discourses are conducted are not philosophically

reconcilable with each other. Of course, there exists no method of interpretation, and no translation is able to mediate the interpreted terms from one
discourse into another.

The foregoing characterization of interpretation is designed to conform
with holistic naturalism in which strong logical and grammatical structures
are not available. The idea is that the experience of nature is a vital part of any
philosophical activity and too interesting to be left to dogmatic natural science
alone (cf. Chapter 2). But suppose that a thoroughly naturalistic, holistic,
eliminatively aconceptual and possibly connectionist (in some nonstandard
sense of *connectionism*) view of neuroscience is available and we attempt to
describe some of our experiences in the language of the theory. The following
question arises: what is the relationship of the language of the theory to other
experiential but nontheoretical discourses which can be used to describe our
experience? So, what should we do with such obviously nontheoretical descriptions of human experience as those provided, say, by religious texts,
music, poetry and other arts?

First of all, they should be submitted to the test of naturalism: they should
be interpreted in the other discourses which we are interested in. We must ask
whether their language or semiotic system, or language in which their language and semiotic system can be adequately described, are naturalistically
understandable. Notice, however, that we are not discussing here what the
artists, poets or visionaries themselves explicitly claim about their own language; neither are we dealing with what naturalists and scientists tell us about
their language respectively. What they explicitly claim may or may not be
interesting or naturalistically comprehensible. Even if it were not, the way
poets and scientists *use* language in order to address human experience may
be naturalistically understandable and philosophically interesting.

We must concede that, at the present phase of neuroscience and physics,
some of our best neuroscientific descriptions of brain processes are relatively
primitive and cannot help us too much in casting light, say, upon poetic
language. But this doesn't imply that a view of language which can adequately deal with poetry must be incompatible with modern naturalism (cf.
Pylkkö, 1993a); or that a genuinely naturalistic view of language, which is
inspired by neuroscience, biology and physics, couldn't be reconciled with an
interesting view of, say, poetic language. Even if some of the best poems or
religious texts deal with experiences which seem to have little or nothing to do
with modern naturalism, neuroscience or physical sciences, the impression of

philosophical distance may have been accepted hastily (cf. Pylkkö, 1996a, where the relation between Heidegger's thinking and that of Wolfgang Pauli's is studied). The experiences themselves belong to nature, and the language or semiotic system which is used in the description of the experiences may be naturalistically understandable; and the language of the adequate theory of the language and semiotic system where the experience is described may be naturalistically understandable.

A view which takes language as holistic and associative neural processing and which deals eliminatively with strong logical and grammatical structures provides in many respects a more proper approach to poetic and religious language, and other fields of human experience, than what traditional logic and grammar can ever do (cf. Chapter 1). But in order to reach this much, naturalism, and the way it pictures language, must distance itself from realism and reductionism. Human experience can be approached within different conventions and described in different discourses, including neuroscience and poetry. Yet no identity-preserving translation can be established between these discourses and no identity between the units of experience which these discourses are supposed to utilize can be established. No meaning-preserving translation ever captures the expressions of one discourse and codes them into the expressions of the other.

The view of connectionism as a computational formalism which is mathematically equivalent with a Turing machine formalism (or with any other equivalent symbolic formalism) and which can be used to implement higher level logical, computational and grammatical structures is basically a reductionist view which presupposes that literal identities and equivalences between the aconceptual and conceptual level are available. (I will not deal here with what is called 'token identity theories,' 'antireductionist materialism' and 'supervenience' because I believe that they are not coherent positions.) But this view runs blatantly against naturalism as it is here understood. For example, it seems implausible that any regular connectionist formalism will be able to describe comprehensively what brain processing is. This is so because every regular connectionist model, as a formalism, is mathematically equivalent with some Turing machine, whereas it is plausible that brains are not mechanical systems at all and, therefore, not adequately describable in terms of any Turing machine. It is, of course, possible to design a nonstandard version of connectionism which would allow not-Turing-computable numbers and functions to appear, say, as the output functions of a network unit. That would make the network less trivial but would not yet render networks as useful for describing aconceptual experiences.

What may guarantee a philosophical reconciliation and mutual interpretation of two discourses, say the discourses of neuroscience and poetry, is that both of the discourses, as well as all descriptions of the discourses, are naturalistically understandable, that is, interpretable in a proper version of naturalism. This amounts to finding philosophical compatibility by eliminating ungainly and conflicting elements, not to establishing reductions. But it may also mean that poetry will expose itself to severe philosophical criticism. Just as standard natural science is corrupted by mechanical thinking habits, a great deal of poetry is corrupted by humanism, universalism, formalist tricks, progressive and enlightened attitudes, and by highly ambiguous attitudes toward modern Western technology.

Language experience, surprise and their neural description

As for a more detailed example, it is possible to develop a view of natural language (cf. Pylkkö, 1992; see also Chapter 5) according to which names are associations from some sounds to other stimuli and back, such that the associations can be used for survival purposes in a social setting. Naming associations are realized by neural networks and experienced internally by the speaker. Theoretically speaking, neural networks consist of relatively simple neuronlike processing units which are connected to each other by axonlike connections whose weight values can be altered (for connectionism in general, see Smolensky, 1988). Regardless of their apparent simplicity, neural networks are here understood as descriptions of biological and experiential processes, not as computational formalisms. We do not assume that the units and connections are purely external, classical objects. They are as neutral with respect to the external-internal dichotomy, and as inseparable and observer-dependent, as the best interpretation of modern physics, including quantum theory, modern biology and neuroscience allows and requires. Neither is it assumed here that neural networks implement some high-level conceptual and contentful symbolic structures. Even with every standard network formalism which is mathematically equivalent with infinitely many high-level symbolic representations, we are not able to guarantee that there exists a high-level representation which is able to carry any interesting, empirically credible or intuitively conceivable content, for example any folk-psychologically comprehensible content. With genuinely holistic nets, the lack of intuitively comprehensible content is even more prominent.

Natural language, music and many other semiotic activities are games which cannot be described adequately as long as gaming (movements, signs, rules, and so on) is approached in purely conceptual terms. Ultimately, even the notion of *player*, in the standard sense which takes players to be identity-preserving and rational individuals, must be eliminated or, at least, strongly modified, because a view or theory of games which is developed in a natural-istically understandable way should not confer to rationality any central role in the definition or characterization of man (see Chapter 6). Semiotic knowl-edge is incorporated, among other things, into the weight values of the connections along which inhibitory and excitatory impulses move from one unit to another in a neural network, and perhaps into the chaotic bursts and fluctuations which such nets are able to produce. Perhaps that kind of nets are able to maintain some kind of *holistic field of meaning* which may assume the mode of superposition too. The field is something that is immediately experi-enced by everyone who is engaged in a semiotic game. To be a player isn't more substantial than to be a suitably tuned neural network (consisting possibly of other neural networks consisting of other neural networks... and so on) which is capable of fulfilling its role as an opponent in a game situation. A biological brain which is capable of fulfilling the role of a participant in a game can be separated from other neural networks only due to the role which is conferred on it by the game, that is, through the activities which it, as a neural network, carries out in a network of neural networks. In other words, communities and groups in which games are realized are nothing crucially more substantial than networks of neural networks which support a field of meaning.

But being a man is crucially more than just being a subject. Man is also a preindividual center of experience in a field of meaning. Unlike a subject, a presubjective center of experience (in a field of meaning) is conceptually inseparable from other centers of meaning. A genuinely holistic field is what experience is (before it is organized into subjects). And it just *is*. That is, it is primarily about nothing.

East-African vervet monkeys learn to classify and name their natural enemies and use the names as alarm calls when a predator is approaching the herd (Cheney & Seyfarth, 1990). The primary semiotic difference for the vervet monkey is that between the enemy and nonenemy, and it is quite obvious that the use of the difference in naming associations would never have taken place had naming not had a high survival value for the monkey, and had there not been a relatively complex social environment where the game of naming could be established. What we are not assuming here is that a high survival value refers to the survival *only* under the threat of predators, or that a high survival value implies a high representational value. Monkeys have surprisingly 'useless' mental capabilities too, and the evolution of the monkey brain was not necessarily guided or enhanced by the allegedly realistic or truth-preserving correspondence or reflection relation which the brain is said to attain with its environment. For example, chimpanzees are able to learn large fragments of human natural language in a nonnatural laboratory environment. This kind of residual potentialities can hardly be explained with the help of any straightforwardly practical purpose which mental capabilities are supposed to serve in the natural environment of the monkey. Assuming conditionally that there are right or reliable representations, it can be claimed that self-deception, lying and day-dreaming may have been more useful for the survival of man and monkeys than any allegedly structure-preserving or 'truthful' mental representation.

In the anomalous connectionism which was sketched above, the processing units and connections of a network may resemble more Mach's elements which are neutral with respect to the psychical-physical constrast than regular external objects, the idea being that, in some cases, their processing can be experienced immediately. They cannot, however, be conceptually or theoretically defined because conceptuality and the theoretical attitude emerges *in* or *through* them. This kind of associative view of naming captures some of the most appealing features of the experiential view of language, namely, that experience is holistic, diffuse, perpetually changing, schematic and inconsistent. It also makes 'meanings' unique, irreversible, partly chaotic and massively contextual neural associations which are learned and experienced by the speaker. Obviously, there isn't much room for the objectivity of meaning in this kind of view of language. We can name our experiences without assuming that what is named must be an individual or transtemporally identity-preserving object, or a set of such objects, in any classical sense of *object* or *set*. Furthermore, the associative view of naming doesn't presuppose that names themselves are transtemporal object-like constituents with permanent meaning and identity. If elaborated within a proper framework, the naturalist picture of language as neural processing can capture even the most important feature of the experiential view of language, namely, that language experience is primarily, though only partly perhaps, aconceptual in its nature. Due to its access to aconceptuality, the naturalist-associationist-experientialist view of language which accords with the best of neuroscience can also deal adequately with surprise and meaning change, unlike any logico-cognitivist view of language which is based on the view of language as a predication mechanism.

According to this kind of naturalistic and holistic picture, the meaning of a word or any other semiotic unit is diffuse and perpetually changing, such that it cannot be decomposed into any persistent constituents. Furthermore, words and other signs, assuming that we want to talk about such objects at all, are not constituents of larger semiotic sequences, like sentences, because words and other signs change their meaning from moment to another, depending, among other things, on the brain processes which are going on in the speaker's or player's head. When a player is forced to face a surprising situation, he is faced with an experience which is aconceptual or asemiotic with respect to his expectations. If systematicity dominates our view of language, we are forced to ignore the aconceptuality. Surprise can be understood naturalistically in the above sketched naturalist-associationist approach exactly because the viewpoint makes it possible for us to deal with aconceptual and preconceptual knowledge. The aconceptual flux of experience is the source which feeds perpetually the fields of human meaning, and it is the access to this flux that makes it possible for us to view adequately the change of meaning in a semiotic context, in particular when the change is related to surprise.

CHAPTER FIVE

Unique language problem

How to destroy theoretical dichotomies

It was characteristic of Wittgenstein's later work that he picked out a traditional conceptual dichotomy and focused a philosophical spotlight upon it. The result was intended to be, not a theory with new dichotomies, but, rather, a clarification and, perhaps, dissolution of the old and questionable dichotomy. One of his main endeavors was to help us to see how such traditional dichotomies have misguided our thinking. However, it is not quite clear what should happen after the problem has been seen in proper philosophical light. In some places he claims rather straightforwardly that, after the clarification, nothing else, especially not new theories or language improvement, can be expected (*Philosophical Investigations*, Wittgenstein, 1953/1974, for example, sections 120-133); whereas in other places he speaks of philosophy as therapy (section 255 of Wittgenstein, 1953/1974) and as a method of destruction (section 118). Yet, hardly anyone would appreciate a therapy which leaves the disease intact after it has been correctly diagnosed. Also 'destruction' sounds more radical than 'clarification,' and someone might say that by deconstructing dichotomies we improve our language.

A celebrated example of Wittgenstein's approach is his dealing with the so-called *private language problem* where the traditional dichotomy is between the *private* and the *public*. It may be suggested that in this case Wittgenstein tried to do more than just help us to see some of the difficulties which experiential or mental language is bound to create. The therapy appears to be much more radical: it suggests that language, meaning and understanding should not be described ultimately in terms of experiential notions. However, the clarification or dissolution of the dichotomy cannot be said to have happened in a perfectly neutral (cf. *neutral* as it is used in Chapter 2 and Chapter 4) way because Wittgenstein's solution to the problem favored the public aspect of meaning at the expense of the private one. Because it seems that Wittgenstein doesn't here just describe the difficulties of an old theory it is far from obvious that he doesn't eventually end up holding a new theory.

In order to have been a pure or neutral description of the difficulties which are related to mental and private vocabulary, Wittgenstein's work should have handled the internal or mental view of language and meaning with more tolerance than what actually happened. And even active therapy which aims, not only at a pure description of the dichotomy, but at its dissolution, could have ended up with something that is, by and large, neutral with respect to the dichotomy, rather than affirming one of the aspects of the dichotomy at the expense of the other. Therefore, it is possible that Wittgenstein aimed at something which goes beyond a pure description of the dichotomy, and we should ask in which sense, if any, Wittgenstein could, after all, keep himself apart from theorizing about language. If, after the deconstructional philosophical work, we hail so openly the public aspect of meaning, isn't it plausible that there will be room, at least potentially, for some relatively private aspect of meaning, too? If there is no room for private meaning in the proper use of language, then can we now, after the philosophical work, mean by *public* what we used to mean by it when it still was part of the dichotomy? Is it really possible that we, so to speak, annihilate the philosophical import of the private aspect of the dichotomy and, at the same time, leave the public one intact? Isn't it more plausible that we are forced to change the meaning of *public* when its opposite is drained off from all serious applicability? But if we nullify the private aspect and try to leave the public aspect basically as it used to be before the philosophical work, then it seems that either we are forced to absurdity because the notion of publicity wouldn't mean much without the opposite; or, we are unable to free ourselves from the old theoretical view, because the empty aspect is still an aspect. If the bracketing of the private aspect changes the meaning of the word *public* from its original meaning in some more radical sense, then it seems that we are designing a new theory and not just describing the problem.

An atheoretical view of language

The question whether the dissolution of a traditional dichotomy will produce new meaning for the surviving aspect of the dichotomy is closely related to (and has to be studied with respect to) the question of what we are supposed to mean when we say that the resulting view of language, namely the view which follows the destructive philosophical work, is not a theory. In which sense then is the dissolution of the old dichotomy and the possibly new meaning of one of the aspects of the dichotomy not theoretical?

Even if Wittgenstein favored the public, the destructive philosophical work was assumed to guide us toward a state of mind which is characterized by a disillusioned attitude toward the application of the old dichotomy. Seeing the difficulty in the proper light of a disillusioned attitude will, most probably, change also the way in which we use language. One problem here is that it looks now as if meaning could be changed *without* and *before* changes in use. But be this as it may, with this change, the meaning of *public* is altered, and Wittgenstein has shifted his philosophical discourse to a new gear. In order to make sense of Wittgenstein's frequent denouncements of the theoretical and explanatory attitude (sections 109; 126; 133, Wittgenstein, 1953/1974; see also Hilmy, 1987, pp. 202-210), we should say that Wittgenstein intended this shift in gear to be, not just a new theory with new dichotomies, but something *a*theoretical. What is not clear is whether this atheoretical can be purely descriptive and neutral (with respect to theoretical dichotomies).

It is well-known that the later Heidegger (see, for example, *On the Way to Language*, 1959/1971) also didn't want to see his view of language as a new theory. He went even further. He thought that philosophy itself was so much contaminated by the theoretical attitude that it is preferable to avoid the association with philosophy altogether, especially with what was called *Sprachphilosophie* (philosophy of language). He preferred to speak of *thinking*, as in "thinking of language."

Let us say here that any regular theoretical work attempts to describe the structure of its subject matter, say the structure of natural language, as accurately as possible and reach as powerful generalizations as possible. The regular theoretical attitude sees language as an entity among other entities, such that the structure of language is what it is, regardless of the activities of the human mind which, by trying to understand what language is, endeavors to understand itself. The regular scientific attitude is based on the assumption that there is nothing fatally circular, confusing or problematic in the situation in which language tries to describe and understand itself. If necessary, the regular theoretical attitude adopts some metaphysical measures to curb the difficulties, for example, by introducing some additional theoretical dichotomies, like that of the object language and metalanguage. The result of the description and explanation is a set of propositions, the laws of the theory, the terms and predicates of which refer to the entities whose behavior we want to explain. Their behavior is thought to be independent of the theory and its terms. For example, many logical or model-theoretical studies of natural language aim at a theoretical explanation, and typical dichotomies, which are accepted by most of those who work within this paradigm, are syntax vs. semantics; use vs. mention; analytic vs. synthetic; form vs. content; intention vs. extension, and so on.

After the Wittgensteinian therapy, natural language should appear to us in what could be called a *state of innocence*, that is, as it used to be before the theoretical attitude entered the scene and blurred our view with its dichotomies. In order to reach the state of innocence, the descriptive, destructive and therapeutic attitude is available but not the theoretical one. Now, the Cartesian view of language with private meanings which cannot be doubted could be a theory upon which we decide to direct the therapeutic attitude, the result being that the dichotomies of the theory are no longer able to keep our mind under their spell and dominate our thinking.

But even if this all could be accomplished, an obvious difficulty would distort this view of philosophy as therapy. The philosophical work was supposed to free us from the dichotomy by guiding us back to the innocence of the ordinary language and ordinary thinking. Yet it can be claimed that the public-private dichotomy, if anything, belongs to the repertoire of ordinary speaking and thinking habits, at least to the ordinary speaking and thinking habits of the present-day West. So, the nature of the state of innocence is intriguing: if ordinariness implies the private-public dichotomy, innocence shouldn't, perhaps, be so ordinary after all.

How innocent is ordinary language?

Is Heidegger free of this kind of difficulty? If Heidegger's early work (for example, Heidegger, 1927/1992) is interpreted in a way which suggests that ordinary everyday experience could, in some sense, preserve authenticity, then we seem to encounter a difficulty which is quite similar to that of Wittgenstein's. This is so because everyday life experience seems to be dominated by such metaphysical dichotomies as that of the private and public, and it will be hard to protect ordinary language and ordinary experience against the charge that they are already corrupted by dichotomism. After all, Heidegger quite openly associated publicity to inauthenticity, and in most cases seemed to think that the *Dasein* could attain authenticity only in highly exceptional circumstances. If everyday experience is dull and superficial, and saturated with inauthentic attitudes, then nobody would expect that it is everyday experience that philosophical work is looking for in order to get rid of dichotomism. This is, by the way, one of the reasons why attempts to see Heidegger as a philosophical pragmatist must be taken with a special caution (cf. Chapter 1).

If the early Heidegger's view of the possibilities of everydayness is still open to troublesome interpretations, the later Heidegger (for example, Heidegger, 1959/1971), seems to have found a way out of this problem. According to him, common sense and ordinary language are indeed already contaminated by overly technical and mechanical thinking habits. It is not only our *view* of language that is distorted by the theoretical attitude; it is the language itself. In a sense, the disease is much more serious than what Wittgenstein thought. Theoretical work doesn't just picture the language in a misleading way; the theoretical attitude which applies scientific thinking habits to the study of natural language transforms natural language in a direction where it eventually tends to satisfy the theory. In Heidegger's view, theoretical work on language has been very successful indeed. For example, logical, model-theoretical and computational views of language are not just views of what language is; they are not even views of a fragment of natural language. Rather, they, along with other reifying tendencies of the scientific culture, shape natural language in such a way that it will eventually resemble formal languages as much as possible. This attempt prevents us from seeing that language is what we *are* and what we are is, at least as long as it is not completely dominated by a technical-theoretical framework, indeterminate, perpetually changing and something for which the future is genuinely open.

According to Heidegger, the history of this theoretical distortion is long and began already with Plato and Aristotle, but, since the early seventeenth century, it has been particularly intensified by the rise of modern technology

(Technik) and natural science. In philosophy, Descartes advocated the technological-theoretical attitude and brought the modern subjectivity and the certainty of knowledge to the focus of philosophical discussion. This *metaphysics of subjectivity*, as Heidegger calls it, declared that the main function of the human mind is to reflect or represent the external reality of things, and therefore, the reliability of this reflective attitude and its foundation became one of the most central philosophical issues. This view reserved a special technical role for language: language also became a mechanism whose main function was to reflect how things of the external reality are. The public-private (and external-internal) dichotomy comprises one of the most essential characteristics of the metaphysics of subjectivity.

Hence, according to Heidegger, the theoretical attitude is saturated with the metaphysics of subjectivity. By conferring on natural language a special representative role, the metaphysics of subjectivity made it possible for us to turn the theoretical attitude also upon language itself. In the theoretical light, language appeared to be one entity among others, characterized by a structure which differentiates it from other entities. This attitude suppressed the proper view of language as perpetually evolving and unfolding human experience. We should notice that the human experience *precedes* the theoretical attitude, and the theoretical attitude may arise within the realm of human experience only if man adopts a special externalizing, reifying and conceptualizing attitude toward his experience. Therefore, by being a special case of the human experience, the theoretical attitude can never provide us with a comprehensive view of what the human experience is. Similarly, the theoretical explanation cannot cover the language experience as a whole because theoretical language is just one possibility of language experience, and we cannot expect that a special case, that is, theoretical language, could reflect the totality, namely, language that is filled also with such experience which is devoid of structure. The original human experience is pretheoretical, aconceptual and asubjective, whereas the theoretical attitude presupposes a subject who applies some concepts to a structured subject-matter. Conceptual work cannot deal with what precedes concepts, namely, that experience, including language experience, from which concepts arise.

In this light it is naive to assume, as Wittgenstein (and, according to some interpretations, the early Heidegger too) may be said to have done, that there exists a metaphysically innocent or pure colloquial language to which we, through philosophical work, can always return after we have realized that the theoretical attitude has led us astray. According to the later Heidegger's view, colloquial language and common sense are already thoroughly corrupted by the theoretical-technical attitude. Colloquial language and common sense of an epoch are not *a priori* untouchable but can be educated and corrupted to serve the interests of the technology and science of the epoch. For example, it can be claimed that both the public-private dichotomy and the external-internal dichotomy organize ordinary speaking and thinking habits of our modern time, and they do it in order to provide a popular basis for the scientific attitude. At the same time, however, science and technology may have contributed to the rise and rigidity of the dichotomies. In this issue, Heidegger's view resembles that of Feyerabend's who claimed that the theories of the new, seventeenth century natural science forced the scientists to invent a new observation language, and it wasn't until this new language had been adopted that the theories of the new natural science could be seen to agree with observations. Eventually, common sense, or *natural interpretation*, as Feyerabend called it, had to be educated to accept the new observations so that common sense could realize how wrong it had been before it had seen the light of the brave new scientific era (see Feyerabend, 1988, pp. 55-66).

But of course, Heidegger's way to get rid of the restrictions of ordinariness differs from Feyerabend's happy egalitarianism and anarchism. The early Heidegger thought that a special experience, the authentic *Dasein* experience, is needed to liberate the human mind from the dullness of ordinary common sense and from the constraints of the related theoretical attitude. This happens either within everyday experience or not, depending on how much one believes in the possibility of attaining authenticity within the everyday world. The later Heidegger thought that freedom from the technological-theoretical attitude can be reached only by adopting a special poetical view of language and by perpetually creating new, uncorrupted language experience. If it is thought, as seems plausible, that everyday life is too dull to become genuinely authentic, both of Heidegger's ways toward authenticity would lie far from ordinary language and common sense.

Unique, but not necessarily private

From the Heideggerian point of view, Wittgenstein's view of language remains too closely tied to the metaphysics of subjectivity. For example, when

Wittgenstein considers the *speaker* as a player in a *language game* he seems to presuppose that the speaking subject is already characterized by a relatively high degree of rationality which makes itself manifest, for example, as the ability to separate oneself from other persons and the playing environment. In general, the ability of being engaged in social action seems to require a rationally organized subjectivity. Wittgenstein doesn't tell us how these abilities and related rationality arise, and how the subject knows to follow orders and recognize rules. Why do we follow orders and rules in the first place? Furthermore, in his description of meaning and understanding, Wittgenstein mitigates, or even suppresses, the importance of experience, especially such experience which is not fully conceptualized. Therefore, regardless of their intended atheoretical nature, language games seem to remain overly externalizing and mechanical.

It looks plausible that Wittgenstein's notion of language game bore originally a distinct behavioristic flair. This shouldn't be too surprising because radical behaviorism was often antimetaphysically oriented, though its denouncement of metaphysics was not particularly radical. For example, many behaviorists assume a sharp metaphysical distinction between the entity which behaves and the environment which is said to provide the stimuli for the behavior. In the thirties, Wittgenstein didn't hesitate to say that humans learn to play language games in a way which is strictly analogous with how animals are trained to follow orders (see *Brown Book*, 1934-35/1984, p. 117 and 131 where language training is described with such unabashedly behavioristic terms as *Abrichtung, Vormachen, Ermunterung, Nachhilfe, Belohnung* and *Strafe*). One crucial difference between Wittgenstein's views and normal behaviorism is that Wittgenstein, unlike mainstream behaviorists, oriented gradually toward an *a*theoretical view of language and meaning. He had realized that because language games are something through which language emerges, no theoretical explanation is able to exhaust them and illuminate adequately their primordial character. Occasionally he seems to be saying that language games are not what people play but what a philosopher designs in order to reveal a confusion in the use of language. Here too appears a slight ambiguity.

Wittgenstein's own comments on behaviorism (1953/1974, say aphorism 307) can hardly be read as a denouncement of behaviorism. On the contrary, they are attempts to enlighten his own version of behaviorism, namely, *grammatical behaviorism*. Unlike what some radical behaviorists were willing to do, Wittgenstein didn't deny that there are experiences, but he said that meaning in language doesn't arise from experience. Meaning is public, rule-based and necessarily action-related, whereas experience as such is private and has therefore no place in language games.

A typical example of this kind of experience mitigation is Wittgenstein's beetle box example (1953/1974, aphorism 293). An experience, say pain, is like a beetle which everyone of us has in a box of privacy. I, and only I, can see the content, the "beetle," of my own box, but I cannot see what others have in their respective boxes. Therefore, says Wittgenstein, the content could be constantly changing, or the box could even be empty. This privacy is all too wild to be associated with proper meaning and language, and a sensation like pain has no place in the language game of pain; the language game of pain deals with pain-related, publicly accessible behavior and action, or better, with pain *as* behavior and action. The pain-beetle is not even a *something*. Pain is not *something*, but it is not *nothing* either. Wittgenstein himself formulates it as (1953/1974, aphorism 304): "The conclusion was only that a nothing would serve as well as a something about which nothing could be said." Pain as experience is more than nothing but less than some-thing, namely, less than something of which something can genuinely be said. Though we may say that experiences exist in some sense, they do it mostly somewhere beyond the sphere of communicability. I can use experience-related language meaningfully only as long as I keep it public and base it on action and behavior. It is action and behavior that guarantee that language is able to be *about* something. And verbal human action is language only if it is about something. Thus it seems that I can say nothing of experience as (private) experience. Experience can be spoken only of as action and behav-ior, only when experience disguises itself as action and behavior.

Because Heidegger's notion of *Dasein* was intended to weaken the role which the conscious and intentional subject plays in our view of meaning, even Heidegger's *Dasein* notion may unwittingly resemble some behavioris-tic views of mind and meaning. It is not completely implausible that some behaviorists would have attacked the metaphysics of subjectivity in a way which is somewhat similar with Heidegger's attack. Thus an interesting question arises: Does behaviorism, say as regards verbal meanings, commit us to the metaphysics of subjectivity? Not by any necessity, or not at least too obviously. One of the main reasons why behaviorism in practice couldn't avoid the metaphysics of subjectivity is that standard behaviorism was so openly theoretical (often also naively reductionist) and, as such, unable to deal with the aconceptual preconditions of meaning. In this question, Wittgenstein's grammatical behaviorism was doing quite well and could have avoided the worst versions of subject metaphysics. But Wittgenstein relied on something that could be called the *metaphysics of ordinariness*. It was, after all, one of Wittgenstein's most cherished endeavors to guarantee that language can, if purified of conceptual blunders, serve as a reliable medium of communication. According to him, it is not only possible, but acceptable and preferable, to see language as such. This interest is basically technological. It was not, perhaps, Wittgenstein's behaviorism as such which led him to overestimate the permanency and reliability of gaming relations, and eventually to degrade human experience. Rather, it was his technological obsession of usefulness which led him to mitigate the role of experience in language. Experience is useless and unreliable. When not conceptually ordered, it is particularly useless and unreliable. It would have been impossible, or at least utterly strange, for Wittgenstein to think that our gaming activities *belong* inseparably *to* our experience.

If *private* means something to which only one person has access and which, in addition, cannot be doubted, then it is questionable if anything in our experience can be purely private; and, analogously, if *public* means something to which anyone has access in principle and which can be genuinely doubted, then it is equally questionable if language and meaning, especially meaning change and meaning indeterminacy, can be described in terms of pure publicity either. Perhaps this dichotomy isn't that illuminating in the first place. Wittgenstein's bias for publicity preserved an ambiguous and, unwittingly perhaps, potentially active role for privacy as something which can be neither doubted nor communicated. There is something highly paradoxical in this result: the purer our subjectivity is, the more uncommunicable it is! A genuine dissolution of this and other dichotomies would have required a seriously *a*theoretical view of language which would have deconstructed the public-privacy dichotomy by letting both of the aspects diminish with equal pace. This could have happened by allowing behavior and action to belong inseparably to experience. Therefore, it might be interesting to see if it is possible to design a view of language which is, not only atheoretical, but less hostile toward experience, and which would let the dichotomy wither away by being, not privacy-oriented, but experiential in a holistic and *asubjective* way. This would require that experience saturates language and meaning, and serves an active role there, unlike what happens in Wittgenstein's neobehavioristic framework. It is, first of all, language which is able to break into the realm of our experience and make it accessible to 'other' experiences. Language is not, and certainly not *only*, a medium of communication, a device of shared aboutness. Language is primarily experiential influence. With the help of interpretations, we can experience what other people experience, that is, we can experience other people's experience *in* and *as* our own. This is possible, because we all dwell in the collective aconceptual experience and this experience connects us to other human beings. Language is not primarily communication but a collective experiential field in which we can experience by participation what 'other minds' experience, with the condition, of course, that the 'other mind' is not really other with respect to us but, via the aconceptual experience, a distant 'part' of us, or, better, the 'other mind' belongs to the asubjective usness. Subtle and evasive gestures which lovers exchange are not communicative movements of an established game. Yet they are full of meaning. They suggest a belonging together, that is, an interactive belonging to a collective experience in which the boundary between two subjects is dissolved.

Instead of going into the deconstruction of traditional dichotomies, let us begin directly with something that is as neutral as possible with respect to the private-public (internal-external) and other such dichotomies and which, as much as possible, lies beyond the scope of every regular theoretical attitude. Let us say that the human experience originally lacks structure, that is, it is originally *aconceptual* in the sense which has been presented and discussed in the earlier chapters. Such structureless experience cannot be grasped comprehensively by any single conceptual system alone. It is this kind of experience from which dichotomies may eventually arise with the help of *articulation and repetition processes* (see also Chapter 2 and Chapter 6). This articulation happens in parallel, such that the emergence of a dichotomy always requires the emergence of both of the two aspects of the dichotomy, and the aspects always remain partly entangled with each other. Only after the original aconceptual experience has been organized by dichotomies, will the theoretical attitude have a field which it can utilize. But, we must be able to *speak* of the experience also when it is in its neutral, aconceptual phase, and this puts special demands on the language in which it is attempted. In order to avoid such difficulties which Wittgenstein's work encountered (unwitting theoreticalness; ordinariness which is corrupted by dichotomies; bias toward the public, external and rational; negligence of the aconceptual experience; commitment to subject metaphysics; commitment to the metaphysics of ordinariness and usefulness), let us dispense with such traditional theoretical dichotomies as that of the private and the public, and begin directly with something pretheoretical, namely with *uniqueness*.

The unique is not something that is private or internal but, rather, something irreversible, originally irrepeatable and indeterminate (see Pylkkö, 1995a; see also Chapter 8). Thus it cannot be copied or translated. What is originally unique can become less unique and more determined by being repeated and structured. For example, by adding up single quantum phenomena by repetition, the uniqueness is gradually reduced into a statistical regularity, though the quantum effect is never reduced exactly to zero. In other words, the statistical law tries to reduce the uniqueness to the minimum by repeating single unique phenomena. Analogously, repetition provided by the training cycles may stabilize the weight values of a neural network to a harmonious state. The ground of commonality in language is repetition, and publicity and externality, as well as privacy and internality, arise from experiential repetition, whereas repetition cannot be said to result only from publicity and externality (or from privacy or internality). Clearly, *repetition* cannot be a purely theoretical or conceptual notion. Repetition and habituation are ways to control and repress the original indeterminacy and intensity of experience (cf. Chapter 1 and Chapter 3). Because indeterminacy may be genuinely aconceptual, and we sometimes experience its intensity as threatening, even horrifying, habituation provides us with a method to domesticate the threat.

Because we have access to the unique and indeterminate, *pure* privacy (and publicity) and internality (and externality) of experience are not really possible. What appears to us as public remains always partly colored by privacy; and what appears to us as external remains always partly entangled with internality. This is so because what is experientially unique, due to its indeterminacy, destroys the borderline which allegedly separates the public from the private, and the external from the internal. In other words, indeterminacy saturates our experience with holism. Thus Wittgenstein's argument against privacy doesn't apply directly to uniqueness.

What is holistic doesn't have composite parts or constituents. Especially, language as aconceptual experience has no constituents, and, in general, holistic experience cannot be explained adequately as consisting of systems which consist of subsystems, such that the behavior of a system could be explained comprehensively in terms of the behavior of its alleged subsystems. Therefore, a borderline is able to separate neither subsystems from each other nor a system from its alleged environment, and there is no way to tell strictly what is external with respect to a given system, be it a brain, language or mind. Separate individual minds, if there were such, would never be really unique because what is unique can never be contained inside the boundaries of a separate individual. Here the word *individual* is used in a sense which covers (or, better, reinterprets) also the standard logical and grammatical use. The unique is perpetually open to influence and is perpetually influenced by the environment with which it is entangled, but the influence cannot be fully conceptualized. For example, it is not mediated by a causal channel which can be cut into definite causally efficacious units. In order to emerge, logical kind of individuals have to be articulated from the aconceptual experience by reducing their preindividual uniqueness by repetition. Thus individuality, what it takes to be a logical or grammatical individual, or — as we should perhaps say — *surrogate individuals*, as well as subjectivity in general, that is, the conceptual device which makes it possible for us to experience individual entities, is possible only if uniqueness is suppressed. This suppression provides the imperfect ground of commonality which is utilized by the concepts and propositions of intersubjective communication.

Experiential repetition and interpretative interaction

The extreme forms of commonality, such as objectuality, what it takes to be an object, and such objectivity which is required by the theoretical-technological attitude, arise from indeterminate and holistic experience through repetition, for example, through repetitious and stabilized associations. External description often renders the object-forming repetitions as conditionings, but a purely external description, if it were possible in the first place, would never be comprehensive and adequate because it is unable to reach the neutral level of experience. In a neutrally attuned language, we can say that a repetition is caused by experiential interaction in a social setting, and, from the external or theoretical point of view, the repetition appears to us as conditioning. However, to describe repetition purely as conditioning would amount to describing repetition from the point of view of its conceptually structured end product. Here we must be careful with such words as *cause* and *influence*. Experiential action is not *causal* in any theoretical sense (say that of classical physics), because the experience which 'causes' a reaction in an experiential context loses its identity by becoming inseparably entangled with that experience which is 'caused' by it, namely, with that which is traditionally called 'effect.' Therefore, in the experiential realm, we cannot keep the cause and the effect separated and they become intertwined into an indivisible whole, and it is this that we, in our atheoretical language, call *experiential interaction*.

Suitable repetition in experience can bring about the impression that we are surrounded by external objects which maintain their identity over time. Similarly, repetition is able to create the impression that one portion of the mind is organized as a subject which consists of concepts, for example, of the concepts with the help of which we recognize external things and refer to them. The subject is a conceptual totality, the hierarchies and perspectivities of which make it possible for us to organize the flux of our experience into objects. Both subjectivity and objectivity arise in parallel from the aconceptual experience through experiential interaction and repetition. As the articulation has attained the proper level, we experience ourselves as subjects who perceive and think of the world as if it consisted of mind-independent objects.

Both the subject with its concepts, and the objects which the subject represents, are so stable forms of experience that they are able to create the impression that they preserve their identity over time, and they may do this so successfully that we do not hesitate to speak of the *common, external world*. But the world is not out there; neither is it particularly common, at least not up to the level of identity. Strict logical identity is a relation which no experience, due to the holistic nature of experience, can satisfy or attain. In a practical context, it is often quite harmless to refer to some repetitions of our experience as 'identities,' such as 'meaning identities,' 'personal identities' and 'identifications or reidentifications of objects,' and so on. But because experience acknowledges no identities, this concession may, in a philosophical context, prove fatal. Individuals and identities appear to us as real and permanent only so far as the original aconceptuality of the human experience is suppressed, if it is *forgotten* (vergessen), as Heidegger might have put it. Perfect identity would require perfect forgetfulness. Experience is basically unique, and what is unique cannot be exhausted by any sort of identities.

Games and the emergence of subjects

Unique experience is originally, not only aconceptual, but asubjective. It doesn't acknowledge the *subject* of perception, action and thinking, until suitable repetition creates *presubjective experiential centers* within the asubjective experience, and these centers become sufficiently articulated in order to adopt such a controlling attitude towards the rest of experience which characterizes the full presence of the subject. After some self-organization, these centers are able to create the impression that their experience is structured into relatively permanent conceptual hierarchies and perspectivities which include minimally some identity and causality conditions upon which the impression of time and space is founded. The hierarchies and perspectivities of the subject render the things of the world for the reason which makes the world look intelligible. Thus the hierarchies and perspectivities serve as the foundation on which the representations of the subject lie. The presubjective experiential centers emerge gradually from agonistic relations in which they are engaged with other emerging centers. These agonistic relations can be viewed as games, and we may say, in accordance with G.H. Mead, that opponents and partners are the primary objects of our evolving environment (Mead, 1910). In parallel with the articulation of the subject, the subject's environment becomes organized. This is experienced by the emerging subject as the appearance of objects within the environment, other players being, of course, its foremost objects (see Chapter 4 and Chapter 6).

Such hierarchy and perspectivity which is characteristic of the presence of subjectivity arise when some originally presubjective centers of experience become engaged in gamelike situations where they have to react to the challenge which *other* presubjective centers provide. The organization of the subject, when it reacts to the challenge, has nothing 'subjective' in it, if 'subjective' is used in the colloquial sense of the word (say, as the opposite of objectivity, presuming some kind of volatileness or unreliability, and so on). On the contrary, the subject is a conceptual structure which allows us to organize our experience into the internal and external subdepartments, and the organization of the subject is just as permanent and reliable as the world of objects because it is the subject that makes the emergence of objects possible. So, how could the organization of the subject be somehow more volatile than the structure of objects? It cannot be so, because the subject and the object are mutually dependent on each other: no objects without a subject which makes the appearance of objects possible; and no subject without the objects which provide the subject with the world which the subject is supposed to represent with its conceptual structure. For example, emotions are not more subjective than concepts. Therefore, aconceptual experiences are *not* emotions! And if there is occasionally something aconceptual in some emotions, that can happen to some concepts too.

The notion of subject bears a distinctive pre-empirical connotation (for the meaning of the word 'pre-empirical,' see Chapter 2). Though the subject is a conceptual structure which makes the appearance of objects possible, the subject is not, unlike what Kant teaches, literally *a priori*, because the subject itself is a kind of experience. Being a subject is a peculiar kind of experience which conceptualizes and organizes itself, and, due to the moderating effect of the emerging structure, loses its intensity. One consequence of this is that we have, contrary to Kant's view, nonperceptual experiences, and what is even more interesting, some of our nonperceptual experiences are not subjective, that is, they have no conceptual structure.

When the game situations with which an experiential center is engaged gradually evolve and become more complex, the center of experience becomes more structured, complicated and persistent, and, eventually, the center experiences itself as something that is, due to its peculiar perspective, separated from others: It has become a competent participant of social games with a considerable repertoire of gaming skills. This experiential separation from other subjects into which every subject is doomed is experienced with strong nostalgia. It is not the conceptual structure of the subject as such which causes the experience of separation from others. Actually, the subject is well connected to other subjects via concepts. The origin of the nostalgia with which the separation is colored lies in the aconceptual origin of the subject, in the conceptually inaccessible underground from which the subject arises. Due to the imperfect or impure nature of its conceptual structure, the subject cannot feel itself fully satisfied with the regimented and formal connections to other subjects which the concept-based communication provides. The subject becomes indirectly aware of the surrounding local presubjective experiential center and realizes eventually that some of the experiences around its Self, due to their primitive, aconceptual nature, are inaccessible to the subject. They are almost *transcendental* (in the Schopenhauerian sense of the word) to the subject. But the subject experiences also that other subjects, though they are conceptually accessible, are separated from it by the sea of aconceptual experience. Of course, from the point of view of the aconceptual experience, this is no clear-cut separation at all! But for the subject, surrounded by uncontrollable aconceptual experience, it appears as total separation, as if a stormy ocean of aconceptual experience had separated the solitary dwelling place of the subject from other subjects. In this sense, one subjectivity excludes others in a way which deserves to be called transcendental, though, at the same time, the subject as a purely conceptual structure is open to concept-based communication from other subjectivities. But clearly, neither of these transcendentalities (the subject's relative separation from its aconceptual origin; the subject's relative separation from other subjects) makes aconceptual experiential influence impossible. The experiential sphere of a presubjective center is *not* closed to experiences coming from other centers, as long as we do not try to approach other centers only as subjects. In general, asubjective and aconceptual experience is not closed to foreign influence, though foreignness is always quite a relative notion in a context which lacks definite boundaries. Originally all experiences belong together and the partition of experience into subjectivities was never strict and perfect in the first place.

But we can say that the subject is experientially, if not completely separated from aconceptual experience, at least distanced from the most intensive varieties of it, because the conceptual level at which the subject is forced to operate is experientially weak, almost devoid of intensity. Thus the subject lives in an incorrigible and hopeless state of perpetual nostalgia: the subject is an island embedded in the ocean of aconceptuality which remains hostile and dangerous and with which the subject never really becomes familiar. The only channel to others which the subject recognizes at the representative level is that of the concept-based communication, but, at the same time, the subject realizes that the communicative channel is experientially weak. It may also notice that it is only the experiential center as a whole, not the subject alone, that is able to recognize other than purely conceptually organized influences moving to and from other centers. The subject which sticks to its representations is able to notice anything other than conceptual influences only indirectly, for example, when its own conceptual organization occasionally fails or breaks down.

The degree of separation from aconceptual experience which a subject-like center is able to establish, even when it is almost transcendental, remains always imperfect. This is often experienced as uneasiness, embarrassment

and anxiety. And when the subject is occasionally forced to face the aconceptuality of its own origin, the encounter may be experienced as pure dread.
Because the subject is always partly entangled with its low aconceptual
origin, it is misleading to refer to experiential centrality with such theoretical
notions as "personal identity" or "identity-preserving subject" even when the
centerization has attained the level of seemingly perfect rationality, autonomy
and health. The aconceptual experience is perpetually changing, and its
holistic flux, including its most permanent part, the subject, cannot be captured by identities, not even by self-identities. It varies with respect to *all*
contexts.

The interaction between the subject — or perhaps we should call this
kind of weak subject only a *surrogate subject* — and the aconceptual makes it
impossible for us to equate the human mind with consciousness. One pitfall of
Wittgenstein's notion of language game is that, in spite of its behavioristic
background, the final conception of gaming rests too heavily on the notion of
a rational and conscious subject, and is, therefore, unable to illuminate how
the subject-object boundary is actually articulated. This is seen already in
Wittgenstein's Cartesian definition of "privacy" as something which cannot
be doubted (see, for example, Section 246, Wittgenstein, 1953/1974). Unlike
what Wittgenstein claims (for example, in Section 288), it sometimes makes
good sense to say that I doubt whether what I am experiencing is pain or
pleasure. Therefore, I may make good sense by saying about myself that I am
doubting whether I am actually in pain. For example, if it were nonsensical to
say that "he is deeply in love but he doesn't yet know it," then a great deal of
our folklore, lyrical poetry, novels, drama, opera and popular songs would be
nonsensical too. They are not. Different regions of our experience do not
always communicate well with each other. Actually, difficulties of communication, even within 'one' mind, can be serious and attain the degree of
transcendentality.

Of course, the above sketched way of doubting one's own experiences is
not really an epistemic attitude of a conscious subject. Rather, it is doubt
which precedes the emergence of genuine subjectivity and originates from a
peculiar, superposed kind of experience. In other words, we can be in an
ambiguous state of mind in which several, mutually incompatible experiences
are simultaneously activated. But there are limits for asubjective doubting
too. When we are experiencing something intensively, even when our field of
experience is superpositionally attuned, we can hardly doubt that what we are

experiencing is intensive, though there may be doubts about what it is that we are experiencing and how to describe and classify it. Typically, when a person experiences for the first time that which is, in the Western psychiatric termi- nology, called "panic attacks" (of the assumed neural basis of which, see Thompson, 1985, pp. 105-108), he may be completely unable to understand and describe what he is experiencing. Yet, he is hardly able to doubt the intensity of the experience.

Language as aconceptual experience

Language is, first of all, aconceptual experience which, in certain social and historical contexts, may appear to us as a medium of communication (for more about these circumstances, see Chapter 8). The view of language as communication, that is, as transportation of ideas, concepts or propositions from one subject to another, is a Western, culturally specific theory or myth which is held for obvious social and political reasons. We may, of course, choose to shape language as much as possible in a particular direction, for example, in the direction where it begins to resemble a communicative medium. Western academic institutions have done this kind of regimentation for more than two millennia. The result is not necessarily a perversion of language, but it is a fallacy, to say the least, to present language solely, or primarily, as a communicative medium with a conceptual structure. What logicians and grammarians have studied is not language itself but that portion of language which has resulted from the two millennia of academic reifica- tion, formalization and purification. Therefore, we may say that logicians and grammarians first designed the very structure which they later pretended to have found and which they now are studying, as if the structure had been there already before and independently of the influence of their work.

Language is experience and speech is experiential influence. When I speak, something happens in that region of the experiential field which is conventionally called 'my subjective experience,' but which should be called an 'experiential center,' and that something tends to spread, not only within my subjective experience, but also to and in 'other minds' and other subjects. Western folk psychology tends to equate the mind and the subject, but it would be better to say that the influence spreads from an experiential center to another within a collective experiential field. The human mind is more than just the subject, and the subject's control over the rest of the mind is not perfect. Of course, it would betray the whole view to assume that the experiential influence is purely causal in some classical sense. Causal effects work in a world which is already divided into separable objects or individuals. A purely causal relation is an impossibility, analogous with the impossibility of pure externality.

There is also language influence which fluctuates only between pre-subjective experiential centers, without reaching the subject and its concepts. But, on the other hand, there exists conceptual exchange between subjects which deserves to be called "communication." In communication, the subjective aspect of an experiential center attempts to exchange ideas with the subjective aspects of other experiential centers. But we cannot guarantee that the experiential and aconceptual language influence among experiential centers, even within allegedly 'one' language game, preserves any kind of persistent meaning similarities, let alone meaning identities. Thus the influence remains always partly unpredictable and uncontrollable, evading all systematic approximations. Actually, the meaning field itself may already be inconsistent or superposed, and, therefore, it may lack classical units and boundaries, including the boundaries of persons and games. Human experience is originally an indivisible collective whole into which local experiential centers gradually appear through self-organization in game situations. The centers, after their articulation in agonistic confrontation with other centers, also remain floating on the sea of aconceptual collective experience from which they emerge as perpetually changing perspectivities and hierarchies whose fictitious boundaries fluctuate chaotically from moment to another. Therefore, even the most well-articulated conceptual exchange between subjects remains partly entangled with its low aconceptual origin, frustrating and distorting the ideal of perfect communication.

Wittgenstein overestimates our possibility of establishing meaning-preserving communication channels in language games. Though social pressure stabilizes experience and shapes it into objective-looking form, the pressure is unable to regiment all of the varieties of language experience. In addition, nothing guarantees that games themselves would not change chaotically or uncontrollably, that is, change into other games or stop being games altogether. Therefore, the shift from the private mind to social action is no salvation as such. Similarly, Wittgenstein never seriously calls into question the speaker's ability to remain identical with himself over time, or his ability to determine in which game he is participating. Why is a language game, that is, the public control of meaning, able to provide the player and his meanings with such a degree of stability that his identity would be preserved and the rules of language established and maintained? What is it that makes two minds so much more powerful than one mind? Or alternatively, what is it that makes one mind's game with nature so much more powerful than the mind's game with itself.

Wittgenstein tried to answer these questions by switching the focus of discussion from meaning entities to game entities. But doesn't the same or similar problem of identity and stability arise with games as well: how do we know that, within a speech community, we are playing one and the *same* game at different moments, or one and the same game as our alleged partners and opponents? And if we disagree as to what the rules of the game are, that is, what the identity of the game actually is, who settles the issue? Also within one speech community, meanings can shift and become fluid to such an extent that the players do not share a common view of which game they are playing. This happens frequently, for example, in political discourses. People *seem* to be participating in one and the same language game, but the experiences which they associate to their apparently common expressions may vary quite uncontrollably, and it may be a matter of utter political controversy which are actually the rules of the game. Now, a Wittgensteinian may protest by saying that this is exactly the reason why meanings must not be seen to rest on experiences: 'If a speaker relies only on his experience, language and meaning will vary uncontrollably.' The anti-Wittgensteinian experientialist might answer: 'Well, what else except experience could connect the speaker's mind with language games? If experience is unreliable, then language and meanings are that too.' It is far from clear that public action alone is able to make meanings converge, unless we isolate them from the realm of experiences. For example, two governments, which are engaged in one and allegedly the same conflict, may not be able to find convergence of meaning in their conversations. Should we say that because there is no convergence, say in the form of shared rules, there is no meaning either? No, this would be an overreaction which would almost completely wipe meanings out of the world. Meanings are not the same as ideally shared and happily converging meanings.

In short, the Wittgensteinian speech community remains too classical, and it relies too uncritically on its own perseverance and identity. The

Wittgensteinian community is divided into identity-preserving speaker individuals who participate in nicely identifiable and separable language games. But this is all too nice and well-behaving in order to characterize the human experience with language in its full variety, flux and indivisibility. It is an inalienable feature of the human condition that we do speak meaningfully also when we fail to recognize which game we are playing and what we actually mean. Even when we know that we are breaking the rules and we are unable to identify the objects which we are speaking about, we are still moving within the sphere of language. Though the objects which are handled by the language games of the Wittgensteinian world may be said to arise within a game, and therefore the objects can be said to be game-relative, they still do often arise and, as they arise, they preserve their identity as long as the game is played. Thus, says the Wittgensteinian, there is no meaning without language-relative objects. But this, too, is an overly rigid and optimistic attitude which would prevent us from speaking, among other things, of the conditions in which objects are formed.

Language influence is mostly intercentral (between experiential centers, but not public!) experiential action which spreads within the sphere of collective aconceptual human experience. Often the result of the influence, say speech understanding, resembles more recreation and interpretation than communication. Sometimes it seems to collapse into an arbitrary misreading which we classify easily as 'misunderstanding,' but this shouldn't prevent us from noticing that arbitrary interpretations also belong to our language. Even experience which is uncommunicable and remains untranslatable may belong to the language. That kind of language may lack the structure which a rule-governed activity would establish. Wittgenstein may have been on the right track in insisting that it is experience which endangers the success of communication in language. But he failed to appreciate that the collapses and errors of communication don't push the speaker out of language, and that meaningfulness is not limited to the communicatively correct and successful situations. Wittgenstein was obsessed with efficacy, success and clarity, to get things done properly, as Brian McGuinnes suggests, referring to the lucrative business background of the Wittgenstein family (McGuinness, 1988, p. 8).

Contrary to the collective and asubjective view, the metaphysics of subjectivity sees language as a system of rational and translatable communication. And indeed, there happens exchange between subjects of experience which may attain the permanency of communication. But if we limit our view of language to the communicative aspect of language, it will be hard to explain what meaning change, indeterminacy, inseparability, locality and temporariness are. For example, the proper understanding of the language of poetry would be precluded. As Arthur Rimbaud put it once: "I witness the birth of my thought" (1871/1957) ("... j'assiste à l'éclosion de ma pensée...", Rimbaud, 1871/1991). He meant that the provenance of verbal creativity doesn't lie within the jurisdiction of the subject and his consciousness. The subject witnesses the happy accidents of the creative mind only as a by-stander. How new verbal ideas appear in the vast and collective human experience is something that goes beyond the control of the subject and its intentions.

As a neural activity, language dwells, not only in 'one' human brain, but in a network of brains which spreads out both spatially and temporally beyond the boundaries of any single brain. Thus, the neural perspective to experience should not try to translate experiential interaction into some kind of common neural code. That would be the neural correlate of correctness and communicative success. Also the neural world consists of local cultures which do not share a common universal code of communication with one another. And just as the boundaries between experiential centers are conventional and, in practice, always inseparably enmeshed, so are those between human brains. The asubjective collective experience, including language experience, can be divided into units which we call "subjects" according to different culturally determined conventions just as the network of brains can be divided into relatively separate individual "central nervous systems" according to different practical conventions, including many academic and other theoretical conventions. But experiential influence, moving both between cultures and between experiential centers, as well as within 'one' center and its brain, is holisticly enmeshed, unpredictable and untranslatable, and requires always a creative interpretative amplification in order to retain its intensity.

Naming indeterminacies

Most theories of naming are conceptualizations of the name-named relation, such that both the name and what is named are separate and nicely individuated classical objects. In addition, whatever it is that connects the name and the named, it is thought to be a mechanism which consists of separate components. In this regard Wittgenstein makes no exception. Wittgenstein's attempts to escape the metaphysics of the theoretical attitude was not completely successful because his view of naming is purely classical: what is named are primarily hammers and apples, that is, classical separable things which can be picked out from a shelf, the rest being secondary. Also Wittgenstein's games are basically classically individualized entities, though occasionally with fuzzy boundaries. But fuzzy objects comprise a conservative extension of the metaphysics of classical objects. In the less fortunate realm of human experience we have to be able to speak of such fugitive phenomena as the passion of erotic love, mythical creatures by which we are possessed and superposed electrons of the quantum-theoretical two-path experiment (for the latter, see Albert, 1992), just to mention some troublesome examples, and, in these examples, hammers and apples are of no, or only of little, help. In addition, some non-Western languages are able to express experiences which are not closely related to the public sphere of human action and which are, therefore, impossible to understand in the light of Wittgenstein's language game metaphor. We are not supposing here that 'expressing' presupposes a subject that expresses itself. Rather, it is the language which expresses itself. Anyway, such expressions are related to the various apersonal modes of being which man can assume (see Chapter 8).

A theorist of naming who sees naming as a mechanism which connects a thing-like name, like the name 'Ann' as a syntactic entity, to a thing, like Ann as a seemingly well defined individual, is like a person who believes that his or her erotic love is caused by or directed to the entity whom he or she loves. But actually, thinking of how names work should be more like thinking of how suppressed childhood memories are begotten: we must begin with the question of what there actually is to be remembered (and named) in these cases. Suppressed memories are creatures which are often invoked by our present conflicts; the beloved 'one' is to some extent a creation of our own imagination which is enhanced, excited and obscured by our passions; a mythical or religious idol which a person imitates to the extent that he becomes possessed by it cannot be easily separated from the person himself, assuming that there was such a thing as a person to begin with; the electron is a phantom of our theoretical cum observational framework; prepersonal and preontological non-Western expressions express (or — assuming that we want to hide the unavoidable redundancy of the preceding words — belong to) collective experiences which precede the appearance of persons and things; and, eventually, external things are fictitious projections of our neural processes, and their naming is a much more difficult problem than what the classical thing-based view of naming assumes. And all of these experiences must be named and spoken of.

Yet they cannot be completely conceptualized, and no *theory* of naming is able to explain how such indeterminacies as love or electrons are named (see Pylkkö, 1995a; Pylkkö, 1996a; Pylkkö, 1996b). This is so because every conceptualization and theory rests on the assumption that both the name (language) and what is named (objects of the reality or the model of the language) consist of things which can be kept clearly separate. (With the exception, of course, that sometimes the syntactic entities of a language are chosen to comprise the reality or the model of the very language itself. But also in this case the language as syntax consists of nicely separable objects, and the objects of the model of which the syntactic objects speaks about and the syntax itself are conceptually clearly separable issues.) But such a separability is a theoretical luxury which the holistic chaos of the human experience cannot afford. Neither are Wittgenstein's language games able to help us here. The meaning of the Finnish expression *ollaan* (see Chapter 8) cannot be reduced to rule-governed action because the action-based publicity of language games is bound to marginalize or even destroy the subtle aconceptuality of the experience which has found its expression in the word *ollaan*, or, better, to which the expression *ollaan* belongs. The meaning of the word is simply not only the use of the word in some action-related and rule-governed social contexts; rather, *ollaan* represents an apersonal and preontological mode of the human way of being which precedes the emergence of rule-following agents. As long as our conception of games has no access to this kind of ontologically nihilistic mode of being, it will be unable to deal with words like *ollaan*.

Words are experiences which often carry with them a conceptual aspect, too. It is this thin layer of conceptualized meaning which is utilized in the intersubjective and intercultural communication. But words carry also associations which never become fully conscious and which, even if they are fully conscious, may be conceptually inaccessible. The conceptual aspect of a word is transcendentally distanced, though not perfectly separated, from the aconceptual origin of the word. This means that words as conceptual tools of representation are unable to exhaust their own aconceptual meaning. Yet the aconceptual aspect of language is able to influence the conceptual one indirectly, that is, in a way which doesn't go through the conceptual channel and may remain unconscious too. At the same time, words influence each other. Also this influence happens partly conceptually, that is, concepts change other concepts. But, in addition, there exists a word-to-word influence which is not conceptual. Just as the aconceptual aspect of a word is able to feed, vitalize, attract, distract and tease the conceptual one indirectly without the help of representations, words influence each other through aconceptual influences which remain uncontrollable by all rational means.

Assuming that we decide to violate Wittgenstein's frequent suggestion that language games are neither theories nor theoretical entities, we may be inclined to say that quantum physicists play a language game of their own in which such words as *electron* and *spin* are used, and this game doesn't satisfy the individuation and separation conditions of the classical physics and classical logic. But this view only transforms the problem into a new philosophical and theoretical terminology which doesn't tell us how the quantum-theoretical language game and the language game of classical physics are to be related. Can one play both games simultaneously, or not? How much complementarity and contradictoriness can there be between two language games? In order to solve these questions, a genuinely aconceptual conception of language is needed (see Pylkkö, 1996b).

Neither can any regular neural or connectionist theory explain how names work. But, must neural explanations of the naming association be based on the naiveté of the standard theoretical and conceptual attitude? And, in general, is the scientific attitude necessarily tied to externalism, objectivism and classical rules of individuation? After all, neurons may not be so external and thing-like as first meets the eye.

Experience and neural association

We must be careful with such words as *brain, neuron* or *association* because in regular use they are so openly external, nicely separable and mechanistic notions. And even if we acknowledge their external, mechanical and separable nature, it would be desirable if we could explain how and why this kind of mechanical thinking arose. For example, Yrjö Reenpää (1959) would have seen the recent neuroscience as a branch of Western metaphysics which has reached the stage of quantitative exactness. Similarly, Bohr would have said that neural events are complementary to microphysical events (see Bohr, 1933). It is interesting to notice that Bohr's notion of *complementarity* bears a clear atheoretical connotation. It is not a term of the quantum theory proper, let alone classical physics or common sense physics. It is a new atheoretical notion with the help of which Bohr tries to cast some light upon the relations between different theories. We may have to concede that, in some field of inquiry, there appears a set of consistent theories which are mutually incompatible but all of which are needed in order to form a comprehensive picture of the phenomena of the field. Therefore, if *language game* is understood as a notion which itself is not theoretical, but can be used to study the properties and relations between some theories, then *language game* resembles Bohr's notion of *complementarity*, at least as regards the atheoreticity. Perhaps the relationship between different language games is sometimes that of complementarity (or transcendentality or untranslatability).

According to Bohr, purely classical thinking habits, which require that the phenomena which we observe must be strictly separable and that the observer must be an impartial bystander, have proved to be inadequate if they are applied to biological phenomena. Bohr (1933) reminds us of the fact that living organisms cannot always be observed without interfering with their life, tampering their reactions, and sometimes this act of interference means that we have to kill the organism in order to study it. In addition, we know that a living nervous system needs a perpetual connection, not only to the rest of the body, but to the so-called environment too. It needs these connections, say neuroendocrinological connections, in order to be a genuine organ with a mature structure and full-scale abilities. Because of perpetual fluctuations and ambiguities, the determination of the boundaries of the nervous system is a matter of convention and convenience, serving the interests of academic and theoretical classifications, not necessarily the interests of a tenable view of what brains are (see also Dewey, 1925, p. 230).

But, if fixing the brain-nonbrain boundary is often a matter of convention, and the boundary, like the boundary between the macrophysical and microphysical levels, can be drawn practically anywhere in the universe, also the boundary of representation and what is represented must be conventional. Therefore, the prospects of scientific objectivity and realism which require the separability of representation and what is represented are not particularly promising. For example, if it is not possible to give an adequate explanation of the retina without quantum-theoretical notions, then the strict classical separation of the brain and non-brain isn't possible any more. If the retina is sensitive to single photons, as has been suggested (Baylor, Lamb & Yau, 1979), all of the inseparable and indeterminate properties of photons (of the nonclassical properties of photons, see Chapter 2) are passed from the quantum theory down to the study of the retina, and, eventually, it is not possible to give a purely classical description of the human perception and behavior any more. The cell membrane and the synaptic cleft of the neuron do not comprise a serious candidate condition for the individuation of neurons, especially if the membrane and the cleft themselves are not classical systems but must be described in some holistic or inseparable terms. It is not right to say that a neuron consists *only* of what goes on within its cell membrane. Like the neuron, we are, and our experience is, strictly speaking everywhere.

Thus, we are not only inside of our neural nets, assuming that saying that would make sense in the first place. We must admit that when we look at a person or landscape we literally see also something of ourselves. Contrary to the kind of holism which was just sketched, the received view of naming and communication is intended to satisfy the classical individuation and separability conditions. Of course, such presuppositions are often applied to the regular individuation of neurons, neural nets and brains too. Thus a neural perspective to experience complies with the view of experience as aconceptual, irreversible and irrepeatable phenomenon only if the perspective doesn't rest on such classical presuppositions. If the classical presuppositions are abandoned, nothing in the brain can be said to return literally to a previous state, and every brain and brain event is a unique phenomenon. Therefore, the uniqueness of experience and the uniqueness of neural phenomena can be made to comply with one another, and the respective discourses are able to attain, at least to some extent, a philosophical agreement. (For more about the relations of different discourses, see Chapter 1.) This is not to deny that repetition, conditioning and stabilized associations create experiential patterns and habits, and some of the patterns and habits can be extremely persistent, rigid and even boring. But nonetheless, experiential repetitions, including the most rigid ones, are not based on strict identity, and therefore stabilized associations and habits also rest on genuine experiential aconceptuality and neural indeterminacy.

Both experiential and neural phenomena are originally unique and irreversible, and it is relative repetition which helps the commonality to emerge from the original uniqueness and irreversibility. Only purely classical systems, if there were such, would be purely common (that is, strictly not unique). In the human experience, it is uniqueness which is primary, and commonality, objects and entities are *derived* from originally unique phenomena by lessening their uniqueness by repetition, such that the lessening never actually reaches zero. Now, from the neural point of view, assuming that it is not tied to naive externalism and classical conditions of separability, it is easy to understand what we mean by uniqueness of experience: just as every neural phenomenon is unique, every experiential phenomenon is unique, and commonality arises from uniqueness by repetition and habituation. Wittgenstein's ejaculation (Section 110, Wittgenstein, 1953/1974) which condemns experiential uniqueness as superstition, is hasty. This hastiness may have been the main reason which prevented him from understanding how language games arise, evolve, merge and diverge. In order to handle these questions, one must have access to aconceptuality. Otherwise such experiential issues as *power, community* and *nationality* have to be handled purely from a classical, externalist and relational point of view.

Wittgenstein's hostility toward experience originates from his obvious behavioristic tendencies. He seems to admit that we have experiences, but he was not willing to give them a vital role in the description of meaning. Every view which associates meaning purely to public activities and separates meaning too sharply from human experience is somewhat behavioristic. In Wittgenstein's meaning behaviorism, the mitigation of experience borders occasionally on suppressive degradation. His urge to secure a public arena for meanings and his eagerness to regiment experiential language in order to make language look like a communicative medium is not only a metaphysical enterprise, but almost a metaphysical obsession.

Nationality as asubjective experience

Also national and ethnic language experience is pervaded by unique meanings. But here, too, uniqueness and individuality are mutually complementary notions, and just like uniqueness cannot really be attributed to a person as a single individual or subject, it cannot be attributed to a local community, clan, tribe or nation as a definite set of individuals. Yet man's interaction with the cultural and natural environment results often in a unique and aconceptual experience, the experience of native language, which no translation can mediate comprehensively into another language. Nationality, including linguistic nationality, is experienced as nearness of meaning which precedes all conceptualizations and the emergence of subjectivity. Thus if there is something unique in personal style, it is not a result of personal achievement but an almost unwitting repercussion from the asubjective national experience (cf. von Humboldt, 1836/1974, for example, pp. 20; 40-43; 143). Language, not the subject, creates poems.

The linguistic uniqueness of a nation, or any other local community for that matter, can hardly be captured by the limited variability which is provided by the Wittgensteinian language game metaphor. Wittgenstein's language games are played by relatively rational and identity-preserving subjects who deal with classical objects. It is sufficient to think about the lists and examples of primitive language games which Wittgenstein gives to us. The indeterminacies which were discussed above cannot be understood in terms of such games which appear on Wittgenstein's lists. The consequence is that those indeterminacies do not belong to the realm of meaning. If the word 'object' (or 'individual') is used in the sense which refers to something that preserves its identity and can be reindividuated, then, obviously, the origin of uniqueness doesn't lie in the objectuality or individuality, or in any combinations of objects and individuals. Therefore, the games which rational subjects play with classical objects and other subjects, are unable to produce anything genuinely unique either, that is, anything genuinely irrepeatable and untranslatable. In addition, Wittgenstein's examples indicate that his idea of the language game was intended to be a *universal* idea, almost an *a priori* notion, and local variation was supposed to be derived as instantiations from the underlying universal pattern. In other words, action-based rationality is something that allegedly reigns everywhere and in all times among humans and, regardless of local cultural variation, provides the foundation for the possibility of correctness and error and, therefore, of meaningfulness, too. This view realizes, unwittingly or secretly, a unifying agenda. Unruly meaning variation annoys Wittgenstein and he reacts with vehement disciplinary measures.

But is the emergence of subjectivity a universal phenomenon? Or in the Wittgensteinian language, is language, in every situation and every cultural context, game-like public action which is governed by rules? Does the subject-object articulation happen along lines which are interculturally commensurable and basically independent of local variation? Is the rationality of gaming a universal property of man everywhere and in all times, without which no language can arise? One could suggest that the aconceptual ground of language, say its national or local dimension, is indeed unique and untranslatable, but the conceptual layer (including the kind of rationality which is encoded into language games) which is controlled by the subject is universal and interculturally translatable and communicable. For example, if language is reducible to such elementary and external language games which Wittgenstein deals with, then meanings seem to be basically translatable, and translations can approach the intended meaning with desired accuracy. The rest, namely, experience which is not domesticated by public rules, doesn't really belong to language. It suffices to reveal what the proper rules of the underlying elementary language games are, and we have found the basis for intercultural communication. Perhaps the rules are difficult to discern, impossible to learn for an outsider, and perhaps we are unable to describe the rules properly and understand how they works. But still, a pattern of behavior would not constitute a rule if it were in principle untractable, ineffable, unlearnable and untranslatable, that is, incorrigibly unique and irrepeatable.

This suggestion is, however, undermined by a difficulty. It separates too categorically the conceptual layer from the aconceptual experience, and, thus, makes the emergence of conceptuality and subjectivity ultimately incomprehensible. It would make the emergence of rules incomprehensible too. It is more plausible that the conceptual layer remains always partly entangled with the aconceptual experience, and, therefore, a unique and untranslatable ingredient remains always effective within the so-called conceptual realm too. This comprises a problem area with which Wittgenstein is unable to deal. Individuality, rationality, and subjectivity (in the sense of what it takes to be a conceptually organized subject), as we are familiar with them, are local Western notions which, regardless of their wide applicability, may be experientially alien to many non-Western cultures and thus carry a hidden streak of intolerance (cf. Chapter 1). This holds also for Wittgenstein's conception of the primacy of the goal-directed rationality of action. Thus these notions (action, rationality, subject, individuality, democracy, and so on) can be used to justify the global policy of unification which the West and its technology realizes with no constraint. In addition, the Western conceptuality, rationality and subjectivity cannot be separated from the Western academic tradition of grammatical and logical studies, and these studies are ineradicably intertwined with the Western technology and science and with the Western economic, religious, political and social organizations. It is implausible that any purely universal gist can ever be distilled from the experience which is to such an extent marked by local and culturally specific ideas. In other words, it is not possible to subtract all Western and Indo-European ingredients from the prevailing notions of conceptuality, rationality and subjectivity without destroying them. Not even the 'purest' mathematical, let alone logical and grammatical, notions, including the notion of language game, are fully universal. They are products of a language-dependent local Western culture. Neither the mind with its aconceptual origins and resources nor biological brains with their unique, irreversible and irrepeatable events which realize the mind can bring about anything so perfectly pure that it would be independent of the local, natural as well as cultural, environment.

In this light, the scientific study of non-Western experience appears almost as a paradox or absurdity. For example, cultural experience which itself didn't produce academic logic, grammar, science and rational philosophy cannot really be explained in terms of these notions without destroying its original aconceptual nature. Also the notion of language game is basically a ratio-centered Western notion, the application of which to non-Western cultures should be carried out with a special vigilance. Our observations, especially scientific observations, are shaped by our theoretical and conceptual expectations to such an extent that we may even fail to observe the presence of non-Western experience in us and in our environment, and, therefore, we tend bluntly to deny its existence. This danger is particularly vital with such aconceptual experience which lacks the rationality of gaming. Because experience is not the same as perceptual experience, say, the synthesis of perception, as Kant would have said, we have to learn to deal with experiential meanings which arise from the dissolution of contrasts and opposites, even from the dissolution of the whole subject and its games. We may feel the presence of the non-Western experience only indirectly, as failures, perversions and mistakes: the experience evades the conceptual analysis but may surface unpredictably as misbehavior, misunderstanding, madness, aggression, anomaly, anxiety, and so on. It may also surface as the breakdown of the rules of a language game. Because of the evasive and subtle nature of the non-Western experience, it becomes gradually more and more difficult to address it in the context of the Western human sciences and cultural studies. We must design, not only a philosophy of rule-following, but also that of rule-breaking, that is, we must endeavor to reach the philosophical understanding of means-endlessness and uselessness. It is only by chance, at the moment of failure, embarrassment, shock, dread or intensive surprise, that we may experience the nearness of a non-Western experience. But as soon as we try to conceptualize and utilize it, it disappears or disguises its meaning again. Therefore, the meaning of a word is also its uselessness.

CHAPTER SIX

Gaming without subjects

Gaming, hunting, and philosophizing

In his *Treatise of Human Nature*, (1739-40/1987, Book II, Part III, Section 10, pp. 451-454), David Hume compares the pleasure of philosophizing with that of gaming and hunting and finds some similarities. The pleasure of gaming and hunting consists of the action of the mind and body, of the engagement of attention and of the overcoming of difficulties and uncertainties. What is easy and obvious is never valued, obstacles are overcome only by action, and, in the games of knowledge, too, it is passion that is needed to motivate action. As in all games, in the games of thinking too, reason alone is unable to move us.

If *hunting* is here used in the regular meaning which relates it to human outdoor activities, and not merely to instinct-driven preying, hunting obviously requires decision making, problem solving, planning, and, eventually, the ability to evaluate alternatives and to choose a good one. Similarly, *gaming*, in its regular sense, is analyzed in terms of rules, movements, strategies, utilities, payoffs, and so on. In all usual treatments, the analysis of both hunting and gaming presupposes that there is a *unit* of decision making which is said to be responsible for the final behavior, and the unit is usually thought to be the hunter or the player himself, that is, the conscious and rational subject himself.

But now Hume's thinking, or any thinking along the Humean line, has to face the following difficulty: No intentional, conscious and consistent subject as a central unit of decision-making is theoretically available within the Humean sphere of notions (see especially, Book I, Part IV, Section VI, *Of Personal Identity*, pp. 251-263). Hume's view was that speaking of players and hunters, as rational subjects or Selves, begs the question of what playing and gaming is because such notions introduce an explanatorily empty *homunculus* into the theory. The *homunculus* is usually introduced as an identity-preserving subject, as the ultimate site of decision and choice, from which action is generated and which defines the person's identity. Hume attacks all such theories which posit an identity-preserving Self and suggest that the Self is able to reify the perpetually changing flow of impressions and ideas into permanent structures. But more interestingly perhaps, the whole idea of a permanent Self is, within Hume's sphere of ideas, impossible already for the plain reason that the subject as a decider, as a reasoner who calculates the proper choice, couldn't affect the action and behavior anyway, because, according to Hume, reason is impotent as the mover of man and unable to initiate action (see Book II, Part III, Sections I -IV, especially Section III, *Of the influencing motives of the will*, but see also Book III, Part I, Section I, pp. 456-470).

But a rational *homunculus* which moves itself with the power of reason is how common sense wants to see man and, perhaps, itself. Common sense says that decision making presupposes that someone intends to reach a goal, and whoever wants to be taken as an intentional subject must maintain this intention with considerable persistence and consistence. Folk psychology and many theoretical refinements which take folk psychology for granted assume that the subject must be conscious, capable of making the required reasonings, comparisons, evaluations and calculations, and that the subject, in order to be a subject, must aim at reaching a goal, say, an advantage in a game situation, with considerable perseverance. But, if we ask what the subject actually is, the answer is usually that the subject is exactly that which intends, is conscious, evaluates alternatives, and so on, and this is not a satisfactory response. Besides the intention, consciousness and evaluation, is there someone, something that we tend to call the *Self*, who intends, is conscious and evaluates? And if there isn't, can we say that it is the intention that intends something, consciousness that is conscious of something and evaluation that values something, and so on? The young Hume renounced all such folk-psychological and metaphysical speculations which posit an intentional, identity-preserving, conscious and consistent subject, and he did that exactly in order to break the aforementioned circle of explanation which resorts to an empty *homunculus*. But then, who or what is doing the gaming or hunting, or philosophizing for that matter? Or, is it the question itself, say, its grammatical form, which enforces the shape of a *homunculus* upon our thinking and thus leads us astray?

The standard answer is, of course, that Hume's inability to explain intentional human action is one of the main reasons why Hume was wrong with his skeptical views as regards the existence of the Self. The Self, says the anti-Humean, is something that we have to assume and with which we have to begin our thinking, even if we don't actually know what it is. In particular, the Self, or the identity-preserving, conscious and consistent subject, who is capable of self-reflection, is needed to keep Passions under the control of Reason. Reason is the main source or faculty to which a responsible person must resort in order to be able to direct his behavior toward an acceptable goal. Passions are not always consistent or acceptable. A person whose life is governed by passions is not really a person at all, that is, he is not *one*, and his experiences diverge and decline to assume a consistent form.

But let us take the young Hume seriously and ask: Is there any line of thinking of gaming and hunting, and other similar human activities, without assuming that the activities are controlled by a classical rational, intentional and conscious subject? Doesn't the suggestion that it is primarily reason that moves us, sound implausible because reason is, indeed, too indifferent, if not impotent? Reason and its representations, as they are usually presented, are empty, void of pain and pleasure, horror and love. Take any action whatsoever, and a good reason, or a whole chain of reasons, for it or its negation can always be found. For example, reasoning is not afraid of anything and doesn't care about itself, not even about its own annihilation or survival. How could anything so indifferent move us to action or impose a choice upon us?

We have assumed that the young Hume was really the anti-realist skeptic, and not the intentionalist, representationalist or realist as some recent revisionists have envisioned him (for references concerning the new Hume interpretations, see Capaldi, King and Livingston, 1991). Therefore, the young Hume, and all Young-Humeans so to speak, are exposed to the problem of the absence of subject which was sketched above. For them there exists no necessary connection between reasoning and action. This is so because it is the Self that is supposed to constitute the connection, and the Self is not theoretically available for them. The anti-Humean might say that only the Self of which the Humeans are deprived would be able to make the originally indifferent and impotent reasoning *someone's* reasoning, and by that, bring the reasoning into a contact with desire, fear and care. But, is the anti-Humean able to tell us *how* the Self is supposed to do that? Probably not. Usually he just posits the ability, and begins to think in terms of it. But he may also suggest that the Self is something genuinely irreducible, something essentially more than just a subject thinking about itself.

But perhaps the idea of a rational and autonomous Self isn't much more than an unwarranted myth which we conceive in order not to be forced to admit that it is passions that run us. Perhaps the Self is nothing but an artificial and impotent edifice which is scaffolded by the social pressure of conformity, and which is constructed in order to save us from the legion of embarrassments which passions always inflict. We pretend to be rational just in order not to look so ridiculous. Perhaps the Self is exactly the opposite of what it pretends to be: it is not the autonomous and rational initiator of action, but only an extension of others in us, a long-distance monitoring activity which others exercise over us, that is, what others, as subjects, exercise over us as subjects. The Self is the influence which others are able to generate in the allegedly own mind of ours. In order to do that, the subject, and its reason and representations, must be able, minimally, to monitor and inhibit the intensity of passions. But, they don't have to be able to represent, understand or explain passions. They may not be able to *control* them either, not even in cases in which we are seemingly dealing with the reason and representations of highly rational, healthy and decent persons. This is so because there exists a peculiar kind of passion which is experienced as submissiveness to reason and control. Submissiveness to reason and control *is*, indeed, a passion, because reason is actually unable to capitalize on the threat to which it, nevertheless, constantly resorts. Reason is unable to reach a rational control over passions, and, therefore, those who *serve* the reason do not have any rational grounds for their servile attitude. Only if nature and the human mind were rationally explainable, that is, only if they would appear to us as comprehensively intelligible in purely rational terms, it would, indeed, be reasonable to serve reason.

A glimpse at the history of asubjectivism

It is not so surprising, perhaps, that Hume's problem with the subject, or rather with the absence of the subject, reappears with such phenomenalists and anti-realists as Ernst Mach (1897) and Wilhelm Ostwald (1901), but it may be somewhat surprising to note that the problem is central also in the Schopenhauer-Nietzsche tradition. Both Schopenhauer and Nietzsche owed much to Hume, especially as regards what they considered philosophically interesting and problematic. Schopenhauer's Kant critique was, among other things, an attack on Kant's notion of the autonomous subject who deliberates on the alternative ways of action and tries to evaluate them in the light of some abstract moral principles (Schopenhauer, 1819/1969, see especially the Appendix). *Der Wille* was supposed to be all too powerful and unconscious (unbewusste) to be controlled by the good and regimented intentions of the subject. And Nietzsche (1884-8/1967), too, partook in the rebellion against the status of the subject as the sovereign of the human mind. He questioned the autonomy of the rational subject as a site from which behavior is controlled and where permanent concepts are stored for the purpose of representation and communication. In an interesting way, Nietzsche equated the subject as an intentional agent and the subject as a grammatical and logical category, and renounced both views as untenable pro-Indo-European myths.

It seems that Schopenhauer's and Nietzsche's aversion to the autonomy of the subject can be traced, to some extent, back to Hume whom they both admired. But if their Hume-connection can be established, as I believe it can, we can also claim that the recent French debate on the role of the subject in philosophy (for which, see Ferry & Renaut, 1985) is of English, or better, of Scottish, origin. Of course, the modern French anti-humanism does not originate directly from Nietzsche alone, but indirectly from Heidegger too. But again, Heidegger's anti-humanism (1947/1977), that is, his hostility toward the subject-centered Western metaphysics, was partly of Nietzschean origin, and, if we acknowledge the influence of the young Hume's nihilism on Schopenhauer and Nietzsche, we are allowed to conclude that David Hume may be partly responsible for Heidegger's anti-humanism, too, and, therefore, for the surprisingly high degree of popularity which anti-humanism has reached among French philosophers since the 1960's.

Power, democracy, technology

But let us go back to the problem of the subject and illuminate it from a restricted angle, namely, from that of power. Hume's problem with gaming and hunting was that, without access to the intentional subject, one is, or seems to be, unable to explain what gaming and hunting are. Consider the notion of power with respect to this problem. The standard view of power is that it is some kind of dominance or control relation among conscious and rational individuals. If this is so, then we would expect some standard game-theoretical notions and metaphors to help us explicate this view. Most of such studies require a rational subject who participates in the power game. Even such alternative notions of power, like that of Macpherson (1973, pp. 8-12 and 40-52), which define power as 'man's potential of developing his capacities,' define power, nevertheless, in terms of *individual subjects* and their capacities.

But one can approach power also from an *asubjective* point of view, not just as a control relation among rational subjects. For example, Michel Foucault's view of power (1976) which rejects the relational model ("power as legal transaction," as he calls it), tries to question, weaken and even get rid of the notion of an autonomous subject. In accordance with Foucault, we might suggest that power should be seen more like an experiential kind of totality, as a kind of independent energy, which is spreading and fluctuating in the field of collective human experience, than as a relation into which a person becomes engaged when he tries to pursue some selfish goals. Power would consist of experiential, asubjective energy which moves both the master and the slave, regardless of their personal reasons to control and be controlled. Power could dissolve boundaries between discontinuous subjects and enhance the collapse of a subject back to the originally continuous, collective experience which lacks personal boundaries. It seems that this kind of view of power complies also with the Humean view of the mind in which the role of the rational subject as the initiator of action has been reduced to the minimal.

But now, a difficult question arises. How would the asubjectivist ever be able to deal with such a political phenomenon as *democracy*, where the notion of the autonomous subject is traditionally thought to be an ineradicable ingredient? This is a power-related version of Hume's problem with the absence of subject.

It seems that all standard views of democracy ('liberal-democratic theories' as they are sometimes called) require that there are autonomous subjects who evaluate alternative scenarios of action in political choice situations. Even Macpherson says (1973, pp. 54-55) that the democratic theory has been traditionally optimistic in the sense that only such human characteristics which are not destructive and which do not *contradict* one another are accepted as essentially human. And, if by *democracy* we mean such social arrangements which allow us to maximize nondestructive and mutually compatible individual powers, it is still individual subjects and their essentially human capacities that we are speaking of. This makes the notion of democracy, including the so-called 'ethical' version, very problematic indeed, because if the conception of democracy is tied to and depends on the rational and autonomous subject then, obviously, it is implausible that we can ever question and challenge in a democratic way such social and political phenomena which rest on the very notion of the autonomous subject and its rationality.

For example, the nature of modern technology, especially information technology, and the notions of knowledge and progress which are related to it, seem to ascend, to some extent, above the range of issues which an autonomous and rational subject can genuinely address, question and criticize. They seem to remain particularly inaccessible if they are addressed in a democratic or ethical way. This is because the structure of experience which such an enlightened subject is, lies itself in the very heart of the technological attitude, and is, in may ways, inseparably entangled with it. The interface of the Western subject and Western technology consists of the attitude of control, manipulation, reification and maximization which we direct to the objects of nature in order to utilize them in our pursuit of welfare and happiness. A typical characteristic of the interface is its inability to control its own growth. It is this same attitude which we adopt when we try to build a social arrangement which maximizes man's possibilities for personal development. Actually, it is possible that the modern Western information technology is needed to maximize the modern individual's developmental potentials. If the modern Western subject is an experience-shaping conceptual structure which was designed by Western technology (and which itself also utilizes and shapes technology), then it is understandable that regular democratic games (persons, institutions and thinking habits) are not really capable of challenging the powers of technology. Challenging or radically questioning the technological attitude would amount to challenging and questioning the democratic games themselves and, through that, the very roots of democracy, namely, the notion of rational subjectivity. The alliance of technology and democracy is too tightly knit, that is, too strong, to be broken without breaking both of the partners of the alliance simultaneously.

This unsolved problem defuses also Feyerabend's *democratic relativism* (see especially *Notes on relativism*, which is the first essay of *Farewell to Reason*, 1987, pp. 19-89). Feyerabend's thesis *R2* (p. 39) demands that societies which are dedicated to freedom and democracy must treat science as one tradition among many others, without conferring any privilege to scientific truths, and without allowing science and scientists to decide social or political issues outside of scientific communities. The main unaddressed problem with this view is that it is far from obvious that democratic persons, thinking habits and institutions can, even in principle, treat technology and science as one tradition among others, let alone challenge the power of technology and science in any other than a superficial and diluted manner. This is so because, on the one hand, democratic thinking and the related individualistic notion of freedom, which Feyerabend cherishes, and, on the other hand, the modern technological and science-inspired conception of man and man-nature relations, are parallel outgrowths and mutually depending derivations from the very notion of Western subjectivity. Thus, if we expect democratic persons, thinking habits and institutions to question seriously the role of technology in our societies and in the global arena in general, we are, most probably, expecting, not only too much, but also something impossible.

A classical example of the notion of the autonomous subject appears in Kant's essay on Enlightenment and maturity (*An answer to the question: 'What is enlightenment?'*, 1784/1991). The subject is a unit of decision-making which confronts a spectrum of possible alternative ways of action and uses his reason to compute the right choice. Our will is free only when the reason of the subject is able to overcome sensuous desires (see for example, Kant, 1803/1964, p. 12). Kant's categorical imperative is one of the most powerful unifying intellectual inventions of the modern epoch. Its crux is behavioral unification in behalf of cultural integration. Moral goodness is not only thought to be one and the same for all cultures, but no intrinsic mechanism to prevent the growth of goodness is designed in Kant's unwittingly totalitarian vision of the perfect world. Kant's view of man may seem somewhat naive to us today because he equates freedom all too straightforwardly with the capability of reason to exercise control over the rest of the mind. Kant failed to see the possibility that some of our impulses are unconscious and aconceptual, and in this respect he anticipated the hyperintellectualist kind of naiveté which characterizes Husserl's view of man too. Any attitude which tries to establish the control of reason over the desires of the unconscious and aconceptual mind should be prepared to encounter unpredictable and uncontrollable reactions. In addition, Kant lacked the access to non-European cultures which, at least at the superficial level of intercultural communication, is a commonplace today, and he was also innocent and lucky not to have witnessed the collapse of maturity which we know as National Socialism and Fascism. It would have been extremely difficult for him to understand such revolutionary movements as Nazism because he declined to ponder over the possibility that man has intensive experiences which are not perceptual and which cannot be comprehensively conceptualized. Unlike Kant's naiveté as regards the nature of man, the possibility of Nazism, or any intensive national passion which would reign outside of and regardless of the control of reason, complies well with Hume's vision of man as he writes: "[...] when we wou'd govern a man, and push him to any action, 'twill commonly be better policy to work upon the violent than the calm passions, and rather take him by his inclination, than what is vulgarly call'd his *reason*." (*Treatise*, 1739-40/1987, Book II, Part III, Section IV, p. 419).

Therefore, it may be difficult to avoid the impression that Kant actually pictured, not a man in any general sense, but, rather, a decent academic citizen of the eighteenth century Königsberg, whose behavior and opinions were shaped by the ideals of the Enlightenment. But human life in general is not limited to the life form of the eighteenth century Königsberg as it was viewed by a hyperdecent and overly rational professor of metaphysics. Something is missing: the asubjective and aconceptual, culturally varying, unique human experience which may have some irrational, mutually incompatible and destructive drives too. These drives may belong to the nonperceptual experience which cannot, not even in principle, be explained in any conceptual or theoretical way.

For example, could this overly decent and rational Kantian person ever radically question the benevolent role which modern technology plays in our society? It seems that he would lack almost all means to do so. If the status of the ultimate decision-maker is conferred upon reason, and the Self is said to mediate the results of reasoning to action, it becomes almost impossible to understand how reason, for example in the disguise of the technological attitude, could have its own veiled interests and sinister passions. How could science and technology, in their seemingly perfect rationality, entertain a dream in which they attain an unconstrained sovereignty over all other forms of experience and culture? More than once has this dream of sovereignty turned into intolerance, and even cruelty, toward nonrational and arational ways of thinking and living.

But the sinister nature of technology may be a difficult problem for the Humeans too. If reason is separated from action by such a sharp cut as is the case with Hume, then how can we ever understand the enormous growth and expansion which characterizes the modern Western technology? Modern Western technology, the brightest outgrowth of the very human reason, reigns globally, governs whole nations and excites them to pursue the dream of universal cultural unification and dominance with an energy which borders on nothing less than an ardent passion. Could Hume ever have been able to predict this passionate hold with which modern technology has embraced the human mind almost globally? How can we become so attracted by reason if it so impotent and indifferent as Hume claims? The least the Humean should admit is that the uncritical submissiveness, if not servility, with which people surrender to the technological way of life, knowing that technology blatantly depletes the quality of their life, is not a rational choice. The attraction of the technological way of life arises from intensive passions. Though concepts, including technological concepts, are, *as experiences*, experientially weak in intensity, the modern Western technology is able to free us from the hardships of the life struggle, and this is a matter of intensive passions. Life without struggle is an alternative which paralyzes our mind and shuns all less comfortable, rivalling scenarios of life. Thus, assuming that the modern Western technology actually is an outgrowth of reason, both the Humeans and the Kantians have great difficulties in explaining why some of the outcomes of the modern technology have turned out to be so disastrous and destructive.

Yet there seems to be a natural connection between Kant's notion of maturity and the ideals of technology and democracy. Does this imply that the notion of democracy, too, is hopelessly naive? Not necessarily, if we are able to design an *asubjective notion of democracy* which views democracy as a power struggle between *centers of experience* which are not always intentional, conscious and rational. But in order to attain that much, we should be able, in general, to deal with games without resorting to overly intentional, rational and conscious subjects. Only this would distance democracy from the fatal alliance which ties it to the modern Western technology.

The dangers of asubjective views of the mind

Let us say that gaming is a social activity with the help of which subjects are organized from the aconceptual experience. By increasing the complexity of the game relations in which a center of presubjective experience is engaged, the structure of the center, namely its perspectivity and hierarchy, becomes increasingly organized too. The major pitfall of nearly all regular theories of democracy (equality, tolerance, and so on) is that they deal only with the end product and upper layer of the organizing processes through which the subject emerges. This end product, the enlightened, rational and autonomous Western subject, is not only a culturally and historically specific local commodity, but a thin upper layer of the Western mind itself. It is far from obvious that this layer which makes itself manifest in conceptual and theoretical thinking and rational planning can picture the rest of the mind in an unbiased way.

But let us not picture the task of envisaging an asubjective view of democracy easier than it is. Those who have worked with asubjective theories of power, and of the human mind in general, have been playing with fire. Martin Heidegger, who guided the phenomenological movement toward an openly asubjective direction, was also notoriously *anti-democratic* in his political inclination (see Heidegger, 1966/1988). In addition, his views of the prospects of intercultural relations, especially during the later stage of his thinking, were so shamelessly Europo-centric, or even Germano-centric, that they bordered on cultural solipsism and couldn't provide us with any viable view of intercultural exchange. For Heidegger, such notions as "intentionality" and "autonomous subject" belonged to the Western tradition of hopelessly misguided metaphysics, and democracy, with its peculiar subject-centered conception of man, mind and truth, associates itself with this tradition. The Western metaphysical tradition has forgotten the only serious question into which a philosopher can put his mind, the question of Being (Seinsfrage). The history of this forgetfulness (Seinsvergessenheit) had begun already with Plato but it has become particularly intensified with the rise of modern natural science, technology and the related Cartesian metaphysics. This metaphysics separates the subject from the object and dictates that the main role of the subject is to represent the objects of the world. But this representative role reifies the human mind into a system of internal entities (a system of concepts) which will eventually begin to resemble the external objects which the system is supposed to represent. Just as the internal is said to be structured by intentionality, the external is said to be structured by causality.

But even in those glorious but lost days when the forgetfulness was not yet able to overwhelm the human mind, Western culture was closed by the barrier of untranslatability. Following Heidegger's line of thinking, we could even say that it is the emergence of the Western subject with its conceptual organization that created the impression that intercultural communication is indeed possible, and that the cultural barriers can be surpassed. The possibility of successful communication was founded on the conceptual structure of the subject, the idea being that the structure is ultimately universal, something that is shared by all people everywhere, regardless of local linguistic, ethnic and cultural differences. The first steps in the development of Western subjectivity were taken when the early Greek science and philosophy emerged and proclaimed to have found the universal truths about man and nature. Thus, paradoxically, one of the ingredients of the Western conception of man is that it is universal. Along with the rise and further development of the conceptually organized subjectivity, the separation of one human mind from other human minds was encouraged, enforced and eventually established. Thus simultaneously, the need for communication between subjects arose. The notion of argumentation, for example, requires such established conditions in which the human experience has already been cut into separate subjectivities. The hope that such communication and argumentation are possible rested on the idea that different subjects, including subjects with different linguistic and cultural backgrounds, are organized by a common universal rationality, even by a common conceptual structure, or, minimally, by different concepts which, however, consist of common conceptual primitives. Thus, before the rise of modern Western subjectivity, the need for communication, as an exchange of conceptual content between subjects, could not have arisen.

According to Heidegger, *Seinsvergessenheit* can be overcome through a special experience of authenticity or through a special appropriation (Ereignis) in which man belongs to Being. Because these experiences are hard to produce and endure, only a chosen few have access to them. In this group those who speak German as their native language have a privileged role to play. This entails a sort of elitism in Heidegger's thinking (see Zimmerman, 1990) and makes the experience too closed for foreign cultural influence (cf. Chapter 1). Thus overcoming the metaphysics of subjectivity almost necessarily results in the breakdown of communication between men and between different cultures. And in general, any view of the human mind, including that of Heidegger's, which doesn't render a central position to the intentional and conscious subject, seems to block the way to such virtues of the Enlightenment as tolerance and equality, at least as they are normally understood. Those who find this kind of view of man threatening will, most probably, suggest that already by adopting the view one may also inhibit the inclination to moral scruples and the rational calculation of alternative payoffs. Without the protection of the rational subject, we seem to open the door to ethnocentric cultural solipsism, irrationalism and nihilism.

Between naiveté and nihilism

So, the question is this: If we deconstruct or eliminate (in some sense, or to some extent) the classical subject and relativize it to the aconceptual aspect of experience, are we bound to plunge into ethnocentrism, linguistic isolationism, cultural solipsism and local nihilism? As with the question concerning the naiveté of the democratic attitude, the answer is: not necessarily, perhaps. There may remain a narrow area which lies between radical nihilism and the naiveté of the Kantian Enlightenment. It is opened by holistic naturalism. It is naturalism which eliminates (or crucially weakens) the strong intentional and conscious subject, relativizes its power with respect to such experience which is not controllable by the reason of the subject, and maintains that the human mind and language is basically aconceptual and asubjective experience. Such naturalism is not external but, rather, experiential. It focuses on the man-nature relationship, without reifying the human experience of nature only into objects. It keeps the human mind and culture open to foreign influence and exchange, and to the possibility of radical change. Foreign influence can occasionally induce a change of meaning which is genuinely unpredictable from and irreducible to the old knowledge. It is not antirealism in the subject-centered sense, but experientialism, according to which nature is primarily an experiential notion. It is only one aspect of nature (as experience) that it can be seen as a collection of entities. Objectivity and subjectivity together comprise a special kind of human attitude, a way to organize human experience into a persistent and feasible form. It is exactly our interest in nature that forces us to reject realism and objectivism, as well as question the subjective conception of experience. If the human experience is inseparably entangled with natural events, our picture of nature is always also a picture of ourselves, and all hopes to attain a man-independent conception of nature are illusory. (For more about such naturalism, see Pylkkö, 1993a; 1993b; and Chapters 1 and 2).

This kind of naturalism has a conscious Humean streak in its orientation. It also questions Heidegger's view of Western thought as a history of *Seins-vergessenheit*. The young Hume deconstructed the reality of both external and internal objects. He also abolished the boundary which allegedly separates perception and thinking. But if this is so, with which kind of view of the human mind did he eventually end up? According to Hume, the human mind consists primarily of aconceptual experience in which no sharp dichotomy between the internal and the external can be drawn; where the subject cannot be sharply separated from the objects; where the so-called environment, perception and thinking comprise an indivisible whole. But doesn't Hume's view of the human mind clash with the mainstream of Western metaphysics and its agenda of reification, and thus come quite close to the spirit with which Heidegger deals with metaphysics? Is Hume's thinking, for example, seriously undermined by the forgetfulness of Being? *Yes* would be an all too obvious and easy answer to the latter question. It would be convenient indeed to classify Hume's thinking as naive naturalism which is unable to deal with the problem of Being. But actually, the difference between Being and entities *can* be characterized within the Humean sphere of thinking, and a proper interpretation of Hume's work, which would distance the phenomenal from the subjectivity of the Self, and which would deal with impressions and thinking as a holistic flow of indivisible aconceptual experience, could face Heidegger's challenge quite well.

At this stage, this isn't much more than a provocative sketch for a possible rereading of some part of the history of Western thinking. The rereading has to overcome some obvious obstacles. The *direction* from impressions to ideas is too rigid with Hume, and the separation of impressions from one another too crisp. But as a starting point to an ametaphysical thinking exercise it is as good as anything: Hume's anti-metaphysics could be turned into ametaphysics. And, just as Heidegger can be said to have had serious difficulties in relating Being and the human way of being, namely *Sein* and *Dasein*, with one another, such followers of Hume as Mach and Ostwald had serious difficulties when they tried to characterize the neutral area between the physical and the psychical. Whatever is chosen to play the role of the neutral elements, it seems that it must be described either in a physical language or in a psychological language. Human intuition, especially folk intuition, doesn't seem to acknowledge any psycho-physically neutral language of experience.

Surrogate subjects in holistic naturalism

Though holistic naturalism has some eliminative traits in it, it doesn't have to deny that Western persons usually experience themselves as separate, intentional individuals whose mental life consists mostly of mental representations and calculations with which they evaluate different behavioral alternatives. Certainly, the experience is there, and it may even be the predominant one. For example, people feel that they are experientially separated from one another. There are many reasons why people want to be experienced, and want to experience themselves, as such. For example, people want to belong to a social group, and the separability and rationality of the members may be a necessary condition for the full membership of the group. One of the main issues is whether the folk-psychological interpretation even of this representable and calculable aspect of experience is adequate. Folk psychology, as well as scientific psychology which takes folk thinking for granted, are, for example, equally unable to explain how subjects arise. This inability holds for the subject both as a logical and grammatical category and as an intentional being. For example, different branches of developmental psychology do not address the problem adequately because they unhesitatingly approach the issue from the point of view of the mature, conceptually organized subject.

But perhaps there is something else to the human experience, something that is not captured by representations and calculations. Holistic naturalism begins with experience which is so primitive and primordial that it doesn't even acknowledge the contrast between the subject and the object. The experience is so unarticulated that it lacks all permanent organization, and therefore the contrast of the internal and the external is not yet effective in it. Therefore we can say that the experience is structured neither by external objects nor by the internal subject whose meaning entities and intentional structures are said to represent the external objects. Thus the experience is not fully conceptualizable. In other words, if we try to conceptualize such an experience, we will end up with *another* experience, and that is not something that we expect a good description to do. In holistic naturalism we are able to avoid the viciously paradoxical situation in which the rational subject tries to explain in some conceptual terms its own emergence from something that precedes the subject and its conceptual organization. Thus the aconceptual view of the human mind is not a conceptual enterprise, let alone a theory about the human mind.

Aconceptuality is not the same as the unconscious either, if the word is used in any regular psychological, say in the Freudian, sense. Freud's unabashed endeavor was to conceptualize the unconscious, a mission which is straightforwardly impossible with respect to the aconceptual experience. In one sense of the word *conscious*, though not perhaps in the standard one, we may be said to be primitively and immediately conscious of an aconceptual aspect of our experience. For example, with the help of certain mind-altering drugs it is possible to produce experiences in which one lacks most of the central characteristics of a rational, conceptually organized subject: one lacks language, is unable to reidentify time and place, doesn't know who one is, and so on. Yet a mind in this state may experience that it is alive *as* a body within a primitive kind of space, or prespace. In other words, one may be said to be primitively conscious, assuming that consciousness doesn't always require self-consciousness, reasoning or conceptual thinking.

Experiential aconceptuality is also needed to relate such consistent conceptual systems with one another which, from a purely conceptual point of view, would be mutually incompatible. For example, we can be *conscious* of the meaning (associated experiences, images, visualizations, imagined experiments, and so on) of some statements which refer, on the one hand, to classical physical systems, and, on the other hand, to quantum-physical phenomena. Assuming, as we actually do, that these two research traditions and related theories clash conceptually with each other, a mind which is able to bring into consciousness statements from both of the belief systems cannot itself be one unitary system. Yet there is a natural sense in which we can say that the mind (and consciousness) nevertheless comprises *one* mind (and consciousness), and it is this mind that is able to deal with the ideas and statements of the two belief systems. Here *one* can, however, refer neither to the standard natural number nor to any result of normal logical individuation processes. Therefore, consciousness is not unitary (that is, one in the regular mathematical meaning of *one*, or in any sense of logical individuation) but something genuinely holistic, and, in order to understand how the different, mutually incompatible but equally conscious departments of the mind should be related, we must use an aconceptual approach which *precedes* the emergence of the conceptual subdepartments. Nonunitary, holistic consciousness differs crucially from the standard view of consciousness which prevails in common sense and in common sense-based theoretical discussions. Thus, the word *consciousness* is ambiguous.

If a more familiar example is needed, consider the following. A perfectly bilingual person, if there is such, who speaks both English and Finnish with native fluency, decides to consider two expressions, one from English and another from Finnish, the idea being that the two expressions are the closest counterparts with respect to meaning which the languages can provide. Yet it is possible that these closest counterparts as regards meaning fall short of being translations or even good approximations. The only satisfactory way to deal with this situation is to say that both of the expressions carry along and around them an aconceptual field of meaning which relates the expressions to the local natural and cultural environment of the respective language. This field is unique in the strong sense of being irrepeatable and nonsystemic (not consisting of some translatable elementary meaning units). This is so not the least because the environment itself is unique and language lives in its neighborhood.

In order to be more specific, let us suggest that the Finnish expression *ollaan* and its allegedly nearest English counterpart, *one is*, exemplify the above sketched situation (for more about this example, see Chapter 8). *Ollaan*, the so-called passive form of the Finnish verb *olla* (to be), lacks person, number and gender, and its original meaning is ontologically almost nihilistic to such an extent that it cannot be reproduced in English without distorting or destroying it. No matter how desperately the English-speaking subsubject, so to speak, of the bilingual person attempts to translate the Finnish area of his mind, the attempt is doomed to remain unsuccessful, or at least inadequate. It is as if the other consciousness, the Finnish thinking and its field of meaning, though perfectly active and present (or 'conscious' in one sense of the word), would remain inaccessible for the English department of the mind, because the Finnish expression and the experience to which it belongs evades the conceptual and ontologically definite touch of the English mind. The touch would necessarily bring with it the grammatical subject-predicate structure which is not present in the experience to which the Finnish word belongs.

We may also try to illuminate aconceptuality by providing empirical analogies. From the point of view of the human ontogeny, aconceptuality may be seen as the experience of a very young child before the emergence of language and before the child is able to differentiate itself from the mother. As to the phylogenetic point of view, the experience is what might be called *lower-order* or *mammalian consciousness*, that is, consciousness as it is experienced mainly by non-human mammals, or by humans below the level which is dominated by complex forms of human language and reasoning. These analogies are somewhat misleading because they presuppose a conceptual perspective and thus assume that aconceptuality can be conceptualized comprehensively and described adequately in theoretical terms. However, with respect to aconceptual experience, no conceptualization is adequate and is bound to preclude some aspects of the experience. If we want to understand the aconceptual experience in its totality, a major philosophical reinterpretation of human experience is necessarily in order, and the reinterpretative approach must surpass the empirical-theoretical attitude which governs the standard studies of the human ontogeny and phylogeny.

Now, it is suggested that the subject arises from this kind of aconceptual experience through gaming activities. The subject, that is, the end product of the game-enhanced articulation process, is also the main unit of action in the regular view of power as a control relation. In the familiar language of *homunculus*-thinking, we are inclined to say that it is the subject which plays these games. But clearly, if it is the environment of gaming within which the subject can emerge and become what it is, the standard view of power as a control relation among subjects is bound to remain inadequate.

It was George Herbert Mead (1910) who used to underline the interactive origin of the subject, but here we want to emphasize also a peculiar aconceptual point of view. The aconceptual experience becomes gradually articulated into the subject (player) and objects (other players and the game environment) as the gaming experience of the evolving center of experience (the emerging proxy subject) becomes more complex and requires articulated responses. Also the experiential subcenters *within* one experiential center, that is, the emerging subsubjects so to speak, can be seen to be related to one another by gaming relations. Perhaps the articulation of subjectivity is experienced as a kind of increased perspectivity and hierarchy in the flow of experience. Part of the organization is what we experience as intentionality, as the direction, perseverance and array of consistent preferences in the activities of our mental life. This (directedness, perseverance and preferences) can be understood as different possible gaming relations among subsubjects. Thus, subjectivity is the conceptual organization which a presubjective center of experience adopts in order to play successfully against other evolving centers of experience. A higher stage of that articulation process may be felt by the subject as a kind of isolation from the primordial experiential communion which only a community can provide. Thus *community* is not synonymous with a *group of subjects* but a name for a collective aconceptual experience which is not yet cut into separate individual subjective experiences.

As long as we want to adhere to naturalistic views, we must concede that intentionality plays a very weak causal role in the explanation of behavior. In certain cultural situations we tend to resort to intentional explanations, but, nevertheless, we should say that an intentional explanation of behavior is like a culturally enhanced hindsight of what is happening to us and in us. Intentionality is not a genuine future-shaping causal power. Benjamin Libet's famous experiments with readiness potentials (Libet, 1985) show that cerebral initiation of spontaneous voluntary action arises unconsciously. This lends support to a kind of Schopenhauerian view of the initiation of human action, and this is in concert with holistic naturalism as it is here understood. The initiation of action begins in the neural unconscious, in the *Unbewusste*, as Schopenhauer would have put it, which is not controlled by the conscious and rational subject, his conceptual schemes and intentions. This does not mean that intentional action would not differ in any way from unintentional action. Though they can be said to have different neural histories, the nature of intentionality is not primarily and purely an empirical or theoretical question. Yet such an actively initiative role which many Kantian, phenomenological and even functional theories confer to reason and conscious intention doesn't comply nicely with neuropsychological evidence. Perhaps the subject's reason is occasionally able to play an inhibitive role as a monitoring center which tries to oversee the events of the aconceptual aspects of the mind. But because inhibition can always turn into suppression, some consequences of the monitoring activities, as well as human behavior in general, will always remain rationally unpredictable.

From connectionism to aconceptual neural naturalism

Human experience is holistic and undergoes perpetual changes. Therefore, we would expect distributed and eliminative connectionism to provide a more appropriate way to model such experience than any symbolic representation. But standard connectionism may also be unable to deal with such incessant change, unpredictability and inseparability which characterize the experiential realm of man. This is especially so if the connectionist formalism is defined, either consciously or unwittingly, to be mathematically equivalent with the Turing machine formalism. Without a proper critical discussion, it would be hasty to view the events of the human brain solely as mechanical processes, that is, as processes which are comprehensively describable in terms of computable numbers and functions.

Up to a certain point, connectionist models, even mechanically computable connectionist models, can be used to approximate the processes in which the hierarchy and perspectivity of the subject, or, rather, the naturalistic proxy of the common sense subject, arises from the aconceptual experience. A distributed and nonlinguistic model, with no central processing unit, and which may even fail to carry symbolic content, provides a possibility to model the naturalistic surrogate subject as a neural network whose connection weight values have been organized by the demands of different gaming situations. But, due to their ultimately mechanical nature and lack of neurobiological credibility, standard connectionist models are bound to remain inadequate, though the degree of their adequacy is, in some respect, higher than that of any symbolic representation. It is far from obvious that connectionist networks are able to approximate human experience *with any desired degree of accuracy*. And if something is lost in the mechanical approximation, we can never be sure that what is lost would not constitute the crux of what we are looking for, that which is most characteristic of the human mind. Furthermore, connectionist models seem to be quite weak in the sense that a great deal of the information which a network possesses lies already in the preliminary setup of the network's weight values *before* it moves to the training phase. How this information is actually gathered goes often unexplained.

We have, at least, two options available if we want to destroy the Hydra of Mechanicalness which threatens connectionism and other theories of the human mind. The first is the most popular one: the Gödelian line of thinking, according to which there are truths and structures which are accessible for the human mind but inaccessible for any mechanical device or system. According to this argument, the ability of the human mind to demonstrate informally the incompleteness of formal arithmetic already shows that the human mind is not constrained by the grid of mechanicalness. Unfortunately, this line of thinking is, for several reasons, unavailable for any genuine naturalist. A connectionist who wants to remain a naturalist should be able to tell us, among other things, what would follow from the assumption that one activation function of a network unit is not Turing-computable. How would, say, a biological brain realize the function?

A naturalistically more viable alternative might be to question the credibility of the contrast between the mechanical (formalizable) and the non-mechanical (nonformalizable). This option is naturalistically more attractive because the claim that there are *any* strictly mechanical processes in nature is not particularly well founded in the first place. Not only brain events, but all natural events, may be ultimately holistic in the sense that they cannot be accounted for as systems which consist of subsystems. But it is equally uncertain that holistic natural events are always describable and explainable in noncomputable mathematical terms either. Thus, natural phenomena may ultimately be amechanical, that is, they are neither Turing-computable nor non-Turing-computable (cf. Chapter 3). Even if this is so, it may still be possible to design both mechanical (Turing-computable) and nonmechanical (non-Turing-computable) approximations of natural phenomena and experiences. This is fully legitimate, as long as we do not claim that the approximations are able to approach the phenomena and experiences with *any* desired accuracy. This means, among other things, that even with the best approximations the distance between the approximating law and what it approximates is, in principle, unknown.

There are some trends in the recent literature of neuroscience which might be developed toward this kind of radically aconceptual direction. In particular, Edelman's theory of consciousness (Edelman, 1989) and Globus's view of noncomputational neuroscience (Globus, 1992; 1995; see also Chapter 3) might be modifiable into naturalistically acceptable theories, even in terms of the kind of radical version of naturalism which is suggested by holistic naturalism. This is not to claim that this direction is that which Edelman or Globus have in mind or will ever pursue.

But only in holistic naturalism are we able to sketch the history of

subjectivity as a gradually emerging phenomenon, beginning with the aconceptual experience, in which presubjective centers of experience arise as
responses to the increasingly challenging gaming situations, and eventually,
ending up with fully conscious subjects which try to understand themselves.
For example, we may want to trace the evolution of the subject's hierarchy
and perspectivity from the mammalian consciousness up to the full human
consciousness, the latter being characterized by the ability to bring something
(a reified, consistent belief, memory, and so on) to mind and manipulate it in
a linguistic context. At the level of the full consciousness, the mind may also
turn toward itself and try to understand itself. Within genuine naturalism, we
must be aware of the peculiar circular character of this situation and be
cautious of not approaching the problem of consciousness from the biased
perspective of full consciousness alone. A consciousness, especially if it is
fully developed, which turns its attention to itself, is hardly able to attain a
comprehensive vision of the human mind and experience. It is not even clear
that the Self or selfhood is exhausted by self-consciousness. But a fatally
biased view of the human mind is to be expected from any attempt of the
consciousness to describe the aconceptual mind in purely conceptual terms.

A typical feature of full human consciousness is its strong inclination to
satisfy the conditions of classical separability and sequentiality: only one
thought or belief seems to enter the mind at any one moment. This inclination
doesn't always find a realization, which is one reason for the ambiguity of the
term *consciousness*. According to a widely accepted view, thoughts and
beliefs consist of separable constituents, just as the external world is supposed
to consist of separable things and systems of things. If this is what thoughts
and beliefs really are, it must be almost impossible for two nonidentical
thoughts or meanings to occur simultaneously in consciousness. For example,
in the standard sense of the words *thought* and *belief* we cannot, indeed, think
about a contradiction, that is, no conscious experience represents a contradic-
tory state of affairs. We could even say that it is exactly the main task of the
regular Western consciousness to suppress the inseparable and superposed
aconceptual experience and reduce it to mental objects which are as classical
as possible. For such objects, it holds that one place can be occupied only by
one object at a time. As a thought object, that object must be consistent,
because an aggregate of incompatible objects couldn't be *one*, and couldn't,
therefore, occur simultaneously in one consciousness. This may be one of the
reasons why the whole idea of consciousness as a classical system (covering

both the Turing-computable or non-Turing-computable structuress) with linear time is untenable.

One of the tendencies of the human nervous system is to divide our experience of the "external environment" into separable things, and our experience of the "inner environment" into separable concepts. But it would be an anti-naturalistic fallacy to equate the human experience with its reified, classical department. One consequence of the fallacy is the inability to account for the *emergence* of the classical department itself. Human experience is not the same as the conscious and conceptual part of the experience. Experience covers something more, namely, the aconceptual, nonintentional and asubjective side too. And finally, the department, which first gives the impression of being classically ordered, turns, in a closer consideration, to be more like a fictitious conceptual projection which rests inseparably upon the aconceptual aspect of the mind. It is characteristic of one aspect of the human consciousness that it is able to exercise a kind of reifying and moderating censorship upon the rest of the mind, as if the holistically superposed and inconsistent human experience which lacks definite space, time, objects and causality would have to be disambiguated by the illusion of permanency and relative immutability which only the projected structures of consciousness are able to create.

It is plausible that the conceptualizing and reifying inclinations of the human brain have a solid evolutionary and genetic foundation. Objectivization of experience into separable things must have had a relatively high survival value. For example, contour enhancement, color constancy and other neural mechanisms of the human visual system support a thing-oriented visual ontology. But still, conceptualization and reification of experience is only *one* possibility to deal with our experience. Experience is originally aconceptual, and, even if reification has had a high survival value in the course of the human evolution, we do not have to let it dominate our philosophical conception of experience. No *a priori* reason forces a naturalist to concede that an information handling process, say that of reification, which evolution has authorized, must be philosophically unquestionable too.

First of all, the evolution of the human brain has produced several rivalling and mutually incompatible ways of experiencing and knowing, and there is no necessity to legitimize only one of them, even if the one had passed the evolutionary selection processes better than the others. Only an extremely cynical opportunist claims that it is the survivor who, in most cases, possesses the best knowledge too. Our view of early human evolution tends to reflect our present-day, technologically biased view of man. Therefore, we tend to overemphasize the technological aspect of the evolutionary survival story: that we survived as a species because we were clever enough to invent tools with the help of which we could manipulate nature and defeat those of our competitors who were less technologically advanced. But even within the standard evolutionary framework, quite a different kind of story could be told as well. Assume, for example, that man survived hundreds of thousands of years because he had created myths, religious beliefs and poetry to save him from lethal boredom, loneliness, social anomaly and destitution, and that it was the invention of tools and early technology with which man's descent toward destruction began, because the tools provided man with an illusory and pretentious view of his possibilities to control the ultimately uncontrollable nature.

Reification of experience into external and internal objects, and the related technological view of nature, may have been useful in some practical contexts, but it cannot serve as a foundation for an adequate notion of human knowledge and experience in general. This is so because the aconceptual department of our knowledge cannot be adequately understood only in the light which a conceptual system sheds, and the standard evolutionary perspective is itself only a theoretical and conceptual undertaking which is hardly able to deal with its own origin in any comprehensive way. Of course, there exists an evolutionary view of the origin of human intelligence, too, including theoretical thinking. But this picture can hardly be expected to be impartial when it has to deal with nonintelligent and nontheoretical aspects of experience.

In order to avoid this partisanship of theoreticalness and conceptuality, we should, perhaps, first design a seriously regressive view of the biological origin of species, a view which would deal with our natural history as a perpetual process of death-seeking regression: the goal of a species is, not to survive the competition of scarce resources, but to idle, destroy and eventually disappear as fast as possible. In addition, nothing as such is able to preclude the possibility that the evolution of the human brain has been based on a terrible, eventually even fatal, systematic mistake, and that which we cherish as the best of our knowledge is just a ridiculous confusion produced by the early counterparts of engineers, scientists and philosophers. Of course, the words 'mistake' and 'confusion' carry with them a great deal of the normative sense which the ratio-centered view of man associates with them. (Because we want to question the ratio-centered view of man, we use here the normative words just for the sake of argument.)

Thus, the least we can do is that we will not ignore or "forget" (in the Heideggerian sense of *vergessen*) the aconceptual, regressive, primordial, unhealthy and suicidal aspects of our mind. What we call *madness*, *diseases* and *death*, regardless of their unpleasant normative connotations, refer to phenomena which are just as natural as regularity, health and vitality. The bias of health, intelligence and vitality which the modern theory of evolution teaches to us is, not only uncritical, but anti-naturalistic. What has survived during the evolution doesn't possess any common 'positive' property (except the empty property that it has indeed survived) which would explain why it has survived. Just as well as we can say that we have survived because of our superior intelligence we could say that we have survived because of our superior stupidity. Only after we have designed an unbiased view of human evolution, that is, a view which concedes that there is no intrinsic rationality in human evolution, we can try to understand the relationship between the conceptual and the aconceptual of our mind. In this work, one of the pitfalls into which we all too easily fall is that we separate them by a cut which is too sharp and therefore not naturalistically credible.

Gaming and reification

The notion of gaming might shed some light upon the problem of object formation, too. It is, after all, in the service of intersubjectivity (object-ivity as the foundation for the communication and exchange between subjects) that objects are needed. As a game world evolves, the subject which participates in it becomes gradually more complex, that is, the degree of the hierarchy and perspectivity, which constitutes the subject, increases. But simultaneously, the conception of *otherness*, namely, that which the subject experiences as not being immediately a part of itself, becomes more articulated. Other people comprise the most important part of the otherness, as the articulateness of the subject's store of objects grows in parallel with the degree of hierarchy and perspectivity of the subject itself. From the point of view of object formation, other people are particularly important, not only as objects, but because it is, first of all, other people that are able to frustrate and humiliate the subject's expectations in a surprising, and even excruciating, way (cf. Chapter 4). For the subject, other people comprise both an important store of objects and the main source of aconceptual unpredictability. Inanimate matter is too indifferent to do that. Nonhuman animals may be threatening, but only humans in their viciousness and desirability are able to attain the utmost peak of otherness, objectuality and aconceptuality which a subject can encounter.

In this kind of *parallel model*, experience is not originally subjective, only some experiences are subjective, and the human experience, including subjectivity, is open to foreign social and cultural influences. Therefore, we will not expect any serious difficulties to arise with respect to solipsism, privacy and the status of other minds and other cultures. In the beginning, there are neither Me nor Others. The aconceptual experience is collective in the sense, and only in the sense, of lacking personal boundaries. It is created neither by a subject nor by a group of subjects. Thus, *collective* doesn't here mean "a group of separate subjects," and, therefore, *asubjective*, or, if we want to emphasize the temporal order, *presubjective*, might a better term. We could say that aconceptual experience is created by more than one pre-subjective center of experience, assuming that it makes sense, which it doesn't, to count such holistic experiences. However, collectivity as an aggregate of separable and well individuated subjects is how Western political philosophy, including most of the democracy theories, has usually understood the notion of collectivity. It was one of Foucault's central points that power is not, or at least, not only, a collective notion in this standard sense. Therefore, the above-sketched holistic naturalism complies with this aspect of Foucault's work. According to Foucault, we should say that individuals or subjects arise as a result of a particular kind of power struggle. Therefore, obviously, we cannot characterize power in terms of individuals and subjects alone.

Subjects disintegrated

From the foregoing point of view which utilizes the game metaphor, we are able to understand, not only how subjects arise, but also how they may be destroyed or become disintegrated. We don't want to say, for example, that a subject's disintegration would necessarily push a person beyond the boundary of humanity. Actually, temporary and partial dissolution of the subject is almost an everyday experience. Utmost exhaustion, some diseases, dreaming, hallucinations, erotic passion, mind-disturbing drugs, lethal danger, and so on, to mention some of the most frequent cases, may cause a temporary confusion in the boundaries and organization of the subject, and threaten the illusion that the subject is the master and command center of the mind, and, in serious cases, destroy the illusion and dethrone the subject from the apparent leading role for an indefinite time.

Partial disintegration of the rational and conscious subject may be what some social practices and religious rituals endeavour to reach. Even art, to some extent at least, may attempt to question some uncritically established thinking and experiencing habits. In order to do that, entrancing art experience, an ultimate surprise in artist context, or in its periphery, may also shatter the hierarchy and perspectivity of which the subject consists (cf. Chapter 4). We tend to think that only something new can offer such an experience to us, but this may be a mistake. What surprises us most may just as well be something very old and primordial which we have forgotten and tend to forget constantly. But perhaps it is not art as such that is able to surprise us. Art may be, after all, too tightly tied to the metaphysics of artistic technologies in order to be able to provide us with something more than just a starting point toward asubjective experience.

Also several therapeutic and religious traditions, which attempt to prepare us to encounter intensive and rare experiences, are prone to destroy overly rigorous and inauthentic reaction habits within us and, through that, dissolve some of the socially conditioned experiencing mechanisms of which the subjectivity in that particular culture consists. Also this kind experiential destruction can be understood as a return to primordial and even primitive layers of the human mind and language. However, this return to aconceptuality must not be understood *merely* as a return to a temporally (historically, developmentally) preceding stage of human experience.

Gaming against metaphysics

Game has been one of the leading anti-metaphysical metaphors of the Western thinking (cf. Spariosu, 1989). Even in its purely mathematical form, game theory is delightfully dynamic and antireificational. Due to its incessantly changing and evolving character, the notion of game can be used to deconstruct too immutable and atemporal structures of the Western metaphysical tradition. This includes Kantian *synthetic a priori* structures, though games themselves may as well incorporate some *a priori-like* experiences of ours which precede specific empirical knowledge and which require a special atheoretical approach in order to be adequately described (cf. Chapter 5). Of course, we are assuming that there are also nonperceptual experiences and, especially, nonperceptual experiences which are not conceptual. This kind of experience may turn out to precede some other experiences, for example, some more reified forms of experience. But because aconceptual and pre-empirical experience, if anything, is still experience, the term *a priori* is in this context a misnomer. Some of our aconceptual experiences may always remain transcendentally inaccessible to the conceptual aspect of our experience. Nevertheless, games are the site where concepts are formed, and therefore knowledge is always related inseparably to the *human* experience and activities, and cannot pretend to offer to us any man-independent conception of nature.

However, this thorough entanglement of games with human affairs cannot be conceptualized *only* as the entanglement of games with the affairs of a rational, conscious and autonomous subject. It is through games that the subject's relative existence and survival as an opponent becomes established. Gaming requires and provides such repetition which can regiment experience into the hierarchies and perspectives of which conceptual expectations consist. Similarly, intentionality needs a game context in order to be experienced. It is the misguided folk-psychological explanation which in vain tries to picture intentionality as a causally efficacious source from which action is initiated. Intentionality is basically a rationalizing and moderating mechanism which tries to keep aconceptual experience under the control of reason, while never really succeeding. From the external and ratio-centered point of view, it may look as if the players of a game realize an intentional plan in their activities, but, actually, it is the game which creates this impression of intentionality. Intentionality can hardly be understood properly without understanding the role which pleasure, pain, horror and passion play in initiating action, for example, such pleasure which a satisfied desire to win a game can induce. And this can be understood only in the light of an even more primordial and aconceptual urge to live and die.

From this perspective, there is not much point in saying that one subject inhabits strictly one body-brain. Rather, every subject's being is distributed onto a social network, and therefore onto several brains and bodies too. A subject can inhabit more than one brain, and a brain can be inhabited by more than one subject. What holds for the subject, holds even more for the pre-subjective center of experience. You can say as literally as it is possible, in general, to characterize such issues that, say, your father or lover lives in your brain too. Therefore, it is not metaphoric to say that we are able to experience what others experience. What we misleadingly call 'others,' lives in us, just as it lives elsewhere at the same time too.

Though subjects, among other metaphysical structures, emerge via gaming, games provide also the setting in which they can be dissolved. It is the gaming environment where we can encounter surprise, shock, bewilderment, embarrassment, horror and other aconceptual experiences which challenge our conceptual expectations and force us to face the limits of our ability to cope with the future (cf. Chapter 4). Thus, it is loss rather than victory that is able to intensify our experiential life, and it is only at the conceptual level, at the level of the rational subjectivity, that we play in order to win.

Eugen Fink (1960, see especially pp. 187-9) has suggested that Nietzsche used the notion of the *Dionysiac* play in order to destroy the remnants of Western metaphysics in his thinking. In accordance with this view, we could say that the experience of being a subject arises as a result of gaming, not *vice versa*, but, at the same time, we may be attracted by a hard, surprising and dangerous life, the Dionysiac challenge. As an experience, a loss following a hard struggle is more intensive than an easy, clean and predictable victory. At the moment, say, of a shattering humiliation or lethal danger, which anticipates an inevitable and final loss, we do live momentarily without the edifying and protective structure of the subject.

The terror of goodness

If we assume that subjects not only play games, but emerge via gaming, we can understand better what power is: power is ultimately the ability to influence and shape the processes in which the subject is organized and disintegrated, and in which it self-organizes and disintegrates itself. Thus clearly, power is not primarily a dominance relation among already existing rational and conscious subjects which satisfy some classical individuation conditions. Rather, it is the ability to create and destroy subjects by influencing the articulation processes in which subjectivity emerges and dissolves itself.

Also the *democratic subject* arises in a certain kind of gaming environment. It is not the intentionality of mature individuals that creates the adequate preconditions for democracy. Rather, we call certain social activities and institutions democratic because of their particular game arrangement, and the democratic subject is a result of the constitution and activation of this arrangement.

The best that democracy can offer to us is variety, perpetual change, tolerance and such struggle which enhances change and allows the variety to flourish. (For the nonstandard sense of *tolerance*, and for the themes of tolerance and cultural variety in general, see also Chapter 1 and 8). This doesn't necessarily suggest peaceful or nonviolent action, because peace is often utilized as a powerful method of cultural unification. Thus, at their best, democratic gaming arrangements might influence and shape the emergence of subjectivity in a way that would enhance the intuitively important goals of variety, change and tolerance. In doing that, democracy should neutralize all such trends of power processes which tend to unify our experience and reach a totally comprehensive grip of our minds. For example, one possible unification tendency in the processes of a subject's emergence is that the center of experience from which the subject arises becomes exclusively and one-sidedly rational and concept-oriented. In other words, the subject begins to inhibit the rest of the experience in an unduly manner. Or at least, it pretends to be able to inhibit the aconceptual aspect of the mind. The result could be, for example, an autonomous individual in the sense of the Kantian Enlightenment. This individual would have a limited, if not naive, understanding both of itself and of human nature in general. Therefore, the dissolving and destroying aspects must also be available and hopefully active in every democratic context where the subjectivity emerges, and a small-scale chaos and anarchy should be allowed to flourish there. Only that may prevent society from becoming a control system with definite global rules. In that kind of locally anarchic context, the subject would not necessarily be doomed to the developmental track, at the end point of which lies the ratio-centered, autonomic individual which suppresses all aconceptual and arational aspects of its experience.

Without a proper notion of *suppression*, we will be unable to understand what the difference between *controlling* and *monitoring* the aconceptual is, and, therefore, the relationship between the conceptual and aconceptual will remain incomprehensible. The inhibitory monitoring can be extremely powerful, and the world, as well as our mind, may eventually appear to us as a huge machine. This may even hold man in a global grip. Yet it is not the same as controlling the human mind. It is far from certain that the aconceptual aspect of the human mind can really be controlled because the notion of control itself seems to require a conceptual organization. Any control may turn into suppression, and the controlling effect is suddenly lost. Unfortunately the word *suppression* is overly shadowed by its Freudian connotations which are heavily loaded with metaphysics. The aconceptual is strictly outside of the reach of any theoretical attitude, including the theory of the unconscious. Often the aconceptual lies openly before us, on the surface, so to speak. Yet it may be without language or expression. It needs no analysis. What it needs is proper language, a proper way of listening to language. This can easily be destroyed by any analytical or theoretical attitude which tries to reveal the structure of the allegedly latent meaning. In addition, freedom from the suppression of the aconceptual doesn't guarantee health or well-being.

However, freedom may occasionally require also some radical and violent means in order to be realized, and therefore we are here already distancing ourselves from the regular view of democracy as a decent and well ordered decision-making procedure for autonomous individuals. Thus, contrary to what regular theories of democracy recommend, it is often in the best interests of democracy *not* to regiment the human mind into the mould of a perfectly organized conceptual structure, into a mature and responsible individual. For example, a perfectly rational individual may be unable to question the dominating role which modern technology has assumed in our society. A perfectly rational mind will note the disastrous consequences of modern technology all too late. The modern Western technology and modern rational subjectivity are too dependent on each other in order to allow the subject's free questioning about the foundations of the technological attitude. They are almost one and the same thing seen from two different angles. Therefore, we can neither hold nor question one without holding or questioning the other, too. Even ethics, including the so-called professional ethics, is seldom anything else but a branch of techniques and technologies, that is, goodness-promoting techniques and technologies which try to make other techniques and technologies more feasible, convenient and flexible. For example, the Kantian categorical imperative is a powerful unification mechanism which shares with other technologies the inability to control its own growth. Thus its allegedly universal form serves as a cultural unification program which is intolerant and ultimately bound to destroy rivaling non-Western ideas which do not assume a rational and autonomous subjectivity to make sense.

One of the reasons why the existing Western democracies do not deserve to be called genuinely democratic any more is that they have allowed technology to assume the role of a global organizing principle. Democracy is unable to control and inhibit its own growth, which has resulted in a series of ethnic and cultural genocides all over the world, some of which are presently going on. It should be the main task of genuine democracy to prevent *any* principle, including democracy itself, from assuming the commanding attitude over our minds. Only success in that task would allow the struggle between experiences and ideas to continue and proliferate. The prevailing Western democracies have failed in this task and they are unable to provide an alternative to what exists: they are unable to challenge the power of technology. And here *power* is (and must be) used in the above-sketched asubjective sense. Democracy *is* able to monitor and, to some extent perhaps, inhibit the overwhelming grip that technology has on our minds. But this monitoring and inhibition doesn't amount to adequate understanding of the nature of technology because the view of man on which the standard democratic thinking and action is based is inadequate. It is inadequate because it is unable to relate the aconceptual and the conceptual in the human experience. Because of this inability, the normal democratic man, as well as his view of man, treats the conceptual aspect of the human experience with unbalanced favor.

Because it is not the good intentions of mature individuals which make democracy work, but the democratic game which makes it possible for us to experience good intentions, it is justified to predict that good intentions alone will never prove sufficiently strong to help us to attain proper understanding of technology, let alone genuine challenging its power. Challenging the power of technology is not primarily an ethical issue, an issue of choosing between values. Neither is it only an issue of choosing between the actions which are assumed to realize values. Thus the fatal alliance of democracy and technology, that is, the prevailing conception of Western man and society, has betrayed the primordial spirit of genuine democracy which *should arise from the collective and aconceptual human experience of nearness and which should make ineffective all good intentions which are too global.* Even Feyerabend's democratic relativism (see *Notes on relativism*, Feyerabend, 1987), which so delightfully tries to limit its own jurisdiction within the Western world and thus denies its global applicability, fails to deprive itself of good intentions (which he attributes with such words as 'free,' 'beneficial,' 'reasonable,' 'fruitful,' and so on) and therefore inadvertently ties itself to the conceptual organization of local Western values. This locality of values as such is, of course, what relativism teaches and cherishes. But, at the same time, these values are hardly able to challenge, question and destroy the essentially good-willing and well-intending core of modern Western technology. This core *is* ethical, that is, it is intended to pursue and promote a special technological kind of goodness. Thus, Western ethics is ultimately a technological enterprise, and it is not so surprising that modern Western technology so unabashedly promotes its own uninhibited growth.

When democracy works properly, no global idea, including democracy itself, no matter how filled with good will it seems to be, should be able to overwhelm our experiences. In order to survive, the spirit of democracy should not attempt to distance itself from the abyss of asubjectivity and aconceptuality where the origin of all human struggle and suffering lies. If successful, this survival attempt would turn the spirit of democracy unavoidably into a local, untranslatable experience, without global or universal claims. We should admit that all claims of universality are pretensions, even, and especially, those which are based on good intentions. Genuine goodness is always local, and no goodness is good enough to be proclaimed universal. Goodness which assumes a universal and global mission turns eventually into terror.

CHAPTER SEVEN

Is Nazism humanism?

Overview of the problem

One of the most fascinating and disquieting issues raised by the recent French Heidegger debate has been the question whether or not Nazism is humanism, and one of the main motivations to defend the implausible-sounding positive answer to the question has arisen from the desire to distance Heidegger's thinking, and perhaps the deconstructionist movement too, from Nazism. If it could be shown that Nazism belonged to the philosophical tradition of subject-centered humanism, or metaphysics of subjectivity, it would be much easier to say that Heidegger took Nazism as something that it actually wasn't, namely, that he mistakenly saw Nazism as a genuine dethronement of the subject's leading role in thinking, experiencing and acting. According to the defense, Heidegger misinterpreted the character of Nazism by not realizing that actually Nazism represented the Western metaphysical tradition because Nazism was both subject-centered, enhanced the subject-object dichotomy, and presupposed strong objectivization and reification of experience, and, therefore, conformed with, rather than challenged or opposed, the demands of the modern Western technology. After realizing that actually Nazism is humanism, Heidegger rapidly distanced himself from Nazism. Therefore, runs the defense, Heidegger's Nazism was a short and not too serious interlude, dating, perhaps, from the beginning of the rectorate of 1933-34 to 1935. After that Heidegger's intellectual bonds with Nazism were casual and eventually broke off. Obviously, if this view is tenable, the a(nti)metaphysical and a(nti)humanistic core of Heidegger's thinking would remain relatively unscathed by Nazism.

This strategy of apology has been authored most powerfully by Philippe Lacoue-Labarthe (1987; see also Lacoue-Labarthe and Nancy, 1991), but a version of it has been defended also by Jacques Derrida (1987), and repercussions of it can be discerned, for example, in Dreyfus and Hall (1992) and Vietta (1989). Also Hans Sluga's work, *Heidegger's Crisis* (1993), belongs to this branch of literature. Sluga sees Nazism basically as a modern phenomenon because, according to him, the Nazi conception of crisis commits Nazism to the directedness to the present and to the discontinuity of the past and present (p. 68). If this view of Nazism were tenable, Nazism could be attached to the metaphysics of subjectivity in Heidegger's sense and, thus, to humanism too.

According to Lacoue-Labarthe's interpretation, Nazism was the Nazi myth. The conception of myth which Nazism realized was *onto-typological*, that is, Nazism resorted to a special kind of logic with a strongly reifying *Gestalt* of a typology, and this led eventually to the absolutization of the subject. The typology which Nazism endorsed was a rigorous race typology which required that the Germans, by adopting a particular mimetic attitude, were able to identify themselves as a nation only by decisively excluding non-Germans. With the Jewish people this exclusion was so obtrusive that they were said to lack identity altogether. According to Lacoue-Labarthe and Nancy, the kind of national identification which Nazism required was possible only because the state assumed the role which normally belongs to the subject; the state became a kind of surrogate, macro-sized subject, *State Subject*. Because the Nazi myth was a powerful identification apparatus which constructed a new kind of subject with a strong *Gestalt*-like shape, Nazism obviously belonged to the tradition of subject-centered Western metaphysics. As it is known that Heidegger did criticize Jünger's notion of *Gestalt* and connected it to *Gestell*, the essence of technology, Lacoue-Labarthe attempts to argue that Heidegger must have denounced Nazism as a version of the metaphysics of subjectivity.

However, the apology rests heavily on a simplistic conception of Nazism which is unable to picture Nazism as a political revolution, ignores its social and cultural background and trivializes it as a philosophical and esthetic movement. In order to evaluate Heidegger's political engagement, we should, first of all, try to understand Nazism as an *experiential revolutionary mass movement*; second, we should try to understand better the cultural and philosophical background from which Heidegger's thinking of the twenties and thirties arose; and, third, we should try to clarify how the literary, philosophical and esthetic Nazism relates to that very background. From this kind of triple perspective, Heidegger's engagement in Nazism can hardly be presented as a short period of confusion and misinterpretation. Nazism, as an experiential social, political and philosophical movement, is ametaphysical and anti-subject-centered if anything is; only some of its trivialized versions are clearly humanistic. In addition, Heidegger's own philosophy of Being bears a close family resemblance with certain philosophical and esthetic movements which were popular in the Weimar Germany and from which also Nazism arose. These movements, of which Expressionism is, perhaps, the most important, were often consciously antihumanistic and antilogocentric, and it is plausible that Heidegger's bend toward Nazism originates from his overall affinity to these movements.

Lacoue-Labarthe's Heidegger is a kind of soft and tolerant Heidegger, a fictive character designed to distance French Heideggerianism and deconstructionism from its unholy roots. It is a construction of considerable hindsight because Heidegger's critique of Nazism was mild and focused at certain naive, peripheral and trivial variants of Nazism and can, therefore, be classified as self-criticism of the movement rather than as clear denouncement. It seems also that, for Lacoue-Labarthe, Nancy and Derrida, Nazism doesn't comprise anything more than just these marginal and trivial variants, whereas Heidegger saw in them only a degenerated branch of Nazism. Therefore, it is understandable that for Heidegger Nazism was an antihumanistic movement *par excellence* and, among political movements of his days, perhaps the *only* seriously antihumanistic movement. It is, indeed, possible to argue that the naive, peripheral and trivial variants of Nazism which Heidegger criticized remained relatively close to their humanistic origin. But it is far from clear, for example, that the atrocities, human rights violations and genocides of which the Nazis were responsible originated *only* or even *mainly* from the humanistic aspects and versions of Nazism. In any case, there is not much evidence for the interpretation that, after 1935, Heidegger would have thought that the Nazi movement as a whole represented the metaphysics of subjectivity and served as an errand boy to promote the veiled interests of nihilistic technology. Not only was Heidegger's Jünger critique written twenty years after Heidegger's alleged turn against ontology, but Heidegger's *Question of Being* (1955/1958) doesn't actually connect Nazism to onto-theo-logic, technology, Gestell, onto-typology, or to any other form of logocentrism. That connection is a figment of Lacoue-Labarthe's own mythology. Similarly, it was not until in the fifties that Heidegger saw Nietzsche's and Schopenhauer's attempt to overcome metaphysics as seriously inadequate (Heidegger, 1954/1993). This critique of dualistic metaphysics can be read, among other things, as a critique of naive, peripheral and trivial Nazism, that is, as a critique of the humanistic misinterpretation and misrepresentation of Nazism.

So, my exploration of the apology interpretation has two columns: first, I will interpret Nazism as a revolutionary and experiential mass movement with residual cultural, philosophical and esthetic programs, and I will connect this picture to the cultural and intellectual life of the Weimar Germany and show that Nazism was definitely *not* subject-centered and pro-ontological but violently critical of the modern Western conception of subject and of the technologization of the human mind and thinking; for the second, I will relate Heidegger's philosophy of Being to certain central trends of the intellectual and cultural life of the Weimar Germany, first of all to Expressionism and German *Dasein* philosophy, and show that these trends also were hostile to the modern Western conception of subject. These trends comprise the common cultural denominator of Heidegger's thinking and Nazism. Because of this denominator, Heidegger was prone to see Nazism as the only genuinely a(nti)ontological and anti-subject-centered political movement of the thirties and, perhaps, of his times in general. The conclusion will be that Heidegger never turned against the movement. Rather, from Heidegger's point of view, the party bureaucrats, due to a lack of philosophical insight, betrayed the original antilogocentric spirit of the National-Socialist revolution. The movement itself was eventually destroyed by a powerful logocentric enemy, the technologically advanced Democracy and technologically oriented Bolshevism.

The intellectual, philosophical and esthetic themes of the anti-humanistic Weimar culture comprise a sort of forum or theater of cultural discussion which doesn't lack controversy or struggle but which, nevertheless, is thematically unitary. Heidegger's *Dasein* philosophy cannot be separated from this thematic whole without distorting the unity and coherence of his thinking. Philosophical and esthetic Nazism was only one version of the very anti-subjectivistic and anti-humanistic mainstream philosophy of the Weimar culture. Embedded into this background, Heidegger's philosophy will not appear as original and unique as the prevailing ahistorical French interpretation suggests but only as one version of the German *Dasein* philosophy. Actually Heidegger wasn't even the only academic *Dasein* philosopher who joined the Nazi movement.

A glimpse at the literature of the Heidegger controversy

Many authors have hinted at a similar approach to the Heidegger controversy, though their problems and notions have not been identical with the forgoing ones. Pierre Bourdieu (1988) was one of the first Frenchmen to connect Heidegger to what Bourdieu called *revolutionary Weimar conservatism*. However, it may be difficult to say what *conservatism* should mean in the Weimar political context, and it seems that the left-right dichotomy is seriously inadequate for the proper characterization of Heidegger's thinking, as well as the Nazi revolution in general. The Nazi movement was definitely directed against the Bourgeoisie and was highly critical of the influence which the big international Capital exercised upon the German people and society.

However, Bourdieu's view, unlike that of Lacoue-Labarthe's and Nancy's, must be credited for its ability to deal with an impressive variety of textual sources. In this respect, Michel Zimmerman (1990) and Richard Wolin (1990) have contributed to a similar critical tradition. Unfortunately, none of them has tried to understand Nazism as a deep and entrancing experience which a whole generation of Germans went through, including many writers and philosophers, though Zimmerman has correctly pointed to the relationship between Heidegger's *Dasein* notion and that of Ernst Jünger's, and Wolin has underlined the antirationalistic features of Heidegger's decisionism.

Nazism is not directly addressed by Bourdieu's Heidegger book (1988) either, though Bourdieu tries to embed Heidegger's work into the very soil of the Weimar culture out of which Nazism also arose. Bourdieu calls for a historical view of Heidegger's thinking but the political and economic history of Germany is hardly ever mentioned by him. While Bourdieu crisscrosses painstakingly the Weimar cultural scene, he forgets to tell us what this all has to do with the National-Socialist revolution, the Nazi experience, the collapse of German society, genocides, atrocities, and so on. Or is the connection supposed to be clear to everyone without specification?

It seems that our question, namely whether or not Nazism is humanism, is addressed by Bourdieu only indirectly. He pinpoints the philosophical origin of Heidegger's political thinking to the aversion to neo-Kantianism which Heidegger clearly expressed. Because Heidegger's Kant interpretation tried to capitalize on certain arational features in Kant's work, Heidegger's attack on neo-Kantianism can be seen as an early stage in his development toward antihumanism. If it is also true that Nazism as a philosophical movement originated from the same antihumanistic sources of the Weimar culture as Heidegger's Kant interpretation and his attack on neo-Kantianism, then we have found a ground for explaining why Heidegger was fascinated by Nazism, the Nazi revolution and Hitler's personality: it was the antihumanistic political alternative that only Nazism, in Heidegger's opinion, could offer to the German people in its way toward the realization of its destiny.

Luc Ferry and Alain Renaut (1990) have attacked Derrida's and Lacoue-Labarthe's apology by pointing out that Nazism was primarily a version of *antimodernism*, and it was the antimodernism in particular which attracted Heidegger. By *modernism* they refer to the tradition of Enlightenment, especially to the democratic institutions and the kind of critical attitude which modern science and philosophy can provide. But Ferry and Renaut have not followed the line of their argument to the bitter end. If it was antimodernism that characterized Nazism, then we should consider the possibility that this means that Nazism was also antihumanism in the particular sense which denounces the metaphysics of subjectivity and which questions the role of the subject as the central philosophical category and explanatory principle. Surprisingly, Ferry and Renaut don't want to acknowledge this. Their Nazism is primarily antimodernism, but they seem to downgrade the force of Nazism as an experiential and philosophical movement which attacked the core notion of all modernity, namely, the notion of rational subjectivity. In general, they don't take Nazism seriously as a philosophical and esthetic movement, and address some peripheral branches of the Nazi doctrine as genuine Nazism. A typical mistake is to take Nazism primarily as *biological racism* (a view which is accepted also by Lacoue-Labarthe). From that point of view, Nazism appears as rather harmless, pseudo-scientific nonsense, and it is hard to understand how some of the best minds of the twenties and thirties could ever have taken it seriously.

Ferry and Renaut also regret the use to which Lacoue-Labarthe and Derrida have put the word *humanism*, and recommend Sartre's definition of *humanism* which deprives man of essence: the essence of man is that he has no essence (Renaut and Ferry, 1990, p. 4). The idea is to save us from the absurd-sounding conclusion of Lacoue-Labarthe's definition, namely, that Nazism is, indeed, humanism. Unlike Ferry and Renaut, I will adopt, by and large, but not accurately, Lacoue-Labarthe's, Nancy's and Derrida's way of using the word *humanism*, and associate it to the attempts to define humanity through autonomous and conscious subjectivity (for additional explication, see Nancy's interview of Derrida, in Derrida, 1989), because this use accords with that of Heidegger's, and because Ferry's, Renaut's and Sartre's definition is highly confusing and doesn't eventually help us to distance Nazism from humanism.

Actually, already in an earlier book, Ferry and Renaut (1985) investigated the possibilities of nonmetaphysical humanism, but, in what follows, both *nonmetaphysical humanism* (Ferry and Renaut) and *antiessentialistic humanism* (Sartre) would be self-contradictory terms if the notion of humanism is not modified by considerable antimetaphysical qualifications. Chapter 6 presented and discussed some of the possible qualifications. Thus, if *ametaphysical democracy* (or, rather, ahumanistic democracy) is intended not to be a straightforward contradiction, *democracy*, in *ametaphysical democracy*, will, of course, mean something quite different from what *democracy* in the usual humanistic context is thought to mean.

Anyway, humanism which implies that the essence of man is that man has no essence sounds much more paradoxical than the phrase "Nazism is humanism." Man without essence must also be man without ethical and rational essence, and it is incomprehensible how such a nonessential creature can represent Western humanism in any regular sense of *humanism*. For example, Sartre who openly proclaims in *Existentialism and Humanism* (Sartre, 1946, p. 44) that his point of departure is the subjectivity of the individual, resorts to a vocabulary which is hardly nonessentialistic: *dignity; moral responsibility; choice; cogito; universal human condition*; and so on. In other words, how could any of the traditional humanistic values, such as democracy and equality, ever be even characterized, let alone defended, with the help of the Sartrean definition? A man without essential character could quite consistently be a relativist racist (say, of Wilhelm von Humboldt's sort) or a genocidal mass murderer (say, of Himmler's sort), whereas it could be hard for a man without essence to defend the benefits of intercultural communication or the equal rights of all men. In addition, Kojève's and Sartre's Hegelian view of freedom as the human ability to wrench man above the determinacies and determinism of nature, is simply based on a mistaken conception of nature (cf. Chapter 2 and 3).

On the other hand, it is not intrinsically obvious that Nazism is *not* humanism (in the Heideggerian sense of the term). Serious crimes have been committed and racism has been (and is) advocated in the name of Socialism, Christianity, Enlightenment, Democracy, Equality and Human Rights, and it may be impossible to characterize, say, *democracy* in such a way that it would definitely block totalitarianism, racism, intolerance, inequality, and so on. A good and interesting definition will, most probably, remain too weak to do that much. It is always good to remember that the expansion of one of the leading modern democracies, the USA, was made possible only with the help of the genocide of the native population; and that Hitler's ambitious plans to reorganize Eastern Europe to serve the economic interests of the *Third Reich* were inspired by the example of the British colonial administration in India (see Hitler, 1941-44, for example. p. 23). In addition, it remains a mystery how any denouncement of Nazism can be derived from Ferry's and Renaut's overly abstract and empty definition of humanism, and why it is supposed to be obvious that Nazism should appear as antihumanism (as the colloquial use demands) in the light of the definition. One of the ironies of the debate is that even if some of the leading Nazi philosophers might have questioned the motivation and historical credibility of Ferry's and Renaut's definition, they would have said that, in terms of the very definition, but not in terms of Lacoue-Labarthe's and Nancy's definition, Nazism indeed is humanism.

Contrary to Lacoue-Labarthe, I will suggest that Nazism was antihumanism *par excellence*, almost, but not perfectly, in the sense in which Lacoue-Labarthe, Nancy and Derrida intend *antihumanism* to be used, though in my vocabulary which hasn't yet been used here, *ahumanism* would be a better word. The resemblance of my thesis with that of Ferry and Renaut has to be evaluated in the light of the fact that our definitions of *humanism* are not identical. Nazism was, among other things, an attack on the Enlightenment picture of man as a rational and autonomous person, and it was especially the boundary of the subject and the object which Nazism attempted to deconstruct. This was supposed to happen by giving in to the *a*subjective urge to surrender to a national, *völkisch* experience. This surrendering is not an identification with a definite class of people but an experience of mythical nearness. This is not *only* an antimodern experience; it is also amodern and ametaphysical. Because I will criticize Lacoue-Labarthe's, Nancy's and Derrida's view of Nazism, I have to alter slightly (but not perhaps essentially) the meaning of *antihumanism* which they have in mind. The alteration takes the term more in the experiential direction.

I have found Ernst Nolte's article, "Philosophie und Nationalsozialismus," (1988), particularly valuable. The most striking feature of Nolte's article is, perhaps, that it makes Heidegger's thinking and political commitment look comprehensible by embedding it into the wider background of theoretical and philosophical Nazism. In this respect it resembles Bourdieu's work.

Nazism as aconceptual experience

The spiritual core of Nazism consisted of the urge to go through powerful aconceptual experiences. During these experiences, that which used to be a regular subject collapsed or withered away by giving way to a collective experiential flow which is indivisible and selfless (see Pylkkö, 1996c). Thus *collective* in the preceding sentence doesn't mean 'a group of individuals' but, rather, suggests the collapse of individuality and, along with that, the collapse of the boundaries which separate individuals from one another. Those who experienced Nazism as a revolutionary mass movement, longed for belonging together with this primordial experiential flux in which the rational subject doesn't inhibit action and dilute experience, and one feels *free* to surrender to the mythical powers which are simultaneously both *subpersonal* and *superpersonal*, and which guide man toward authentic life. According to National-Socialist thinking, international logocentric ideas prevented the German people from living authentically and realizing its destiny. Therefore, the national revolution had to destroy the uppermost structure of the German mentality, its alien or international layer, under which the uncorrupted German experience was said to hibernate. It was thought that the destruction of the foreign international influence would resuscitate the original German experience. The course which this national awakening would take was thought to be partly unpredictable and rationally uncontrollable.

Within the Nazi sphere of ideas, the human *Dasein* was seen as a scene of a historical struggle between *Life* and *Logos*. The authenticity of the *Dasein* could be attained only if the demands of Life were not suppressed or ignored. The authenticity was either straightforwardly identified with Life, or thought to consist of a balance between the demands of Life and Logos. In both cases, the experiential Life energy requires a special *life form* (Lebensform) in order to be released. But the life form of a nation could also be exposed to a constant threat of corruption which could prevent the national *Dasein* from reaching authenticity. For example, a wide-spread modern disease threatened to corrupt the German *Dasein*, its spirit (Geist), and its life form, and to the symptoms of the disease belonged, at least, selfishness, means-end-rationality, Christian ethical scruples, technologically ordered urban life style, capitalist market interests, internationalism, parliamentary rules, ideas of equality, bourgeois code of manners and regular scientific thinking. Only an experiential national revolution could help the Germans to curb the tidal wave of this corruption, and the revolution would be able to do this only by resuscitating an experience which is much older and more primordial than the aforelisted table of modern values, an experience which can be traced back to the prehistorical heritage of the German people (Volk). Thus one of the subject-object-boundaries which Nazism was assumed to deconstruct was the boundary which separates a modern individual from his ancestors. Only the original experience of the *Volk* is sufficiently sane and healthy in order to realize the Life principle, and only the national revolution can eventually generate the vigor which the German nation needs in order to accomplish its destiny.

But *Volk* is not to be understood in this context primarily as a biological notion. As Alfred Rosenberg (1934-40, see especially Dokument PS-1749, pp. 209-212) argues, the mythical experiential energies were *not* supposed to have such a plastic structure or *Gestalt* which can be studied by regular science. The mythical powers were definitely something that lie outside of the scope of the standard scientific attitude, including such structural methods which anthropologists use. The mythical powers were assumed to be unique and to arise from the local natural and historical environment. Every nation (Rosenberg mentions also the Japanese, Chinese and some African peoples) should remain faithful to its original life forms and thus sustain a contact to its own source of vitalizing powers. In order to capture the original experiential flair of the epoch, testimonies of those who actually partook in the movement or followed it from a short experiential distance, like Alphonse de Chateaubriant (1937), are of special interest. In de Chateaubriant's words (1937, p. 63), every nation has to find its own *unconscious inner way* (la voie intérieure du peuple). That the powers are still alive in the life forms of a nation is something that can be experienced as a peculiar authenticity by those who belong to the nation, though, on the other hand, we may have to say, somewhat circularly, that those who lack the experience do not really belong to the nation. For example, the German life form was supposed to be authentic as long as it endorses selflessness, courage, friendship, faithfulness and solidarity, and doesn't hesitate to resort to uninhibited hardness and violence if the vital interests of the *Volk* have to be protected.

Volk is something that cannot be approached only from an intellectual point of view, from the point of view of the *Logos*. It is not something with which an individual may identify himself with the help of logical or dialectical reasoning alone. An academic, scientific and intellectual way of approaching the *Volk* is based on logical identity principles, and, if the approach is acceptable at all, it must be derived from the primordial *völkisch* experience, not *vice versa*. First the *Volk* has to be experienced subconceptually; then, if necessary, it can be theorized about, and the intellectual attitude of controlling and the related identification mechanism can enter the scene. When you experience the communion with your *Volk*, and you begin to realize the experiential energies of the *Volk* in your own life, then you also know immediately and without intellectual reasoning that this is what is happening. It is unconscious (unbewusste) love, as Max Wundt, a philosophy professor from Jena, once put it in his article "Was heisst völkisch?" (see Wundt, 1924, p. 13). But perhaps it could just as well be unconscious hate. In both cases, your personal bourgeois identity begins to wither away. The experience is immediate, asubjective, revelatory and so powerful that no doubt of its nature and origin can arise. The *völkisch* experience of communion with the *Volk* is also so overwhelming and aconceptual that it may be difficult to describe it in any rational terms. But nonetheless, this lack of rational accessibility doesn't undermine the revelatory certainty, the *truth*, with which the experiencer is possessed whenever the experience of communion overtakes him.

Philosophical Nazism was characterized, not only by a certain kind of moral relativism, namely, that anything goes as long as it serves the interests of the national authenticity, but also by antirealism in the sense that, when a subject plunges into the indivisible whole of the collective national experience, the subject's boundary with objects will become somewhat obscure and may even become dissolved. Therefore this collective experience produces its own kind of experiential categories and classifications. Such categories and classes as *German*, *Jewish* or *bourgeois* were not intended to be scientific, empirical or reified sets of objects, but notions of experiential nearness and distance which made themselves 'real' through the high intensity of the experience. They were real if they were genuinely believed in, and as long as they helped to produce an authentic national experience.

Nazism and anti-Semitism

National-Socialist anti-Semitism wasn't primarily biological of its origin but, rather, cultural, economic and social. According to Alfred Bäumler (1942, see for example, p. 65), race is not a natural class but a social notion which describes the essential unconscious and instinctive relations among the members of a community. According to Hitler's view (Hitler, 1925), the Jewish people threatened the vitality of the German *Volk* and its spirit (Geist). This threat was not primarily, and certainly not only, a threat against the racial (biological) purity of the German people, but an attack on the authenticity of the *völkisch* experience. In *Mein Kampf* (1925) Hitler describes at length the Vienna of his youthful years, and one of the leading ideas is that the social, economic and political life of the Habsburgian Monarchy was corrupted by a Jewish conspiracy. In a conversation with Rauschning, Hitler openly denies the scientific validity of the concept of race (Rauschning, 1940a, pp. 210-211). Rauschning's reliability has sometimes been questioned (see Irving, 1977, p. xxii), but some present-day specialists have also defended his interpretation of Nazism (Broszat, 1987). A person with a spotless Nazi background could be accepted to the highest Nazi elite even if he, like Reinhartd Heydrich, could be classified as a biological jew. Hitler's speeches seldom address racial hygiene as such but he returns, instead, with almost obsessive tenacity, to art, history and other spiritual issues. The Jews were responsible for a much more fearful plot than just poisoning the German Blood, and that was the cultural, social and political conspiracy they had allegedly launched in order to weaken the authenticity of the German *Geist*. The primary agents of this conspiracy were Bolshevism and Capitalism, and the spiritual core of the conspiracy was the internationally-oriented intellectualism of the Enlightenment.

Typically, logocentric intellectualism pictured man as a rational and morally conscious subject who attempts to cultivate his maturity and decency by letting his behavior be guided by abstract and universal ideas, including the ideas of equality, tolerance and democracy. These ideas are definitely internationally oriented, and intended to be universally applicable, which often means the suppression of the local cultural, linguistic, racial and historical variation. Because the Nazis contrasted such words as *Blut* or *Rasse* with the logocentric international ideology, it is far from clear that the meaning of the German *völkisch* vocabulary was ever intended to be interpreted in any strictly theoretical, scientific or biological way. This would have betrayed the National-Socialist ideology, because the theoretical rationality, not the least as it has found its expression in the modern natural sciences, belongs, if anything, to the mental equipment of the modern enlightened subject.

Due to the lack of any own national identity, the Jewish people were believed to be particularly responsive to the temptations of such international, abstract, universal and intellectualist ideas. The alleged Jewish intellectualism, internationalism and logocentrism was said to weaken the German *Volk* by depriving the local German spirit of the sources of national revitalization. For example, overly rational, formal and intellectualist science and philosophy belonged to the enemies of the German spirit. Furthermore, Christianity as a version of the normative Jewish thinking; British-French Enlightenment as misconceived and pretentious universalism; French Cartesianism as foreign intellectualism; and, eventually British empiricism as technologically oriented antispiritualism, were labelled as enemies of the national spirit (see for example, Böhm, 1938). It is ironic that the German-French-British cultural and philosophical triad which dominated the Nazi discussion has resurfaced recently in Deleuze and Guattari's geophilosophy (see Deleuze & Guattari, 1991). Also the view that the Jewish cultural heritage was somehow weakened by its inclination to adopt overly abstract metaphysical ideas which are void of creative vitality seems to have been quite popular between the Great Wars. Even Wittgenstein elaborated it at length in the thirties (see Wittgenstein, 1980, for example p. 18-20).

It is often difficult for academic scholars to admit that world-historical events are inspired and shaped by openly nonacademic ideas, that is, by ideas which must appear to them as immature, inadequate, unscientific, and often almost ridiculous. Contrary to these, academic theories themselves are usually highly intellectualist and tend to picture man as overly rational, goal-directed and autonomous. Therefore, they often fail to find a balance between rational, irrational and arational ingredients of human experience and behavior. When academic theories are forced to deal with such partly obscure, violent, arational and even partly irrational events as, for instance, Nazism, the World Wars and recent genocides, they give in to the temptation to introduce some "hidden variables" with the help of which these obscure and obnoxious events are rationalized. Typically, the intellectualist bias tends to suppress the experiential aspect of Nazism and replace it by the agenda of secret but rational motives. A popular explanation along this line is to see Nazism as a conspiracy of Capital against the Workers. It is hard for us to admit that, from the Nazi point of view, Hitler's war was a war against the International Jewry (Judentum), and against Bolshevism and the International Capital as special manifestations of the Jewish conspiracy, and that the rationality of the war, however thin it may have been, was in Hitler's endeavor to save the authenticity of the German culture. Yet this is what Hitler and the other Nazi leaders seriously believed they were doing. In order to understand the Nazi movement, this must not be ignored and replaced by profound and overly rationalizing hidden motive explanations.

The national revolutionary experience had its hidden, unconscious and aconceptual aspects, too, but these aspects cannot be reduced to some intellectually controllable variables. The Germans were not searching for their missing identity so desperately that they became second-rate, almost schizophrenic, imitation Frenchmen, as Lacoue-Labarthe's and Nancy's theory suggests (1991, p. 40). There was no hidden logic, unconscious (Freudian) code or other veiled agenda. Instead, there was something thoroughly aconceptual involved, and it seems that every purely intellectualist theory, like that of Lacoue-Labarthe and Nancy's, is in serious trouble as it attempts to deal theoretically with something which remains strongly, though not completely, atheoretical. Actually, it is questionable whether *any* theory of Nazism can be adequate, assuming that the word *theory* is used in a regular logical and conceptual sense. Only certain relatively rational aspects of Nazism are theoretically accessible, and every thinking that lacks access to the genuine aconceptuality will always fail to comprehend Nazism adequately. What is needed for the proper understanding of Nazism is an access to the experiential asubjectivity and aconceptuality which may be so intensive that even the identity of the understanding subject is in danger. Thus, it is not the theoreticity of the theoretical attitude alone that makes the explanation of Nazism impossible; what makes it impossible is that the theoretical attitude, as a manifestation of reason, accepts and utilizes the inhibitive role which the monitoring subject exercises upon the rest of the human experience. Reason is always selfish, and, therefore, a biased judge when it has to encounter some aconceptual experiences. Nazism as such lies relatively open and unhidden before anyone who is not *afraid* of adopting the asubjective approach.

If Hitler's war was a war against the International Jewry, it is obvious that the *difference* between the Aryan race and other races must have been vital in the Nazi thinking. But it is far from obvious that this difference was able to differentiate and identify reified and external racial classes in any realistic, logical or well defined sense, or that it was even intended to do that. Thus it is not clear that the Nazi version of racism was really pseudoscientific, because it was never intended to be scientific in the first place. By their education, most of the Nazi leaders were artistically, literarily, politically and historically oriented, and, therefore, unable, though occasionally willing perhaps, to develop a seriously biological version of racism. In practice, the racial distinctions which appeared in the Nazi thinking were either sociohistorical or purely experiential in their kind, and arose mainly because they were passionately believed in. Because it was the passion and urge to experience something ravishing that carried the racial and national revolution onward, the racial difference bore a strongly prelogical experiential flair.

In Hitler's opinion, the Jews in the multicultural Double Monarchy comprised an isolated ethnic group which didn't *belong to* the German nation and never wanted to belong to it either. As many examples of *Mein Kampf* (1925) show, the racial key words, like *German* and *non-German*, expressed *experiential nearness and distance* to Hitler, and were thought to organize both the German and Jewish mind before any conceptual, scientific and typological rationalizations enter the scene. In a language which is similar with that of the later Heidegger, we can say that the intraracial similarities among the Germans were based on the experiential *Nähe* (nearness), not on the logical identity or inclusion relation, and, as such, the experience of similarity (nearness) and difference (distance) can be said to precede all reificational or ontological typologies which may indeed be onto-theo-logical in their nature.

Hitler as a man without essential subjectivity

Hitler was a revolutionary socialist who believed that he was chosen to save the German *Geist* from the oblivion to which the international Jewry had planned to send it. In this saving mission, a special role was reserved for socialism, because bourgeois selfishness as an internationally acclaimed ideological attitude was thought not to serve the national interest. At the beginning of his career, he had, like Mussolini, a distinct proletarian identity, but after an incident to which he referred as a "mystical conversion" he transformed himself into a *völkisch* leader. Later Nazi literature used to describe the incident in mystical or pseudo-mystical terms because it was said to be colored by a peculiar apersonal experience. Alphonse de Chateaubriant's *La Gerbe des Forces* (1937, see especially chapter *Hitler*, pp. 61-78) depicts a legend according to which Hitler lost his accidental personal identity and was some-how first absorbed and later guided by the will of the German people. After that Hitler begun consciously to suppress the characteristics of his bourgeois person and distance himself from his family background and earlier personal contacts. As the Nazi literature sometimes presented it, he was mystically unified, or even married, with the German *Volk* and its *Geist*. He was no longer supposed to be a person or a citizen but, rather, a subpersonal power submitted directly to the service of the *Volk*. (For Hitler's own words, see Domarius, 1965, Band I, erster Halbband, p. 19, and zweiter Halbband, p. 606; but see also Rauschning, 1940b, pp. 202-220.) He was not Musil's phenomenalist *der Man ohne Eigenschaften*, the man without essential personal properties, but rather, the Schopenhauerian man who has sidelined his rational, autonomous and accidental subjectivity, and whose actions are dictated by the *völkisch* uncon-scious (das Unbewusste; de Chateaubriant's "la voie intérieure du peuple"). It is tempting to apply Heideggerian terms again and say that Hitler's *Wille* and the *Wille* of the German people dwelled in the same spiritual region and, by coming to the nearness (die Nähe) of one another, eventually belonged together (zusammengehören).

And this is how Hitler was experienced, not only by de Chateaubriant and Heidegger (see Heidegger, 1933), but by many a sensitive and intelligent contemporary. Göbbels describes his first encounter with the Hitler phenom-enon with a messianic language which doesn't hide its openly erotic connota-tions (see Bärsch, 1987, pp. 212-233). Leni Riefenstahl (1987) describes with ecstatic and visionary terms her first exposure to Hitler's power of suggestion (p. 152). This took place in the Berlin *Sportpalast* in February, 1932. When she later made personal acquaintance with Hitler, he used to emphasize that his devotion to the salvation of the German *Geist* was unconditional and apersonal, and he even compared his own political work to the artistic calling by which he sensed, quite correctly I think, that Riefenstahl was possessed. In a similar vein, he is said to have discredited Himmler as a possible successor because Himmler lacked artistic vision.

Though less literally articulate than Mussolini, Hitler was highly sensitive to music, visual arts, and architecture, and especially to the suggestion of cinema, and he seems to have been aware of his Schopenhauerian connection. In a conversation with Riefenstahl, he exalted Schopenhauer as a profound visionary but downgraded Nietzsche as a mere verbal artist. Hitler's Schopenhauer connection may have arisen from his affection, or rather, addiction, to Wagner's music (see Matter, 1977). Wagner's music drama, especially its rich chromatic harmony, was widely presented, for example in Ernst Kurth's music esthetics, as the major manifestation of the Schopenhauerian *Unbewusste*, and, as such, it was assumed to be able to affect the human unconscious directly, without the mediation of concepts.

In this light Lacoue-Labarthe's characterization of Nazism as "absolute subjectivization" is not credible. Rather, the Hitler phenomenon was a Schopenhauerian phenomenon which, just like music in Kurth's esthetics, could bring the Germans experientially close to their Will (Wille), the conceptually inaccessible urge to live and die, create and destroy. This comprised a violent attack on the autonomy and identity of the modern Western subjectivity.

National Socialism as a cultural rescue movement

The asubjectivist nature of Nazism was widely noted, not only by de Chateaubriant, but by a number of other contemporary commentators. It is typical of reports which were written in the early and mid thirties that they present a vast, though often critical, panorama of Nazism as a revolutionary cultural and social movement. Hitler, Göbbels, Heyse, Heidegger, Bäumler, Jünger, Benn and Rosenberg, and many other Nazi leaders and nationalist intellectuals were obsessed by the critical condition of the German culture and its spiritual revival. In addition to the rather arational experientiality, the commentators also underline certain more rational aspects of the Nazi revolution. Nazism was seen as a rescue movement to save the German culture and protect Germany against the international enemy which was led by Bolshevism and Capitalism. In order to illuminate this point of view, I will resort to three non-German authors (Paavolainen, 1936; Böök, 1933; Koskenniemi, 1937) who all wrote in the thirties.

Olavi Paavolainen was a brilliant Finnish writer who visited Germany in 1936 as an official guest of the *Nordische Gesellschaft*. Immediately before the Second World War he travelled extensively also in the Soviet Union and Latin America. In his book on Nazi Germany, *Kolmannen Valtakunnan Vieraana* (Paavolainen, 1936), he presents Nazism as a revolutionary social mass movement with complex esthetic and philosophical implications. For him, Nazism is a movement which tries to change the German life style and thinking habits by directing them back to the national, mythical and collective roots. It was obvious for Paavolainen that the Nazis were preparing the German people for a total war against Bolshevism, Christianity and Democracy. But Paavolainen was particularly skillful in describing the semiotics of everyday life, habits, taste, fashion, rhetoric, propaganda and myths. The twenties had been overly liberal and international, saturated by individual indulgence in sexual liberation, drugs, commercial excitement, urban life styles and international ideas and contacts. A few years earlier Paavolainen had published a book on these individualistic and nihilistic themes. But now, Nazism had changed all that. Nazism was national, collective, puritan, devotional, but not less experientially intensive. The intensity was aroused by a new experiential attitude, by the unconditional surrender to the apersonal national will. This surrender had, according to Paavolainen, a distinct, though unconscious and often suppressed, sexual character, and it was enhanced by the pre-Christian German mythology which exalted vitality and the asubjective experience of power as the dialectics of domination, submission and violence. Paavolainen says explicitly, not only that he tries to expose the reader to *Nazism as an experience* (in addition to the Finnish word *elämys*, he uses the German word *Welterlebnis*), but that no purely intellectual explanation of this experience is possible (p. 228). He went so far that he called Nazism the first originally European religion. He found particularly abhorrent, incidentally, the puritan code which was supposed to control personal sexual relations in the new Germany and which, according to Paavolainen, unabashedly repressed the German woman.

Fredrik Böök, a Swedish author, published in 1933 a book on Hitler's Germany. He devotes three chapters of his book to anti-Semitism. According to Böök, the Nazis and other German ultranationalists thought that the Jewish influence in the mass media, literature, universities, and publishing business amounted to a conspiracy against the spirit of the German Culture. According to Böök, German anti-Semitism was a reaction to the Jewish anti-Germanism and, in general, to the international influence which the Jewish community actively spread in Germany. The international Jewish intellectuals had waged an ideological war against the German spirit, and this served as the main fuel for German anti-Semitism. Böök presents Heinrich Heine as a typical German-speaking advocate of international anti-Germanism. It is ironic that even Lacoue-Labarthe's argumentation seems not to be completely free of anti-Germanism (1987, p. 80, "Germany still does not exist."), as if you couldn't oppose someone successfully without adopting, to some extent, your opponent's categories. Even Adorno, in his vicious attacks on Stravinsky, Sibelius, Heidegger, and other national figures, cannot help adopting a tone which, in its disciplined aggressiveness and intolerance, is not so far from the sublimated hate of the fascistic rhetoric.

What is not obvious is that, if there was such a struggle between the alleged Jewish anti-Germanism and the German anti-Semitism, it was primarily a battle of two races. Perhaps it was rather a battle of two chosen nations and cultures, as Hitler is said to have put it in his interview with Rauschning (1940b, p. 227), a battle to settle the question which one of the two nations was, so to speak, more chosen. According to the Nazi philosophy, the Jewish influence upon the German culture was overly intellectualizing and sterilizing, and remained all too closely tied to the Jewish religion which was controlled by lifeless norms, complex but ultimately empty symbolism and formalism, and by overly abstract and logocentric theology. It was said to poison the roots which nourished the German *Geist* and connected it to the genuinely aconceptual *völkisch* experience. We are familiar with a similar theme of cultural purity in the recent French context too. For example, it is often said that the American culture industry is one-dimensional and superficial, and its impact upon the European culture is destructive. It is not seldom that we hear leading French intellectuals criticizing the American culture in terms which are not far from cultural racism.

The propaganda war between anti-Germanism and anti-Semitism was described and commented also by the Finnish author and university professor V.A. Koskenniemi (1937) who was, not only a Nazi-sympathizer, but also a poet and Goethe scholar, and a specialist in German literature. According to his view, the situation in German universities and professional life was alarming and the Jewish influence had to be sidelined. Also, some recent scholars have been surprised by the statistics of the Jewish influence. It has been claimed, for example, that half of the medical doctors of Berlin in 1933 were of Jewish origin (see Bourel, 1994). It must be added that Koskenniemi viewed the Jewish culture with sympathy and conceded that the deep-going Jewish ingredient and influence in the present and past German culture had been fruitful and definitely ineradicable. The question was whether or not the influence had now become too big.

It is not easy, however, to discern the rational, goal-directed aspects of Nazism from the less rational ones because the rationality, namely the need to protect or save the German culture which was said to be threatened by vicious Internationalism, fueled, in a complex way, the fire of arationality and eventually irrationality too. This was so because the Nazi thinking equated the authenticity of the German culture with the peculiar aconceptual and asubjective *völkisch* experience.

Nazism as Expressionism in politics

Because it can be claimed that Nazism attempted to estheticize and poeticize the political sphere in quite a similar way as the German romanticism had attempted to do earlier (for Romanticism and politics, see Schmitt, 1919), we need to turn our attention to those esthetic movements of the twenties and thirties which shared some common philosophical interests and goals with Nazism. This may help us to appreciate the peculiar intertwinement of the rational, ecstatic and irrational ingredients in the Nazi experience. In particular, we should consider German Expressionism and illuminate its role in the Weimar culture and in the emergence of Nazism.

Expressionism, in painting, drama and poetry, was one of the most prominent esthetic movements of the Weimar and Nazi Germany. The philosophical core of Expressionism was the nihilistic attitude it had adopted toward the Western notion of rational and moral autonomy. In its attack on the hegemony of the autonomous and rational consciousness, Expressionism brought anomalous experiences and social marginality into the artistic spotlight, revealed ambiguity and absurdity in everyday "small life," and depicted man as a primitive creature who longed for surrendering to such primordial experiences which were not controlled by rational calculations, moral scruples, the taste of the bourgeoisie or the classical conception of beauty. Such primordial experiences were supposed to originate from the preconscious existential urge either to stay alive or die, and the urge was supposed to be so primitive that, under its spell, the instincts of sex and aggression, and the drives toward domination, pleasure and self-destruction, which could hardly be distinguished from one another, dictated what man is and how he behaves. Expressionism was saturated with the new *Lebensgefühl* of *Angst* and nihilism. Perhaps Egon Schiele and his work could be mentioned as an example of such an artistic attitude and thinking.

Now, an interesting question arises: How did the Nazi revolution, cultural administration and esthetics deal with Expressionism?

They seem to have applied double standards. On the one hand, the Nazi esthetics with its emphasis on apersonal and asubjective experience was quite close to the Expressionist philosophy of primordial experience; on the other hand, it wasn't easy for the Nazi cultural administration to accept the openly satirical and partly nonrealist dream-like world which the Expressionists had created, especially when it was filled with open eroticism. Yet both Expressionism and Nazism attacked the Enlightenment picture of man as an autonomous subject, and rejected the bourgeois life style and code of behavior. Especially Göbbels, who was also a novelist and literary scholar, and whose literary work was inspired by Dostoyevsky (see Bärsch, 1987, pp. 216-218), accepted the Expressionist program and was sensitive to the visions of Expressionism, even to the avant-garde ones, whereas Hitler's artistic orientation and taste were obviously less cultivated and more conventional than Göbbels's.

A Swedish journalist, Christer Jäderlund, who published in 1937 a book on Nazi Germany (Jäderlund, 1937) describes the mutual appeal of the Nazis and the Expressionists (see especially pp. 181-182). The Expressionists were often fascinated by the antibourgeois revolutionary thrust of the Nazis, and the Nazis were eager to utilize the powerful Expressionist machinery of artistic suggestion. A typical case of the former was the Expressionist painter Emil Nolde who quite early became a member of the *NSDAP*. He is said to have proclaimed that instinct is ten times more than knowledge (Instinkt ist zehnmal mehr als Wissen, for which see Froning, 1990, p. 10). One of the most characteristic features of his art was, perhaps, his extremely intensive handling of color, especially in flower paintings. He is said to have proclaimed that the one who paints flowers paints their deep-seated life (ihr tiefenliegendes Leben.) This unconscious but intensive life seems to have attracted Göbbels who, to Hitler's consternation, not only bought some of Nolde's paintings, but exhibited them openly in his home collection (Guyot and Restellini, 1983, pp. 58 and 208).

The obvious Nazi affinity for Expressionism has been recognized by some art historians too (see, for example, Gordon, 1987, pp. 178-185). Nevertheless, they seem to be unable to explain the sudden turn from affinity to aversion which the Nazi policy adopted. It is not that Göbbels's view of man differed so much from, say, Beckmann's, Grosz's or Dix's views; rather, the question was that, according to the later Nazi policy, it was not proper, especially after the success of the National-Socialist revolution, to show to the German people their *previous*, that is, pre-revolutionary portrait.

Hitler who was a frequent movie-goer and admirer of Fritz Lang's work seems to have utilized in his speech performances the ostensive acting gestures of the Expressionist drama. It has also been claimed that Albert Speer's architecture, especially his design and decoration of the *NSDAP* conventions, resembled the gloomy, colossal and consciously artificial night scenes of the early Expressionist movies. And it is obvious that Leni Riefenstahl applied and further developed the Expressionist movie esthetics and techniques, especially those of Arnold Fanck's, in her suggestive *Parteitag* movies. Though Riefenstahl struggled painfully toward the esthetic perfection of her art, and invented new and even revolutionary techniques of documentary film, she recognized the unconscious origin of her work and described it as "instinctive" and "chaotic" (Riefenstahl, 1987, see especially the lecture she gave in 1938 in Paris on cinema as art, pp. 333-335). For her, documentary film was not an attempt to reflect external events, and neither did Hitler ask her to do anything like that. In her book, *Hinten den Kulissen des Reichsparteitag-Films*, she says that her films tried to help the German nation to re-experience the original *Parteitag* experience (Riefenstahl, 1935, see especially p. 15). In this search for experience and re-experience, she utilized the Expressionist film and drama esthetics which she had adopted during her acting and directing career. It is a nice example of a circle of mutual influence that the visual setting of the party conventions (Reichsparteitag), and therefore the setting of some of Riefenstahl's movies, had been designed by a man, Albert Speer, whose esthetic thinking had been shaped, among others, by Expressionist ideas, not the least by the Expressionist movie itself.

In order to understand the a(nti)subjectivistic tendencies of the Nazi esthetics, it is crucial to acknowledge the connection between the Nazi esthetics and the Expressionist movie, especially Fritz Lang and his scriptwriter and wife Thea von Harbou (who later lent her support to the Nazi movement). One of the main themes on which the German movies of the twenties and early thirties, and Lang's and von Harbou's work in particular, concentrated was the relationship between power, sexuality and the unconscious. Full power *in* or *with* people could be reached only if those who participate in the power *Erlebnis*, become one with each other by surrendering to the unconscious, aconceptual and collective experience of nearness. Such an experience bears a distinct sexual flair and cannot be controlled by intellectual plans or rational calculations. The experience and related energy are subpersonal and remain conceptually and morally uncontrollable. As soon as power is exercised *from* one individual *over* another in the sense of a *control* relation, the intensity of power is immediately diminished by separation, selfishness, calculations and critical attitudes (cf. Chapter 6).

It is understandable that Lang, who soon after his immigration to the USA had proclaimed himself an anti-Nazi, wanted to distance his work, not only from Nazism, but eventually from Expressionism too. This latter distancing must have been motivated by the fact that Lang was, to some extent, conscious of the connection between Nazism and Expressionism. But regardless of Lang's attempt to separate his work from Expressionism, it is not by chance that Göbbels, who immediately after January 1933 assumed the ideological control over the German movie industry, offered the highest administrative position of the future Nazi movie administration to Lang. Simultaneously Göbbels forbade the distribution of one of Lang's movies (see Schrader & Schebera, 1987). This ambiguity reveals almost transparently the dualism which characterized the relationship of Nazism and Expressionism. Lang who soon after the incident left Germany had earlier become famous for his Expressionist movie dramatization of the *Nibelungen Lied*, a specimen of the *völkisch* German mythology if anything.

Peter Gay (1968, pp. 107-118) has recognized the political ambiguity which characterized the Expressionist movement. This is how he associates the Expressionist esthetics with Nazism: "...the Expressionists returned to the animal through art [...] the Nazis would return to the animal in life..." (p. 113). Both the Nazis and the Expressionists envisioned man as a creature who is driven by subrational instincts. Perhaps we should distinguish two schools of Expressionism, *avant-garde Expressionism* and *conventional Expressionism*, and concede that, after all, the so-called *Entartete Kunst* and the straight Nazi art may not have been so serious enemies as may first appear but, rather, rivals who shared several central goals and have a common philosophical and esthetic background.

They both saw man as an irrational *Doppelgänger* who dreams about a power which would make people resemble puppets, the idea being that a machine-like puppet is an inseparable part of the collective power experience. As happens in some of E.T.A. Hoffmann's short stories, this ultimate power destroys the conventional boundary which separates normal persons from one another. It seems that the dualism of the avant-garde and conventional branches within the Expressionist movement represents a kind of *narcissism of small differences*, as Freud would have put it. Analogously, close philosophical relatives, like Marxism and Nazism, who had turned against each other mainly because of the question of nationalism, express their diversion in terms and tones which are far more ferocious than what the philosophical difference itself would suggest. Of course, Marxism and Nazism were separated also by other issues than nationalism, but Marxism had also its asubjective branches. Alfred Müller-Armack (1933, pp. 16-19) argues that the philosophy of history with which Nazism wanted to associate itself was far less deterministic than that of the mainstream Marxism. The Nazi view of history denied the existence of strict, let alone deterministic, historical laws. But he also says that both Marxism and Nazism originate from the nineteenth century German Romantic historicism (Historismus).

Expressionism touched Heidegger too, because Ernst Jünger, especially in his early works, was strongly influenced by Expressionism, and it is known that Heidegger followed keenly Jünger's work (Zimmerman, 1990). Especially, Heidegger's views of modern Western technology owe much to Jünger's seminal work *Der Arbeiter: Herrschaft und Gestalt* (1932/1981). But already *Der Kampf als inneres Erlebnis* (Jünger, 1922), betrays Jünger's close association with the leading Expressionist poet, Gottfried Benn, who himself later openly supported the Nazi movement (for which, see, Kunnas, 1972, p. 11) and didn't resign to *internal exile* until the late thirties. (For Jünger's connection to Expressionism, see Meyer, 1990, pp. 41-61). Heidegger's themes of nihilism and antimodernism cannot be fully comprehended without Benn's Expressionist vision of the modern society as a morgue. It was beyond the nihilistic modernity, as it appears in Benn's and Jünger's Expressionist visions, that Heidegger wanted to find his way as a thinker. But, in order to surpass nihilism, one must first understand it and live by it.

Nazism was Expressionism of politics, or Expressionism *in* politics. Nazi *Appells* were ceremonies where the Germans could unhesitatingly surrender to an asubjective and subpersonal *völkisch* experience, as Paavolainen had witnessed. Such collective experience is never completely controllable by consciousness. The Nazi political apparatus controlled the Germans as subjects, as separate citizens with rational goals and interests, but not as a collective of preindividual experiential centers which dwell in the flux of asubjective revolutionary enthusiasm. Rather, Nazism itself expressed and followed the movements of the German collective and aconceptual experience. Our understanding of Nazism as a power experience remains inadequate as long as we consider power only as an external relation in which some autonomous subjects exercise control and domination over other subjects (cf. Chapter 6). Therefore, Nazism is almost impossible to understand for any theory or view in which the aconceptual and the subconscious play no role and which, therefore, has, by definition, to present man as a rational being and power as an external relation between conscious and rational individuals.

In his *Risti ja Hakaristi* (1938), Paavolainen compares the Nazi society with the pre-Columbian American societies. Both the Nazi society and the pre-Columbian societies were, according to Paavolainen, characterized by a strong tendency to annihilate all symptoms of personal individuality and destroy the calculative rationality upon which this kind of individuality rests. Paavolainen ends his second book on Nazism by teaching us that we should not only try to *think* about Nazism; we should have courage to *see* it. By *seeing* he seems to suggest an asubjective experiential touch with Nazism. Without such a touch, which may occasionally resemble surrendering or assimilation, our understanding of Nazism will remain inadequate. No analysis or theory alone will ever reveal us the essence of Nazism. Revelation is an experiential event which requires that the rationality and conceptuality which always characterize the presence of the thinking subject have to be undermined or sidelined. We must have courage to experience Nazism.

The rational, irrational and arational in Nazism

However, the decision to surrender to the national or *völkisch* aconceptuality seems to have been partly consciously chosen because the Nazis had actually received a full parliamentary mandate for their plan to destroy parliamentarianism (cf. Eitner, 1990; see also Oakes, 1986). The destruction of democracy was planned democratically. We must concede that any attempt to save parliamentarianism in that situation would have been antidemocratic! But the Nazi power elite could not have stayed in power had the leaders themselves not surrendered to the collective asubjective experience which they had helped to arouse, and had they not followed, rather than guided, the Nazi revolution as an experiential *Volk* movement. Purely selfish calculations of the Nazi elite and administration could not have carried the movement to such peaks of mass popularity as happened. It is also compatible with this view that the *NSDAP* itself wasn't a particularly successful economic enterprise. In general, Hitler seems to have thought that the national economy was a side issue, something that takes care of itself as soon as more serious problems, such as the crisis of the German spirit and culture, have been solved. He used to ridicule everyone who suggested that the crisis was originally economic. The Nazi alliance with Capital, to which Lacoue-Labarthe refers several times, is another myth which hasn't found much documentary or empirical support (see Turner, 1985).

Alfred Müller-Armack's lucid study on the National-Socialist conception of state and national economy, *Staatsidee und Wirtschaftsordnung im neuen Reich* (1933; see also Haselbach, 1994), separates Nazism, on the one hand, from bourgeois-liberal capitalism and, on the other hand, from Marxism. In National-Socialism, the corporative work organization provides the basis for the reconciliation of the interests of the economy with those of the state. The reconciliation is not possible in the Marxist or in the bourgeois-liberal state. The Nazi state is sufficiently strong in order to intervene, even with violent measures if that is required, in the economy, for instance by the policies which slow down inflation or too rapid economic growth, but, at the same time, the state remains elastic and sensitive to the entrepreneurial needs. Unlike the Marxist state which is bureaucratic, the Nazi state is able to react to the demands of the economy without violating the needs of the *Volk*.

According to Müller-Armack, the idea of the bourgeois-liberal state rests on a mistaken conception of freedom. Freedom is understood as *individual* freedom, the freedom of an individual from state control. The National-Socialist state acknowledges the entrepreneurial initiative as long as it promotes the interests and the unity of the national community, but the state is also ready to assume the role as a leader of the national-economic totality by providing a vision of the nation's future. Unlike the Marxist theory and bourgeois-liberal model, the Nazi thinking envisions the future as genuinely open, indeterminate and partly unpredictable. The future lies hidden in the unfolding national experience waiting to be disclosed. For this disclosing it needs the *Führer* who serves as the mediator between the national will and political action. Thus freedom as a notion applies to the *Volk* and community, rather than to separate individuals. The *Führer* must be seen as an ineradicable and apersonal power ingredient which belongs to and serves the *Volk* community.

In Finland, similar ideas were presented and discussed by professor Yrjö Ruutu, the leader of the Finnish National-Socialist party (see Klinge, 1972, pp. 132-152). Like Müller-Armack, Ruutu preached for the unity of the national community and resorted to the unifying myth of national origin. Both of these men were also corporativists who accused parliamentarianism of inefficiency but didn't eventually reject it altogether. It is interesting to note that both of them continued their career successfully after the war as organizers of the forthcoming welfare state system, Müller-Armack as a high official in Ludwig Erhard's ministry of economy (see, Haselbach, 1994) and Ruutu, among many other positions, as a high-level executive at the Finnish ministry of education (see Klinge, 1972, p. 152).

The *Führer* promised to give the German people what it really longed for. The Germans wanted to live through a heroic drama of freedom which concluded either with unconditional victory or with a national collapse, a collective suicide, the *Götterdämmerung*. The victory would change, not only the history of Europa, but the history of the world. This dramatic vision had originally only little to do with economic issues, though the revolution, of course, had some economic implications too. But the possibility of a national collapse was anticipated already in 1933 by some commentators, like Fredrik Böök, who were, by and large, sympathetic to the goals of the revolution (see Böök, 1933, p. 21). Among other sympathizers, Louis Ferdinand Céline seems to have never really believed in Hitler's prospects of reaching the final victory. Because Hitler's was not a drama of identification, but an Expressionist drama of destruction of all identifications, we can resort to the notion of *Dionysus* as it was presented by Nietzsche. At the beginning of *Die Geburt der Tragödie* (1872/1939, pp. 50-53), Nietzsche defines the *Dionysian* principle as the annihilation of the individual, as a violation of the *principium individuationes*. In this sense Nazism was the ultimate Dionysian experience, and Expressionism was its artistic counterpart: the autonomy of the individual, one of the most central metaphysical principles of Western thinking, was questioned and undermined. Many sensitive and acute observers, including, Céline, recognized the Dionysian energy of the revolution, and thus strongly sympathized with it, but, nevertheless, understood its dangers and didn't really believe that the future of Europe would be Dionysian. The future would be that of the average man whose conduct of life is inhibited by reason. And reason, by its nature, is selfish, never impartial. It is reasonable to try to prosper, and it is usually profitable to be ethical. Arational goodness is not really ethical.

This is not to say that Hitler's total war against the International Jewry was based on no rational reasoning at all. It certainly had its reasons too, and, for example, the preliminary parliamentary work of the *NSDAP* relied clearly also on many rational calculations. Therefore, in order to understand Nazism, we need to find a view which preserves a due role for the rational, irrational and arational aspects of Nazism respectively. For example, if we decide to characterize the Nazi policy in expressions or metaphors of gaming, they should not ignore the aconceptual and arational aspects of Nazism, for example, the unpredictable course of events of the revolutionary movement. Therefore standard game theory is inadequate in this area (cf. Chapter 4). The need to defend the German culture could, in some contexts, be transformed into quite rational goals and policies, whereas the Nazi view of the authenticity of the German *Geist* as a Dionysian experience was already quite arational, often almost ecstatic. And finally, to use genocide as a rational method toward the national authenticity was a miscalculation and, as such, way beyond the boundaries of any rationality. However, miscalculations can be seen as irrational acts because they are based on the possibility of correct calculations. This doesn't mean that the Jewish genocide was *only* a miscalculation. Partly it was no calculation at all. The arational aspect of Nazism reveals itself in the tenacity with which the genocide was carried out even though it was known to be an act of useless revenge. Reason is not impartial but favors ethics and morality, because ethics and morality serve, in the long run, always the best interests of the subject. Genuine goodness and badness are arational, selfless and a-ethical, and serve no calculative interests.

According to Lacoue-Labarthe (1987, see especially pp. 35-36), the Final Solution breaks the rules of historical rationality and descends below all comprehensibility. This is an exaggeration and doesn't comply nicely with Lacoue-Labarthe's and Nancy's overall view of Nazism as the Nazi myth because, according to their view, the Nazi myth was shaped by an overly rational logic of onto-typology. The logic of the Nazi myth which the authors present doesn't sound incomprehensible at all, and it is hard to see how Lacoue-Labarthe's and Nancy's theory could ever reconcile the strict logic of the onto-typological Nazi myth with the absolute historical uniqueness and incomprehensibility which they also associate with Nazism. Logic is not supposed to be something unique and incomprehensible. Therefore, the gap, on the one hand, between the rational and the irrational and, on the other hand, between the rational and the arational, is not bridged by Lacoue-Labarthe's and Nancy's theory. This is so because their theory deprives their approach of any access to the experiential aconceptuality.

The aconceptual *völkisch* experience represents the *a*rational aspect of Nazism, whereas the national suicide attempt belongs, perhaps, already partly to the irrational side. In spite of this, we can find economic, political and social arrangements which were intended to provide a framework for both of the aspects of Nazism, but which themselves were, to some extent, rationally organized and planned. This all could be described with the help of such game metaphors (see Chapter 4) which allow the participants occasionally to weaken, and even dissolve, their rational subjectivity and plunge into the aconceptual dimensions of experience. The road to the proper social and political arrangements were cleared up by the Nazis when they destroyed those of the central social and political institutions of the Weimar Germany which were thought to be foreign or alien to the German spirit. Metaphorically speaking, the uppermost layers of the German national *Dasein* were separated and annihilated. This meant, among other things, that the ardor of hate which only a national revolution can arouse was directed to the juridical, parliamentary, educational, military and religious institutions which were thought to be non-German. One by one, they were destroyed, sometimes also reorganized and rebuilt (Gleichschaltung), in order to make them satisfy the alleged interests of the German *Volk* and race. And, of course, the university system, in the nazification of which Heidegger took part, was one of the most central and visible institutions in the agenda of the National-Socialist revolution. But the consequences which the annihilation of the uppermost cultural layers of the German man induced were not, and could not have been, fully predictable. The arousal of the aconceptual national energies which the annihilation released and which had been inhibited by the institutional and social establishment of the bourgeois-liberal Weimar state and society were genuinely unpredictable.

If a nation which is in the middle of a total war decides to allocate a considerable part of its resources to the mass extermination of some of its ethnic minorities, the nation's policy can hardly be taken as a purely rational enterprise. Rather, it indicates suicidal desperation, especially if the genocide is realized with the help of a relatively primitive technology. But even in their despair, the Germans were not externally forced to follow Hitler; nor did Hitler lead the revolution in the intentional sense of the word *lead*. Rather, he expressed the will of the asubjective revolutionary totality. The Germans did follow him because they had eventually become themselves, reached the authentic openness and nearness to their Being. Both Hitler and the Germans served and belonged to the German national *Dasein*, but the unfolding and disclosure of the *Dasein* lay outside of the control of any man, that is, any man as an intentional and rational subject of action. The Germans wanted to follow themselves, their *Geist* and destiny, even to the ultimate genocide, massive destruction and self-destruction, because they felt that it is better to die as what you are than to live as a foreigner in your body, mind and country.

The Weimar culture and the temptations of the Unreason

Many writers have associated Nazism as a cultural movement with the "right-wing" ultranationalistic radicalism of the Weimar Germany. However, in order to make sense, the "right-wingness" should not exclude revolutionary, anti-Capital, anti-Bourgeoisie, anarchistic and nihilistic tendencies. The connection between radical nationalism and "German philosophical irrationalism" has been studied, among others, by Bourdieu (1988) and by Lucács (1974), but we will not consider their views here in detail because the main line and motivation of their polemics remains otherwise alien to the present approach. For example, unlike what Bourdieu and Lucács suggest, the Nazi revolution grew out of a socialist and proletarian movement with strong anti-Capitalist tendencies, and the *NSDAP* economic policy was watched by the German Big Business with suspicion rather than with enthusiasm. The Nazi emphasis on the countryside, the antimodern ideal of a noncommercial life style, and even the strict environmental measures of the Nazi administration, enhanced the atmosphere of *Volk*-socialism rather than that of the efficiency and rationality of the modern business attitude.

One of the most interesting views which Bourdieu presents in his Heidegger-study (1988) is the claim that Heidegger's bend to the conservative radicalism of the Weimar era had its philosophical roots in his Kant critique and in his attack on neo-Kantianism. Bourdieu's view accords with the idea that it was exactly antihumanism and the possibility to find a political realization for it that attracted Heidegger in Nazism. Heidegger's Kant interpretation may have been one of the first similarities between Heidegger's work and National-Socialist philosophy, but certainly it wasn't the only one. Bourdieu could have chosen just as well Heidegger's philosophy of *deinon* from *Introduction to Metaphysics* (1935/1978) or the *Angst*-filled view of authenticity from *What is metaphysics?* (1929/1988).

Hans Sluga (1993, pp. 9-16; 247-8; but see also pp. 97-100) has tried to question and undermine Bourdieu's thesis by showing that the political polarization of the German philosophical community into the Nazi and non-Nazi camps didn't reflect its division into the non-Neo-Kantian and Neo-Kantian camps. Some philosophers who criticized Neo-Kantianism were not attracted by Nazism at all, unlike what Bourdieu's thesis seems to predict. In addition, Neo-Kantianism was also criticized, say, by some neo-positivists, as well as by some scientific and conceptual realists, and this happened for reasons which are not closely related to the spirit of Heidegger's Kant interpretation. For example, it is known that Gottlob Frege was a Nazi-sympathizer, but it can hardly be claimed that it was his critique of Kantianism that led him to lend his support to Nazism. Whatever his reasons were, it doesn't look plausible that they originated from his logical studies alone.

One problem with Sluga's position is that his view of Nazism as a philosophical and revolutionary movement rests on considerable hindsight and hyperintellectualist academic attitudes. He acknowledges the heterogeneousness of Nazism's philosophical makeup, but ends up presenting a thesis (p. 16) which is, in its inclusiveness, almost trivial: philosophers who subscribed to the National-Socialist cause shared certain common ideas which they interpreted in different ways. Who would deny this platitude? Thus, something is missing here, namely, Nazism as a revolutionary experience and the eagerness with which many philosophers wanted to modify their own ideas in order to make them serve the spirit of the revolution. From the experiential point of view, what should interest us in the political engagement of the Weimar philosophical community is not such external and accidental facts as who belonged to the *Deutsche Philosophische Gesellschaft* and possibly contributed to its journal, but, rather, what they wrote, how they related their philosophical work to the national revolution, and how they *themselves* saw the relationship between their work and the ideas which they believed to characterize National Socialism. Purely statistically speaking every political movement, let alone a highly popular national revolution, always adheres to itself a number of people whose ideas and thinking are only superficially related to the revolutionary experience, and there exists a legion of reasons, from simple error to pure opportunism, why such people bother to join the revolution. From a strictly nonexperiential point view, revolutions remain incomprehensible, and wouldn't even exist. They are simply *too* heterogeneous and aconceptual to be subsumed under a definite umbrella of externally or empirically discriminative criteria. Thus Sluga's Frege ticket is a *nonsequitur*. Only a detailed analysis and experiential interpretation of Frege's reasons to lend his support to Nazism could reveal whether or not the reasons were closely related to his proper philosophical work, that is, logical studies. Only after the interpretation we could evaluate whether Frege's affinity to Nazism supports or undermines the thesis that Heidegger's affinity to Nazism originated from Heidegger's Kant interpretation. Unfortunately, this analysis and interpretation is not put forward by Sluga.

Similarly, the fact that some neo-Kantians supported the revolution is, as such, quite uninteresting, as long as we don't know *how* they related their philosophical work to the experience of the national revolution. In Heidegger's case we know, by and large, how he saw the relationship between his *Dasein* philosophy and the *Dasein* of the German nation at the prime of the revolution. But clearly, Sluga is unable to address these questions because his approach to Nazism is too ratio-centered and individualist. The list of features (crisis; nation; leadership; order) which he suggests that we should consider if we want to understand political movements is simply inadequate. First of all, experience is missing.

The connection of National-Socialist thinking to the early German Romanticism, and to the Romantic poeticization of the political sphere, is vital for the understanding of Nazism. Nation, race, mother tongue and homeland as revitalizing sources of experiential authenticity inspired the asubjective branch of the Romantic movement, and this authenticity-seeking spirit spread its influence also upon the political field. Political ideas and arrangements which were thought to promote national authenticity were received with special affinity. The Romantic spirit was mediated to the twentieth century by Schopenhauer, Wagner, Hoffmann, Nietzsche and many others, and one of its later manifestations was German Expressionism. Though it is an open question how far this German tradition was eventually able to distance itself from the mainstream of Western metaphysics, its antimetaphysical and ametaphysical traits were conspicuous, and the antimetaphysical and ametaphysical tendencies of the German *Dasein* philosophy and existential philosophy of the 1920' and 1930's, for example the contrast of Life and Logos, can be traced back to this tradition.

It is true that Schopenhauer's notion of Idea still bore a conspicuous Platonic flair which Schopenhauer never could or wanted to get completely rid of, and it seems likely that this notion and some of its Platonism were passed over to the Nazi philosophy too. In addition, Nietzsche's skeptical attacks on such central notions of the Western metaphysical tradition as grammar, logic, truth, subject and substance were inconclusive and, due to its aggressive attitude, remained in many respects bound to its logocentric philosophical enemy. But still, the ametaphysical and the asubjectivist attitude with Schopenhauer and Nietzsche is distinct (cf. Nolte, 1990, pp. 196-197), and both the Weimar and the Nazi culture were strongly inspired by their work. It is this tradition of German Romanticism, Nietzscheanism, Existentialism and Expressionism to which also Heidegger's philosophical work most naturally associates itself. For example, Wolin has argued that the background of Heidegger's decisionism (in *Being and Time*) lies in Nietzsche's notion of *will to power* (Wolin, 1990, see especially, pp. 39-42; see also Löwith, 1940, especially, pp. 27-45).

Now, in order to understand better these connections, let us review briefly some main representatives of German Existentialism from the twenties and thirties. Some of the academic philosophers whom we will consider, like Hans Heyse and Alfred Bäumler, were National-Socialists, whereas others, like Ludwig Klages, were associated to the movement by many ideological and philosophical bonds.

Hans Heyse's antihumanistic existentialism

Almost at the same time when Heidegger assumed the rectorate at Freiburg, Hans Heyse assumed the rectorate of the University of Königsberg. In 1935, Heyse published a book, *Idee und Existenz*, in which he sketched a broad and highly critical picture of the modern Western culture. Modern culture is characterized by the undue dichotomy of Existence and Idea, Bios and Logos. If these powers remain polarized to such an unhealthy extent as presently happens, Life tends to turn to pure subjectivity and Ideas tend to become abstract and lifeless. The life forms of a culture which is in the polarized state remain fragmented, and life itself turns inauthentic and tends to center on the satisfaction of selfish interests. Eventually, Being becomes alienated from itself.

The theme of alienation was, most probably, introduced to German Existentialism by Emil Lask who used the term *Seinsvergessenheit* to denote this kind of human situation (see Nolte, 1992, p. 38), and it is probable that Heidegger, who passed the notion onto Heyse, adopted his respective notion of forgetfulness of Being from Lask. According to Heyse, the Greek tragedy, the World War and the National-Socialist revolution are examples of experience in which the polarization of Bios and Logos has been successfully overcome and the authenticity of Being regained. Hence, in the political situation of the thirties, the authenticity can be realized only in the National-Socialist revolution, and in the future, perhaps, in a new war experience.

Heyse's philosophy of the authentic existence attempts also to reach a dissolution of the subject-object dichotomy. The subject is an artificial metaphysical category the separation of which from external objects has to be overcome through the asubjective experience of Being as Being (Sein als Sein). During this experience, the contrast of the subjective and the objective disappears, and is replaced by the experience of an unfragmented totality (see, for example, Heyse, 1935, pp. 284-288). Just like Heidegger who, in his rectorial address, "The self-assertion of the German university" (1933/1990), had built a philosophical bridge from his *Dasein* notion to Hitler's fight for the freedom of the German *Geist*, Heyse proclaims that it is only in the National-Socialist state in which the unity of Idea and Existence can be attained. Therefore, says Heyse, German philosophers have to choose the right side in the world-historical fight in which the Germans attempt to save the authenticity of their national existence (see for example, Heyse, 1935, p. 294).

Ludwig Klages's antilogocentrism

Ludwig Klages was one of the German *Dasein* philosophers whose work in the early twenties anticipated both Heidegger's work and Nazi thinking in general. In a series of books (Klages, 1921; 1922; 1934), Klages painted a panorama picture of the downfall of Western thinking. According to him, the present state of the Western culture is dominated by logocentric thinking which is characterized by the inability to overcome intellectualism and dualism. First of all, antilogocentric thinking should never equate Consciousness (Bewusstsein) and Experience (Erlebnis). Consciousness is only one part of experience, and not just any part, but often the most corrupted one. Consciousness has compromised itself by making an unholy alliance with the logocentric Spirit (Geist) whose secret agenda is to pull the living human Body (Leib) apart from the Soul (Seele) and, by doing that, transform the human Body into a mechanical (soulless) Body (Körper). A logocentric culture, such as our present culture, is dominated by the psycho-physical dualism which sterilizes the human experience by depriving it of the connection to the body and to the revitalizing sources of sexual energy which only the body can provide. Only sexual energy which doesn't originate from the conscious subject, and isn't thus controlled by it, is able to attract the Soul and Body back together and overcome dualism.

Klages's notion of antilogocentric experience anticipates Heidegger's authentic *Dasein* experience (see Heidegger, 1927/1992) and continues the path opened by Schopenhauer and Nietzsche for whom the notion of Will (Wille) represented the aconceptual urge to stay alive and affirm the Life principle. The Will is authentic because it has not yet divided experience into the external world and the internal subject. The Will is instinct-driven but not intentional, that is, it is not guided by the conscious subject who chooses between alternative options according to some rational or moral principles.

Alfred Bäumler's asubjectivism

Unlike Klages, Alfred Bäumler was an active member of the *NSDAP* and an ardent supporter of the Hitler regime. He was one of the leading academic administrators and re-organizers of the Reich education system after the revolution of 1933 (Gleichschaltung), and he wrote extensively about theoretical and philosophical issues of National Socialism. He was also professor of philosophy at the University of Berlin and a specialist in Kant and the Kantian tradition, and his early works had concentrated on what he called "German Irrationalism" (Bäumler, 1923). For Bäumler, *irrationalism* was a version of subjectivism, and irrational judgments were subjective taste judgments. Therefore, the irrational is not, with Bäumler, related to the destruction of subjectivity. On the contrary, Bäumler attacked irrationalism (subjectivism, subject-centered thinking) and intellectualism simultaneously. In general, Bäumler's life work seems to comprise a vast attack, not only on individualism and subjectivism, but also on Humanism and Enlightenment. The German philosophical tradition of individualist irrationalism (subjectivism) and idealism has to be overcome through a Nietzschean version of National Socialism in which individual and personal experience will be dissolved into the will of the *Volk*. Man cannot become fully a man by being only a person. He must also be a non-person, something distributed among "ourselves" (Bäumler, 1942, p. 198), that is, the *Volk*. For the Germans in the situation of the 1930's, this *völkisch* nonpersonal authenticity means partaking in the National-Socialist revolution. This requires voluntarism, but the right kind of voluntarism is not subject-centered but something where personality, nation and race become an indivisible whole (Bäumler, 1942, p. 188). Only this kind of new, mythical and heroic personality which is energized by a strong non-personal Nietzschean Will (Wille) can overcome the powers of the Logos.

Bäumler's National-Socialist Nietzsche interpretation which he presented in *Nietzsche, der Philosoph und Politiker* (1931) is famous for its attempt to shun the Dionysian aspect of Nietzsche's work. The political motivation for this is quite transparent. The openly ecstatic and sexual connotations of the mystery cults of Asia Minor were found less than reputable and 'Nordic' by many Nazis. In Bäumler's opinion, the Dionysian aspect was too 'Asiatic' (asiatische) or 'Egyptian' (ägyptische) and therefore not Aryan enough in order to serve as the philosophical background for German nationalism. Nazis, as well as many other German nationalists, wanted to use the ancient Greek culture as a source of inspiration for the revitalization of the German national spirit, but not everything in the Greek experience was thought to be equally useful. Bäumler's selectiveness has given good reasons for the rivalling Nietzsche interpretations to accuse Bäumler of one-sidedness and even of censureship mentality.

Bäumler wanted to see the real weight of Nietzsche's work in his later philosophy, especially in his philosophy of *will to power*. Because the early Nietzsche had characterized the Dionysian aspect of human experience by saying that it challenged the *principle of individuation*, it might be suggested that Bäumler's interpretation is openly metaphysical. No doubt, the principle of individuation belongs to the core of the Western metaphysical tradition (cf. Chapter 2). But this characterization of Bäumler's work is hasty and can hardly provide a tenable view of Bäumler's Nietzsche interpretation. If it could be shown that Bäumler's aversion to the Dionysian aspect would have implied that he was inclined to accept the metaphysics of subjectivity, say, in his philosophy of *will to power*, there might be some ground for the view that at least one of the most influential Nazi thinkers belonged to the humanist tradition of metaphysical subjectivity. But this cannot be shown. Though Bäumler wanted to distance Nietzsche's life work from his youthful Dionysianism, Bäumler's view of *will to power* was definitely antihumanistic, focusing strongly on the asubjectivistic tendencies in the Nietzschean *will to power*. In *Nietzsche, der Philosoph und Politiker* (pp. 73-78), Bäumler attacks the philosophy of subjectivity, the primacy of things, normative thinking and the idea of progress, and associates the will to knowledge with the will to power. Thinking is a drive (Trieb) to power, knowledge is a unit of power (der Erkennende ist ein Machtquantum) and even philosophy is will to power, not an activity of the rational consciousness in the regular autonomous sense. Thus Bäumler's reluctance to accept the Dionysian aspect of Nietzsche's work did not imply any overall tendency to adopt a metaphysical stance. Actually, even Heidegger, who was willing to emphasize the importance of Nietzsche's view of *eternal recurrence*, tends to suppress the openly sexual flair with which Nietzsche colors his teaching of the affirmation of Life and eternal recurrence.

Franz Böhm's German Geophilosophy

Heidegger's conviction that only German philosophy, or better, German thinking and poetry, will be able to reveal the essence of technology, challenge the power of the *Gestell*, and save the Western man from *Seins-vergesseinheit* continued a whole tradition of ultranationalism which was cherished, among many others, by Franz Böhm. The main goal of his book, *Anti-Cartesianismus* (1938), was to search for the essential national character of German philosophy. Böhm found the essence of German thinking in the special oppositional and rebellious role which the German philosophy had played in the history of thought, especially with respect to French philosophy. Only German philosophy could challenge and overcome the dualism with which the French Cartesianism had poisoned the European culture. In Böhm's geophilosophical perspective, the German nation had a special task to carry on the tradition which the Greeks had passed over to them. In Cartesianism, philosophy was seen as an enterprise to secure a reliable foundation of knowledge for a rational individual. German philosophy had to replace this setting by putting the national community (völkische Gemeinschaft) first (p. 191). The experience of communion with people is the site where the essence of man reveals itself. According to Böhm, the idea of a harmonious personality which traditional Humanism had developed overemphasizes the importance of the individual person and suppresses the collective origin of man (p. 200). The individualist Humanism of the Enlightenment is originally a French idea, and its claim of universality is pretentious. Especially within the German culture, individualist humanism will eventually lead to sterile intellectualism. Intellectualism and individualism can be overcome only by adopting the attitude of personal sacrifice which means that the individual personality is submitted to the service of a community.

Was Nazism onto-typological?

Even this brief excursion into the German Existentialism and *Dasein* philosophy of the twenties and thirties should raise doubts about Lacoue-Labarthe's (1987; but see also Lacoue-Labarthe and Nancy, 1991) interpretation of Nazism. Because German *Dasein* philosophy comprises a part of the background from which Nazism grew up, it is difficult to believe that Nazism was simply an onto-typological myth. Rather, we should see National-Socialist thinking as a nationalist branch of the antilogocentric German *Dasein* philosophy which grew up from the cultural soil of German Romanticism, Nietzscheanism, Expressionism and Existentialism. This formed also Heidegger's foremost spiritual landscape. Lacoue-Labarthe's interpretation is a misconstruction which is designed to serve an obvious apologetic function with respect to Heidegger's philosophy, and, through that, with respect to the origins of deconstructionism too. But there are too many crucial aspects of Nazism and the National-Socialist Revolution with which this design cannot be reconciled. In this respect Lacoue-Labarthe's own interpretation reflects, if not dishonesty — the quality he seems to abhor most in philosophical work — at least lack of proper vigilance as regards the amount, relevance and credibility of the texts which he has chosen to use as his sources.

Lacoue-Labarthe's and Nancy's view of Nazism (1991) rests on a very narrow selection of sources, mainly on a couple of theoretical or pseudo-theoretical texts. Yet it is just a platitude to say that the theoretical literature of National-Socialist thinking is enormous and includes texts, not only from philosophy and esthetics, but from practically every area of human interest. Even if the theoretical aspect of Nazism, as the theoretical activity in general, is based partly on rationalization and hindsight, we cannot afford to ignore it when we want to move toward a philosophical understanding of Nazism. Our understanding of Nazism should be based on a spectrum of sources which is as broad as possible, and it should include minimally the writings of such leading Nazi thinkers as Hans Heyse, Alfred Bäumler, Carl Schmitt, Franz Böhm, Hans Freyer, Alfred Müller-Armack and Hermann Schwarz, just to mention some of the most famous names. It seems that Lacoue-Labarthe's and Nancy's theory of Nazism falls short of satisfying this elementary condition.

Alfred Rosenberg was a kind of half official *NSDAP* race philosopher, but the National-Socialist Revolution was something more than just Rosenberg's texts. Nor did Rosenberg's texts guide the revolution. The revolution and the Nazi movement were vast political, cultural and social events the core of which was power struggle and national experience. Power, struggle, suffering and experience are not texts. Neither do Rosenberg's texts reflect or cover the enormous variety of Nazi philosophy and esthetics. Nazism as a philosophical, esthetic and artistic movement was heterogeneous, rich and complex, and its variety ranges from Benn's Expressionist poetry and Jünger's visionary and philosophical prose, through Heidegger's thinking and Riefenstahl's movie esthetics to Hitler's and Göbbels's orations. And Rosenberg's texts do not reflect faithfully even the official Nazi ideology because the ideology, if there ever was one, was, due to unexpected turns of the power struggle, too heterogenous, heterodox and perpetually changing in order to be covered by any single contemporary interpretation, no matter how close to the views of the *Führer* and the party elite the interpretation is assumed to have been. For example, it is quite well known that Hitler himself frowned on Rosenberg's *Mythus* (see Domarius, 1965, Band I, zweiter Halbband, p. 892), the source on which Lacoue-Labarthe and Nancy rely most.

According to Lacoue-Labarthe (1987) and Nancy (Lacoue-Labarthe & Nancy, 1991), the Nazi myth is characterized by a figure, *Gestalt*, which serves as a racial identification mechanism. In particular, their argumentation rests heavily on the assumption that Rosenberg's *Gestalt* notion is onto-typological, and imposes a strict racial typology, which classifies people into reified classes and requires also that the classifier himself has internalized a rigorous racial identity. Therefore, a German nationalist who applies Rosenberg's notion of race individuates the Germans, including himself, with the help of distinct Aryan properties which will also separate the Germans from non-Aryans, especially from the Jews. But this is hardly a tenable view of one of Rosenberg's central notions. Rather, Rosenberg's *Gestalt* seems to have been a popularized version of Schopenhauer's *Idea*. If this is so, Rosenberg's *Gestalt* may turn out to be much less onto-theo-logical, onto-typological or onto-anything than what first meets the eye.

To make a long story short, Schopenhauer's *Idea* was an intermediate notion between *Wille* (Will) and *Vorstellung* (representation). Ideas were supposed to preserve something of the vitality, creativity and energy of the Will, and, at the same time, be detached from the obvious dangers which are related to the uncontrollability of the Will. Because Ideas had preserved something of their perceptual and sensual origin, they had inherited some ingredients of the aconceptuality of the Will too. As Schopenhauer points out, one characteristic feature of this aconceptuality was the dissolution of the subject-object contrast (Schopenhauer, 1819/1969, section 34). Therefore Rosenberg's *Gestalt* is not particularly obviously an onto-typological notion. Rather, the flair of anti-subject-centered metaphysics is actually quite distinct in it, as it is already in Schopenhauer's notion of Idea, and in Schopenhauer's thinking in general.

Rosenberg's thinking in *Der Mythus des 20. Jahrhunderts* (1930) is dominated by the dichotomy of Intellect (Intellekt) and Instinct (Trieb) which is a repercussion of Schopenhauer's dichotomy of Representation (Vorstellung) and Will (Wille), and Rosenberg's work can be seen as an attempt to reconcile these disconcerting tendencies into a balanced and vigorous whole. The leading idea is that the German culture can regain its vitality only by reaching up to such a reconciliation (p. 343). Without the Will, as an instinctive drive, artistic work, for example, is doomed to futility (p. 348); and even a personal growth process will remain inauthentic if the Will aspect is suppressed (p. 338). At the end of a section called *Wille und Trieb* (p. 344), Rosenberg says that the *life form* of a culture can bring Intellect and Instinct together into a living whole only by resorting to the right racial myth. In other words, only the life form which incorporates the proper racial myth is able to provide the site where conceptual thinking (Logos) and aconceptual experience (Leben) meet. For the Germans, the proper myth is the myth of the Aryan race.

Unlike what Lacoue-Labarthe and Nancy suggest, the mythical experience, as it is understood by the German post-Romantic thinking, especially in the Nazi context, isn't necessarily an experience which requires an identification to a permanent and strict type or class. For example, to experience revolutionary enthusiasm doesn't mean that one imitates a particular model, say that of a racist German nationalist, let alone an Apollonian hero model. On the contrary, mythical experience can be partly a *Dionysian* experience, or in some other sense an ametaphysical experience, in which one loses the old identity. Actually, Nietzsche (1872/1939, for example p. 53 and p. 138) defines the *Dionysian* by referring to the annihilation of individuality in a wholeness or totality experience. Interestingly, *individuality* may here refer, not only to a logical or grammatical category, but to personal identity as well. Later the *Dionysian* is explicitly associated with the *mythical* (pp. 141-143). In the context of the Nazi revolution, this could mean, among other things, that one loses the old bourgeois identity, say that of a selfish capitalist speculator whose ideology is colored by the international ideas of liberal business thinking. The dissolution of the old identity can sometimes happen rapidly, for example, by adopting a mythical role in a ritual or mass spectacle. Among other things, it can mean that the subject-object boundary attached to a person becomes ambiguous, and the experiential boundaries of the person with other persons begin to fluctuate and eventually to wither away. Therefore, surrendering to the revolutionary *völkisch* experience was interpreted, not only by Heidegger, but by many a German *Dasein* philosopher, as an antilogocentric experience which represented a radical departure from all previous imitative attachments, for example, from the *Gestalt* of the bourgeois identity.

On several occasions, Heidegger suggested that the more irrational something appears to us the more strict and exclusive our notion of *ratio* must have been. In this respect Heidegger's view came closer to Rosenberg's thinking than that of Bäumler's who unabashedly extolled Life and Power. Anyway, in both of the cases, namely, with Rosenberg and Bäumler, surrender to the racial or *völkisch* myth requires the dissolution of the bourgeois identity and destruction of the autonomous subject which is all too effectively contained and monitored by conceptual thinking, selfish calculations and overly intellectual and abstract attitudes. This kind of experience can hardly be classified as onto-typological. It requires a de-ontologization of all too strict typologies and individuations.

Neither should we accept Lacoue-Labarthe's and Nancy's contention that the Germans with their 1933 revolution were searching for a firm identity by *imitating* the Ancient Greeks (Lacoue-Labarthe and Nancy, 1991). Rather, in 1933 the Germans were trying to reach a collective state of mind which would liberate them from the intentional imitative attitude by destroying all models of identification. Not only the Apollonian imitation, but also the Dionysian drive away from imitation belongs to the sphere of the Greek experience.

Perhaps we are eventually forced to concede that the German ameta-physical national dream was naive. But even if this were so, it was neither the "mimetic logic" of the Nazi myth nor a "State Subject" with which the mythical experience ended up. The *Führer*'s Germany was not a totalitarian fascist state of the Italian style but a *Volk im Werden*, a nation in the experiential mode of a perpetual revolutionary flux in which it had liberated itself from the bourgeois and Christian inhibitions, and from many rational constraints which are typical for the Western metaphysics of subjectivity. For example, unlike what Lacoue-Labarthe suggests, Heidegger of the thirties didn't associate *techne* and *imitation* with metaphysical subjectivity. On the contrary, in *Introduction to Metaphysics* (1935/1978, p. 159-160), Heidegger's view of these notions associates them, not with technique or skills, but with *aletheia*, openness, truth and *deinon*, all notions with a strong ametaphysical flair. Thus, in the thirties, Heidegger could entertain a mythical vision of the German destiny, and even see the destiny as an imitation of the Greek, without plunging into the metaphysics of subjectivity.

For Lacoue-Labarthe (1987) and Nancy (Lacoue-Labarthe and Nancy, 1991), Nazism is a myth with an ontologically effective structure with the help of which the German people endeavored to constitute a new identity for themselves. In general, they see myth as an individuation apparatus which utilizes mimetic procedures. The Nazi myth, in particular, was a racist indi-viduation mechanism which was used by the Germans to construct a strong *subject-like state* structure. If this picture were right, it would be hard for us to understand how some of the best writers of the thirties, including such brilliant French writers as Céline, Brasillach and Drieu la Rochelle, could have ever been attracted by the spell of Nazism. It is plausible that these French writers were attracted by Nazism exactly because they, quite justifi-ably, saw a connection between the Nazi thinking and antilogocentrism. For example, Tarmo Kunnas (1972) has shown that it was the openly antirational and instinctive nature of Nazism, its unabashed recourse to primitive aggressive, sexual and suicidal instincts, which attracted, not only Céline, Brasillach and Drieu la Rochelle, but many other famous writers, including Ezra Pound and Knut Hamsun. They were hardly looking for a German or Italian national identity which crystallized itself in an onto-typological myth or State Subject. In a proper interpretation, aggressiveness, sexuality and suicidal instincts can be seen as representing the ametaphysical aspects of human experience.

The flux of the revolutionary experience was energized, not only by violence and terror (deinon), but also by anarchist spontaneity and plasticity as regards the organization of the state. According to Hitler's conception of state, the state lacked all conceptual independence and was almost instrumentally submitted to the service of the *Volk* and race (see Jäckel, 1981, pp. 79-95; Müller-Armack, 1933, p. 36-37; see also Hitler's *Mein Kampf*, 1925, second volume, section two which deals with the notion of the state). This doesn't mean that it had the stable identity of a regular hand tool. The *Führer principle* itself bore considerable anarchist ingredients, and the state had to accommodate itself to the perpetually varying revolutionary needs. It was not the idea or structure of the state which dictated what was best for the Germans; it was the racial Will which expressed itself through the *Führer's* will and found its way occasionally also into the varying structures of the state. This Will was not supposed to be dominated by any ideology or political doctrine, let alone by selfish bourgeois interests. Rather, the *Führer's* will reflected the needs, moods, movements and inner drives of the German *Volk* faster and more reliably than any constitution, ideology, doctrine or state apparatus. The *Führer's* will overtook and replaced the state, its constitution and bureaucracy, and, in the Nazi thinking, this could not mean anything other than that Hitler's preconscious and asubjective mind was directly connected to the spirit of the German *Volk*.

Had Hitler's connection to the *Volk* been mediated by a constitution, bureaucracy, state, doctrine or ideology, Hitler as a historical phenomenon would not have been irreplaceable. When Carl Schmitt (1929) characterized a total state as a state in which the contrast between the state and society is dissolved, and later (Schmitt, 1934) proclaimed that Hitler is the protector of justice (and that Hitler's will be the only source of all future jurisprudence), this wasn't interpreted by the Nazis as suggesting that the Weimar legislative and juridical system had to be replaced by a new system, the Nazi system. No, the main idea was to get rid of all such systems and related doctrines.

Therefore, the Nazi state lacked the essential metaphysical identity or sub-jectlikeness. Also Hans Freyer (1931) contrasted the state and the people (Volk), and proclaimed that the original revolutionary energy of the *Volk* lacks all structure, order and system (p. 53). The energy which shapes the future is pure eruption and process. Because Lacoue-Labarthe's and Nancy's picture of Nazism ignores also the most characteristic opposition of the Nazi philosophy and literature, namely that of Life and Logos, they fail to appreci-ate that the state, especially the pre-revolutionary bourgeois-liberal state, was often seen by the Nazis as an inhibitive structure which suppresses the will of the *Volk* and, therefore, the Life principle itself. For Freyer (1931), it was the industrial society and its state structure, and the modern machine technology which they supported, where the suppressive power was incorporated. The primordial revolutionary energy of the *Volk* was to be directed against them. Thus, those who participated in the 1933 revolution and helped to shape its thinking did not experience it as an act of designing a new state subject. Rather, the revolution was about surrendering to an asubjective or postsubjec-tive experience of belonging to a *Volk*.

In the revolutionary situation of 1933, it was far from obvious or predict-able what the practical consequences of the surrendering to the racial and *völkisch* myth would turn out to be. We don't expect the destruction of the enlightened Western subject to induce only fully predictable, let alone nice, consequences. After all, the national revolution was supposed to make the future of the *Volk* genuinely open. Only hindsight, not historical necessity or even high probability, connects the revolutionary enthusiasm of 1933 to the pseudo-technologically organized genocide of the Jewish people and other minorities. Lacoue-Labarthe's and Nancy's Nazi logic suggests that the vio-lent events of the final phase of the Nazi epoch could have been predicted. This emphasis on logic and prediction is in conflict with their overall view of the Jewish genocide as something unique and incomprehensible.

Derrida and the deconstruction of quotation marks

In *Of Spirit* (1987), Jacques Derrida has put his finger upon Heidegger's use of quotation marks around the word *Geist*, and we should credit Derrida for noticing a detail which is rife with complex possibilities of interpretation. Derrida's work is painstakingly involved, and it is obvious that there is much at stake now. His main goal is to show that the early Heidegger's way of mentioning the notion of *Geist* connects it to the metaphysics of subjectivity, and, therefore, Heidegger, quite correctly, avoided using it in his proper philosophical work. But, during his Nazi engagement, Heidegger failed to avoid the notion, though he, as Derrida puts it, knew that he *ought* to have avoided it. Now, the issue is whether Heidegger knew that, that is, whether Heidegger, after *Being and Time*, ever associated *Geist*, or Nazism in general, to the metaphysics of subjectivity. However, Derrida's work is, not only painstaking, but also painful to follow because the reader is embarrassed to note Derrida's inability to admit the obvious: that Heidegger omitted the quotation marks as soon as he was sure that the National-Socialist Revolution of the 1933 contributed to the openness of the German national *Dasein*. After that realization, he adopted the word *Geist* from its original Hegelian and Nazi context, and modified it in order to make it serve the purposes of his own thinking.

The seeds of this modification can be found already in the section 82 of *Being and Time*. It is obvious that in earlier sections of *Being and Time* Heidegger had recommended that the word *Geist* should be avoided because some of its standard meanings are contaminated by the Cartesian metaphysics of subjectivity. But so is the average *Dasein* of the Western man! As long as the power of Modernism is overwhelming and the veil of *Seinsvergessenheit* unbroken, the German *Dasein* and the *Dasein* of the average German will remain closed. It is not misleading to characterize this kind of *Dasein* by saying that it is actually dominated, not only by the attitude of *Vorhandenheit*, but by the inner experience of being a Soul, consciousness and, perhaps, a *Geist* in some traditional sense of the word. But the possibility of disclosure lies hidden in the average, dull and misguided *Dasein* too. Because of the ambiguity of the word *Geist*, it is possible to characterize the authentic *Dasein*, not only as a dissolution, but also as the openness of the *Geist* toward Being. In Heidegger's view, this became possible at the unique historical situation of the 1933 Revolution.

Some ingredients of this kind of interpretation can be discerned in Krell's review of Derrida's *Of Spirit* (Krell, 1988), but Krell turns away from it as soon as he has indicated some of its implications. The credibility of Derrida's interpretation depends on the credibility of the thesis that Hegel's *Geist* and the Nazi application of it is a continuation of the Cartesian metaphysics of subjectivity. But, if it is the case that already the Hegelian-Nazi view of the possibilities of the *Geist* contained crucial ingredients of asubjectivism and antihumanism, Derrida's stance loses much of its thrust. And this brings us back to our original question, namely, whether Nazism is humanism or not. Anyway, the last paragraph of section 82 of *Being and Time* lends itself also to the reading that the originally inauthentic *Geist* which is caged by the metaphysics of subjectivity lies in the average *Dasein* waiting for the epoch of openness, the time of the revolution.

Heidegger's attitude toward decisionism seems to have been highly ambiguous, and around January 1933 something crucial happened. Before that fatal date, the prospects of achieving authenticity through political action seemed to have been scarce. But during the year of the Revolution, it had become clear to Heidegger that National Socialism might be the way, and perhaps the only and last possibility, for the disclosing of the German *Dasein*. Therefore he decided to commit himself to the cause of the Revolution. That was a good reason to drop the quotation marks: Now the German *Geist* could eventually be taken seriously as a path toward national authenticity. After 1945 the spiritual landscape in Europe was gloomy again because the only possibility for a genuinely ametaphysical turn in the political history of the West had been lost. Now only God could help us. The German *Geist* had returned to its state of inauthenticity, and therefore the word *Geist*, once again, deserved to be surrounded by the quotation marks.

Heidegger and the temptations of the Nazi antihumanism

Heidegger was fascinated by the destructive and creative revolutionary thrust and drive of the Nazi movement and, in particular, by Hitler's ecstatic, devotional and selfless style of leadership. It is plausible that he saw in it a present-day representative of antihumanistic Dionysianism, the only political power of creative destruction (deinon) which was active in his epoch. In order to belong to the movement, Heidegger's attempts to understand the movement from a philosophical point of view did not have to comply particularly faithfully with the views which more official Nazi ideologists, like Rosenberg, happened to put forward. Heidegger's thinking didn't have to follow any particular, well defined *doxa*, alleged "Nazi logic," because the movement, like any ongoing revolution, was heterodox, heterogeneous and undogmatic. Heidegger's Nazism was just one option, though obviously a highly subtle one, in the spectrum of different and mutually conflicting versions of Nazism, and, as such, represented only one attempt to understand and shape the historical events. For most of the party leaders, Heidegger's philosophy was simply too difficult to understand and too detached from the everyday conduction of political action to be really interesting. Obviously, Heidegger himself thought that his version of Nazism was the only genuine one and provided the most profound view of what was going on and, therefore, illuminated better than the average Nazi views the possibilities which the historical situation opened for the German people.

Heidegger was attracted by Nazism because he thought that, in the particular historical situation of the early 1930's, the authenticity of the German *Dasein* was best served by the National Socialist revolution. He hoped, among other things, that the revolution would create circumstances in which the essence of modern technology could be understood and its uninhibited global growth contained. It is obvious that during and after his rectorate Heidegger became gradually aware of the differences between his own thinking and other versions of Nazi thinking. Bäumler, Heyse and Rosenberg were competent philosophers and writers but not, of course, as original, radical and creative as Heidegger himself. Nevertheless, Heidegger thought that the philosophical foundations of Nazism should not be left for a mediocrity, not even for a competent mediocrity, and he accepted the challenge of defining and shaping the Nazi thinking into a form which he himself could take seriously, and, by doing that, he defended his own vision of what the revolution was about. In his Nietzsche lectures, he argued against Bäumler's Nietzsche interpretation but this can hardly be taken as an adequate evidence for Lacoue-Labarthe's thesis that Heidegger's increasingly critical attitude toward Bäumler and certain other famous Nazi philosophers after 1934 eventually amounted to a definite denouncement of Nazism.

True, something happened around 1935. Heidegger criticized Bäumler for disregarding Nietzsche's thesis of the *eternal recurrence* (Heidegger, 1936-37/1991, see for example, vol. I, pp. 21-24). But there remains a long way to go from this critique up to a full-fledged denouncement of Nazism. Nietzsche was an important figure to *some* Nazi philosophers and writers, including Bäumler, but not to all of them. Hitler himself saw in Nietzsche also a verbal acrobat, not only a serious German Thinker. Though Nietzsche was conveniently anti-Semitic, his frequent analyses of the retardation and brutality of the German culture are never far from anti-Germanism either. In his

Nietzsche lectures, Heidegger wanted to distance himself from the most irrational trends of German Existentialism and from too straightforward National-Socialist readings of Nietzsche, as if his experiences with political engagement had made him cautious and, perhaps, a bit worried about the philosophical insight of his political allies. Therefore, it is understandable that he wanted to inhibit the full force of the thesis of *will to power* by emphasizing the importance of the thesis of the *eternal recurrence*. This is not so surprising because some aspects of Nietzsche's Dionysianism remained always alien to Heidegger, just as they remained to Bäumler. Especially, Nietzsche's eroticism, naturalism, skepticism and psychological self-analysis played only a minor role in Heidegger's thinking.

Heidegger's psychological self-insight was not particularly acute, or, to say the least, its area of application was limited. Among other things, it seems to have excluded the sex life. What Heidegger had found in the Dionysian experience was mainly horror, violence and death (deinon), though his vision didn't necessarily lack unwitting sexual connotations. Heidegger's Dionysus was the God of destruction and pain whose main weapon was terror, not the God of sexual ecstacy, unconditional and aconceptual love, intoxication and reproduction. Along with Nietzsche's eroticism, Heidegger ignored also Nietzsche's empiricism, relativism, naturalism and skepticism. Neither did Nietzsche's devilish humor excite Heidegger. But this bias doesn't amount to a definite denouncement of Nietzsche's work, let alone of Nazism. On the contrary, in the thirties Heidegger tried to coin a philosophically valid version of both Nietzscheanism and Nazism, and perhaps it was his erotophobic interpretation of Nietzsche that was reflected in his eagerness to accept Nazism, even though he must have been aware of some of its philosophical limitations.

In the thirties, he saw in Nietzsche a major philosophical thinker who had been able to illuminate the question of Being with the help of the philosophical theme of *will to power*. Heidegger's authoritarianism, urge toward purity and discipline, his intolerant personal constitution, lack of humor, and his suppressed aggressiveness, aggressive sexuality, lack of relativism and tendency to elitism and cultural chauvinism made it possible, and perhaps even easy, for him to understand also the metaphysical aspects of Nazism which, especially during the war, became gradually more conspicuous and eventually even dominant in the movement. Unfortunately, Heidegger's own version of Nazism was not welcomed by the party executives with such enthusiasm as Heidegger would have expected. However, this did not prevent him from defending his own view with an attitude which was never far from jealousy, and which didn't lack suppressed erotic overtones, as if he had tried to downplay the influence of his competitors by claiming that they had not been really faithful to the spirit of the *Führer*.

Neither does biographical or textual data lend support to the view that Heidegger, in 1935 and after, had criticized the movement as an outsider. In summer 1936, Heidegger still thinks that Hitler's revolution began a counter-movement against nihilism (see Pöggeler, 1992). This indicates, unlike what Lacoue-Labarthe attempts to demonstrate, that Heidegger, at least in 1936, did *not* associate Nazism to a technologically oriented nihilism.

In *An Introduction to Metaphysics*, (1935/1978), Heidegger teaches that violence and terror (deinon) belong to the essence of the human Being (see pp. 150-52). Violence, hardness, nearness of death, horror and *Angst*, so dear to Heidegger, are still advocated by him as viable ways toward authenticity of the human *Dasein*. In political life, the ability to elicit terror and horror is associated with historical greatness, and political creativity and the ability to spread destruction are equated. Because we know that Heidegger was an ardent Hitlerist, it is not far-fetched to think that we are reading here a philosophical defense of Hitlerism. In the *Origin of the Work of Art* (1935-36/ 1971), authenticity is associated with what sounds almost like a *völkisch* experience with slight biological tones. *Erde* (Earth) is not only a *völkisch* notion but seems to bear a close resemblance with the Nazi doctrine of the primacy of *Leben* (Life), *Blut* (Blood), *Boden* (Soil) and *Heimat* (Homeland), notions which were not usually intended to be taken too biologically.

Heidegger's work as a whole can be seen as a fight against the temptations and illusions of the Western Metaphysics. Yet it is far from obvious that *deinon, Erde*, and *Welt* of the middle Heidegger or *Erfahrung* and *Nähe* of the later Heidegger are free of the shadow of metaphysics. In this light, Heidegger could hardly have condemned Nazism just because it was unable to reach its ultimate *a*metaphysical goal. Perhaps it was the mutual aversion of Metaphysics that made Heidegger and the Nazis so close political allies, and perhaps it was eventually the mutual inability to overcome metaphysics that made them able to share the experience of spiritual neighborhood and, after the war, the destitution and disillusive resignation from the political arena.

After the War, especially during the late forties and early fifties, when Heidegger's philosophy and thinking evolved, his National Socialism grew deeper too. Now he saw Nazism in the light of his new vision of 'technology as *Gestell*,' and, indeed, Nazism, as well as his own earlier version of Nazism, began to appear much less ametaphysical and less asubjectivist than what it used to look like in the thirties and, in particular, what it should have been in order to have been able to challenge the essential nihilism of the modern Western technology. Perhaps Nazism had been philosophically immature quite in the same way as his own thinking. After all, both Heidegger's early thinking and Nazi thinking were, to some extent, metaphysicalized by all too rigid dichotomies. For example, with Heidegger the dichotomy of the authentic and the inauthentic was developed in a dualistic manner (cf. Chapter 1); in the Nazi thinking, the dualism of Life and Logos was sometimes presented in an overly categorical way. Because in the early and mid thirties Heidegger himself had not been too sure about his own, still evolving attitude toward metaphysics, he could hardly expect the Nazi leaders to be that either, i.e., he could not expect the Nazi leaders to be philosophically more mature than the leading young philosopher of the *Reich*.

Also after 1935, the Nazi movement appeared to Heidegger as the only political movement that could challenge Western metaphysics and pursue asubjectivism and antihumanism in politics, and even after the war he thought that Nazism had been the best political alternative in the situation of the early 1930's. Among the variety of political movements, only Nazism had any chance of challenging the global power of the modern scientific technology. Perhaps the Party had been too engaged in the power struggle and too intoxicated by the revolutionary violence to have taken the final jump into the actual overcoming of nihilism and metaphysics, but, certainly, Nazism was the only political movement which came even close to the understanding of the essence of nihilism and technology, and, through that, to the possibility of overcoming them. Due to the limited philosophical insight, the Party elite wasted the vital revolutionary energy of the *Volk* and let the ardor slack off. And it is possible that all this, in Heidegger's view, was a consequence of immature philosophy which ran against the originally antihumanistic and authentic core of Nazi thinking. Hitler and the party leaders had to give in to the demands of modern technology, and this happened because otherwise they wouldn't have been able to challenge their metaphysically well-equipped enemy, the governments of the USA (Capitalism) and the Soviet Union (Bolshevism).

Though Heidegger would not have said that Nazism is humanism, he might have said in the fifties that the trivial and stupid versions of Nazism incorporated something of the metaphysics of subjectivity. Hitler's apersonal and dramatic exorcism which, by raising the *völkisch* ecstasy, had expelled the Devil of Internationalism from the German soul, had been shamefully misused and vulgarized by crude biologism and superficial techno-humanism: Hitler's spirit had been wasted in the obscurity of a pseudo-technologically accomplished genocide which was, neither arational nor morally wrong, but purely irrational and therefore, to some extent, metaphysical. It was not morally wrong because morality, as an application of the metaphysics of subjectivity, doesn't apply to a national revolution which tried to destroy the structure of the rational and autonomous subjectivity in the German mind. Morality applies only to something predictable, to those courses of possible events which a moral agent can reason about. Moral reasoning doesn't apply to a genuinely open and unpredictable future, for example, to the future as it is disclosed by a national revolution. When the uppermost cultural layer of the German man, his internationalism, modernity and rationality, has been wiped off, his future lies open and unpredictable, and it is possible that it is open also toward war, mass murder and genocide.

In his "Overcoming metaphysics" (1954/1993, but based on notes from the years 1936-46), Heidegger attacks harshly Schopenhauer's, Wagner's and Nietzsche's attempts to overcome metaphysics, and the leading idea seems to be that these predecessors of his remained all too much tied to metaphysical dichotomies, such as that of 'instinct' and 'reason.' It is indeed possible to read here a critique of political modernism too, especially such modernism which is unable to understand the essence and global power of technology. The target of the critique could cover both the modern welfare society of the West Germany and the last, moderately technologized and suicidal stage of the Nazi period. But even here it seems that Heidegger still believes that there exists an authentic version of Nazism which is free from the metaphysical dualism which undermined the credibility of the misguided versions of Nazism. And in addition, "Overcoming metaphysics" is, to a great extent, an unwilling, occasionally even unwitting, exercise in self-criticism too. Many of the dichotomies which Heidegger now labels as metaphysical used to be his too, and we could pile upon them a whole bunch of his own dichotomies, all of which were not used by those whom he criticizes: authentic/inauthentic; *die Erde/das Welt*; Being/*Dasein*, and many others. Just as it is an open question to what extent Nietzsche actually was able to free his thinking from its metaphysical load, it is an open question how much

Heidegger could do that. And eventually we can ask the same question as regards Nazism too, and the answer is no less obvious.

The humanistic misuse of Nazi thinking actualized during the war, especially after 1942, when the possibility of defeat in the war could already be anticipated, that is, more than twenty years after the movement was initiated in Munich and nine years after the 1933 revolution. This is not to say that the atrocities, mass murders and genocides of the years 1942-44 originated only from the metaphysical aspect of Nazism. Without the overall asubjective and violently antihumanistic atmosphere which dated back to the Weimar culture, Expressionism and Romanticism, the machinery of the German technology which was, after all, quite primitive if compared with that of the Allies, could not have been applied with so disastrous consequences. But still, the downfall of the *Reich* was basically caused by the strong metaphysical, logocentric and technologically much more advanced international enemy, led by the governments of the United States and the Soviet Union. And the reason for the downfall was that the Nazi Germany didn't rely, didn't want to rely, and wasn't able to rely, so much on modern Western technology as its enemy. The last gloomy events of the Nazi epoch could not, in Heidegger's mind, obscure the fact that the *NSDAP* was the very political party whose vision of the German man and the nation complied better with Heidegger's own thinking and political views than any other political movement of the thirties or later. Around 1942, the Nazi elite eventually realized that the International Jewry had succeeded in reaching its ultimate goal, the destruction of the German nation and its spirit, and, in the light of this realization, the Jewish genocide can be seen as a massive act of retaliation which the remnants of the Nazi movement launched, if not directly against its international enemy, at least against the local representatives of it. Yet, in Heidegger's opinion, not even the genocide of the Jewry could obscure the inner greatness of the National-Socialist movement.

CHAPTER EIGHT

Nationally unique meanings

Ollaan

It is not particularly difficult to explain in English what Rimbaud had in mind when he wrote to his friend: "...j'assiste á l'éclosion de ma pensée..." (Letter to Paul Demeny, Charleville, May 15, 1871, Rimbaud, 1871, p. 187). In case of difficulties, we can always consult a translation by Luise Varèse (1946, p. xxix): "... I witness the birth of my thought..." Perhaps the idea of asubjectivism is difficult to envision, but at least Rimbaud's metaphor is not impossible to capture in English. The metaphor seems to be saying that somebody is witnessing the emergence of his thought, though it may sound somewhat paradoxical that we *only* witness, or at most attend or assist, the emergence of our thoughts, instead of begetting them. Perhaps Rimbaud is saying that, unlike what we want to believe, we, as conscious agents, are not mothers of our thoughts but, rather, their fathers or, even less, namely their midwifes. Perhaps we *are*, among other things, our thoughts, or better, our words, but, even if that is the case, we do not produce consciously what we are.

Though an asubjective experience is immediate and overtakes us frequently, it is somewhat symptomatic that Rimbaud has to resort to a metaphor in order to describe it. The experience tends to defy straight language which is often a prisoner of rigid metaphysical attitudes, like that of the subject-object contrast. One gets the impression that the languages of the Indo-European family in particular do not easily lend themselves to listening to and speaking of such meanings in which the power of the conscious subject and its rationality is undermined. It is not easy to find examples of grammatical constructions the meaning of which would openly question the ontology of objects and individuals. Analogously, the Indo-European grammar seems to rely heavily on the rationality, goal-directedness and awareness of the agent whose action a sentence describes.

In order to notice that we are not dealing here with a universal property of languages, let us consider a Finnish example. *Erällä* is one of the last poems of Aaro Hellaakoski (1893-1952) and it appeared in the series *Sarjoja* (1952). It is also one of the best examples of asubjectivist thinking in recent Finnish literature. It describes how a Westernized man enters a Finnish wilderness area, witnesses a gradual dissolution of his familiar identity and rational subjectivity, and eventually finds himself lying fatally wounded side by side with a dying lynx. The poem is a rather disillusioned journey into the Finnish psyche, through its thin Westernized surface, into an endless flux of non-Western asubjective experience. It is a poem about the origin and limits of rational subjectivity. Being a rational and autonomous Western subject is, in the original Finnish landscape, basically an alien experience. Like a recently imported cultural disguise, it covers the ancient Finnish experience which dates back to the days before the Finnish life and land were occupied by Christianity, Western technology and commercialization.

However, every interpretation of the poem in English will be frustrated by a difficulty. There exists a single, apparently harmless expression, *ollaan*, which seems to be impossible to translate into English. In standardized grammatical terms we are expected to say that this is the passive form from the infinitive *olla*; similarly, *olla* is supposed to be the Finnish counterpart of the English *to be*. The problem is that there is no obvious active sentence from which *ollaan* can be derived; especially, there is no topicalization of the object of a respective active construction; there is neither grammatical nor logical subject in *ollaan*; there is no person, or number, let alone gender. It would almost completely betray its meaning to offer *one is* (or *it is*; *we are*; *there is*) as a translation of this kind of amorphously primitive way of being. There is no *one* present in *ollaan* because being one presupposes oneness, that is, unity and identity, and the Finnish utterance doesn't suggest anything like that. Yet a vaguely collective sense is alluded: whatever is there is not alone, and, in addition, the so-called Finnish passive is always related to human affairs. Nonetheless, it is not quite right to say that there is *one*, say a person, who shares the collectiveness of *ollaan* with some other *ones* or persons. Rather, the impression is that when we are in the mode of *Ollaan* we are there pre-individually, *before* the processes of individuation apply.

Untranslatable uniqueness

If it is claimed that it is impossible to translate *ollaan* into English, quite a lot is claimed. One might protest by saying, for example, that actually the above sketched description of *ollaan* delivers its meaning quite well, in particular, what it is supposed to mean in Hellaakoski's poem. In the poem, *ollaan* is contrasted to the personal way of being which is expressed by the sentence *minä olen* (I am). This construction is easy to accommodate into the standard personal inflection paradigm and it seems to have the regular subject-predicate structure. But what we have suggested above about the meaning of *ollaan* is not quite what we usually mean by *translation*. Rather, we should call it *interpretation* because it is too long and unique to be a translation. Actually, the interpretation is indefinitely long because it is unfinished, and will probably always remain so. Unlike a genuine translation, it is also irrepeatable and irreversible. Probably no one else will — or would even like to — produce anything identical, and, assuming that the will appeared, there wouldn't be any common method to do that either. Unlike regular translations, interpretations, including the above interpretation of *ollaan*, are always more or less controversial and tied to many background assumptions.

Now, one may concede and say: "All right, a good poem can be quite unique and hard to translate, and its uniqueness may require a reading which, in order to be successful, must also be unique. But what is *unique* supposed to mean here? How unique can a poem be? Also a computer program can be unique in the obvious sense that, take any relatively complex program and, most probably, no other program is identical with it, especially not syntactically identical. Yet programs are translatable, if anything is."

But that is not what we have meant by *uniqueness* in the earlier chapters (see, for example, Chapter 5). If we use here the word 'program' in the normal way, then a finite computer program is never genuinely unique because its semantic content (in the sense in which 'programming language semantics' is used, say, by Tennent, 1981) can always be expressed comprehensively in any other programming language, at least if the expressive power of the latter is that of a Turing machine. And, in addition, there always exist, in one programming language, an enumerably infinite number of programs which are semantically identical with a given program but which differ syntactically from one another. Therefore, the uniqueness which a computer program can reach is not what we have been looking for.

Unique happens only once, it cannot be repeated, and we cannot return to it either. No relation of identity, not even self-identity, applies to it. Now the big question is, of course, can meanings ever be *that* unique — and still, in some sense, be meanings. Or, what amounts almost to the same: can *anything* be that unique.

Consider native or local cultures, that is, cultures which have had no (or have had only superficial) contacts with Western technology and the related commercialized way of life. They seem to be unique if compared with other cultures, native or not. The uniqueness of native cultures may originate from the peculiar gamelike experiential interaction which the communities (which support the cultures) have developed with the local natural environment. This interaction is assumed to have a unique history, that is, the relation of the community to nature has changed gradually. We haven't assumed here that native cultures necessarily conceive nature as if it consisted of external, reified objects which can be used for different purposes. That would be a distinctly Western conception of nature. The social games of a native community, linguistic games included, arise from the unique experience of nature which makes living in the natural environment meaningful and feasible.

The uniqueness of the games from which meaning arises doesn't stop at the environmental or communal level. It flows down to the neural events which are active during the games, and from there back to different cultural and semiotic activities. In other words, the related brain events of the players must also be unique. We haven't assumed here that, in order to be a member of a community, or a player in a social game, one (sic) has to satisfy any classical individuation or separability conditions (see Chapter 4 and 6). Similarly, we do not assume that brains are classical systems which consist of subsystems, such that the behavior of the system can be explained in terms of the subsystems. Eventually the uniqueness saturates the whole semiotic sphere of the culture, including such areas as myths, religious beliefs, music, arts and crafts, construction of tools and buildings, and so on.

The unique meaning view can be developed to the ultimate stage where we have to say that a player of a communal game can never mean by (what we conventionally call) 'one word' one and the same thing twice; actually, he cannot mean one and the same thing even once, though every attempt to interpret the preceding idea in an ametaphysical language would take a hopelessly large space. Obviously, if this inalienable lack of meaning identity holds, then language is not primarily a medium for the transportation of ideas, concepts and propositions from one person to another. Language is not primarily communication. We should not even say that language always needs persons or subjects to arise, because personhood and subjectivity require processes where persons and subjects are individuated, and, the individuation requires that the conception of identity is available. Therefore, persons or individuals are neither unique nor anything from which the unique originates. Uniqueness precedes personhood and individuality, and originates from local and native experience (cf. von Humboldt, 1836/1974).

Neural indeterminacy

If we want to envisage experiential uniqueness from the neural point of view, we can begin by acknowledging that a living brain never returns to a previous state, and a state in which the brain happens to be is something to which even self-identity doesn't apply. The unique brain is also a brain with no *communication* between different areas: each area of the brain lives, so to speak, like a culture of its own. The cultures are not connected by communication or translation; they are mutually influenced by ways which resemble interpretations. In interpretations, new and unpredictable meanings are designed, and the design is often based on incomplete and misleading hints which arrive from distant brain cultures through less than causally reliable channels.

Let us use the word *mechanical* by and large as it is used by Kreisel (1974). Almost in Kreisel's sense, we may say that something, either a theory, system or phenomenon, is mechanical if it can be simulated, with *any* desired accuracy, by a Turing machine. If we use the prefix *a* as has been suggested earlier (Chapter 1), something is *amechanical* if and only if it is neither mechanical (Turing-computable) nor nonmechanical (not-Turing-computable) (cf. Chapter 3). This characterization deconstructs the traditional dichotomy of the mechanical and the nonmechanical. It has been proposed earlier that single quantum phenomena are amechanical and, therefore, they can serve as the physical originators of the unique. For example, they can serve as the physical origin of such neural events which are active during some of our experiences, especially during such experiences which are aconceptual.

An experience is aconceptual if it doesn't arise only through the activation of concepts or representations; therefore, no conceptual description can fully capture its nature either (for the development of intuition about aconceptuality, see *l'expérience intérieure* in Bataille, 1943/1988; and Chapter 1). The aconceptual experience is holistic in the sense that it cannot be explained comprehensively in terms of the properties or behavior of its (alleged) components or constituents. Typically, aconceptual experiences lack content and tend to relativize or dissolve, to some extent, the subject-object boundary. Thus, we associate subjectivity strongly to conceptuality: the subject is that which organizes the not-necessarily-conceptual experience into a conceptual form; or better, the subject *is* the conceptual organization in our experience which is not originally and completely conceptual. First of all, space, time and causation arise from this regimentation of experience; later preferences and intentions also appear into the organization of subjectivity. An experience in which such structures are dissolved is aconceptual and has no organization, structure or content. It is about nothing.

Now, it may be suggested that connectionist and chaos-theoretical concepts and methods (Skarda & Freeman, 1987; 1990) can help us distance language theory from the structure-oriented theoretical tradition of grammatical and logical studies. Clearly, this sounds like a step in the right, that is to say, less metaphysical direction. This is especially so if 'connectionism' and 'chaos' are defined in a way which allows reference to non-Turing-computable numbers and functions. Unfortunately, the available nonmechanical alternative is not what is usually opted for. Either consciously or unwittingly, connectionists and chaos-theorists define their systems in terms of Turing-computable numbers and functions, which is an unnecessary constraint. The reason is easy to understand but hard to accept. But, even if the boundary of mechanicalness is surpassed, the access to the aconceptual aspect of language is not yet available. We need something genuinely amechanical.

If we believe that some neural events cannot be explained without reference to quantum-sized phenomena, as, for example, Beck and Eccles (1992; see also Eccles, 1989) have suggested, then it is possible that the inseparable properties of quantum phenomena (for which, see d'Espagnat, 1981; 1984; Howard, 1989) provide the physical origin for the holistic nature of the aconceptual experience (cf. Chapter 3). So, contrary to Roger Penrose (1994), quantum events of the brain, if such things have to be considered, would be associated, not to the nonmechanicalness, but to amechanicalness, that is, to inseparability, indeterminacy and randomness. Actually, Penrose's approach would block our access to the description of aconceptual experience because the nonmechanical (noncomputational), in the above sketched sense, is conceptually structured and completely determined in advance. Of course, Penrose and many others would protest by proclaiming that everything (that exists) is either mechanical (Turing-computable) or nonmechanical (non-Turing-computable). In other words, nothing lies outside of their union. But this is, if not pure superstition, a stance that needs to be discussed.

Some aspects of conceptual thinking may, to a certain extent, be explained in terms of macro-sized neural processes, such as action potentials and hyperpolarizations. But even if we have, say in an academic context, the impression that our thoughts and language are conceptually organized and that our ideas and sentences are completely determined by previous ideas and sentences, we have to concede that this conceptual, sequential and determinate aspect of our experience requires an aconceptual origin to arise. Classical physics and chemistry, as well as the noncomputable mathematical structures of nonclassical physics and chemistry (Penrose), are unable to provide the origin. The initiation of conceptual thinking remains partly indeterminate and unpredictable, even if the emergence of consciousness and conceptual understanding, as Penrose (1994) and Hameroff (1994) claim, had something to do with quantum coherence in microtubules (see Chapter 3).

In a sense which was suggested by Wolfgang Pauli (1954; see also Pylkkö, 1996b; and Chapter 3), single quantum events are unpredictable and even 'irrational:' there exists no rational explanation why something which appears to be purely deterministic, namely, the evolution of a quantum system according to the Schrödinger equation, 'collapses' into something which is only probabilistic, namely, into a result of a measurement. 'Irrational,' or better, *arational*, refers, in this context, to the absence of a rational explanation for how something deterministic ends up producing something random.

Now, if quantum phenomena, that is, phenomena which are not reducible to classical physics and which may remain irreducible to noncomputable physics too, are effective in our brains when we experience something, it can be suggested that it is their randomness which serves as the origin of the freedom of our mind (cf. Chapter 3). Obviously we are here trying to capture a particular connotation of the word *freedom*. *Freedom* refers to the unpredictability of the course which thinking and other experiences may take. For rather obscure reasons, the freedom of will has traditionally been associated to the autonomy and rationality of conscious choice, not, say, to sexual desire or suicidal drives. The underlying idea must have been that nature is mechanical and deprived of freedom, and that only a rational choice is able to ascend man above the constraints of nature. Sexual and destructive drives arise from the bodily life of man, and that kind of life is governed by unfree obsessions. Contrary to the traditional view, here freedom means that we *cannot* know, not even in principle, which direction we, our thoughts and actions, are going to take. This relates freedom to such aspects of our experience which are not completely conceptually organized, and to such events of our body and brain which are not fully conceptualizable. Some of such experiences may also remain inaccessible to consciousness (cf. Libet, 1985).

Kokea and the limits of conceptual thinking

Perhaps an expression like *ollaan erällä* alludes to an experience which is, not only unique and untranslatable, but also aconceptual in the sense that it precedes the emergence of concepts. Björn Collinder (1977, p. 118) lists *ole-* in the Proto-Fenno-Ugric vocabulary, whereas the root *koke-* (experience) belongs to the Proto-Uralic vocabulary (Collinder, 1977, p. 45), that is, to the earliest layer of the Finnish language. Presumably *koke-* had originally very little to do with conceptual or propositional attitudes. Rather, its meaning seems to have been associated to the examination of fishing nets and game traps. (We still say that *verkot koetaan*, that we *experience* a fishing net.) Contrary to this, *ajatella* (to think) which is probably derived from *ajaa* (to drive), is an Indo-European loan, though an early one (Collinder, 1977, p. 140).

In this light, we are led to encounter an interesting quandary if we try to analyze the meaning of such passive-like constructions as *ollaan erällä* or *koetaan* in any purely theoretical or conceptual framework. These utterances may be related to experiences which, at least partly, precede the emergence of conceptual thinking. (Note that *preceding* is not used here *only* in the historical or temporal sense.) If this is so, every theoretical or conceptual explanation of the utterances and experiences is bound to remain somewhat inadequate. It may be this area, the conceptually inaccessible experience, where uniqueness dwells. Therefore it would represent a fallacious approach to such an experience to decide in advance that, say, *verkot koetaan* means simply that we bluntly collect the net up from the water. That is what a modern Western man does with his fishing nets. Also *hunting*, in the present-day context, has a special technological meaning: an animal is killed in order to transform it into a body which, say as meat or leather, can be used for different purposes. But the ancient experience of fishing and hunting may have been different. It wasn't necessarily permeated with and structured by the technological attitude which we almost automatically project upon the ancient mind. Even if the human mind was shaped by the survival struggle, the struggle wasn't *only* a technological issue.

Also the word *erä* may turn out to be inaccessible to any theoretical approach. The word *erä* hints to *eräs* (something indefinite; someone) (cf. Collinder, 1977, p. 93) and perhaps to *eri*, that is, to something that is different, the idea being, possibly, that *maa* (land) which is *erä*, namely *erämaa* (wilderness), differs from the cultivated land by being, among other things, a source of wild game. Yet the nature of this difference seems to be conspicuously aconceptual, alluding perhaps to the peculiar experiential unfamiliarity or even anonymous threat which such a land may offer to someone who is accustomed to a more domesticated way of life. We can almost sense a hint to a kind of secrecy here, perhaps to the unconscious, though not in the Freudian, but rather in the Schopenhauerian sense: *erämaa* is something else, the Other, which, like Schopenhauer's *Wille*, is hard to domesticate and which cannot be reduced to the familiarity of the conceptual life. Remnants of the uncontrollable uniqueness will always survive in the distant wilderness.

Finnish as aconceptual experience

Now, at least some reasonable people would say: "Give me a break! Some poems may be hard or impossible to translate, but this doesn't give us good reasons to believe that language as a whole is just a flux of unique meanings. A great deal, perhaps almost all of language is rational and communicable. Language consists, after all, of sentences which express propositions. Sentences have a universal grammatical structure which reflects an equally universal logical structure. Either *Ollaan* and other similar examples have the standard grammatical or logical structure, or, if not, they must represent a marginal case."

Indeed, we are so accustomed to think of language in terms of grammatical and logical structures that we may be inclined to say that without such structures there remains no language at all. Language simply disappears. But where is the subject-predicate structure in the *ollaan* utterance, which is, in terms of meaningfulness or fullness of meaning, just as complete as any grammatical sentence or consistent proposition of the Indo-European languages? For example, *ollaan erällä* is not elliptical, let alone incomplete. Nothing in the utterance hints to a missing or underlying grammatical (or logical), form. Yet, even without the subject-predicate structure, the utterance belongs to the Finnish language.

Recent grammatical and logical studies of language have committed themselves to the ontology of separable objects and individuals to such an extent that I am skeptical of their prospects of ever reaching an adequate explanation of such utterances as *ollaan erällä*. Neither are we quite on the right track if we suggest, as Quine (1969) might do, that we have here an ontology which competes with the Indo-European one. No, the situation is even more radically competitive, not sportive but belligerent: There seems to be no ontology at all! When we enter the landscape of originally Finnish thinking we also leave the Western ontology behind us without replacing it with a new one. This is *ontological nihilism*, not relativism. *Nihilism* seems to be a particularly fitting word if the lack of ontology in Finnish meanings is contrasted to the ontology-oriented meanings of the Indo-European languages.

In the context of the modern Finnish welfare state life, it is hard to address such an experience directly. However, remnants of this Finnish experiential nihilism can still be encountered indirectly as alcoholism, anxiety, excessive suicidal obsessions, feelings of marginality and inferiority, overall tendency to mutiny, mutism, gaps in communication, and so on. Perhaps this should be understood as a reaction to the suppression which the alien ontology and the related conception of man exercises upon the native mind. The academically scaffolded sentential or propositional structure, as well the conception of a rational and autonomous person, which all educated Finns learn to imitate, is basically an alien, imported layer in the Finnish language experience, and it is experienced by many native speakers as foreign and inauthentic. This is what also Hellaakoski's poem witnesses. The language which is spoken by men who are in the mode of *ollaan erällä* is separated from the school language of the educated man by an enormous experiential gap.

If language can emerge without ontology, then we should be careful to not define language by saying that language consists of sentences (or propositions) which satisfy a grammatical (or logical) subject-predicate structure. Perhaps we should say that language is, at least originally, aconceptual experience, and what we call 'communication' of concepts, ideas or propositions is just one aspect of language, a direction in which language *can* be guided under certain cultural, social and political circumstances. In order to make language resemble communication, we can let it become more and more like a formal or conceptual code, for example like predicate logic. This can be continued so long that eventually, in Heidegger's sense of *Vergessenheit*, all of the aconceptual origin of language is 'forgotten.' This doesn't mean that aconceptual meanings are originally marginal, only that they have been marginalized for different political and social reasons.

Philosophical nationality

Even if the meaning of *ollaan erällä*, due to its uniqueness, is conceptually inaccessible and untranslatable, this doesn't imply that we cannot talk about its meaning, or that we cannot describe its meaning to non-Finns. But it does imply that an adequate description of its meaning is bound to be more like an unpredictable and irrepeatable interpretation than a translation or communication of regimented ideas. An interpretation, unlike a translation, is able to deal also with aconceptual experiences and address the issue of ontological nihilism. However, a language in which a successful interpretation is carried out cannot be a theoretical or conceptual language which pretends to have established an objectivist or neutral point of view. Languages, cultures and minds are separated from one another by a kind of 'creativity barrier,' that is, a barrier that can be crossed only with the help of creativity, and human minds of different origin do not share a common conceptual forum where they could meet as equals. For example, rational action is unable to provide such a forum. The medium of communication which the modern Western technology, science and philosophy offers isn't neutral either. In that medium, the transportation of ideas runs only in one direction, even though that is often pretentiously called 'objective knowledge' or 'intercultural communication.'

Concepts always remain entangled with their local, historical and environmental soil, their experiential aconceptuality, even if they try to surpass it. Though they can succeed in ascending above their low origin by increasing their articulation, concepts can never purify themselves completely from the aconceptuality. Thus, it is not a tenable position to claim that the human experience consists of two sections, namely, of the universal meanings and of the local ones, because this kind of dualism would obscure the relationship between the conceptual and the aconceptual in our mind. For example, almost all of our prevailing philosophical and scientific concepts are originally Greek-German-British-French concepts, that is, European ideas, not universal. The cultures which created modern technology, science and philosophy have tried to purify their language and experience from the embarrassing and bizarre local aconceptualities, and, indeed, they have succeeded in creating the impression that the resulting knowledge is more than just a local commodity. This cultural achivement has made it easier for them to market their technology, science and philosophy as universal products. Analogously, the related conception of man as a rational and autonomous being is offered as a universal model of man.

Before the Second World War the local nature of culture, including the technological, scientific and philosophical culture, was still a widely accepted view, perhaps even the dominant one, and the local origin of language and culture was acknowledged and encouraged, not suppressed. The American way of life was American, not a universal model; the rational, democratic and autonomous subject was a product of the European Enlightenment, not a universal idea; transcendental philosophy and symphonies were a German privilege which could only be imitated, more or less succesfully, by Frenchmen, Englishmen and Finns (see for example, Böhm, 1938).

After the war it has become increasingly difficult, nowadays almost impossible, to address this problem field. Repercussions of philosophical localism can still be heard in Heidegger's *Der Spiegel interview* (1966/1988) where he said that serious philosophical problems, like the essence of modern Western technology, can be thought creatively only within that cultural sphere from which the technology originated. This sphere covers mainly the Central-European scene, especially the German culture which, according to Heidegger, was the only genuine heir of the Ancient Greek civilization. Japanese, Finnish or other non-Western thinkers cannot cope seriously and creatively with problems, like the essence of technology, which are basically alien to their cultural background. If they want to think seriously and creatively they have to address problems which have arisen within their own cultural sphere.

The interview was Heidegger's philosophical testament. It was not a spontaneous ejaculation, as has sometimes been suggested. The views which are expressed there continue a long tradition both in the European philosophy and in Heidegger's own thinking. Already in *Introduction to Metaphysics* (1935/1978, p. 50), Heidegger had reserved for the German nation the special task of saving the European spirit (Geist) from the darkness and destitution into which America and Russia (the Soviet Union) were trying to push it. In *...poetically man dwells...* (1951/1971, p. 218), Heidegger suggested that poetry and thinking must come near each other. Because original and creative poetry is practically always written in a native language, the obvious implication is that also thinking can be carried out only in a native language. In *Language in the poem* (1953/1982, p. 195), Heidegger again proclaims that meanings, especially meanings in language, always arise in a context of race, tribe, clan and family. In short, one needs the earth, soil and original native community in order to create and cultivate authentic meanings. According to Hans-Georg Gadamer (1981, p. 114) Heidegger did not only see this line of development as a general possibility but actually realized it in his own thinking. Eventually Heidegger's language became just as untranslatable as the language of poetry: "Sie ist am Ende so völlig unübersetzbar wie das Wort des lyrischen Gedichts..." (Here 'sie' refers to Heidegger's language.)

Is it possible to think about philosophical problems in Finnish?

With a little help from Heidegger, we can now ask our final question: Is it possible to think originally, surprisingly and creatively about such philosophical problems which were begotten in a language which one doesn't speak as a native speaker?

The answer must be negative, or, at least, more on the negative side than on the positive one. If the meaning of such expressions as *ollaan erällä* or *koetaan* becomes understandable only through the annihilation of ontology, especially through the annihilation of the ontology of human beings and autonomous subjects, then it can be expected that their meaning is impossible to learn by anyone who has not grown up in the local and unique experiential situations to which the expressions belong. It is impossible to initiate a grownup outsider who doesn't belong to the community with such experiential situations.

But the view that the proper acquisition of language requires that one grows up within the community in which the language is spoken doesn't apply only to the Finnish passive-like utterances but can be extended to cover practically any area of language, and even beyond language to the acquisition of any meaningful experiences whatsoever. Just as we can hardly say that a person born blind knows what color terms mean, we shouldn't say that a person who has grown up in the urban West knows what such Finnish words as *lumi* (snow), *järvi* (lake) or *metsä* (forest) mean. Their meaning cannot be learned in any academic context. What a modern city man who hasn't experienced the wilderness as a child has in mind is either some half-urban counterpart experiences or some artificial reproductions (from books, movies and so on). Thus, just as the proper understanding of Hellaakoski's poem requires that one understands experientially what the difference between *minä olen* (I am) and *ollaan* is, the reader is also assumed to have an experiential touch with the basic Finnish vocabulary which includes many words which are used to describe the environment of the arctic wilderness. This touch is not something which can be comprehensively conceptualized and cut into constituents. It is too subtle, holistic and amorphous to serve that purpose. That kind of meaning cannot be explained as goal-directed action either, especially not if the action is defined in terms of rational individuals, or groups of such individuals. We can use, if that is what we want, the words *game*, *player* and *movement* in order to describe the experiential situation of *ollaan* and other local aconceptual experiences, as long as we don't suppose that games are played and movements are made *only* by well individuated and rational subjects (cf. Chapter 4 and 6).

Thinking which hopes to satisfy such attributes as *original*, *surprising* or *creative* must have an experiential touch with the native vocabulary, and in many cases acquiring the touch requires that one is either born in the community or has moved to its sphere of influence sufficiently early during the formative years. Only then can thinking utilize the seeds which lie hidden in our words and which have been passed over to us from our ancestors. These seeds are aconceptual and unpredictable, and they remain out of the control of the rational and autonomous subject, its conceptual organization and conscious intentions. The seeds are local, ethnic, environmental and even racial (cf. von Humboldt, 1836/1974). They are also unique and untranslatable. However, it is not necessary that the ancient speakers of the native language understood or experienced intensively every potentially vital aspect of their language. They may have passed the language forward, or the language may have moved forward in their minds, even if they themselves were unable to establish a contact to the seeds. Even if the ancient speakers themselves were not always able to listen to the energizing aconceptual meanings of their language, the possibility may still be with us today.

Unique meanings need not be closed to foreign influence either (cf. Chapter 1). Uniqueness is not privacy and doesn't thus bound us to cultural solipsism (cf. Chapter 5). Experiential uniqueness is open to perpetual influence and change which may, however, be unpredictable and conceptually uncontrollable. Some influences may arise from straight confusion and misunderstanding; others are based on more careful thinking, even on interpretations which try to shift meanings over cultural barriers from one language into another. Genuine intercultural dialogue which is not one-directional is based on interpretation. The interpretative influence lacks method and rules, and it may be partly accidental, sometimes almost miraculous, but, at the same time, it may be the only way to preserve cultural variety under the pressure of global unification, and even the future of democracy may rest on its prospects (cf. Chapter 6). But, nevertheless, intercultural interpretation may not always succeed peacefully. Actually, authentic human relations, including the intercultural ones, can be harsh, painful and even violent, as already Väinämöinen's and Vipunen's conflict in the seventeenth song of *Kalevala* indicated (see Preface).

Thus what we need is local thinking which is relativistic enough in order to appreciate foreign influence. This is something that Heidegger's thinking fails to accomplish when the appreciation of uniqueness leads him to cultural purism and solipsism. His thinking is open neither to foreign cultural, ethnic and linguistic influences (cf. Chapter 1) nor to influences arising from the Western scientific culture. Not all of the latter influences need be onto-theological (cf. Chapter 2). Analogously, universalism is an illusion, not much more than a misnomer for the globalization of Western ideas, and its practical consequence will be cultural unification, even if universalism is advocated under such seemingly well-intending banners as 'intercultural communication' and 'global human rights.' Modern Western technology and science, including logic and grammar, as well as the related ideals of the Enlightenment, are products of local Western culture whose claim of universal validity is pretentious.

All thinking, including philosophical and scientific thinking, rests on the aconceptual human experience, and the acquisition of language with the help of which aconceptual experiences can be spoken of takes place in infancy. Thus, if philosophical thinking is not carried out in the philosopher's native language it may fail to be anything more than an uncritical repercussion of original thinking. Such residual thinking has borrowed its light from the original thinking which emits its radiance from the cultural power centers toward the periphery. To suggest that there exists a conceptual or rational level of language which is universal and common to all cultures would obscure our view of how concepts emerge. This obscurity would imply either a version of dualism, namely an untenable separation of the conceptual and the aconceptual, or a straightforward repression of the aconceptual mind.

References

Albert, David, 1992. *Quantum Mechanics and Experience*. Harvard University Press: Cambridge, Massachusetts.

Arnaud, Alain & Excoffon-Lafarge, Gisèle, 1978. *Bataille*. Seuil: Paris.

Bärsch, Claus-Ekkehard, 1987. *Erlösung und Vernichtung. Dr. phil. Joseph Goebbels. Zur Psyche und Ideologie eines jungen Nationalsozialisten, 1923-27*. Boer: München.

Bataille, Georges, 1943/1988. *Inner Experience*. Translated by Leslie Anne Boldt. State University of New York Press: Albany. The original title *L'Expérience Intérieure*. Gallimard: Paris, 1992.

Bäumler, Alfred, 1923. *Kants kritik der Urteilskraft. Ihre Geschichte und Systematik. Erster Band: Das Irrationalitätsproblem in der Ästhetik und Logik des 18. Jahrhunderts bis zur Kritik der Urteilskraft*. Max Niemeyer: Halle.

Bäumler, Alfred, 1931. *Nietzsche, der Philosoph und Politiker*. Reclam: Leipzig. Zweite Auflage.

Bäumler, Alfred, 1942. *Bildung und Gemeinschaft*. Junker und Dünnhaupt: Berlin. Zweite Auflage, 1943.

Baylor, D.A.; Lamb, T.D. & Yau, K.-W., 1979. Responses of retinal rods to single photons. *The Journal of Physiology*, volume 288, pp. 613-634.

Beck, Friedrich & Eccles, John, 1992. Quantum aspects of brain activity and the role of consciousness. *Proceedings of the National Academy of Sciences*, USA, vol. 89, pp. 11357-11361, Dec, 1992.

Bohm, David, 1952. A suggested interpretation of the quantum theory in terms of "hidden" variables. I & II. *Physical Review*, vol. 85, Num. 2, January 15, 166-193.

Bohm, David, 1957. *Causality and Chance in Modern Physics*. Routledge and Kegan Paul: London.

Böhm, Franz, 1938. *Anti-Cartesianismus. Deutsche Philosophie im Widerstand*. Felix Meiner: Leipzig.

Bohr, Niels, 1933. Light and life. *Atomic Physics and Human Knowledge*, pp. 3-12. John Wiley: London, 1958. First published in *Nature*, *131*, 421, 1933.

Böök, Fredrik, 1933. *Hitler's Tyskland. Maj 1933*. P.A. Norstedt & Söners: Stockholm.

Bourdieu, Pierre, 1988. *The Political Ontology of Martin Heidegger*. Polity Press: Cambridge, 1991. First published in French as *L'Ontologie Politique de Martin Heidegger*. Editions de Minuit: Paris, 1988. A slightly different version was published already in *Actes de la recherche en sciences sociales*, 1975.

Bourel, Dominique, 1994. Un rencontre ineffacable. *Le Monde des Débats*, March 1994, p. 15.

Broszat, Martin, 1987. Enthüllung? Die Rauschning-Kontroverse. *Nach Hitler: Der schwierige Umgang mit unserer Geschichte. Beiträge von Martin Broszat*, edited by Hermann Graml ja Klaus-Dietmar Henke, pp. 249-251. Oldenbourg: München.

Capaldi, Nicholas; King, James & Livingston, Donald, 1991. The Hume literature of the 1980's. *American Philosophical Quarterly*, Volume 28, Number 4, October 1991, pp. 255-272.

Cassidy, David, 1992. *Uncertainty. The Life and Science of Werner Heisenberg*. W.H. Freeman and Company: New York.

de Chateaubriant, Alphonse, 1937. *La Gerbe des Forces. Nouvelle Allemagne*. Éditions Bernard Grasset: Paris.

Cheney, Dorothy L. & Seyfarth, Robert M., 1990. *How Monkeys See the World. Inside the Mind of Another Species*. University of Chicago Press: Chicago and London.

Collinder, Björn, 1977. *Fenno-Ugric Vocabulary. An Etymological Dictionary of the Uralic Languages*. Helmut Buske: Hamburg.

Cortes, Alberto, 1976. Leibniz's principle of the Identity of the Indiscernibles: A false principle. *Philosophy of Science*, 43, 1976.

Couliano, Ioan P., 1984. *Eros and Magic in the Renaissance*. The University of Chicago Press: Chicago and London, 1987. Translated into English by Margaret Cook. Original French title *Eros et Magie à la Renaissance*. Flammarion: Paris.

Crane, Tim, 1992. The nonconceptual content of experience. *The Content of Experience. Essays on Perception*, edited by Tim Crane. Cambridge University Press: Cambridge.

Cussins, Adrian, 1992. Content, embodiment and objectivity: the theory of cognitive trails. *Mind*, Vol. 101.404, October, 1992.

Deleuze, Gilles & Guattari, Félix, 1991. *Qu'est-ce que la philosophie?* Les Éditions de Minuit: Paris.

Derrida, Jacques, 1987. *Of Spirit*. Translated by Geoffrey Bennington and Rachel Bowlby. University of Chicago Press: Chicago, 1989. Original French title, *De l'esprit*. Editions Galilée: Paris, 1987.

Derrida, Jacques, 1989. Eating well, or the calculations of the Subject: An interview with Jacques Derrida. *Who Comes after the Subject?*, edited by Eduardo Cadava, Peter Connor and Jean-Luc Nancy. Routledge: New York and London, 1991. The interview was published originally in *Cahiers Confrontations*, no. 20, Winter 1989.

Descombes, Vincent, 1980. *Modern Fransk Filosofi, 1933-1978*. Translated into Swden by Gustaf Gimdal. Röda Bokförlaget: Göteborg. The original title *Le Même et L'Autre*.

Dewey, John, 1925. *Experience and Nature*. Revised edition, 1929. Open Court: La Salle, Illinois, 1989.

Domarius, Max, 1965 (ed.). *Hitler. Reden und Proklamationen, 1932-45. Kommentiert von einem deutschen Zeitgenossen*. Süddeutscher Verlag: München.

Dreyfus, Hubert L., 1991. *Being-in-the-World. A Commentary on Heidegger's 'Being and Time'*. Division I. The MIT Press: Cambridge, Massachusetts and London, England.

Dreyfus, Hubert & Hall, Harrison, 1992. Introduction. *Heidegger: A Critical Reader*, edited by Hubert Dreyfus and Harrison Hall. Blackwell: Oxford.

Eccles, John, 1989. *Evolution of the Brain: Creation of the Self*. Routledge: London and New York.

Edelman, Gerald, 1989. *The Remembered Present. A Biological Theory of Consciousness*. Basic Books: New York.

Eitner, Hans-Jürgen, 1990. *Hitlers Deutsche. Das Ende eines Tabus*. Casimir Katz Verlag: Gernsbach.

Engel, Andreas & König, Peter, 1992. Paradigm shifts in neurobiology. Toward a new theory of perception. *Philosophy and the Cognitive Sciences*, edited by R. Casati and G. White, pp. 131-138. The Austrian Ludwig Wittgenstein Society: Kirchberg am Wechsel.

d'Espagnat, Bernard, 1981. *À la Recherche du réel. Le Regard d'un Physicien*. Gauthier-Villars: Paris.

d'Espagnat, B., 1984. Nonseparability and the tentative description of the reality. *Physics Reports*, vol. 110. no. 4, Aug 1984, pp. 201-264.

Evans, Gareth, 1982. *The Varieties of Reference*. Edited by John McDowell. Clarendon Press: Oxford.

Faye, Jan, 1991. *Niels Bohr: His Heritage and Legacy*. Kluwer: Dordrecht.

Ferry, Luc & Renaut, Alain, 1985. *La Pensée 68. Essai sur l'anti-humanisme contemporain*. Gallimard: Paris.

Ferry, Luc & Renaut, Alain, 1990. *Heidegger and Modernity*. Translated by Franklin Philip. University of Chicago Press: Chicago. The original title *Heidegger et les Modernes*. Grasset & Fasquelle: Paris, 1988.

Feyerabend, Paul, 1987. *Farewell to Reason*. Verso: London and New York.

Feyerabend, Paul, 1988. *Against Method*. Revised edition. Verso: London and New York.

Fink, Eugen, 1960. *Nietzsches Philosophie*. Kohlhammar: Stuttgart.

Fodor, Jerry & Pylyshyn, Zenon, 1988. Connectionism and cognitive architecture: A critical analysis. *Connections and Symbols*, edited by Steven Pinker and Jacques Mehler, pp. 3-71. The MIT Press: Cambridge, Massachusetts.

Foucault, Michel, 1976. Two lectures. *Power/Knowledge. Selected Interviews and Other Writings, 1972-1977*, pp. 78-108. The Harvester Press: Brighton.

Frank, Manfred, 1995. Mental intimacy and epistemic self-ascription. A copy of an unfinished manuscript.

Franklin, Stan & Garzon, Max, 1991. Neural computability. *Progress in Neural Networks*, Vol. 1, edited by Omid Omidvar, pp. 127- 145. Ablex: Norwood, New Jersey.

Freud, Sigmund, 1905/1976. *Jokes and Their Relation to the Unconscious*. Translated and edited by James Strachey, revised by Angele Richards. Pelican Freud Library 6. Penguin: Harmondsworth, England, 1976. Original title *Der Witz und seine Beziehung zum Unbewussten*, 1905.

Freyer, Hans, 1931. *Revolution von rechts*. Eugen Dieterich: Jena.

Froning, Hubertus, 1990. *Europäischer Expressionismus*. Berghaus: Kirchdorf/Inn. Sonderausgabe für Artbook International.

Gadamer, Hans-Georg, 1981. *Heidegger's Wege*. J.C.B. Mohr: Tübingen.

Gay, Peter, 1968. *Weimar Culture*. Penguin: Middlesex, 1974. Appeared originally in *Perspectives in American History*, II, 1968.

Geroch, Robert & Hartle, James, 1986. Computability and physical theories. *Foundations of Physics*, vol. 16, no. 6, pp. 549-566.

Globus, Gordon, 1990. Heidegger and cognitive science. *Philosophy Today*, Spring 1990, pp. 20-28.

Globus, Gordon, 1992a. Toward a noncomputational cognitive neuroscience. *Journal of Cognitive Neuroscience*, vol. 4, num. 4, pp. 299-310.

Globus, Gordon, 1992b. Derrida and connectionism: différance in neural nets. *Philosophical Psychology*, vol. 5, no. 2, pp. 183-197.

Globus, Gordon, 1995. *The Postmodern Brain*. John Benjamins: Amsterdam.

Göbbels, Joseph, 1929. *Michael. Ein deutsches Schicksal in Tagebuchblättern*. Franz Eher Nachf. GMBH: München. 3. Auflage, 1933.

Gödel, Kurt, 1944. Russell's mathematical logic. *Philosophy of Mathematics. Selected Readings*, edited by Paul Benacerraf and Hilary Putnam. Cambridge University Press: Cambridge, 1985, pp. 447-469. Printed originally in *The Philosophy of Bertrand Russell*, pp. 125-153, The Library of Living Philosophers, edited by Paul A. Schilpp. Northwestern University Press: Evanston, Illinois, 1944.

Gordon, Donald, 1987. *Expressionism. Art and Idea*. Yale University Press: New Haven and London.

Groos, Karl, 1899. *Die Spiele der Menschen*. Gustav Fischer: Jena.

Guyot, Adelin & Restellini, Patrick, 1983. *L'art Nazi. Un Art de Propaganda*. Editions Complexe: Bruxelles, 1987.

Hämäläinen, M.; Hari, R.; Ilmoniemi, R.; Knuuttila, J. & Lounasmaa, O., 1993. Magnetoencephalography - theory, instrumentation, and applications to noninvasive studies of the working human brain. *Reviews of Modern Physics*, vol. 65, no. 2, April 1993, pp. 413-497.

Hameroff, Stuart, 1993. Quantum conformational automata in the cytoskeleton: nanoscale cognition in protein connectionist networks. Paper without references written for the Abisko (Sweden) Conference on *Towards a material basis for cognition*, May 10-14, 1993.

Hameroff, Stuart, 1994. Quantum coherence in microtubules: A neural basis for emergent consciousness. *Journal of Consciousness Studies*, vol. 1, no. 1, pp. 91-118.

Hamlyn, D.W., 1980. *Schopenhauer. The Arguments of the Philosophers*-series. Routledge and Kegan Paul: London.

Haselbach, Dieter, 1994. Nation, Gott und Markt - Mythos und gesellschaftliche Integration bei Alfred Müller-Armack. *Politikwissenschaft als Kritische Theorie. Festschrift für Kurt Lenk*, edited by Th. Greven, Peter Kühler and Manfred Schmitz, pp. 215-230. Nomos: Baden-Baden.

Heidegger, Martin, 1927/1992. *Being and Time*. Translated from German by John Macquarrie and Edward Robinson. Blackwell: Oxford, 1992. The original title, *Sein und Zeit*. Max Niemeyer: Tübingen, 1986.

Heidegger, Martin, 1929/1988. What is metaphysics? The translation from German, by Hulland Crick, is included in *Existence and Being*, with introduction and analysis by Werner Brock. Gateway Editions: Washington, 1988. The original title "Was ist Metaphysik?" *Wegmarken. Gesamtausgabe*, Band 9. Vittorio Klostermann: Frankfurt am Main, 1976.

Heidegger, Martin, 1933/1990. The self-assertion of the German university. *Martin Heidegger and National Socialism. Questions and Answers*, pp. 5-13, edited by Günther Neske and Emil Kettering, translated by Lisa Harries. Paragon House: New York, 1990. Originally published in German as "Die Selbstbehauptung der deutschen Universität," 1933.

Heidegger, Martin, 1935/1978. *Introduction to Metaphysics.* Translated by Ralph Manheim. Yale University Press: New Haven and London, 1978. Original title, *Einführung in die Metaphysik,* 1935.

Heidegger, Martin, 1935-36/1971. The origin of the work of art. Translated by Albert Hofstadter, in *Poetry, Language, Thought,* Harper: New York, 1971. The original title "Der Ursprung des Kunstwerkes," *Holzwege. Gesamtausgabe,* Band 5. Vittorio Klostermann: Frankfurt am Main, 1977.

Heidegger, Martin, 1935-36/1977. Modern science, metaphysics, and mathematics. *Martin Heidegger. Basic Writings,* edited by David Farrell Krell. Harper: San Francisco. This is a translation by W.B. Barton and Vera Deutsch of sections B.I.5.a-f$_3$ of *Die Frage nach dem Ding* which consists of lecture notes from winter semester 1935-36. Max Niemeyer: Tübingen, 1962.

Heidegger, Martin, 1936-37/1991. *Nietzsche.* Volumes one and two. Translated by David Farrell Krell. Harper: San Francisco, 1979. The first volume of the paperback edition, 1991. Originally, lectures mainly from the winter semester 1936-37, published in German with the title *Nietzsche* by Günther Neske: Phullingen, 1961.

Heidegger, Martin, 1938/1977. The age of the world view. *The Question Concerning Technology and other Essays,* translated by William Lovitt. Harper and Row: New York, 1977. Originally "Die Zeit des Weltbildes," a lecture given in 1938, and published in *Holzwege. Gesamtausgabe,* Band 5. Vittorio Klostermann: Frankfurt am Main, 1977.

Heidegger, Martin, 1941/1993. *Basic Concepts.* Translated by Gary E. Aylesworth. Indiana University Press: Bloomington, 1993. Original title *Grundbegriffe,* lectures conducted during the winter semester 1941. *Gesamtausgabe,* vol. 51, Vittorio Klostermann, 1981.

Heidegger, Martin, 1947/1977. Letter on humanism. Translated by Frank Capuzzi and Glen Gray in *Martin Heidegger. Basic Writings,* edited by David Farrell Krell, Harper: San Francisco. The original title "Brief über den 'Humanismus,'" *Wegmarken. Gesamtausgabe,* Band 9. Vittorio Klostermann: Frankfurt am Main, 1976.

Heidegger, Martin, 1947/1993. A letter to Herbert Marcuse. *The Heidegger Controversy: A Critical Reader,* edited by Richard Wolin, pp. 162-163. The MIT Press: Cambridge, Massachusetts and London, England.

Heidegger, Martin, 1951/1971. ...poetically man dwells... English translation by Albert Hofstadter in *Poetry, Language, Thought.* Harper and Row: New York, 1971. The original title "...dichterisch wohnet der Mensch..." in *Vorträge und Aufsätze.* Neske: Phullingen, 1954. Originally a lecture given in 1951.

Heidegger, Martin, 1953/1982. Language in the poem. A discussion on Georg Trakl's poetic work. English translation by Peter Hertz in *On the Way to Language.* Harper and Row: New York, 1982. Original title "Georg Trakl. Eine Erörterung seines Gedichtes," first published in *Merkur,* no. 61, 1953.

Heidegger, Martin, 1954/1975. Moira. In *Early Greek Thinking,* translated by Frank Capuzzi. Harper & Row: San Francisco, 1975. Published originally in *Vorträge und Aufsätze.* Neske: Pfullingen, 1954.

Heidegger, Martin, 1954/1977a. The question concerning technology. *The Question concerning Technology and other Essays,* translated by William Lovitt. Harper and

Row: New York, 1977. Originally a lecture titled "Die Frage nach Technik," which is included in *Vorträge und Aufsätze*. Neske: Pfullingen, 1954.

Heidegger, Martin, 1954/1977b. Science and reflection. *The Question concerning Technology and other Essays*, translated by William Lovitt. Harper and Row: New York, 1977. Originally a lecture titled "Wissenschaft und Besinnung," in *Vorträge und Aufsätze*. Neske: Pfullingen, 1954.

Heidegger, Martin, 1954/1993. Overcoming metaphysics. The English translation by Joan Stambaugh, in *The Heidegger Controversy: A Critical Reader*, edited by Richard Wolin, pp. 67-90. The MIT Press: Cambridge, Massachusetts and London, England. Published originally under the title *Überwindung der Metaphysik* in *Vorträge und Aufsätze*. Neske: Pfullingen, 1954.

Heidegger, Martin, 1955/1958. *The Question of Being*. Translated by William Kluback and Jean T. Wilde. Twayne: New York, 1958. The original title *Über 'Der Linie'*, 1955.

Heidegger, Martin, 1957/1969. *Identity and Difference*. Translated by Joan Stambaugh, Harper and Row: New York, 1969. Includes the original German text *Identität und Differenz* which was published by Neske: Pfullingen, 1957.

Heidegger, Martin, 1957-58/1971. The nature of language. Translated by Peter D. Hertz, in *On the Way to Language*, Harper and Row: San Francisco, 1971. The original title "Das Wesen der Sprache," *Unterwegs zur Sprache. Gesamtausgabe*, Band 12. Vittorio Klostermann: Frankfurt am Main, 1985.

Heidegger, Martin, 1959/1971. *On the Way to Language*. Translated by Peter D. Hertz. Harper and Row: San Francisco, 1971. Original title, *Unterwegs zur Sprache. Gesamtausgabe*, Band 12. Vittorio Klostermann: Frankfurt am Main, 1985.

Heidegger, Martin, 1966/1988. *Der Spiegel* interview with Martin Heidegger. *Martin Heidegger and National Socialism. Questions and Answers*, edited by Gunther Neske and Emil Kettering, translated by Lisa Harries, pp. 41-66. Paragon House: New York, 1988. The original interview, "Nur noch ein Gott kann uns retten," was published in *Der Spiegel*, 23/1976 (May 31, 1976), pp. 193-219. Also available in *Antwort. Martin Heidegger im Gespräch*, edited by Günther Neske und Emil Kettering, pp. 81-111. Neske: Phullingen, 1988.

Hellaakoski, Aaro, 1952. *Sarjoja*. Werner Söderström: Helsinki.

Heyse, Hans, 1935. *Idee und Existenz*. Hanseatische Verlagsanstalt: Hamburg.

Hiley, Basil, 1991. Vacuum or holomovement. *The Philosophy of Vacuum*, edited by S. Saunders and H. Brown, pp. 217-249. Oxford University Press: Oxford.

Hilmy, Stephen, 1987. *The Later Wittgenstein*. Basil Blackwell: Oxford.

Hitler, Adolf, 1925. *Mein Kampf*. Translated into Swedish by Nils Holmberg. Askil & Kärnekull, 1970. The first edition of Hitler's work was published in 1925.

Hitler, Adolf, 1941-44. *Hitler's Table-talk 1941-44*. With an introduction by H.R. Trevor-Roper. Oxford University Press: Oxford, 1988.

Hjelmslev, Luis, 1961. Prolegomena to a Theory of Language. Translated by Francis J. Whitfield. University of Wisconsin Press: Milwaukee and London. Reprinted in 1969.

Howard, Don, 1989. Holism, separability, and the metaphysical implications of the Bell experiments. *Philosophical Consequences of Quantum Theory*, pp. 224-253, edited by James Cushing and Ernan McMullin. University of Notre Dame Press: Notre Dame, Indiana.

von Humboldt, Wilhelm, 1836/1974. *Linguistic Variability and Intellectual Development*. Translated by George C. Buck and Frithjof A. Raven. University of Pensylvania Press: Philadelphia. The original work *Über die Verschiedenheit des menschlichen Sprachbaues und ihren Einfluss auf die geistige Entwickelung des Menschengeschlechts* appeared in Berlin 1836.

Hume, David, 1739-40/1987. *A Treatise of Human Nature*. Edited by L.A. Selby-Bigge, with text revised by P.H. Nidditch. Oxford University Press: Oxford. Second edition 1987.

Husserl, Edmund, 1913/1976. *Ideas. General Introduction to Pure Phenomenology*. Translated by W.R. Royce Gibson. George Allen and Unwin: London, 1976. Original title *Ideen zur einer reinen Phänomenologie und phänomenologischen Philosophie*, 1913.

Husserl, Edmund, 1937/1989. *The Crisis of European Sciences and Transcendental Phenomenology*. Translated by David Carr. Northwestern University Press: Evanston, 1989. The original work, *Die Krisis der europäischen Wissenschaften und die transzendentale Phänomenologie: Eine Einleitung in die phänomenologische Philosophie*, was written in 1934-37, edited by Walter Biemel. Nijhoff: The Hague, 1954.

Irving, David, 1977. *Hitler's War. 1939-1942*. Macmillan: London.

Jäckel, Eberhard, 1981. *Hitlers Weltanschauung. Entwurf einer Herrschaft*. Deutsche Verlag-Anstalt: Stuttgart. Erweiterte und überarbeitete Neuausgabe.

Jäderlund, Christer, 1937. *Hitlers Tyskland. Reportage från Tredje Riket*. Bonniers: Stockholm.

Jammer, Max, 1966. *The Conceptual Development of Quantum Mechanics*. McGraw-Hill: New York.

Jammer, Max, 1974. *The Philosophy of Quantum Mechanics. The Interpretations of Quantum Mechanics in Historical Perspective*. John Wiley: New York.

Johnson-Laird, P.N. & Byrne, Ruth, M., 1991. *Deduction*. Lawrence Erlbaum: Hove.

Jünger, Ernst, 1922. *Der Kampf als inneres Erlebnis*. *Werke*, Band 5, *Essays* I. Ernst Klett Verlag: Stuttgart. (The reprint date missing).

Jünger, Ernst, 1932/1981. *Der Arbeiter. Herrschaft und Gestalt*. Klett-Cotta: Stuttgart, 1981.

Kalupahana, David, 1992. *A History of Buddhist Philosophy. Continuities and Discontinuities*. University of Hawaii Press: Honolulu.

Kant, Immanuel, 1784/1991. An answer to the question: 'What is enlightenment?' *Kant. Political Writings*, pp. 54-60, edited with an introduction and notes by Hans Reiss, translated by H.B. Nisbet. Second enlarged edition, 1991. Original German title "Beantwortung der Frage: Was ist Aufklärung?" First published in *Berlinische Monatsschrift*, IV, December 1784, pp. 481-94.

Kant, Immanuel, 1803/1964. *The Metaphysical Principles of Virtue*. The second edition (1803) of *Metaphysische Anfangsgründe der Tugendlehre*, translated by James Ellington. The Library of Liberal Arts-series. Bobbs-Merrill: Indianapolis, 1964.

Klages, Ludwig, 1921. *Vom Wesen des Bewusstseins. Aus einer Lebenswissenschaftlichen Vorlesung*. Johann Ambrosius Barth: Leipzig. Die zweite Auflage, 1926.

Klages, Ludwig, 1922. *Vom Kosmogonischen Eros*. Georg Müller: München.

Klages, Ludwig, 1934. *Geist und Leben*. Junker und Dünnhaupt: Berlin.

Klinge, Matti, 1972. *Vihan Veljistä Valtiososialismiin*. Werner Söderström: Porvoo and Helsinki.

Koskenniemi, V. A., 1937. *Havaintoja ja Vaikutelmia Kolmannesta Valtakunnasta. Kootut Teokset* V, WSOY, Helsinki, 1955. Published originally in 1937.

Kreisel, G., 1974. A notion of mechanistic theory. *Synthese*, 29, 1974, pp. 11-26.

Krell, David Farrell, 1988. Spiriting Heidegger. *Of Derrida, Heidegger, and the Spirit*, pp. 11-40, edited by David Wood. North-Western University Press: Evanston, Illinois, 1993. Appeared first in *Research in Phenomenology*, 18, 1988.

Kunnas, Tarmo, 1972. *Drieu la Rochelle, Celine, Brasillach et la tentation fasciste*. Les Sept Couleurs: Paris.

Lacoue-Labarthe, Philippe, 1987. *Heidegger, Art and Politics. Fiction of the Political*. Translated by Chris Turner. Basil Blackwell: Oxford, 1990. Original title *La Fiction du Politique*. Christian Bourgois: Paris, 1987.

Lacoue-Labarthe, Philippe & Nancy, Jean-Luc, 1991. *Le Myth Nazi*. Éditions de l'Aube.

Laurikainen, K.V., 1988. *Beyond the Atom. The Philosophical Thought of Wolfgang Pauli*. Springer: Berlin and Heidelberg.

Leibniz, G.W., 1704/1985. *New Essays on Human Understanding*. Translated and edited by Peter Remnant and Jonathan Bennett. Cambridge University Press: Cambridge, 1981. Reprinted 1985.

Leibniz, G.W., 1989. *Philosophical Essays*. Edited and translated by Roger Ariew and Daniel Garber. Hackett: Indianapolis and Cambridge.

Levinas, Emmanuel, 1979. *Le Temps et l'autre*. Presses Universitaires de France: Paris, 1991. First edition, Fata Morgana, 1979.

Libet, Benjamin, 1985. Unconscious cerebral initiative and the role of conscious will in voluntary action. *The Behavioral and Brain Sciences*, 8, pp. 529-566.

Löwith, Karl, 1940. *Meine Leben in Deutschland vor und nach 1933. Ein Bericht*. Fischer: Frankfurt am Main, 1989. Written originally 1940, published first by Carl Ernst Poeschel, 1961.

Lucács, Georg, 1974. *Die Zerstörung der Vernunf. Werke*, Band 9. Luchterhand: Darmstadt and Neuwied.

Lucas, J.R., 1961. Minds, machines and Gödel. *Minds and Machines*, edited by Alan Ross Anderson. Prentice-Hall; 1964. Published originally in *Philosophy*, vol. XXXVI, 1961.

Mach, Ernst, 1897. *The Analysis of Sensations, and the Relation of the Physical to the Psychical*. Translated from the first German edition by C.M. Williams, revised and supplemented from the fifth German edition by Sydney Waterlow. Open Court: Chicago and London, 1914.

Mach, Ernst, 1906. *Erkenntnis und Irrtum*. Johann Ambrosius Barth: Leipzig. Second edition.

McGuinness, Brian, 1988. *Wittgenstein. A Life. Young Ludwig 1889-1921*. Duckworth: London.

MacLean, Paul, 1973. *A Triune Concept of the Brain and Behavior*. University of Toronto Press: Toronto.

Macpherson, C.B., 1973. *Democratic Theory. Essays in Retrieval*. Clarendon Press: Oxford, 1975.

Matter, Jean, 1977. *Wagner et Hitler. Essai.* Editions L'Age d'Homme.

Mead, George Herbert, 1910. What social objects must psychology presuppose? *The Journal of Philosophy*, 7, 1910. The essay is included also in Mead's *Selected Writings*, pp. 105-113, edited with introduction by Andrew J. Reck. Bobbs-Merrill: Indianapolis and New York, 1964.

Merleau-Ponty, Maurice, 1945/1971. *Phénoménologie de la Perception.* Gallimard: Paris, 1992.

Meyer, Martin, 1990. *Ernst Jünger.* Carl Hanser: München.

Minsky, Marvin & Papert, Seymour, 1969. *Perceptrons. An Introduction to Computational Geometry.* MIT Press: Cambridge, Massachusetts.

Mukařovský, Jan, 1940. On poetic language. *The Word and Verbal Art, Selected Essays by Jan Mukarovsky, Yale Russian and East European Studies*, 13, translated and edited by John Burbank and Peter Steiner. Yale University Press: New Haven and London, 1977. Published originally with the title "O jazyce básnickém," in *Slovo a Slovesnost*, 6, 1940.

Müller-Armack, Alfred, 1933. *Staatsidee und Wirtschaftsordnung im neuen Reich.* Junker und Dünnhaupt: Berlin.

Nagel, Thomas, 1974. What is it like to be a bat? *Philosophical Review*, October 1974, pp. 435-450.

Nagel, Ernest & Newman, James, 1957. *Gödel's Proof.* Routledge & Kegan Paul: London.

Nietzsche, Friedrich, 1872/1939. *Die Geburt der Tragödie.* Kröners Taschenausgabe, Band 70, mit einem Nachwort von Alfred Bäumler. Alfred Kröner Verlag: Stuttgart, 1939.

Nietzsche, Friedrich, 1884-88/1967. *The Will to Power.* Translated by Walter Kaufmann and R.J. Hollingdale. Vitage/Random House: New York, 1967. Original title *Der Wille zur Macht. Gesammelte Werke*, neunzehnte Band. Musarion: München, 1926.

Nolte, Ernst, 1988. Philosophie und Nationalsozialismus. *Heidegger und die praktische Philosophie*, edited by Annemarie Gethman-Siefert and Otto Pöggeler, pp. 338-356. Suhrkamp: Frankfurt.

Nolte, Ernst, 1990. *Nietzsche und die Nietzscheanismus.* Propyläen: Frankfurt am Main.

Nolte, Ernst, 1992. *Heidegger. Politik und Geschichte im Leben und Denken.* Propyläen: Berlin and Frankfurt am Main.

Oakes, Guy, 1986. Translator's introduction. In Carl Schmitt's *Political Romanticism.* The MIT Press: Cambridge, Massachusetts.

Olff-Nathan, Josiane, 1993. Introduction. *La Science sous le Troisième Reich*, pp. 2-29. The book is written by a research group under J. Olff-Nathan's direction. Deuil: Paris.

Omnès, Roland, 1992. Consistent interpretation of quantum mechanics. *Reviews of Modern Physics*, Vol. 64, No. 2, April 1992, pp. 339-382.

Ostwald, Wilhelm, 1901. *Vorlesungen über Naturphilosophie, gehalten im Sommer 1901 an der Universität Leipzig.* von Veit: Leipzig. Third edition, 1905.

Paavolainen, Olavi, 1936. *Kolmannen Valtakunnan Vieraana.* Gummerus: Jyväskylä, 1936. Reprinted by Otava: Helsinki, 1975.

Paavolainen, Olavi, 1938. *Risti ja Hakaristi. Uutta Maailmankuvaa Kohti.* Gummerus: Jyväskylä.

Pais, Abraham, 1991. *Niels Bohr's Times, in Physics, Philosophy, and Polity.* Oxford University Press: Oxford. The paperback edition, 1993.

Patočka, Jan, 1988. *Qu'est-ce que la Phénoménologie.* Translated into French by Erika Abrams. Millon: Grenoble.

Pauli, Wolfgang, 1954. Wahrscheinlichkeit und Physik. *Physik und Erkenntnistheorie*, pp. 18-23. Vieweg: Braunschweig/Wiesbaden, 1984.

Penrose, Roger, 1994. *Shadows of the Mind. A Search for the Missing Science of the Consciousness.* Oxford University Press: Oxford.

Petersen, Aage, 1963. The philosophy of Niels Bohr. *Bulletin of the Atomic Scientists*, Chicago, September, 1963. Appeared also in *Niels Bohr. A Centenary Volume*, edited by French and Kennedy. Harvard University Press: Cambridge, Massachusetts, 1985.

Pfefferkorn, Kristin, 1988. *Novalis. A Romantic's Theory of Language and Poetry.* Yale University Press: New Haven and London.

Plotnitsky, Arkady, 1994. *Complementarity. Anti-Epistemology after Bohr and Derrida.* Duke University Press: Durham and London.

Pöggeler, Otto, 1992. Heidegger, Nietzsche and politics. *The Heidegger Case*, edited by Tom Rockmore and Joseph Margolis. Temple University Press: Philadelphia.

Pour-El, M.B. & Richards, Ian, 1981. The wave equation with computable initial data such that its unique solution is not computable. *Advances in Mathematics*, 39, 1981, pp. 215-239.

Putnam, Hilary, 1961. Comments on the paper of David Sharp. *Philosophy of Science*, vol. 28, no. 3, July 1961, pp. 234-237.

Putnam, Hilary, 1964. Discussion: Comments on comments on comments. A reply to Margenau and Wigner. *Philosophy of Science*, vol. 31, no. 1, January 1964, pp. 1-6.

Pylkkö, Pauli, 1991. Game-theoretical aesthetics. *The American Journal of Semiotics*, no. 1-2, 1991.

Pylkkö, Pauli, 1992. Connectionism and associative naming. *STeP-92, New Directions in Artificial Intelligence*, edited by E. Hyvönen, J. Seppänen and M. Syrjänen. The Finnish AI Society, Otaniemi, Finland.

Pylkkö, Pauli, 1993a. Eliminative naturalism and artistic meaning. *Philosophy Today*, vol. 37:2, Summer 1993, pp. 193-200. Chicago.

Pylkkö, Pauli, 1993b. Semiotics without signs and rules. *S - The European Journal of Semiotic Studies*, vol. 5-4, 1993, pp. 729-759, Vienna.

Pylkkö, Pauli, 1994a. Gaming without subjects - Some Humean trends in recent philosophical naturalism. *The British Tradition in the 20th Century Philosophy, The Papers of the 17th Ludwig Wittgenstein Symposium*, 1994, edited by Jaakko Hintikka and Klaus Puhl, pp. 371-384. The Austrian Ludwig Wittgenstein Society: Kirchberg am Wechsel.

Pylkkö, Pauli, 1994b. Associative naming and the quantum-theoretical two-path experiment. *STeP-94. New Directions of Artificial Intelligence*, edited by E. Hyvönen, J. Seppänen and M. Syrjänen. The Finnish AI Society: Otaniemi, Finland.

Pylkkö, Pauli, 1995a. Indeterminacy and experience. *Current Trends in Connectionism*, edited by Lars Niklasson and Mikael Bodén, pp. 321-329. Lawrence Erlbaum: Hillsdale, New Jersey.

Pylkkö, Pauli, 1995b. On surprise. *Semiotica*, 109-3/4, pp. 283-309. Bloomington, Indiana, 1996.

Pylkkö, Pauli, 1995c. 'Dasein' naturalized. *Analecta Husserliana*, volume XLIX, edited by Marlies Kronegger and Anna-Theresa Tymieniecka, pp. 203-218. Kluwer Academic Publishers: Dordrecht.

Pylkkö, Pauli, 1995d. Is it possible to think about philosophical problems in Finnish. *New Directions in Cognitive Science. The Proceedings of the Lapland Symposium*, edited by Paavo Pylkkänen and Pauli Pylkkö. The Finnish AI Society: Otaniemi, Finland.

Pylkkö, Pauli, 1996a. Eliminative holism as a solution to Bohr's puzzle of two languages. *Brain, Mind, and Physics*, edited by Paavo Pylkkänen, Pauli Pylkkö and Antti Hautamäki, pp. 140-156. IOS Press: Amsterdam.

Pylkkö, Pauli, 1996b. Wolgang Pauli and Martin Heidegger on the limits of scientific rationality. In *Vastakohtien Todellisuus. Juhlakirja professori K.V. Laurikaisen 80-vuotispäivänä*, edited by Urho Ketvel, et al., pp. 129-135. Helsinki University Press: Helsinki, Finland.

Pylkkö, Pauli, 1996c. Nazism as preconceptual experience. *Current Issues in Political Philosophy. The Papers of the 19th Ludwig Wittgenstein Symposium*, edited by Peter Koller and Klaus Pohl. The Austrian Ludwig Wittgenstein Society: Kirchberg am Wechsel.

Quine, Willard van Orman, 1953. *From a Logical Point of View. Nine Logico-philosophical Essays*. Harvard University Press: Cambridge, Massachusetts. Second revised edition, 1980.

Quine, Willard van Orman, 1969. *Ontological Relativity and Other Essays*. Columbia University Press: New York.

Rauschning, Hermann, 1940a. *Samtal med Hitler*. The original title *Gespräche mit Hitler*, translated into Swedisch by Alf Ahlberg. Fifth edition. Natur och Kultur: Stockholm.

Rauschning, Hermann, 1940b. *Gespräche mit Hitler*. Europa Verlag: New York. Zweite Auflage.

Reenpää, Yrjö, 1959. *Aufbau der allgemeinen Sinnesphysiologie. Grundlegung einer Wissenschaft vom Beobachten*. Vittorio Klostermann: Frankfurt am Main.

Reenpää, Yrjö, 1967. *Wahrnehmen, beobachten, konstituiren. Phenomenologie und Begriffsbestimmung der ersten Erkenntnisakte*. Vittorio Klostermann: Frankfurt am Main.

Riefenstahl, Leni, 1935. *Hinter den Kulissen des Reichsparteitag-Films*. Zentralverlag der NSDAP. Franz Eher Nachf. GMBH: München.

Riefenstahl, Leni, 1987. *Memoiren, 1902-1945*. Ullstein: Frankfurt, 1990. Published originally by Albrecht Knaus: München, 1987.

Rimbaud, Arthur, 1871/1957. Letter to Paul Demeny (May 15, 1871). An English translation, by Louise Varèse, of this letter appeared in *Illuminations, and Other Poems*, pp. xxviii-xxxv. New Directions Paperbook, 1957. The French original in *Oeuvre-Vie*, edited by Alain Borel with the collaboration of Andrée Montègre, pp. 185-194. Arléa, 1991.

Rosenberg, Alfred, 1930. *Der Mythus des 20. Jahrhunderts. Eine Wertung der seelisch-geistigen Gestaltenkämpfe unserer Zeit*. Hoheneichen: München, 1933. 8. Auflage.

Rosenberg, Alfred, 1934-1940. *Das politische Tagebuch Alfred Rosenbergs aus den Jahren 1934/35 und 1939/40*. Edited by Hans-Günther Seraphim. Musterschmidt: Göttingen, 1956.

Rosenthal, Sandra & Bourgeois, Patrick, 1991. *Mead and Merleau-Ponty. Toward a Common Vision.* State University of New York Press: Albany.

Russell, Bertrand, 1903. *Principles of Mathematics.* W.W. Norton: New York. Reprint date missing.

Sartre, Jean-Paul, 1946. *Existentialism and Humanism.* Translated by Philip Mairet. Methuen: London, 1948. Original title *L'Existentialisme est un Humanisme.* Les Éditions Nagel: Paris, 1946.

Schmitt, Carl, 1919. *Political Romanticism.* Translated by Guy Oakes. The MIT Press: Cambridge, 1986. Original title *Politische Romantik,* published by Duncker & Humblot: Berlin, 1919.

Schmitt, Carl, 1929. Wesen und Werden des faschistisches Staates. *Positionen und Begriffe: im Kampf mit Weimar - Genf - Versailles,* pp. 109-115. Duncker & Humblot: Berlin, 1988.

Schmitt, Carl, 1934. Der Führer schützt das Recht. *Positionen und Begriffe: im Kampf mit Weimar - Genf - Versailles,* pp. 199-203. Duncker & Humblot: Berlin, 1988.

Schopenhauer, Athur, 1819/1969. *The Wolrd as Will and Representation.* Translated from German by E.F.J. Payne. Original title *Die Welt als Wille und Vorstellung. Sämtliche Werke,* textkritisch bearbeitet und herausgegeben von Wolfgang Löhneysen. Cotta-Insel: Stuttgart, 1960.

Schrader, Bärbel & Schebera, Jürgen, (eds.), 1987. Lang's interview. *Kunstmetropole Berlin, 1918-1933,* pp. 351-2. Originally published in *Film und Fernsehen,* Heft, 8, 1983, p. 43.

Skarda, Christine & Freeman, Walter, 1987. How brains make chaos in order to make sense. *Behavioral and Brain Sciences,* 10, pp. 161-195.

Skarda, Christine & Freeman, Walter, 1990. Chaos and the new science of the brain. *Concepts in Neuroscience,* vol. 1, no. 2, pp. 275-285.

Sluga, Hans, 1993. *Heidegger's Crisis. Philosophy and Politics in Nazi Germany.* Harvard University Press: Cambridge, Massachusetts and London, England.

Smolensky, Paul, 1987. The constituent structure of connectionist mental states: A reply to Fodor and Pylyshyn. *The Southern Journal of Philosophy,* vol. XXVI, Supplement, pp. 137-161.

Smolensky, Paul, 1988. On the proper treatment of connectionism. *Behavioral and Brain Sciences,* 11, pp. 1-74.

Spariosu, Mihai I., 1989. *Dionysus Reborn. Play and the Aesthetic Dimension in Modern Philosophical and Scientific Discourse.* Cornell University Press: Ithaca and London.

Steegmuller, Francis, 1970. *Cocteau. A Biography.* Constable: London, 1986. First published by MacMillan, 1970.

Tennent, R.D., 1981. *Principles of Programming Languages.* Prentice-Hall: Englewood Cliffs, New Jersey.

Thompson, Richard, 1985. *The Brain. A Neuroscience Primer.* W.H. Freeman: New York. Second edition, 1993.

Turner, Henry Ashby, 1985. *German Big Business and the Rise of Hitler.* Oxford University Press: Oxford and New York.

Varela, Francisco J.; Thompson, Evan & Rosch, Eleanor, 1991. *The Embodied Mind. Cognitive Science and Human Experience.* The MIT Press: Cambridge, Massachusetts and London, England.

Varèse, Luise, 1946. By way of a preface. *Illuminations and Other Prose Poems*, pp. xxv-xxxv. New Directions, 1957.

Vietta, Silvio, 1989. *Heidegger's Kritik am Nationalsozialismus und an der Technik*. Niemeyer: Tübingen.

Wang, Hao, 1974. *From Mathematics to Philosophy*. Routledge & Kegan Paul: London.

Wang, Hao, 1987. *Reflections on Kurt Gödel*. The MIT Press: Cambridge, Massachusetts.

Wittgenstein, Ludwig, 1934-35/1984. *Das Blau Buch. Eine Philosophische Betrachtung (Das Braune Buch)*. Suhrkap: Frankfurt am Main.

Wittgenstein, Ludwig, 1953/1974. *Philosophical Investigations*. Translated by G.E.M. Anscombe. Basil Blackwell: Oxford, 1974.

Wittgenstein, Ludwig, 1980. *Culture and Value*. Edited by G.H. von Wright and H. Nyman. Blackwell: Oxford. The German title *Vermischte Bemerkungen*.

Wolin, Richard, 1990. *The Politics of Being. The Political Thought of Martin Heidegger*. Columbia University Press: New York.

Wundt, Max, 1924. Was heisst völkisch? *Fr. Manns pädag. Magazin*, Heft 987. Hermann Beyer & Söhne: Langensalza.

Zimmerman, Michael, 1990. *Heidegger's Confrontation with Modernity. Technology, Politics, Art*. Indiana University Press: Bloomington.

Name Index

In the series ADVANCES IN CONSCIOUSNESS RESEARCH (AiCR) the following titles have been published thus far or are scheduled for publication:

1. GLOBUS, Gordon G.: *The Postmodern Brain*. 1995.
2. ELLIS, Ralph D.: *Questioning Consciousness. The interplay of imagery, cognition, and emotion in the human brain*. 1995.
3. JIBU, Mari and Kunio YASUE: *Quantum Brain Dynamics and Consciousness. An introduction*. 1995.
4. HARDCASTLE, Valerie Gray: *Locating Consciousness*. 1995.
5. STUBENBERG, Leopold: *Consciousness and Qualia*. 1998.
6. GENNARO, Rocco J.: *Consciousness and Self-Consciousness. A defense of the higher-order thought theory of consciousness*. 1996.
7. MAC CORMAC, Earl and Maxim I. STAMENOV (eds): *Fractals of Brain, Fractals of Mind. In search of a symmetry bond*. 1996.
8. GROSSENBACHER, Peter G. (ed.): *Finding Consciousness in the Brain. A neuro-cognitive approach*. n.y.p.
9. Ó NUALLÁIN, Seán, Paul MC KEVITT and Eoghan MAC AOGÁIN (eds): *Two Sciences of Mind. Readings in cognitive science and consciousness*. 1997.
10. NEWTON, Natika: *Foundations of Understanding*. 1996.
11. PYLKKÖ, Pauli: *The Aconceptual Mind. Heideggerian themes in holistic naturalism*. 1998.
12. STAMENOV, Maxim I. (ed.): *Language Structure, Discourse and the Access to Consciousness*. 1997.